普通高等学校应用型教材

国际贸易

国际商务谈判：双语实训教程

主　编　胡琳祝　段立群

副主编　钟玉嫔

中国人民大学出版社

·北京·

图书在版编目（CIP）数据

国际商务谈判：双语实训教程/胡琳祝，段立群主编. --北京：中国人民大学出版社，2021.4
普通高等学校应用型教材. 国际贸易
ISBN 978-7-300-28631-0

Ⅰ.①国… Ⅱ.①胡… ②段… Ⅲ.①国际商务-商务谈判-双语教学-高等学校-教材 Ⅳ.①F740.41

中国版本图书馆 CIP 数据核字（2020）第 188040 号

普通高等学校应用型教材·国际贸易
国际商务谈判：双语实训教程
主　编　胡琳祝　段立群
副主编　钟玉嫔
Guoji Shangwu Tanpan：Shuangyu Shixun Jiaocheng

出版发行	中国人民大学出版社		
社　　址	北京中关村大街 31 号	邮政编码	100080
电　　话	010－62511242（总编室）		010－62511770（质管部）
	010－82501766（邮购部）		010－62514148（门市部）
	010－62515195（发行公司）		010－62515275（盗版举报）
网　　址	http://www.crup.com.cn		
经　　销	新华书店		
印　　刷	固安县铭成印刷有限公司		
开　　本	787 mm×1092 mm　1/16	版　　次	2021 年 4 月第 1 版
印　　张	20	印　　次	2024 年 12 月第 3 次印刷
字　　数	467 000	定　　价	43.00 元

作者简介

胡琳祝，重庆科技学院法政与经贸学院经济系教师，讲师，物流师，高级国际贸易师，工程管理硕士，芬兰哈格-赫利尔应用科技大学访问学者。从事国际贸易和国际商务类课程的教学工作多年，多次指导学生参加全国性大赛并获奖。发表论文《中小微型企业发展现状及问题研究》《世界经济区域发展趋势下我国对外经济政策的走向》《跨境电商发展对我国对外贸易模式转型的影响》以及 Assessment of International Business Transaction Risk Based on Big Data；出版专著《商务英语翻译理论研究》以及教材《电子商务应用英语（双语）》《国际货运代理》《国际贸易实务》等。参与“国际贸易案例库”“基于应用型本科品牌特色的 CLIL 双语教学模式的应用研究”“基于学科竞赛的国际经贸专业应用型人才派样平台建设研究”等校级项目。

段立群，重庆科技学院法政与经贸学院经济系教师，讲师，物流师，高级国际贸易师，管理学硕士，新加坡南洋理工大学访问学者。从事国际商务沟通类课程的教学工作多年，多次指导学生参加全国性大赛并获奖。发表《应用型大学汽车服务工程专业国际化途径探析》《基于真实工程的应用型特色课程教学设计》以及 Analysis on Trade Complementarity and Competition in CAFTA 等论文。主持校级实践教学考核方式改革；参与“国际贸易案例库”“基于应用型本科品牌特色的 CLIL 双语教学模式的应用研究”“国际经济贸易专业实践教学体系研究与实践”等校级项目。

钟玉嫔，毕业于重庆理工大学市场营销专业，进出口行业资深从业人员，曾任重庆力帆实业（集团）进出口有限公司业务二部部长，拥有 10 余年海外市场开拓与外贸出口管理经验。致力于理论与实践的结合，为重庆多家院校讲授国际贸易实务课程，连续多年被评为优秀外聘教师。

内容简介

本书主要由7章内容构成，具体包括：第1章国际商务谈判概述，第2章国际商务谈判的构成、分类与基本流程，第3章国际商务谈判的准备阶段，第4章国际商务谈判的开局阶段，第5章国际商务谈判的实质性磋商阶段，第6章国际商务谈判的结束阶段，以及第7章不同国家的谈判风格。其中每一章的框架都以导读案例开始，然后分为两大部分：第一部分是本章涉及的国际商务谈判的基础理论知识；第二部分是实训部分，主要包括专业术语的名词解释、对国际商务谈判专业知识的理解与掌握、专业句子的英汉互译、案例分析、国际商务谈判口语练习。其中，在涉及国际商务谈判具体阶段的第3~6章内容中增加了各阶段涉及的商务谈判礼仪知识，这样既可以让学生在掌握国际商务谈判具体环节知识的同时也对每个环节的商务礼仪有所了解，又可以使学生掌握更加全面的国际商务谈判理论和实践知识。

前　言

本书是为应用型本科高校的国际经济与贸易专业、国际商务专业、商务英语专业编写的一本理论与实训相结合的综合性的双语教材。本书以习近平新时代中国特色社会主义思想为指导，全面落实党的二十大精神，本着专业教育“实用为主，够用为度”的原则，在传授学生国际商务谈判基本理论知识的同时，重点培养学生在国际商务谈判情景下的语言应用能力、沟通能力和解决实际问题的能力。

本书主要针对应用型本科的国际经济与贸易专业学生的特点，以国际贸易理论与实务知识为基础，以国际商务谈判知识为主线，集专业知识、专业词汇与短语的积累、案例分析和商务情景口语练习为一体，全方位地训练和提升学生国际商务谈判的综合素养以及分析问题、解决问题的能力。

针对专业教学目标，本书具有如下特点：

1. 实训为主，理论为辅

鉴于目前市面上关于国际商务谈判的教材要么主要介绍理论知识，要么完全是实训内容，本书将理论与实践相结合，尽量浓缩理论知识，将理论知识作为实训的基础，在学生掌握了一定理论知识的基础上，重点培养学生在国际商务场景中运用谈判技巧和谈判策略达成最终目标、取得谈判成功的实战能力、英语口语能力以及对国际商务谈判商务礼仪的运用能力。

教材中的实训部分内容全面，包括专业词汇及短语的运用、谈判专业知识的理解、谈判案例的分析以及国际商务和国际贸易中涉及的各个主题内容的谈判训练。

2. 中英文结合，内容形象生动

针对大部分应用型本科学校的学生英文整体水平不高的情况，本书内容采用中英文两种语言进行编写，避免学生将过多的时间和精力花在英文翻译和理解上，从而忽视了对国际商务谈判专业知识的学习。与此同时，教师可以引导学生通过阅读英文内容，提高学生对专业词汇、短语在商务场景中的运用能力和学生的阅读能力。本书在商务礼仪知识方面采用了形象生动的图形来展示，有助于学生的理解和记忆。

3. 企业人员参与，案例真实新颖

为了提高本书的实用性和时效性，我们邀请了在重庆知名企业重庆力帆实业（集团）进出口有限公司从事了多年外贸工作的专业人士参与本书的编写，提供了大量最新的商务谈判的真实案例，案例生动翔实，贴近生活，特别是在商务谈判具体环节和商务礼仪环节，可以让学生真切地感受到商务谈判随时随地发生在我们周围。

本书由重庆科技学院的胡琳祝、段立群担任主编。胡琳祝负责全书总体设计、审读定稿以及第 4 章和第 5 章的整理和编排，段立群协助审查书稿和补充第 4 章及第 5 章的相关资料。企业人员钟玉嫔担任副主编，主要负责国际商务谈判环节企业真实案例的收集。参编人员的具体分工如下：胡琳祝第 1~3 章，钟玉嫔第 4 章和第 5 章，段立群第 6 章和第 7 章。

由于编者能力水平有限，疏漏之处在所难免，敬请专家、学者以及广大读者批评指正并反馈给我们，便于及时修订。

编　者

目　录

第1章　国际商务谈判概述 …… 1
导读案例 …… 1
模块1　正文 …… 2
模块2　专业术语实战 …… 30
模块3　新单词 …… 31
模块4　有用的表达 …… 32
模块5　练习 …… 32
第2章　国际商务谈判的构成、分类与基本流程 …… 39
导读案例 …… 39
模块1　正文 …… 40
模块2　专业术语实战 …… 70
模块3　新单词 …… 71
模块4　有用的表达 …… 72
模块5　练习 …… 72
第3章　国际商务谈判的准备阶段 …… 81
导读案例 …… 81
模块1　正文 …… 82
模块2　专业术语实战 …… 126
模块3　新单词 …… 127
模块4　有用的表达 …… 128
模块5　练习 …… 128
第4章　国际商务谈判的开局阶段 …… 135
导读案例 …… 135
模块1　正文 …… 136
模块2　专业术语实战 …… 160
模块3　新单词 …… 161
模块4　有用的表达 …… 161
模块5　练习 …… 162

第5章　国际商务谈判的实质性磋商阶段 …… 172
导读案例 …… 172
模块1　正文 …… 173
模块2　专业术语实战 …… 209
模块3　新单词 …… 210
模块4　有用的表达 …… 211
模块5　练习 …… 211
第6章　国际商务谈判的结束阶段 …… 221
导读案例 …… 221
模块1　正文 …… 222
模块2　专业术语实战 …… 251
模块3　新单词 …… 252
模块4　有用的表达 …… 253
模块5　练习 …… 254
第7章　不同国家的谈判风格 …… 264
导读案例 …… 264
模块1　正文 …… 265
模块2　专业术语实战 …… 297
模块3　新单词 …… 297
模块4　有用的表达 …… 298
模块5　练习 …… 298

Contents

Chapter 1 Introductions to International Business Negotiation ······ 1
Case Guide-Reading ······ 1
Module Ⅰ Text ······ 2
Module Ⅱ Terminology Practice ······ 30
Module Ⅲ New Words ······ 31
Module Ⅳ Useful Expressions ······ 32
Module Ⅴ Exercise ······ 32
Chapter 2 Composition, Classification and Basic Procedure of International Business Negotiation ······ 39
Case Guide-Reading ······ 39
Module Ⅰ Text ······ 40
Module Ⅱ Terminology Practice ······ 70
Module Ⅲ New Words ······ 71
Module Ⅳ Useful Expressions ······ 72
Module Ⅴ Exercise ······ 72
Chapter 3 Preparation for International Business Negotiation ······ 81
Case Guide-Reading ······ 81
Module Ⅰ Text ······ 82
Module Ⅱ Terminology Practice ······ 126
Module Ⅲ New Words ······ 127
Module Ⅳ Useful Expressions ······ 128
Module Ⅴ Exercise ······ 128
Chapter 4 Opening for International Business Negotiation ······ 135
Case Guide-Reading ······ 135
Module Ⅰ Text ······ 136
Module Ⅱ Terminology Practice ······ 160
Module Ⅲ New Words ······ 161
Module Ⅳ Useful Expressions ······ 161

Module Ⅴ Exercise ········· 162
Chapter 5 Consultation for International Business Negotiation ········· 172
Case Guide-Reading ········· 172
Module Ⅰ Text ········· 173
Module Ⅱ Terminology Practice ········· 209
Module Ⅲ New Words ········· 210
Module Ⅳ Useful Expressions ········· 211
Module Ⅴ Exercise ········· 211
Chapter 6 Closing of International Business Negotiation ········· 221
Case Guide-Reading ········· 221
Module Ⅰ Text ········· 222
Module Ⅱ Terminology Practice ········· 251
Module Ⅲ New Words ········· 252
Module Ⅳ Useful Expressions ········· 253
Module Ⅴ Exercise ········· 254
Chapter 7 Negotiation Styles in Different Countries ········· 264
Case Guide-Reading ········· 264
Module Ⅰ Text ········· 265
Module Ⅱ Terminology Practice ········· 297
Module Ⅲ New Words ········· 297
Module Ⅳ Useful Expressions ········· 298
Module Ⅴ Exercise ········· 298

Chapter 1

Introductions to International Business Negotiation

Work Objective

After studying this chapter, you will be able to:

- probe into the nature of negotiation;
- master the definition of the business negotiation and international business negotiation;
- familiarize with the characteristics of international business negotiation;
- identify the contents of international business negotiation;
- know the principle of international business negotiation;
- understand the main theories of international business negotiation.

Case Guide-Reading

Egypt and Israel finally reached an agreement on the ownership of the Sinai Peninsula through the principle of equality and mutual benefit.

Since the "Six-Day War" in 1967, Israel occupied the Sinai Peninsula of Egypt. In 1978, when they sat down to discuss peace, their positions were incompatible. Israel insisted on retaining a part of the Sinai Peninsula, while Egypt insisted on fully reclaiming the Sinai Peninsula. People initially divided the boundary between Sinai and Israel on the map. However, no matter how they negotiated, Egypt refused to accept it. Obviously, focusing on the territorial division alone cannot solve the problem. So is there any other method of etiquette distribution? The analysts found that Israel's etiquette lies in security. Once Israel agrees to return the Sinai Peninsula, Egyptian tanks can enter Israel from the Sinai border at any time. Egypt's interest lies in the recovery of sovereignty. Since the Pharaonic era, Sinai is part of the Egyptian territory. Egypt doesn't want to give up the territory to a foreign intruder. The final agreement is as follows: Sinai was completely returned to Egypt, but most areas were required to be demilitarized to ensure Israel's security. The Egyptian flag could fly around, but the Egyptian tanks could not get close to Israel. No one can deny that the Egyptian-Israeli agreement is a solution that both parties are satisfied with.

Source: Wang Fuxiang. *Theory and Practice of Business Negotiation*. Beijing: Science Press, 2008.

Module Ⅰ Text

Ⅰ A Brief Introduction to Negotiation（谈判概述）

Nowadays, negotiation is a common practice in the world. Whether you like it or not, negotiation will revolve around you at anytime and anywhere. In fact, everyone is a negotiator. Negotiation often happens between parents and children, between subordinates and leaders, between colleagues and between friends, when purchasing items, traveling, making work arrangements, purchasing and selling goods, etc., in order to eliminate differences and achieve consensus, and ultimately take joint action. So what is on earth the definition of negotiation? In fact, the so-called negotiation refers to the process of the exchange of information and consultation on agreements between the parties involved, based on certain needs, with a view to coordinate the relationship and win or maintain their own interests.

谈判是我们当今世界上普遍存在的一种行为。无论你喜欢与否，谈判都会围绕着你，无处不在，无时不有。其实人人都是谈判者。父母与子女之间、下属与领导之间、同事与同事之间、朋友与朋友之间为选购物品、旅游、工作安排、商品购销等问题都会进行协商，以消除分歧从而取得一致，最终采取共同行动，这些都是谈判。那么谈判的定义到底是什么呢？其实，所谓谈判是指参与各方基于某种需要，彼此进行信息交流，磋商协议，以协调相互关系、赢得或维护各自利益的行为过程。

Gerard Nierenberg, president of the American Negotiation Institute, believes negotiation is a behavior in which people change their relationships, exchange opinions, and negotiate with each other in order to achieve consensus and directly affect interpersonal relationships. Negotiation is an act, and it is also a process in which parties involved join in consultations on issues of common interest, coordinate and adjust their own economic, political or other interests in order to seek mutual compromise. Every party involved feels that the agreement is reached under favorable conditions, so the purpose of the negotiation is to coordinate the conflicts of interest and ultimately achieve "win-win".

美国谈判学会会长杰勒德·尼尔伦伯格认为，谈判是人们为改变相互关系而交换意见，为取得一致而相互磋商的一种行为，为的是直接影响人际关系。谈判是一种行为，更是一个过程。在这个过程中，参与各方就共同关心或感兴趣的问题进行磋商，协调和调整各自的经济、政治或其他利益，以谋求相互妥协，从而使各方都感到是在有利的条件下达成协议，所以谈判的目的就是协调各方的利害冲突，最终实现“双赢”或“共赢”。

As an important method of coordinating the relations and interests of all parties involved, negotiation is widely used in political, economic, military, diplomatic, scientific and technological fields, especially in the management field of 21st century. Most of the behaviors of modern managers can be called negotiation. The management world is like a negotiating table and the managers are negotiators. A new trend has emerged in the business administration community in the U.S., that is, more and more doctors of literature and art "abandon literature for commerce", and which account for 1/10 of the doctors of liberal arts. The HR departments of major international corporations have a high evaluation for these liberal arts doctors, mainly because they are good at eloquence, strong in organization and good at using various strategies, especially for negotiation.

Please see Figure 1.1 for the essence of negotiation.

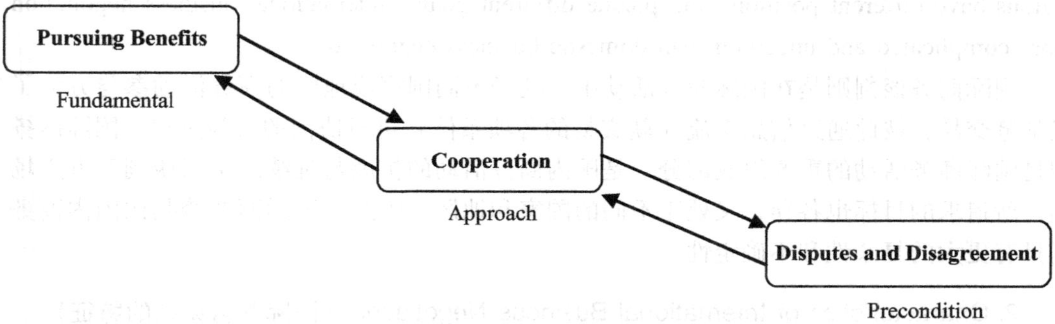

Figure 1.1 The Essence of Negotiation

谈判作为协调各方关系和利益的重要手段，被广泛应用于政治、经济、军事、外交、科技等各个领域，特别是在21世纪的管理领域。现代管理者的大部分行为都可以称得上是谈判。管理世界是张谈判桌，管理者人人都是谈判者。在美国的工商管理界出现了一种新趋势，即越来越多的文学艺术博士“弃文从商”，他们大概占文科博士的1/10。各大公司人事部门对这些文科博士评价很高，主要是因为他们的口才好、组织力强、擅长运用各种策略，特别适合谈判。

图1.1展示了谈判的真谛。

Ⅱ Definition and Characteristics of International Business Negotiation（国际商务谈判的概念与特征）

1. Definition of International Business Negotiation（国际商务谈判的概念）

Before we understand what international business negotiation is, let's figure out what business negotiation is. Business negotiation is mainly concentrated in the economic field. It refers to the behavioral process in which in order to coordinate and improve each others' economic relations, and meet the needs of trade, all parties involved negotiate the transaction conditions of the subject through information exchange and negotiation agreements to achieve the purpose of the transaction. Business negotiation includes commodity trading, investment, service trade, technology trade, economic cooperation, etc.

在了解什么是国际商务谈判之前，我们先弄清楚什么是商务谈判。商务谈判主要集中在经济领域，是指参与各方为了协调、改善彼此的经济关系，满足贸易的需求，围绕标的物的交易条件，彼此通过信息交流、磋商协议达到交易目的的行为过程。具体包括商品买卖、投资、服务贸易、技术贸易、经济合作等。

International business negotiation is a process in which international business activities are conducted by business participants from different countries or regions in order to reach a certain transaction and negotiate with each other through information exchange. International business negotiation is an important part of international business activities and it is also the expansion and continuation of domestic business activities. Since the parties involved from different countries or regions have different positions and pursue different goals, international business negotiation is more complicated and uncertain than domestic business negotiation.

国际商务谈判则是在国际商务活动中，处于不同国家或地区的商务活动参与方为了达成某笔交易，彼此通过信息交流（就交易的各项条件）进行协商的行为过程。国际商务谈判是国际商务活动的重要组成部分，是国内商务活动的扩展与延续。由于谈判双方立场不同，所追求的目标也各异，又处于不同的国家和地区，因此，国际商务谈判比国内商务谈判具有更大的复杂性和不确定性。

2. Characteristics of International Business Negotiation（国际商务谈判的特征）

(1) The Commonality between International Business Negotiation and General Business Negotiation（国际商务谈判与一般商务谈判的共性）

a. The objective of business negotiation is to obtain financial interests.（以获取经济利益为谈判的目的）

The reason for negotiation is to realize certain goals and interests. The purpose of negotiation is to focus on economic interests. Although the parties involved in business negotiation will be constrained by political and diplomatic factors, the primary issue they consider is how to gain more economic benefits under the current political and diplomatic situation. The success of business negotiation is judged by whether the negotiations satisfy economic interests of all parties involved. Without financial interests, business negotiation will lose its values and foundations. Therefore, business negotiation is the negotiation which intends to gain direct economic interests.

之所以要进行谈判，就是要实现一定的目标和利益。谈判的目的就是集中在经济上的利益。虽然参与商务谈判的各方会受到政治、外交等因素的制约，但他们考虑的首要问题还是如何在现有政治、外交关系的格局下获得更多的经济利益。商务谈判是否成功要从谈判是否满足了各方的经济利益来判断。没有经济利益，商务谈判就失去了其价值和基础。因此，商务谈判就是为了获得直接经济利益的谈判。

b. The core of business negotiation is price. (以价格作为谈判的核心)

Although the items and elements involved in business negotiation are not just prices, prices are only one part of the negotiating contents, and the requirements and interests of negotiation are not only reflected in prices, almost all negotiations are based on price. Other terms and conditions, such as product quality, quantity, delivery date, date and methods of payment can be translated into a certain price in many cases, and are reflected or compensated by the price increasing or declining. For example, the price of a first-class apple is 80 RMB per kilo, while the price of a second-class apple is 60 RMB per kilo, so this difference in quality is translated into a difference in price, and the same is true in quantity. For example, the price for one M/T chicken is 10,000 RMB, and the price for ten M/T chicken is 9,000 RMB, which means that the difference in quantity can also be translated into price. But not all cases can do such a translation. In other words, negotiation will not accept such a translation. For example, we've imported a set of equipment and according to the stipulations of previous contract, this set of equipment should have the latest technology of the 21st century. However, after the goods arrived for inspection, it was found that the technology of these equipment is very old from the 20th century. In this case, even if the seller can offer the equipment at a 50% discount, we will not hesitate to reject the proposal, because the technology is too outdated to offset the losses caused by the discounted price.

虽然商务谈判所涉及的项目和要素不仅仅是价格，价格只是谈判内容的一部分，谈判者的需要和利益也不仅仅体现在价格上，但几乎所有谈判都以价格作为核心内容。其他条件，如产品质量、数量、交货期以及付款时间与形式等得失在很多情况下都可以折算为一定的价格，并通过价格的升降而得到体现或予以补偿。例如，一级苹果的价格是每千克 80 元人民币，而二级苹果的价格是每千克 60 元人民币，所以这种质量上的差异就转换成价格上的差异，在数量上也是同样的道理。例如，1 公吨鸡肉的价格是 10 000 元人民币，而 10 公吨鸡肉的价格就是 9 000 元人民币，这也就意味着数量上的差异同样可以转换为价格上的差异。但也不是所有情况都可以做这样的转换。换言之，谈判并不会接受这样的转换。例如，我们要进口一批设备，根据之前合同的规定，这批设备应该具备 21 世纪最新的技术，但货物到达查验之后发现，这批设备所使用的是 20 世纪非常陈旧的技术。在这种情况下，就算卖方可以提供 50%的折扣价将这批设备卖给我方，我方也会因为这个技术太落后无法用价格来抵消其带来的损失而毫不犹豫地拒绝对方降价的提议。

c. Items of contract should keep strictly accurate and prudent. (合同条款应准确严谨)

In business negotiation, the two parties finally come to a conclusion on the rights and obligations by signing a contract or agreement. These terms and conditions should be worded with strict accuracy and prudence, which are the prerequisicy for the guarantee of each party's interests. A negotiator who has gained a favorable terms and conditions may walk into the trap of a tricky contract set by the other parties, especially when they are not careful enough in drafting the contract, failing to ensure the completeness, correctness or accuracy, equitability and legitimacy of the contract.

在商务谈判中，双方通过签订合同或协议最终就双方的权利与义务达成一致。合同条款是保证双方利益的前提，所以应该采用准确严谨的措辞。特别是在起草合同时不够谨慎，不能确保合同的完整性、正确性或准确性、公平性和合法性时，取得了有利条件的谈判一方可能会走进另一方提前设定的合同陷阱。

(2) Features of International Business Negotiation (国际商务谈判的特性)

a. Internationality (国际性)

Internationality is the greatest feature of international business negotiation and the basis for other characteristics. The subjects of negotiation are from two or more countries or regions, representing the interests of different countries or regions.

国际性是国际商务谈判的最大特点，也是国际商务谈判其他特点的基础。其谈判主体来自两个或两个以上的国家或地区，代表了不同国家或地区的利益。

Usually, the abbreviation of the country or region plus specific negotiating objects or things is used to refer to specific international business negotiations, such as "China-US intellectual property negotiations" and "China-Russia negotiations on construction of ×× projects". As the result of international business negotiation will lead to the transactional transfer of assets, it will involve a series of issues such as international trade, international settlement, international insurance and international transportation.

通常是以国家或地区的简称加上具体的谈判对象或事物来称呼特定的国际商务谈判，如"中美知识产权谈判""中俄关于××工程项目建设的谈判"等。由于国际商务谈判的结果会导致资产的跨国转移，因而会涉及国际贸易、国际结算、国际保险、国际运输等一系列问题。

b. Cross-culturality (跨文化性)

International business negotiation is not only cross-border negotiation, but also cross-cultural negotiation. The negotiating parties of different countries or regions represent different social, cultural, religious, economic, and political backgrounds, and the values, ways of thinking, behaviors, modes of communication, and customs of the negotiating parties are also different. If the negotiators do not understand the cultural background and differences of the counterparty very well, it is likely to cause many unnecessary misunderstandings and even lead to negotiation failure. For example, when an Indian businessman shakes his head about the products you displayed, this means he identifies and satisfies with your products. But if you don't understand the Indian culture, you will feel that he isn't interested in your products or doesn't need these products, so you may give up the opportunity of this negotiation.

国际商务谈判不仅是跨国的谈判，而且是跨文化的谈判。不同国家或地区的谈判主体代表着不同的社会、文化、宗教、经济、政治背景，而谈判各方的价值观、思维方式、行为方式、交往模式以及风俗习惯等也各不相同。如果谈判人员不能很好地了解谈判对手的文化背景和差异，就很有可能会造成很多不必要的误解，甚至导致谈判失败。比如，当一个印度商人对你展示的产品摇头时，其实是表示对产品的认同和满意，但如果你不懂得印度的文化，你会觉得对方对你的产品不满意或者不需要这个产品，所以可能会放弃这次谈判机会。

In addition, different religious beliefs and social ideologies can have a huge impact on international business negotiation. An experienced negotiator knows how to avoid these cultural differences, find the common interests of both parties, and deal with these differences properly. If necessary, negotiators need to cater to and praise counter-party's culture for reducing conflicts and obstacles caused by cultural differences, and even turn these differences into an activator for negotiation.

另外，不同的宗教信仰和社会意识形态也会对国际商务谈判造成巨大的影响。一个有经验的谈判人员知道如何去规避这些文化差异，去寻找双方的共同利益并正确处理这些差异。如果有必要，谈判人员甚至需要去迎合和赞美对方的文化从而减少由文化差异带来的冲突和障碍，甚至可以将这些差异转化为谈判的催化剂。

c. Complexity（复杂性）

Complexity is derived from internationality and cross-culturality. Compared with domestic business negotiation, international business negotiation faces a more complicated and changing environment.

复杂性是由国际性和跨文化性派生出来的。与国内商务谈判相比，国际商务谈判会面临更加复杂多变的环境。

People engaging in international business negotiation will spend more time and efforts to adapt to the environment. This complexity is reflected in various aspects, such as differences in language, in communication methods, in legal systems and in negotiation perceptions.

从事国际商务谈判的人员将花费更多的时间和精力来适应环境。这种复杂性体现在各个方面，如语言的差异、沟通方式的差异、法律制度的差异、谈判认识上的差异等。

Whether it is face-to-face communication or written communication, the primary obstacle in international business negotiation is language, unless your counter-party can speak your mother tongue and write in your native language. Since the conventions and terminology of international trade are expressed in English, English is the most commonly used language in international trade and international business activities. But if the counter-party is from a non-English speaking country, then French, Spanish, Russian, Italian, Arabic, etc. will be used in international business negotiation. Therefore, in international business negotiation, the ability to master multilingual skills is very important. However, such talents are rare. Generally speaking, in international business negotiation, negotiators must master at least one foreign language, for example, English. In very formal and significant international business negotiation, all parties have their own translators, and most often hire temporary ones who know the language of the counter-party well which can achieve effective communication and reduce the negotiating costs.

不管是面对面的交流还是书面交流，在国际商务谈判中首要的障碍就是语言，除非你的谈判对手能用你们国家的语言进行交流或用你们国家的语言进行书信往来。由于国际贸易的惯例和术语都是用英语表达的，所以英语是在国际贸易和国际商务活动中使用最广泛的语言。但如果谈判对手是来自非英语国家，那么法语、西班牙语、俄语、意大利语、阿拉伯语等就会被运用到国际商务谈判中。因此，在国际商务谈判中，掌握多种语言的能力就非常重要了。但在现实生活中，能掌握多国语言的人才毕竟是少数，一般来说，在国际商务谈判中，谈判人员至少要掌握一门外语，比如英语。在非常正式和重要的国际商务谈判中，双方都会有自己的翻译，一般是临时雇用能熟练掌握对方语言的人员。这样既可以达到有效交流的目的，又可以节省谈判成本。

International business negotiation is not only subject to domestic legislation, but also subject to relevant international commercial law and international practices related to international trade, international settlement, international transportation and international insurance. For example, you are now preparing for an import and export trade negotiation, and you need to master the trade terms used in international trade and be proficient in it. You also need to fully understand the laws of the the counter-party with whom you are negotiating and the laws and regulations issued by the international economic organizations. As an excellent negotiator, you need to be well informed of the latest laws and regulations with regard to the content of the negotiation at home and abroad, so as to adjust the negotiating strategies accordingly.

国际商务谈判不仅要受到国内立法的约束，而且要受到相关的国际商法的约束，还要受到与国际贸易、国际结算、国际运输和国际保险相关的国际惯例的约束。比如，你现在要准备一个进出口贸易的谈判，你需要掌握国际贸易中运用的贸易术语并能熟练运用，同时你也需要充分了解谈判对手所在国家的法律以及国际经济组织颁布的法律和法规。作为一名出色的谈判人员，你还需要随时了解国内外与谈判内容相关的最新的法律和法规以便及时调整谈判策略。

d. International Policy Factors（国际政策因素）

International business negotiations often involve political and diplomatic relations between the countries or regions where the negotiating subject is located. Therefore, the policies formulated by the government play a crucial role in the negotiation. For example, a foreign company is willing to cooperate with a Chinese enterprise to complete a large-scale project, but the country where the former is located is in conflict with its neighboring country. In this case, the Chinese enterprise not only undertakes the risk of being unable to finish the project, but also inducing diplomatic confrontation. Here is another example: an importer from the Middle East asked a Chinese manufacturer to produce a batch of T-shirts with words of religious discrimination. In this case, no matter how huge the profit of this order is, the Chinese enterprise should refuse this offer. Negotiators must be highly sensitive to international politics in international business negotiation.

国际商务谈判往往涉及谈判主体所在国家或地区之间的政治和外交关系，因此，政府制定的政策会对谈判起着至关重要的作用。假设一个国外的公司要与中方合作共同完成一个大型工程项目，但此时该公司所在的国家正与邻国就边界问题发生冲突，在这种情况下中方不仅面临无法完成该工程项目的风险，而且有可能会卷入外交冲突。又比如，一个来自中东的进口商要求中国的一个企业生产一批T恤，但需要在上面印上带有种族歧视的文字。在这种情况下，不论这个订单的利润有多大，中国企业都必须果断拒绝。谈判人员在国际商务谈判中必须对国际政治有高度的敏感性。

In terms of the process and results of international business negotiation, negotiators must implement the relevant national and foreign policies, especially the implementation of a series of laws and regulations on foreign economics and trade which require negotiators to be familiar with the guidelines and policies of the countries where the counter-party is located and to use them properly.

在国际商务谈判的过程和结果方面，谈判人员必须贯彻执行国家的相关方针政策和外交政策，特别是执行对外经济贸易的一系列法律、法规。这就要求谈判人员熟悉谈判对手所在国家的方针政策并能恰当运用。

e. Difficulty（困难性）

In addition to the above-mentioned features, international business negotiation involves more factors and is more complex than domestic business negotiation.

除了以上提到的特征以外，国际商务谈判比起国内商务谈判而言，还涉及更多的因素，并且更加复杂。

In the implementation stage after the signing of the international negotiation agreement, if there are disputes or other incidents, there are many relationships that need to be coordinated, and there are many issues that need to be handled, it will be quite difficult to resolve them. The negotiators are required to predict all possible problems in advance and to take appropriate measures and preparations.

在国际商务谈判协议签订后的执行阶段，如果出现纠纷或其他意外，需要协调的关系非常多，需要处理的问题也很多，则解决起来会相当困难。这就要求谈判人员事先能预测到某些可能出现的问题并进行相应的防范与准备。

In addition, the cost of travel, meetings, foreign research, etc. is much higher than domestic business negotiation. For example, the value of the subject of the negotiation is very high. In this case, you need to visit the counter-party's company in person and check the quality of the goods. You may also need to conduct multiple rounds of negotiation to ensure that the counter-party can achieve the required credit rating, meet the proposed technical standards and perform the contract efficiently.

此外，在旅途、会议、国外调研等方面的费用也比国内商务谈判要高很多。例如，谈判的标的物的价值非常高，这时就需要亲自去走访谈判对手公司并且查看核实商品的质量等，还有可能需要进行多轮谈判以确保对方公司能达到要求的资信等级，满足提出的各项技术标准并能高效地履行合同。

In a sense, international business negotiation is competition for comprehensive strength in terms of knowledge, skills, perseverance and finance.

从某种意义来讲，国际商务谈判就是在知识、技能、毅力和财务方面综合实力的竞争。

Ⅲ The Contents of International Business Negotiation（国际商务谈判的内容）

International business negotiations usually include negotiations on commodity trading, technology trade, labor service cooperation, contracting, joint ventures, etc., and different types of negotiations have different contents. This chapter will focus on international trade in goods negotiation and international technology trade negotiation.

国际商务谈判通常包括商品买卖、技术贸易、劳务合作、工程承包、合资合作等方面的谈判，类型不同，谈判涉及的内容就会有所不同。本章将重点介绍国际货物贸易谈判和国际技术贸易谈判。

1. International Trade in Goods Negotiation（国际货物贸易谈判）

International trade in goods refers to the trade activities of goods with physical form between two or more countries or regions. Because trade objects are visible and tangible, they are also called visible trade. International trade in goods negotiation is divided into import goods trade negotiation and export goods trade negotiation.

国际货物贸易是指具有实物形态的商品在两个或两个以上的国家或地区之间的贸易活动。由于贸易对象具有看得见、摸得着的实物形态，因此国际货物贸易也称为有形贸易。国际货物贸易谈判可分为进口货物贸易谈判和出口货物贸易谈判。

The negotiation process generally involves enquiry, offer, counter-offer and acceptance or declining. If the counter-offer is accepted by the counter-party, both parties need to sign an international sale or purchase contract. Among them, the offer and acceptance are the two basic necessary steps to close a deal. When a valid offer is accepted by the counter-party within the specified validity period, the transaction is concluded. International trade in goods is generally negotiated in two forms: one is written form, where buyers and sellers communicate and negotiate through telegraph, telex, fax, letter, e-mail, etc.; the other is oral form, by participating in professional trade fairs, China Import and Export Fair, international fairs, trade team visits abroad and customer visits, etc.

谈判及磋商的流程一般涉及询盘、发盘、还盘和接受或拒绝几个环节。如果接受了对方的还盘，双方需要签订国际货物买卖合同。其中，发盘和接受是达成交易必不可少的两个基本环节。当一项有效的发盘被对方在规定的有效期内接受时，交易即达成。国际货物贸易谈判一般有两种形式：一种是书面形式，买卖双方通过电报、电传、传真、信函、电子邮件等方式进行沟通和洽谈；另一种是口头形式，通过参加各种类型的专业性交易会、中国进出口商品交易会、国际博览会以及贸易团队出访、邀请客户访问等方式进行。

The content of international trade in goods negotiation involves various trading conditions, including the name of commodity, quantity, quality, specifications, packing, price, shipment, insurance, payment terms, commodity inspection, claim, arbitration and force majeure, etc. Only after the buyer and the seller have agreed on the above conditions, the transaction can be concluded and the contract can be finally signed.

国际货物贸易谈判的内容涉及各项交易条件，主要包括：商品名称、数量、质量、规格、包装、价格、装运、保险、支付方式、商品检验、索赔、仲裁以及不可抗力等。只有在买卖双方就以上条件达成一致后，交易才能达成，合同才能最终签订。

2. International Technology Trade Negotiation（国际技术贸易谈判）

International technology trade refers to the transfer or licensing of technology across borders between parties in different countries on the basis of normal commercial conditions. Commercial international technology transfer is international technology trade. International technology transfer refers to an international trade behavior between different international enterprises, economic organizations or individuals that sell or acquire software technology use rights from counter-party according to normal commercial conditions. It consists of two aspects: technology export and technology introduction. The subject of technology transfer is technical knowledge and machinery or equipment that is transferred with the technology. The international technology market is actually a kind of "virtual "market that is difficult to determine a fixed place, that is, a multi-functional intangible market integrating technical research and development, technology trading, technology intermediation and technology information exchange.

国际技术贸易是指不同国家的当事人之间按一般商业条件进行的技术跨越国境的转让或许可行为，商业性的国际技术转让就是国际技术贸易。国际技术转让是指不同国际企业、经济组织或个人之间，按照一般商业条件，向对方出售或从对方购买软件技术使用权的一种国际贸易行为。它由技术出口和技术引进两方面构成。技术转让的标的物是技术知识以及随着技术一起转让的机器设备。国际技术市场其实是一种“虚拟”的难以确定固定场所的市场，即集技术研发、技术交易、技术中介和技术信息交换为一体的多功能的无形市场。

The main contents of international technology trade include patent, trademark, and proprietary technologies. The patent is an exclusive right granted by the competent authority of the government to the inventor for its invention within a certain period of time. In recent years, disputes over patent have been particularly prominent in automotive design. For example, BYD F8 and Mercedes-Benz CLK have 40% similar appearance, and Shuanghuan S6 and Mercedes-Benz Smart have 70% similar appearance. The trademark is exclusive right protected by relevant laws applied by users of it in accordance with the law and approved by the department in charge. Proprietary technology also known as technical secret is a method and means of undisclosed production technology, knowledge and experience, and skills and management.

国际技术贸易的主要内容包括专利权、商标、专有技术。专利权是政府主管机构授予发明人在一定时期内对其发明所享有的一种专有权。近年来在专利权方面的纠纷在汽车外观设计方面尤为突出。例如，比亚迪 F8 与奔驰 CLK 的外观相似度达 40%，双环 S6 与奔驰 Smart 的外观相似度达 70%。商标权是商标的使用者依法申请并经主管部门核准所授予的专用权利，受相关法律保护。专有技术又称技术秘密，是一种没有公开的生产技术、知识经验以及技能和经营管理的方法、手段。

The main methods used in international technological trade include permit trading, international cooperative production, technical advisory service, international engineering contracting, BOT and franchise.

国际技术贸易采用的主要方式包括许可贸易、国际合作生产、技术咨询服务、国际工程承包、建设-经营-转让和特许专营。

(1) Permit Trading（许可贸易）

It is also known as license trading which means that the owner of intellectual property or know-how, as a licensor, grants a license to the licensee (importer) by signing a license contract with the latter. Permit trading allows the licensee to use the technology, manufacture or sell the contracted product in accordance with the terms and conditions of the contract, and pay a certain amount of technical royalties to the licensor. According to the regional distribution of its time and scope and the degree of authorization, the permit trading is divided into five types which includes simple license, sole license, exclusive license, sub-license and cross license.

许可贸易也称许可证贸易，是指知识产权或专有技术的所有人作为许可方，通过与被许可方（引进方）签订许可合同，将其拥有的技术授予被许可方，允许被许可方按照合同约定的条件使用该项技术，制造或销售合同产品，并由被许可方支付一定数额的技术使用费给许可方的技术交易行为。许可贸易根据其时间和范围区域分布以及授权程度的大小，可分为普通许可、排他许可、独占许可、分许可、交叉许可五种类型。

(2) International Cooperative Production（国际合作生产）

International companies produce different parts of the same products according to the signed agreement, and then one or both of them assemble the parts into products for sale, or they can separately manufacture the parts required by the other party, exchange them, and assemble them into products for sale, or production is carried out according to the requirements of the other party. International cooperative production is the relationship of rights and obligations between two or more legal entities based on contracts. The parties only have relation of rights and obligations in the production process, and generally do not participate in the preparation and construction of the project. At the same time, the rights and obligations of the involved parties are only reflected in the exchange of technology, the provision of labor and production results.

国际企业根据共同签订的协议，分别生产同一产品的不同零部件，然后一方或双方装配成产品出售，也可以分别制造对方所需的零部件，相互交换，各自组装成产品出售，或者一方按另一方的要求进行生产。国际合作生产是两个或两个以上的法人实体之间建立在合同基础上的权利与义务关系，各方当事人只在生产过程中发生权利与义务关系，一般不参与项目的筹建和建厂，同时当事人的权利和义务也只表现在技术交换、劳务提供和生产成果上。

(3) Technical Advisory Service（技术咨询服务）

It is an activity, in which an independent expert or expert group or consulting agency as a service provider offers the technical analysis, demonstration, prediction, evaluation and technical reports on a specific technical subject at the request of the client. Moreover, the client should pay a certain amount of technical service fees. Technical advisory services come in a variety of forms, such as project feasibility studies, technical program development and review, process and product improvement, personnel training, project implementation supervision and guidance, and bidding documents.

技术咨询服务是指独立的专家或专家小组或咨询机构作为服务方应委托方的要求，就某个具体的技术课题向委托方提供技术分析、论证、预测和评价，提供技术报告，并由委托方支付一定数额的技术服务费的活动。技术咨询服务的形式多种多样，如项目的可行性研究、技术方案的制订与审核、工艺和产品的改进、人员培训、对项目实施的监督与指导、招投标文件的拟定等。

（4） International Engineering Contracting（国际工程承包）

It is also known as "turnkey project". It refers to a government, company or project owner (generally called the project owner or contractor) entrusting a foreign project contractor to undertake the task of completing a certain project according to the specified conditions. International engineering contracting is not only a way of international labor cooperation, and also a way of international technology trade. This method is suitable for large-scale new projects. For example, in recent years, Chinese enterprises have built large-scale projects in countries along "the Belt and Road", including the National Industrial Park of Ethiopia built by Chinese enterprise; the largest steel mill in Southeast Asia completed by China Metallurgical Group in Vietnam; Awasa Industrial Park, the first national industrial park in Ethiopia built by China Civil Engineering Group. International engineering contracting has some features like large scale, huge investment, complex project and has direct relation with technology and the nature of trade.

国际工程承包也称"交钥匙工程"，是指一个国家的政府部门、公司企业或项目所有人（一般称工程业主或发包人）委托国外的工程承包人负责按规定的条件承担完成某项工程任务。国际工程承包既是国际劳务合作的一种方式，又是国际技术贸易的一种方式。这种方式适用于大型的新建项目，例如，近年来中国企业在"一带一路"沿线国家的大型工程的援建，包括：中企承建的埃塞俄比亚的国家工业园，中国中冶集团在越南完成的东南亚最大钢厂，中国土木工程集团承建的埃塞俄比亚首个国家工业园——阿瓦萨工业园。国际工程承包具有规模大、投资多、项目内容复杂、与技术有直接关系和贸易性质的特点。

（5） BOT（建设-经营-转让）

It refers to the construction of an established industrial project or infrastructure, including construction, maintenance, and transfer, operating within a fixed period of time and being allowed to recover the investment, operation and maintenance costs of the project and some service fee, rent and other expenses of the contract during the period. The project shall be transferred to the government of the project party after the expiration of the prescribed time limit. For example, the English Channel Undersea Tunnel, the Sydney Undersea Tunnel in Australia, and the Bangkok Expressway in Thailand.

指建设方承担一个既定的工业项目或基础设施的建设，包括建设经营、维修和转让，在一个固定的期限内运营并且被允许在该期限内收回对该项目的投资、运营与维修费用以及一些合同的服务费、租金等费用，在规定的期限届满后，将该项目转让给项目方的政府。例如，英吉利海峡海底隧道、澳大利亚悉尼海底隧道、泰国曼谷高速公路。

(6) Franchise（特许专营）

The franchise is a new type of commercial technology transfer that has developed rapidly in the latest two or three decades. It refers to a technology transfer by which a company that has achieved successful experience transfers its trademark, business name, service mark, patent, know-how, and management method or experience to another company and allows the latter to use them on condition that the franchise fee will be paid.

特许专营是最近二三十年飞速发展起来的一种新型商业技术转让方式。它是指由一家已经取得成功经验的企业，将其商标、商号名称、服务标志、专利、专有技术以及经营管理的方法或经验转让给另一家企业的一项技术转让，特许方在收取一定金额的特许费的前提下，允许被许可方使用它们。

A franchise contract is a long-term contract in which the parties operate in the same industry, sell the same products, provide the same services, use the same trade name and trademark, and even the stores' decoration, supplies, employee's overall, and production process and service delivery are exactly the same. This method is suitable for the situation that the licensor's products or services can't be exported to the target market, and the enterprise is not willing to invest in the target market, but its production process is relatively easy to be transfered to the other independent enterprise. This method is also the most common way that enterprises of developed countries open up the market in developing countries. It often appears in the catering industry, chain service industry, such as McDonald's, KFC, Starbucks, and Holiday Inn and so on.

特许经营合同是一种长期合同，其合同的双方经营同样的行业、出售同样的产品、提供同样的服务、使用同样的商号名称和商标，甚至店面的装潢、用品、员工的工作服、产品的制作工艺以及服务的提供方式也完全一致。这种方式适合于特许方的产品或服务不能出口到目标市场，企业又不愿意在目标市场投资生产，但其生产过程比较容易转移给另一独立企业的情形，这种方式也是发达国家的企业进入发展中国家市场的最普遍方式。常见于餐饮业、连锁经营的服务业，如麦当劳、肯德基、星巴克、假日酒店等。

3. International Compensation Trade Negotiation（国际补偿贸易谈判）

International compensation trade is one kind of trade which generally refers to one party purchasing machinery, equipment, technology, raw materials or labor services from another foreign party on the basis of credit, and agreeing to use its products, other commodities or labor services to settle the loan in installments within a certain period of time.

国际补偿贸易，一般是指一方在信贷的基础上，从国外另一方购买机器、设备、技术、原材料或劳务，约定在一定期限内，用其生产的产品、其他商品或劳务分期清偿贷款的一种贸易方式。

International compensation trade negotiations are generally divided into three stages: project selection, feasibility analysis, and substantive negotiations. Firstly, in international compensation trade negotiations, you should make adequate preparations before negotiating. In addition to making preparations for personnel and time that should be done in general trade negotiations, for the importer, it is also necessary to consider the supply of raw materials, labor organization, transportation, hydropower facilities and other basic conditions, as well as the determination of the scale of the project, the market positioning of the product, and the project's ability to pay debts. For the supplier, it is necessary to investigate the credit status, production technology level, production capacity of the importer, and the regulations on international compensation trade in the country where the importer is located. Secondly, it is necessary to flexibly choose the compensation form, including buy-back, counter purchase, processing fee compensation, mixed compensation, international trade certificate, and labor compensation, which type of compensation you choose depends on the specific circumstances and needs of the two parties. Finally, determine the compensation products. Because the selected compensation forms are different, the compensation products will also be different. When choosing compensation products, you should avoid choosing resource products, such as oil, natural gas, coal, etc., and try to choose industrial products with high added value; try to avoid occupying export quotas; choose compensation products to the extent possible; make the price reasonable.

国际补偿贸易谈判一般分为三个阶段：项目选择、可行性分析和实质性谈判。在国际补偿贸易谈判中，首先要在谈判前做好充分的准备工作。除了做好在一般贸易谈判中应做好的人员、时间上的准备以外，对引进方而言，还需要考虑原材料供给、劳动力组织、交通运输、水电配套设施等基础条件，以及工程规模的确定、产品的市场定位以及项目偿债能力等。对于供给方，需要调查引进方的资信情况、生产技术水平、生产能力以及引进方所在国家关于国际补偿贸易的规定。其次，需要灵活地选择补偿形式，包括回购、互购、加工费补偿、混合补偿、国际贸易证书、劳务补偿，究竟选择哪种补偿形式取决于双方的具体情况和需要。最后，确定补偿商品。由于选择的补偿形式不一样，所以补偿的商品也会不同。在选择补偿商品时应避免选择资源性产品，比如石油、天然气、煤炭等，应尽量选择附加值高的工业制成品；应尽量避免占用出口配额；在可能的范围内选择补偿商品；补偿商品的作价要合理。

4. International Financial Leasing Business Negotiation（国际融资租赁业务谈判）

The international financial leasing business means that the business where the lessor purchases the leased property from the supplier and provides it to the lessee for use, and the lessee pays the rent according to the lessee's selection of the supplier's leased property.

国际融资租赁业务是指出租人根据承租人对供货商租赁物的选择向供货商购买租赁物并提供给承租人使用，承租人支付租金的业务。

At present, in international equipment investment, financial leasing has become the second financing method after bank credit. In China, the financial leasing started in the early stage of China's reform and opening up, and the financing lease in China is mainly the import financing business, that is, the Chinese enterprises as the lessees rent the equipment for production from foreign lessors.

目前，在国际设备投资中，融资租赁已经成为仅次于银行信贷的第二大融资方式。在我国，融资租赁起步于改革开放初期，而且在中国融资租赁主要是进口融资业务，即中方企业作为承租人租用国外出租人的设备用于生产。

The content of international financial leasing business negotiation involves equipment supply agreement, financial leasing agreement, equipment maintenance service agreement, and loan agreements. Both parties need to negotiate the contents of the above agreements one by one and finally close a deal. Before the negotiation, you need to do the relevant preparatory work, such as selecting the equipment and suppliers for the lease, writing and submitting the project proposal for the rented equipment, selecting the appropriate leasing company, investigating the credit, personnel composition, technical level, the market competiveness of products of the lessee.

国际融资租赁业务谈判中涉及设备供应协议、融资租赁协议、设备维修服务协议、贷款协议，双方需要对以上协议的内容逐个进行磋商并最终达成一致。在谈判前企业需要做好相关准备工作，如选择租赁的设备和供货商；撰写并呈报租进设备的项目建议书；选择合适的租赁公司；对承租人的资信、人员构成、技术水平、产品的市场竞争力等进行审查。

Ⅳ Main Principles of International Business Negotiation（国际商务谈判的主要原则）

1. Principle of Equality and Mutual Benefit（平等互利原则）

In international business negotiation activities, equality and mutual benefit is the foothold for conducting business negotiations. The principle of equality is the basis of business negotiations. In international business negotiations, regardless of the economic strength of the negotiating parities in the countries where the negotiating parties are located, the size of the company, the legal status of the negotiating parties are equal, and they enjoy equal rights and fulfill their equal obligations. The principle of mutual benefit as the goal of negotiation means that the negotiating parties can finally obtain their own interests through negotiation by finally reaching an agreement. The principle of mutual benefit is based on the principle of equality, and only equality can achieve mutual benefit.

在国际商务谈判活动中，平等互利是进行商务谈判的立足点。平等原则是商务谈判的基础。在国际商务谈判中，不论谈判各方所在国家的大小贫富、谈判各方的经济实力强弱、公司规模大小，谈判各方的法律地位都是平等的，并且享有平等的权利，履行平等的义务。互利原则作为谈判的目标，是指谈判各方通过谈判最终达成一致的协议，能获得各自的利益。互利原则是以平等原则为基础的，只有平等才能实现互利。

In international business negotiations, all parties must fully understand and consciously abide by the principle of equality and mutual benefit. Neither party can force bullying and impose its own will on the other party. If one party only wants to get more and pay less, the other party may consider terminating the negotiation. Therefore, all parties should be fully prepared for the negotiation, and try to meet the needs of the other party on the premise of equality and without prejudice to their own interests, so that the negotiation can proceed smoothly and the negotiating parties can reach mutually beneficial negotiation aims.

在国际商务谈判中，谈判各方必须充分认识并且能自觉遵守平等互利的原则，任何一方都不能恃强凌弱，将己方的意愿强加给对方。如果一方只想要得到更多，付出更少，那么对方可能就会考虑终止谈判。因此，谈判各方都应该为谈判做好充分的准备，并且在平等的、不损害己方利益的前提下尽量满足对方的需求，这样谈判才能顺利进行下去，谈判各方才能达到互利互惠的谈判目标。

2. Principle of Trust（信任原则）

Trust is of great importance in business negotiation. Trust between group leader and group members as well as between two negotiating parties is a decisive element of shaping relationship of all parties. There are basically three types of trust in professional relationship：

信任原则在商务谈判中非常重要。谈判组长和谈判成员之间的信任以及谈判各方之间的信任是塑造各方关系的决定性因素。在职业关系中有三种类型的信任：

（1）Deterrence-based trust：people believe or expect that they will be punished if they do not do something based on consistency with past behavior.

基于威慑的信任：如果为了保持和过去行为的一致性而不去做某事，人们相信或期望他们会受到惩罚。

（2）Knowledge-based trust：people believe or expect that the other person will act in a certain way based on what they have learned. Predictability is based on their understanding of the other person's action，thoughts and intents，not just his past behavior.

基于知识的信任：人们相信或期望他人会根据他们所学的内容以某种方式行事。可预测性是基于他们对他人的行为、思想和意图的理解，而不仅仅是其过去的行为。

（3）Identification-based trust：people believe or expect that they can act on behalf of the other person because they share the interests，values and concerns of the other person very well. It involves substantial internalization of the other person's desires，intentions，values，and so on.

基于身份的信任：人们相信或期望他们可以代表他人行事，因为他们很好地分享了他人的利益、价值观和关注。它涉及对他人的欲望、意图、价值观等的实质内化。

Regardless of which kind of the above trust that a negotiation is based on，it is necessary to maintain this kind of trust in business negotiations. Parties should do what they say，and have a basis for speaking. Don't lose trust in the other party，so that the other party will question the sincerity of the negotiation，which may lead to the termination. Once you lose trust，the best way to save it is to admit your mistakes，win the other parties' understanding，get the involved parties back to the negotiating table and continue negotiations to achieve the benefits that the parties expect.

不论是基于以上哪种信任，在商务谈判中一定要维护好这种信任，一定要做到言而有信，出口有依据。万万不可信口开河，失信于对方，这样对方会对谈判的诚意产生质疑，从而可能会导致谈判终止。一旦失言，最好的挽救方法就是承认错误，赢得对方的谅解，使谈判各方重新回到谈判桌上，继续谈判，以实现各方期望得到的利益。

3. Principle of Win-win（双赢原则）

This principle is based on a solution by the negotiating parties to find the possibility of maximizing cooperation. The principle of win-win is important because it usually produces results that are more satisfactory to the negotiating parties than to bargain over the price. Win-win approach is a collaborative process and the negotiating parties ultimately achieve a win-win result by helping each other. The negotiating parties need to make sure that every question raised is not challenging and try to figure out how to defeat the counter-party. What's more, take other interests and benefits into consideration.

该原则是基于谈判各方为寻找最大化合作的可能性的解决方案。双赢原则很重要，因为它通常会产生比就价格讨价还价更令谈判各方满意的结果。双赢是一个协作的过程，谈判各方通过相互帮助最终实现双赢。谈判各方需要确保提出的每个问题都没有挑战性，并试图弄清如何击败对方，更重要的是考虑到其他方面的利益。

As for the methods and ways for the negotiating parties to achieve win-win, many negotiating experts at home and abroad have seriously studied and summarized the following aspects:

至于谈判各方达到双赢的方法和途径，国内外许多谈判专家都认真研究过，概括起来需遵循以下几个方面：

(1) If there is no agreement, what are the possible options? What impact will it have? Make a full assessment of this.

(2) Don't put too much emphasis on their own positions and focus on the interests, needs and cooperation.

(3) Fully communicate with the information and logic behind the interests in order to enhance mutual understanding.

(4) To assess whether the allocation of benefits is reasonable and whether the terms of the agreement are acceptable, standards that are adopted should be agreed by all parties.

(5) A mechanism should be established to allow negotiating parties to revisit the agreement when certain options fail or the situation changes.

(1) 如果无法达成一致，可能的备选方案是什么？会产生哪些影响？对此要做充分的评估。

(2) 不要过多强调各自的立场，将注意力放到利益、需求和合作上。

(3) 就利益背后的信息和逻辑进行充分沟通，以便增强彼此的理解。

(4) 评价利益分配是否合理以及协议条款是否能接受，应采用各方认可的标准。

(5) 应建立一种机制，在某些选择方案失败或形势发生变化时，谈判各方有机会重新探讨协议。

4. Principle of Seeking Common Ground While Putting Aside Differences（求同存异原则）

International business negotiations are different from domestic business negotiations. There are great differences in the negotiating environment and the objects of negotiation. The place of negotiation is likely to be abroad or in a third neutral country, and the objects involved are foreigners. Therefore, the negotiating parties have differences in customs, cultural background, legal system, and negotiating style, but there are also some commonalities. First, although there is a certain degree of divergence and conflict in the interests of the two parties, there is also consistency of interests. Negotiators are required to correctly judge the interests and needs of their own and the other party. For the common interests, they can reach an agreement. For existing differences and conflicts, they cannot be forced to try to close the differences. Second, when there are major differences and conflicts between the two parties, negotiators can adjust to different situations in accordance with the principles of seeking common ground while putting aside differences, so as to achieve the best negotiation results.

国际商务谈判不同于国内商务谈判，在谈判环境和谈判对象上都有很大的区别。谈判地点很可能在国外或中立的第三国，涉及的对象都是外国人。因此，谈判双方在风俗习惯、文化背景、法律制度、谈判风格等方面都存在差异，但是也应该看到共性。首先，谈判双方在利益上虽然存在一定程度的分歧和冲突，但同时也存在利益的一致性。这就需要谈判人员正确判断己方和对方的利益和需求。对于一致的利益，可以达成协议；对于存在的分歧和冲突，不能强求尽力弥合。其次，在双方分歧和冲突较大的情况出现时，谈判人员能本着求同存异的原则，（根据国际惯例和规则）针对不同的情况进行调整，从而达到最佳的谈判效果。

5. Principle of Flexibility（灵活机动原则）

In international business negotiations, it is necessary to flexibly use various negotiation skills to make the negotiations ultimately successful. The process of negotiation is not only a process of continuous zero-sum game between the two parties, but also a process of continuous organizing and thinking. Negotiators need to flexibly use various negotiation skills to speculate on the true ideas of the counter-party, so that the former can make themselves always in a favorable position. In short, during the entire negotiation process, on the premise of adhering to the basic principles of your own party, in order to facilitate the final success of the negotiation, you should have the flexibility to achieve the entire negotiation goals, adopting different negotiation skills according to different negotiation objects, different market competition conditions, and different sales intentions.

在国际商务谈判中，需要灵活运用各种谈判技巧使得谈判最终获得成功。谈判的过程既是双方不断进行零和博弈的过程，又是一个不断组织思考的过程，需要谈判人员灵活运用各种谈判技巧，揣测对方内心的真实想法，使己方在谈判中始终处于有利的位置。总之，在整个谈判过程中，在坚持己方基本原则的前提下，要有实现整个谈判目标的灵活性，要根据不同的谈判对象、不同的市场竞争状况、不同的销售意图，采用不同的谈判技巧，最终促成谈判的成功。

6. Principle of Interest Allocation（利益分配原则）

The purpose of negotiation is to reach agreement between parties with different interests.

Negotiation can be performed in a variety of forms. While the traditional competitive approach to negotiation trying to maximize one party's gain over the other party's loss, the collaborative approach focuses on parties with diverse interests working together to achieve mutually satisfying outcomes. However, no matter what form a negotiation may take, its goal of interest will never change.

谈判的目的是在具有不同利益的各方之间达成协议。谈判可以采取多种形式。传统的竞争性谈判方法试图以另一方的损失为代价最大化一方的收益，而协作方法则侧重于具有不同利益的各方的共同努力，以实现相互满意的结果。但是，无论谈判采取何种形式，其关注的目标都不会改变。

Any business negotiation occurring at home involves two aspects of interests: personal interest and organizational interest; however, in the international business negotiation, there are three aspects: personal interest, organizational interest and national interest. On what extent these interests can be unified, coordinated and balanced, to a large extent determines the progress and outcome of negotiations.

任何国内商务谈判都涉及两个层次的利益：个人利益和组织利益；但是国际商务谈判会涉及三个层次的利益：个人利益、组织利益和国家利益。在多大程度上这些利益可以统一、协调和平衡，在很大程度上决定了谈判的进展和结果。

（1）Personal Interests vs. Organizational Interests（个人利益与组织利益）

Personal interests mainly include realization of personal value, promotion to higher positions, increasing personal income and pursuing comfortable life. Comparatively speaking, personal interests can be easily brought into line with that of organizations since realization of one's personal value; social status and his reputation in others' expectation are linked closely with his performance and achievements done for the organization. Therefore, there is an interior connection between personal and organizational interests, so the realization of organizational interests means fulfillment of personal interests and vice versa.

个人利益主要包括实现个人价值、晋升至更高职位、增加个人收入和追求舒适的生活。相对而言，自实现个人价值以来，其社会地位和他在他人期望中的声誉与他为公司所做的业绩及取得的成就密切相关，这时个人利益很容易与组织的利益保持一致。因此，个人利益与组织利益之间存在内在联系。组织利益的实现意味着个人利益的实现，反之亦然。

（2）Personal Interests vs. Organizational & National Interests（个人利益与组织利益及国家利益）

Because there is a close internal relationship between personal interests and organizational interests, it is easier for personal interests to be consistent with organizational interests, but under normal circumstances, personal interests and national interests can easily conflict. For individuals, national interests seem to be far away from them, and their actual interests are not closely related. Therefore, individuals only consider the interests of the country as a general guiding principle. However, when an individual negotiates on behalf of a country in bilateral negotiations or multilateral negotiations, he/she is certainly representing the interests of the country and will do his/her best to fight for more benefits for the country. Because under this circumstance, the interests of the country are absolutely first. Once the interests of the country are damaged, it will definitely cause huge losses to organizations and individuals.

因为个人利益与组织利益存在紧密的内在联系，所以个人利益更容易与组织利益保持一致性，但是在通常情况下，个人利益与国家利益就很容易发生冲突。对于个人而言，国家利益似乎离个人很遥远，与个人的实际利益联系也不够紧密，因此，个人仅仅把国家的利益作为一个总体的指导原则来看待。然而，当个人代表国家在双边谈判或者多边谈判中进行谈判时，必定会代表国家的利益并且尽全力为国家争取更多的利益。因为在这种情况下，国家的利益绝对是第一位的，一旦国家的利益受损，必定会给组织和个人带来巨大的损失。

V Main Theory of International Business Negotiation（国际商务谈判的主要理论）

1. Game Theory（博弈论）

(1) Theoretical Basis（理论基础）

The game first appeared in the article "Games in the Living Room" published by American economist John von Neumann in 1928, and in 1944 he coauthored with German economist Oscar Morganstern a book called *Theory of Games and Economic Behavior* which marked the initial formation of game theory. The game originates from the word game, but its meaning is not the same as game in Chinese, but a game activity in which people abide by certain rules and win. In fact, in economic activities, there are also many games that are under certain rules, and the decision-making battles of the participants are games. Game theory is a theory that studies the rational choice between rational opponents in order to maximize their own interests and minimize losses. Game theory studies the conflicts between rational people, that is, games with participants who have perfect logical thinking ability and are interested in win.

博弈最开始出现在美国经济学家约翰·冯·诺依曼在1928年发表的文章《客厅里的游戏》中。在1944年他又与德国经济学家奥斯卡·摩根斯特恩合著了《博弈论与经济行为》一书，该书标志着博弈论的初步形成。博弈（game）源于游戏，但含义并不等同于汉语中的"游戏"，而是指人们遵守一定的规则，并且使自己获胜的游戏活动。其实在经济活动中，也有很多与游戏一样，都是在一定规则下，各参与方的决策较量，这就是博弈。博弈论是研究理性的对手之间旨在使己方利益最大化、损失最小化的策略选择的理论。博弈论研究的是理性人之间的冲突，即有完善的逻辑思维能力、对"赢"感兴趣的参与者的博弈。

(2) Game of Theory and Business Negotiation（博弈论与商务谈判）

The use of game theory is one of the important strategies in business negotiation. The concise and clear analysis of complicated and uncertain negotiations can make the research more scientific, standardized, and systematic. Look for certain regular things to establish a certain analysis mode, and thus build a basic framework for theoretical analysis of negotiations.

采用博弈论是商务谈判的重要策略之一。对复杂的、不确定的谈判进行简洁明了的博弈分析，可使研究进一步科学化、规范化、系统化。寻找某些规律性的东西，建立起某种分析模式，从而构建谈判理论分析的基础框架。

a. Classification of Business Negotiation（商务谈判的分类）

From the perspective of game theory, business negotiation can be divided into zero-sum game negotiation and non-zero-sum game negotiation. Zero-sum game negotiation is also called adversarial negotiation, and non-zero-sum game negotiation is also called cooperative negotiation. The tactics used in these two kinds of negotiations are different. In the zero-sum game negotiation, the interests of the negotiating participants are opposite, that is, the sum of the interests of the negotiating parties is a fixed value. The negotiating parties divide this fixed interest through negotiation. The bargaining in business negotiations are zero-sum game negotiations. An increase in the interest of the buyer means a decrease in the interest of the seller, and vice versa. In non-zero-sum games, the relationship between the negotiating parties is more complicated, especially when there are multiple negotiators involved, the relationship between the negotiating parties is complicated and changeable.

从博弈论的角度看，商务谈判可以分为零和博弈谈判和非零和博弈谈判。零和博弈谈判又被称为对立型谈判，非零和博弈谈判又被称为合作型谈判。在这两种谈判中所用到的战术是不同的。在零和博弈谈判中，谈判参与者的利益是对立的，也就是说，谈判双方的利益之和是一个固定的数值。谈判双方是通过谈判来分割这个固定利益。在商务谈判中的讨价还价环节一般都是零和博弈谈判。买方利益的增加就意味着卖方利益的减少，反之亦然。而在非零和博弈中，谈判各方的关系就比较复杂，特别是在有多个谈判方参与时，谈判各方之间的博弈关系就是复杂多变的。

b. Procedures of Business Negotiation（商务谈判的程序）

The business negotiation process based on game theory mainly includes three aspects. Firstly, establish value-at-risk, that is, preparation for business negotiations. Value-at-risk refers to the evaluation and determination of the content of the transaction to be conducted by the two parties who are intending to cooperate. For example, the estimated value of the goods to be purchased, the ideal price and the total capital required, as well as other additional conditions, the highest price that can be accepted, etc. Value-at-risk is the basis for negotiation between the two parties, and no value-at-risk cannot constitute negotiations. Secondly, determine the surplus of cooperation, that is, the value added by cooperation over non-cooperation. In fact, the bargain between two parties is to determine their respective surpluses. The distribution of the surplus of cooperation generally depends on the strength of the two parties and the use of negotiation strategies and skills. Safeguarding the basic interests of both parties is the basic goal that must be reached in the negotiation, and it is also the key to affect the success or failure of the negotiation. In business negotiations, as shown in Figure 1.2, if the total benefit of the cooperation between the two parties is $A + B$ (flexible space) $+ C$, both parties of the negotiation have their own minimum interests (ie, the critical point). The critical point of Party A is *A* and the critical point of Party B is *C*. If the minimum interests are not met, the negotiation will break. In fact, in the negotiation, the focus of the dispute between the two parties is in the interest elasticity area of *B*. When the interests of any one of the two parties are close to $A + B$ or $B + C$, they must stop, otherwise, they will touch the counter-party's critical point and negotiation will fail. Finally, reach the agreement to share the remaining interests. If the negotiation cannot continue, the negotiating parties cannot cooperate to realize their own interests, and at the same time, their own interests may be damaged. An agreement is a guarantee for the parties to share the remaining interests and a link to maintain continued cooperation.

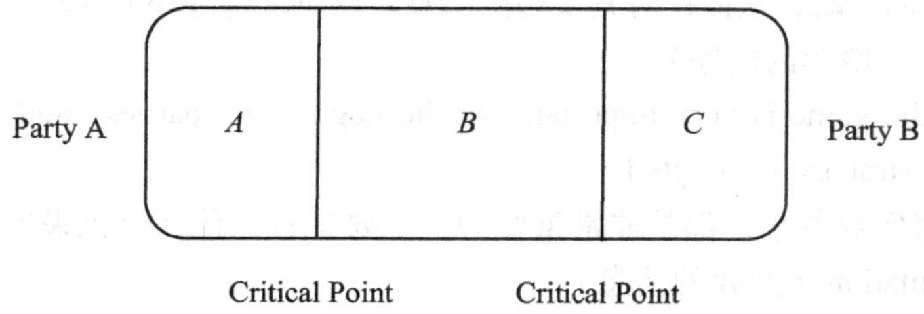

Figure 1.2 Surplus of Cooperation

在博弈论基础上的商务谈判程序主要包括三个方面。首先，建立风险价值，即商务谈判的准备。风险价值是指打算合作的双方对所要进行的交易内容的评估确定。例如，要购买的货物的预估价值、理想价格、所需要的总资金及其他附加条件、可以接受的最高价格等。风险价值是双方谈判的基础，没有风险价值就无法构成谈判。其次，确定合作剩余，即合作相比不合作增加的价值。其实在谈判过程中双方的讨价还价就是为了确定各自的剩余。合作剩余的分配一般取决于双方实力的大小和谈判策略、技巧的运用。维护双方的基本利益是谈判必须达到的基本目标，也是影响谈判成败的关键。在商务谈判中，如图 1.2 所示，假如双方合作所带来的利益总量为 $A+B$(弹性空间)$+C$，谈判双方都有各自的最低利益（即临界点）。甲方的临界点为 *A*，乙方的临界点为 *C*。如果最低利益得不到满足，谈判就会破裂。实际上在谈判中，甲、乙双方争夺的焦点在 *B* 这个利益弹性区域。当甲、乙双方中任何一方的利益接近 $A+B$ 或 $B+C$ 时，都要适可而止，否则触碰到对方的临界点，谈判就会失败。最后，达成分享剩余的协议。如果谈判无法继续进行，谈判各方就无法进行合作以实现各自的利益，同时还有可能使自身利益受损，而达成协议是谈判各方分享合作剩余的保证，也是维系继续合作的纽带。

c. Elements of Business Negotiation（商务谈判中的要素）

• Game Participant（博弈参加者）

Participants in the game may be natural persons, legal persons, or social organizations. Each party has its own strategy, which will increase the difficulty of negotiation. Therefore, when negotiating, it is necessary to clarify the strength of the players and transform the incomplete information into a complete information in order to win the negotiations.

博弈参加者可能是自然人、法人或社会组织，各方都有自己的策略，增加了谈判的难度。所以在谈判时首先需要弄清楚博弈方的实力，将不完全信息博弈转变为完全信息博弈，从而在谈判中取胜。

• Strategy Space（策略空间）

In business negotiations, with the different players, the strategies and skills will vary. Even if the same strategy is used, there will be differences due to different players in the implementation, and there is no exactly the same strategy space. Therefore, at the beginning of the game, you need to pay attention to the strategy adopted by the counter-party, so as to respond to its strategy in a timely manner and change the zero-sum game into a non-zero-sum game.

在商务谈判中，随着博弈方的不同，所采用的策略和技巧也会有所区别。就算运用同样的策略，实施时因博弈方不同也会有差异，没有完全相同的策略空间。所以在博弈开始时，需要关注对方采取的策略，从而针对其策略做出及时反应，将零和博弈转变为非零和博弈。

• Game Order（博弈的次序）

The order of the game is very important for the negotiating parties, and it mainly depends on what time what strategy is adopted.

博弈次序对博弈双方来讲都是非常重要的，主要是看在什么时机采取什么样的策略。

• Game Information（博弈的信息）

The information of the game is also crucial for the negotiating parties. To gain the upper hand in the information age, you must have a stable and reliable source of information to grasp various situations in the game in a timely manner, and at the same time make predictions on the behavior of the players based on the information, so that you can take the initiative in negotiations.

博弈中的信息对于谈判各方也是至关重要的。信息时代要在博弈中占上风，就要有一个稳定可靠的信息来源，及时掌握博弈中的各种情况，同时根据信息对博弈方的行为做出预测，使己方在谈判中处于主动位置。

The negotiating parties should fully understand the game process and interest structure in the negotiation in order to obtain the maximum benefits. The process of business negotiation is actually a game process. The negotiating parties have incomplete information in the game of rotating bids, and each has its own psychological expectations of the transaction price. However, in the final analysis, only through the cooperative game can the two parties obtain the remaining interests share of the transaction.

谈判各方应该充分了解谈判中的博弈过程和利益格局，才能获得最大利益。商务谈判的过程实际上就是一个博弈的过程。谈判各方在轮流出价的博弈中具有不完全信息，都对成交价格有各自的心理预期，但是，归根结底只有双方通过合作博弈，才能实现交易剩余的分享。

2. Theory of Negotiation Strength（谈判实力理论）

（1）Theoretical Basis（理论基础）

The theory of negotiation strength is based on a long-term study of negotiating skills by the famous American negotiator John Winkler, and the book *Bargaining for Results* systematically expounds theory of bargaining power. He believes that the basis for the use of negotiation skills and the basis for success are the negotiation strength. The use of skills has a very close relationship with the growth and decline of negotiation strength. The key to establishing and strengthening the negotiation strength is to fully prepare for the negotiation and fully understand each other. For business negotiations, Winkler also proposed a price-focused negotiation method, that is, price-quality-service-condition-price.

谈判实力理论基于美国著名谈判学家约翰·温克勒对谈判技巧的长期研究，他在《讨价还价技巧》一书中系统地阐述了“谈判实力理论”。他认为谈判技巧运用的依据和成功的基础就在于谈判实力。技巧的运用与实力的消长有着极为密切的关系。建立并加强谈判实力的关键在于对谈判的充分准备和对对方的充分了解。针对商务谈判，温克勒还提出了以价格为中心的谈判方法，即价格—质量—服务—条件—价格。

(2) Negotiating Strength（谈判实力）

a. Definition（谈判实力的定义）

Strength is a social phenomenon that gives people the ability to control others, events or activities. Negotiation strength refers to the comprehensive potential energy possessed by the negotiator relative to the counter-party in the negotiation, not only including the objective strength possessed by the negotiator, such as the economic strength of the enterprise, technological level, uniqueness, reputation, brand, etc., but also including the psychological potential compared with the counter-party, which is the source of negotiation strategies and skills. The negotiation strength exists objectively, but only the negotiation strength perceived by the counter-party is effective. Only the negotiation strength is stronger than the counter-party, you can take advantage of the initiative and master the initiative to achieve a beneficial result in the negotiation.

实力是一种社会现象，它赋予人们控制他人、事件或者活动的能力。谈判实力是指谈判者在谈判中相对于谈判对手所拥有的综合性势能，不仅包括谈判者所拥有的客观实力，如企业经济实力、科技水平、独特性、信誉、品牌等，而且包括谈判者与对方相比所拥有的心理势能，这是谈判策略和技巧的源头。谈判实力是客观存在的，但只有被对手感知到的谈判实力才是有效的。谈判实力强于对手，在谈判中就能占据优势和掌握主动，取得对己方有利的结果。

b. Main Factors Affecting the Negotiation Strength（影响谈判实力的主要因素）

It is very difficult for the negotiating parties to be completely symmetrical or equal in actual transactions. In most cases, the negotiation strength structure between two parties is asymmetric. The criteria for judging the strength of the negotiating parties are not factors such as economic strength and company scale, but it depends on other factors. The importance of the transaction to the two parties determines the negotiation strength. The transaction is more important to which party, indicating the higher the demand of that party. Then the worse the initiative, the weaker the negotiation strength, otherwise, the stronger the negotiation strength is. The endurance of time determines the negotiation strength. Time is an important factor to change the negotiation strength. The stronger the time endurance of the negotiator, the stronger the tolerance and initiative of the negotiation, and the stronger the negotiation strength. Therefore, the negotiator should have sufficient time and patience. The power determines the negotiation strength. The negotiation strength of the negotiators with limited power in the negotiation is strong. The strength of the competitors determines the negotiation strength. The more competitors the negotiator faces, the weaker the negotiation strength; the fewer competitors the negotiator faces, the more obvious his advantages; the higher the uniqueness, the stronger the negotiation strength. The degree of negotiation information determines the negotiation strength. Whoever has the information advantage, who has the initiative and stronger negotiation strength.

谈判双方的实力完全对称或均等在现实的交易中是很难出现的，更多的情况是谈判双方的实力结构不对称。判断谈判双方实力的标准并不是经济实力、公司规模等要素，而是取决于其他因素。交易对双方的重要性决定了谈判实力。交易对哪方更重要，说明该方的需求程度更高，那么其主动权就越差，谈判实力就越弱，反之，谈判实力就越强。谈判时间耐力的高低决定谈判实力的强弱。时间是改变谈判实力的重要因素。谈判者的时间耐力越强，谈判的承受力和主动性就越强，谈判实力就越强，因此，谈判者在谈判中应有充分的时间和耐心。权力大小决定谈判实力的强弱。在谈判中权力受限的谈判方的谈判实力强；竞争对手的强弱决定谈判实力的强弱。谈判者面临的竞争对手越多，实力越弱；谈判者面临的竞争对手越少，其优势越明显；谈判者的独特性越高，谈判实力就越强。谈判信息掌握的程度决定谈判实力。谁具有信息优势，谁就掌握主动权，谈判实力就强。

(3) Application in Business Negotiation (在商务谈判中的运用)

Firstly, set a deadline for structural negotiation conditions and threaten to withdraw from the negotiation to find other partners if the negotiation conditions are not accepted. Secondly, show your tough attitude and maintain a tough position in the negotiation to force the counter-party to compromise. Thirdly, ridicule the counter-party's position, despise or show disdain for its positions, and force it to abandon its claim. Fourthly, highlight your own plan, emphasize the importance of your suggestions through which to force the counter-party to compromise. Fifthly, threaten the relationship between the two parties and warn the counter-party to sever the relationship with it if it does not accept the conditions put forward by your party, so as to put pressure on the counter-party who relies on you and force it to make concessions.

第一，为结构谈判条件设定最后期限，并威胁如果到期不接受谈判条件将退出谈判以寻找其他合作伙伴。第二，显示强硬态度，在谈判中一直保持强硬立场从而迫使对方做出让步。第三，嘲笑对方立场，轻视或对对方的立场表示不屑一顾，迫使对方放弃自己的主张。第四，突出己方的方案，强调己方建议的重要性，并通过这种方法强迫对方做出让步。第五，威胁双方关系，警告对方如果不接受己方提出的条件就断绝与对方的关系，以此向对己方依赖较大的对方施加压力，从而迫使对方做出让步。

3. Theory of Negotiation Needs (谈判需要理论)

(1) Theoretical Basis (理论基础)

Theory of negotiation needs was put forward by Gerard Nierenberg, president of the American Negotiation Institute and barrister on the basis of summarizing the psychologist Maslow's hierarchy of needs. Hierarchy of needs indicates that basic human needs are divided into five types: physiological needs, safety needs, social needs, esteem needs, and self-actualization needs, and they evolve from low to high, as shown in Figure 1. 3. Based on this theory, Nierenberg systematically put forward the theory of negotiation needs in the book *The Art of Negotiating*.

谈判需要理论是由美国谈判学会会长、大律师杰勒德·尼尔伦伯格在总结心理学家马斯洛的“需要层次论”的基础上提出来的。需要层次论认为，人的基本需要分为生理需要、安全需要、社交需要、尊重需要和自我实现需要 5 种，并且是从低到高演进的，如图 1. 3 所示。在此理论基础上，尼尔伦伯格在《谈判的艺术》一书中系统地提出了谈判需要理论。

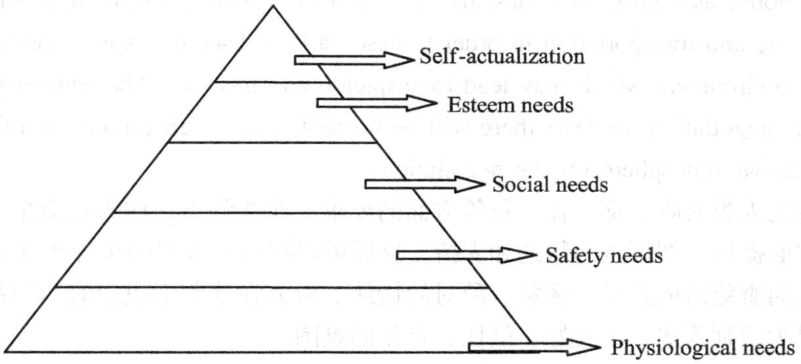

Figure 1. 3 Maslow's Hierarchy of Needs

(2) Contents（谈判需要理论的内容）

According to the theory of negotiation needs, the need is the basis and motivation of the negotiation, because every purposeful action of human beings is to satisfy a certain need. For the negotiating subject, if there is no unmet need, people will not come together to negotiate. Negotiators should discover the needs associated with the negotiating parties, pay attention to various needs that drive the counter-party, and choose different methods to affect the counter-party's motivation. Negotiation can be divided into three levels: negotiation between individuals, organization-to-organization negotiations, and state-to-state negotiations. The negotiator must pay attention not only to the needs of the organization, but also to the needs of the individual. By discovering and inducing the needs of the individual, the negotiator can influence personal position and views, and make the negotiation develop in the direction of benefiting your party.

谈判需要理论认为，需要是谈判产生的基础和动因，因为人类的每一种有目的的行为都是为了满足某种需要。对谈判主体而言，如果不存在某种未被满足的需要，人们就不会走到一起来谈判。谈判者应该去发现与谈判各方相联系的需要，对驱动对方的各种需要加以重视，以选择不同的方法来影响对方的动机。谈判可以分为 3 个层次：个人与个人之间的谈判、组织与组织之间的谈判以及国家与国家之间的谈判。谈判者不仅要重视组织的需要，而且要重视个人的需要，通过发现和诱导个人的需要，进而影响他的立场、观点，使谈判向有利于己方的方向发展。

(3) Application（谈判需要理论在谈判中的运用）

Negotiation not only meets the needs of your party, but also meets the needs of the counter-party. Friendly and cooperative relations between two parties can be further developed and strengthened. Such negotiations are successful ones. Based on the study of Maslow's hierarchy of needs, this theory can find needs that are connected to both parties of the negotiation.

通过谈判不仅使己方的需要得到满足，也使对方的需要得到满足，双方的友好合作关系才能得到进一步的发展和加强，这样的谈判才是成功的谈判。在研究马斯洛的需要层次论的基础上，我们可以看到，该理论可以找到与谈判双方都有联系的需要。

a. Physiological Needs（生理需要）

It is mainly reflected in human requirements for food, clothing, housing, and transportation. During negotiations, as a host, you must pay attention to providing all possible help and support in food, housing, and transportation in order to ease various discomforts and pressures caused by the unfamiliar environment which may lead to suspicion and hostility. The counter-party will also pay back in the negotiation, at least there will be no hostility, which can create a friendly, trusting and cooperative atmosphere for the negotiation.

主要体现为人类对吃、穿、住、行等方面的要求。在谈判中，作为东道主一定要注意在吃、住、行方面提供一切可能的帮助和支持，这样可以减轻对方因陌生环境所带来的各种不适和压力，从而避免造成急躁、怀疑、敌对的情绪。对方在谈判中也会有所回报，至少不会有敌意，可以为谈判营造一个友好、信任、合作的氛围。

b. Safty Needs（安全需要）

Safty needs is mainly reflected in personal safety and status security in the negotiation. When the negotiation is arranged on the guest field, due to the lack of understanding of the local customs, social order, and traffic conditions, the counter-party will feel insecure in action. As a host, you should try your best to give the counter-party as much companionship as possible during the free time outside negotiation, such as private car transfers, escort visits, excursions, etc. Doing so will allow the other party to treat yourself as an acceptable and dependable person, which is beneficial to the smooth progress of the negotiations.

安全需要在谈判中主要体现在人身安全和地位安全上。当谈判安排在客场时，由于对方对当地风俗习惯、社会治安、交通状况缺乏了解，在行动上会感觉缺少安全感。作为东道主的一方，应该尽力在谈判之余给予对方尽量多的陪伴，如专车接送、陪同参观、游览等。这样做可以让对方把己方当作可以接受、可以依赖的人来看待，这对谈判的顺利进行是有利的。

c. Social Needs（社交需要）

The needs at this level are mainly reflected in the hope of the two parties in the friendship and the establishment of friendly relations between the two parties, and their dependence on the enterprise and the desire to strengthen the unity and cohesion within the enterprise. Therefore, negotiators should have a friendly and cooperative mentality and use every opportunity to promote and develop friendship with each other. For example, invite counter-party to a family dinner, give counter-party gifts, and so on. Once the negotiating parties have friendship as the basis, it will be much easier to make concessions and reach an agreement. At the same time, the negotiating team should maintain a high degree of unity. If a negotiating team's internal opinions are not consistent, this will damage the individual's sense of belonging to the organization which will give the counter-party the opportunity to intervene, and will cause great damage to your party.

这一层次的需要主要体现在谈判双方对友谊、对建立双方友好关系的希望；对本企业的依赖以及对加强企业内部的团结与凝聚力的希冀。因此，谈判人员应该持有一种友好合作的心态，利用一切机会促成和发展与对方的友情。例如，邀请对方参加家宴、赠送对方礼品等。一旦谈判双方有了友情作为基础，让步与达成协议就会容易很多。同时，谈判小组内部应该保持高度团结。如果一个谈判小组内部意见不合，就会损害个人对组织的归属感，会给对方乘机而入的机会，给己方带来极大的损害。

d. Esteem Needs（尊重需要）

It is not only to be respected in personality, but also to be respected and appreciated in terms of status, identity, and ability. Do not use insulting language, be polite and do not personally attack negotiators during negotiations. Receiving people should comply with the rules of business etiquette, especially when dealing with the negotiators who have different positions, pay attention to being equal. When you have the upper hand in negotiations, don't be overjoyed or even ridicule the counter-party.

在谈判中主要体现在不仅要在人格上得到尊重，而且在地位身份、学识与能力上要得到尊重和欣赏。在谈判中不能使用侮辱性的语言，要言辞有礼，不能对谈判人员进行人身攻击。待人接物要符合商务礼仪的规范，特别是在处理双方谈判人员的级别职务时，要注意做到对等。当在谈判中占据上风时，不要喜形于色甚至讥讽对方。

e. Self-actualization Needs（自我实现需要）

This is the highest level of needs, and it is mainly reflected in the pursuit of the actualization of the goals of negotiations for the benefit of your own party and its shareholders, and the achievements of the negotiations to reflect your own value. In negotiations, it is almost impossible to abandon one's own interests to satisfy the counter-party's self-actualization needs. When your party gains more benefits, you can emphasize various conditions that are objectively unfavorable to the counter-party, and appreciate the counter-party's subjective efforts and ability in order to help it to maintain a sense of inner balance.

这是最高层次的需要，它在谈判中主要体现为追求谈判目标的实现，为己方和股东争取利益，以谈判中取得的成就来体现自己的价值。而在谈判中，要放弃自身利益去满足对方自我实现的需要几乎是不可能的。当己方获取较多利益时，可以通过强调各种客观上对对方不利的条件，赞赏对方主观上做出的努力和过人的能力，来让对方获得内心的平衡。

Summary

International business negotiations are different from general business negotiations. International business negotiations have the characteristics of internationality, cross-culturality, complexity, international policy factors, and difficulty. The content of international business negotiations involves international trade in goods, technology, compensation, and international financial leasing. The main principles of international business negotia-tions include the principle of equality and mutual benefit, the principle of trust, the principle of win-win, and the principle of seeking common ground while putting aside differences, etc. International business negotiation requires a certain theory as the basis. This book mainly introduces game theory, the theory of negotiation strength, and the theory of negotiation needs.

国际商务谈判与一般商务谈判既有共性又有区别。国际商务谈判具有国际性、跨文化性、复杂性、国际政策因素、困难性等特点。国际商务谈判的内容涉及货物贸易、技术贸易、补偿贸易、国际融资租赁等。国际商务谈判的主要原则包括平等互利原则、信任原则、双赢原则、求同存异原则等。国际商务谈判需要一定的理论作为基础，本书主要介绍了博弈论、谈判实力理论和谈判需要理论。

Module Ⅱ Terminology Practice

1. International Trade: The fair and deliberate exchange of commodity and service across national boundaries.

2. International Settlement: Financial activities conducted among different countries in which payments are effected or funds are transferred from one country to another, in order to settle accounts, debts, claims, etc.

3. International Insurance: Conclude an agreement with an international insurance company in which the insured needs to pay money and the insurer pays the costs if the insured has an accident, injury, etc.

4. International Transportation: Goods to be carried from one country to another by various modes of transportation.

5. Enquiry: Importer intends to make a purchase of some goods and asks some information from exporter, such as price, samples, catalogue, discount, delivery date, terms of payment, insurance.

6. Offer: Reply to an enquiry from customer. It includes firm offer and non-firm offer.

7. Counter-offer: Customers reject any terms or conditions of the original offer and send new terms to customers.

8. Simple License: Also called non-exclusive license. The licensor grants the licensee to use a trademark or a technology to produce, manufacture and sell the product under the technology within the time and regions specified in the contract. The right to continue to use the trademark and the technology to produce, manufacture and sell contracted products will be remained, and the technology may be transferred to the third party for use.

9. Sole License: The licensor permits the licensee to implement the patent exclusively within the time and geographical scope agreed in the contract. At the same time, not only can the licensor no longer permit third parties to implement the patent in the same way, but also the licensor himself cannot implement it.

10. Exclusive License: The licensor gives the licensee the exclusive right to use a certain commodity or a certain technology to produce, manufacture and sell the product under the technology within the time and regions specified in the contract, and may not continue to use the trademark in the region. And the use of this technology to produce, manufacture and sell contracted products, and the technology may not be transferred to the third party.

11. Sub-license: The licensor allows the licensee to transfer part or all of the rights it obtains from the licensor to a third party within the time and regions specified in the contract. The licensee may enter into a sub-license contract with a third party in his own name and within the time and the licensed regions to obtain a technology transfer fee.

12. Cross License: Both the licensor and the licensee will provide their own technology usage rights to the other party. The essence is that both parties are interested in each other's technology, and exchange the use of technology and the right to sell the products on the basis of mutual benefit.

Module Ⅲ New Words

1. win-win *adj.* 双赢的，对各方有利的
2. reflect *v.* 反映；反射（声、光、热等）；显示，表明
3. offset *n.* 开端；出发；抵消；补偿 *v.* 抵消；弥补；补偿
4. equitability *n.* 公平性，公正性
5. accuracy *n.* 准确（性）；精确（程度）
6. values *n.*（商品）价值；用途；积极作用 *v.* 重视；珍视；给……估价
7. legitimacy *n.* 合法性；正统；正统性；嫡系
8. face-to-face *adj.* 面对面的 *adv.* 面对面地
9. multi-lingual *adj.* 多语言的；多语种的；能说多种语言的
10. visible *adj.* 看得见的；可见的；明显的；能注意到的
11. tangible *adj.* 有形的；实际的；真实的；可感知的 *n.* 有形资产；可触知的或具体的事物
12. participate *v.* 参加，参与
13. participant *n.* 参与者，参加者
14. arbitration *n.* 仲裁；公断
15. know-how *n.* 专门知识；技能；实际经验
16. contractor *n.* 承包人；承包商；承包公司
17. trademark *n.* 商标；（人的行为或衣着的）特征；标记
18. patent *n.* 专利权；专利证书 *adj.* 有专利的；受专利保护的；明显的 *v.* 获得专利权
19. licensor *n.* 许可方；授权商；许可人；授权人
20. licensee *n.* 售酒执照持有者；特许制作（使用）……的人（公司）

Module Ⅳ Useful Expressions

1. business negotiation 商务谈判
2. common practice 普遍做法；惯例
3. service trade 服务贸易
4. technological trade 技术贸易
5. domestic business 国内贸易，国内商务
6. financial interest 经济利益
7. terms and conditions （合同）条款
8. delivery date 装运期
9. methods of payment 付款方式
10. discounted price 折扣价，低价
11. right and obligations 权利与义务
12. transfer of assets 资产转移
13. social ideology 社会意识形态
14. mother tongue 母语
15. trade fair 交易会，展销会
16. commodity inspection 商品检验
17. force majeure 不可抗力；不可抗力因素
18. intellectual property 知识产权
19. large scale 大规模的；大范围的；大型的
20. time limit 期限；时限

Module Ⅴ Exercise

Ⅰ. Answer the following questions according to the text.

1. What is the essence of negotiation?
2. What is the purpose of negotiation?
3. What is the core of negotiation? Why?
4. What is international business negotiation?
5. What are the general characteristics of international business negotiation?
6. What are the special features of international business negotiation?
7. How to understand the cross-culturality of international business negotiation?
8. How many types of international business negotiation are there? What are they?
9. What are the specific contents of international technological trade?
10. What is "franchise"? Give some examples of franchise in your life.

Ⅱ. Match the words in Column A with their definitions in Column B.

Column A	Column B
1. negotiation	A. a special name, sign, word that is marked on a product
2. force majeure	B. acceptable or allowed by law
3. accuracy	C. to obtain a special document giving right to sell new products
4. equitability	D. to take part in an activity or event
5. legitimacy	E. a company that agrees to do work for another company

6. participate	F. process of judging officially how an argument be settled
7. arbitration	G. the ability to do something without making a mistake
8. contractor	H. unexpected events, for example a war
9. trademark	I. treating all people in a fair and equal way
10. patent	J. official discussions between the representatives of opposing groups who are trying to reach an agreement, especially in business or politics

Ⅲ. Translate the following terms and phrases into Chinese.

1. nature of negotiation
2. cross cultural
3. consultation agreement
4. negotiating opponents
5. interpersonal relationship
6. religious belief
7. common interest
8. complicated environment
9. good eloquence
10. domestic legislation
11. technological transfer
12. negotiating strategy
13. pursue different goals
14. counter-offer
15. reach a settlement
16. proprietary technology
17. excess capacity
18. trade intermediary
19. turn-key operations
20. license agreement

Ⅳ. Please determine whether the following statements are True or False.

1. In international business negotiation, price is the key point because it concerns the economic interests for both parties. (　　)

2. When negotiating with the counter-party, you only need to focus on your own benefit and interest. (　　)

3. In international business negotiation, both parties always require the translators to obtain their goals. (　　)

4. Both parties should try to understand each other's point of view before making decision. (　　)

5. International business negotiation is totally different from the domestic business negotiation. (　　)

6. International technological negotiation is the main type of international business negotiation. (　　)

7. Burger King belongs to franchise. (　　)

8. Know-how is the same as trademark. (　　)

9. When Indian people nod their heads, it means "yes". (　　)

10. Negotiation is based on mutual understanding and communication. (　　)

Ⅴ. Translate the following sentences into Chinese.

1. Negotiation is a social phenomenon and a special embodiment of human relations.

2. Success in negotiation is seen not to be measured in points scored off one's opponents, but in the contribution that the negotiation makes to the successful operation of the activity as a whole.

3. The entire process of negotiation is founded on the premise that both are interdependent.

4. The unique characteristic of international versus domestic business negotiations is that international business negotiation is influenced by a wide diversity of environments.

5. Win-win approach has proved to be successful and effective in many tough negotiations, because it takes into full consideration of both parties' interests.

Ⅵ. Translate the following sentences into English.

1. 谈判是我们每天生活中都会经历的事情。
2. 谈判者需要就共同的利益和目标交换意见从而调整自己的谈判策略。
3. 只有“双赢”的谈判才是真正意义上成功的谈判。
4. 国际商务谈判主要存在于经济领域。
5. 在谈判中没有所谓的对错，因此我们要忽略讨价还价的立场。
6. 在国际商务谈判中，最根本的原则是平等互利原则。
7. 很乐意收到贵方继续进口我方丝绸的订单。
8. 我们之间一定还有商量的余地。

Ⅶ. Case Study

Case 1: Successful Business Negotiations between Daimler-Benz AG and Chrysler Automobile Manufacturing Company

Case Source: Li Pinyuan. *International Business Negotiation*. Wuhan: Wuhan University Press, 2006.

Preface

Time: 1997-1998

Key Point: Successful Negotiation between Daimler-Benz AG of Germany and Chrysler Automobile Manufacturing Company of the United States

Background

Industry: Manufacturing

Subject: Daimler-Benz and Chrysler

Issue: The successful merger of German Daimler-Benz AG and Chrysler Automobile Manufacturing Company has brought greater benefits to both parties.

In 1994, Daimler-Benz's subsidiary, Medes-Benz Co., Ltd., under the leadership of Helmut Verna, began looking for partners. Because of the Mercedes brand alone, its growth space has reached its limit. To gain new growth points, the brand series must be expanded. At the time, Chrysler was "satisfied with the thirst" for a long time. "Chrysler and Daimler-Benz are the perfect match, I have no doubt about this." said Chrysler chairman Eaton.

During the eight-month negotiation period, Daimler gave the secret operation a name called "Gamma". "Gamma" is the third letter in Greek, and the previous letter represents a joint plan that has been conducted but has not been successful. In May 1998, Daimler-Benz AG of Germany and the Chrysler Automobile Manufacturing Company of the United States announced the merger to form the new DaimlerChrysler Company. The two strong joints determine the fate of nearly half a million people, and will also create an annual turnover of up to 260 billion DM, almost equal to the gross domestic product of Denmark. The news immediately caused a sensation in the global industry and the economic community. On the same day, the *Wall Str-eet Journal* published an article entitled "Daimler-Chrysler's Secret Talks—Two Strong Combinations of $ 35 Billion". When the article was published, Daimler's stock soared immediat-ely from 178 German mark to 201 German mark, and Chrysler's stock also rose from 41 US doll-ars to 53 US dollars.

Questions

1. What is international business negotiation?
2. What is the purpose of the negotiations?

Appendix

Characteristics of international business negotiations include the strong policy nature of state and business negotiations. International business should be handled in accordance with international practices. The factors affecting negotiation are complex and diverse, involving a wide range of issues, and the content of negotiations is diversified and complex.

Case 2: The "Win-win" Principle of International Business Negotiations

Case Source: Han Yuzhen. *International Business Negotiation Practice*. Beijing: Peking University Press, 2006.

Preface

Key Point: The Chinese side negotiated with the supplier on the payment method and finally reached an agreement.

Background

Industry: Project

Subject: Chinese Company and Foreign Company T

Issue: The Chinese company finally agreed to use the letter of credit to pay foreign merchants through negotiations.

In a hydropower project, the Chinese owner won a large amount of concessional loans. When the owner selects the supplier for the purchase of hydropower equipment, in order to facilitate the unification of the standard for evaluation, in accordance with international practice, the company agrees to use the letter of credit by the manufacturers. The payment method is quoted, and finally Company T won the bid. When the contract for the supply is to be signed, there is a disagreement within the owner about the payment method. Under normal circumstances, we use this type of foreign loan to pay by collection. Because we use the letter of credit to pay, we have no right to examine the document, the risk is greater, and the opening of the letter of credit requires a higher certificate. Fees, therefore, were proposed to pay by the collection method. However, Company T expressed strong opposition to this. It proposed that the original quotation was calculated based on the payment by letter of credit. If the Chinese party must change the collection method, the contract price will increase by 1.1 million US dollars. It turns out that if Company T collects money by collection, the interval between them is about 10 days longer than that of the letter of credit. That is, Company T receives more than 10 RMB for each payment from the receipt of the actual payment. About a day, this means that it will take up more than 10 days of funds, which means that Company T has to bear the cost of capital equivalent to paying interest to the bank for 10 days. The entire supply contract is divided into 8 payments, and the winning bidder is added. Almost as much as $1.1 million is bank interest. In order to reduce the risk, the Chinese owner has negotiated with the supplier and obtained confirmation from both opening banks. The terms of the letter of credit ensure that the real payment location is in China. Under such conditions, the Chinese owner quickly and unanimously agreed to use the letter of credit to pay the winning bidder, thereby speeding up the payment time to the outside party and avoiding the extra expenses incurred by the foreign party. We have avoided the losses caused by the increase in contract prices.

Questions

1. In this case, what principles have been followed by the negotiating parties?
2. In what ways can the principles be applied in the negotiations?

Appendix

A win-win situation should include three aspects: first, through negotiations, not only the needs of the parties will be met, but also the needs of the other party will be satisfied. Second, the friendly and cooperative relations between the two sides will be further developed and strengthened. Third, the entire negotiation is highly efficient.

Ⅷ. Role plays practice. Work in pair and converse according to the given information.

Task 1

Background

Your role:

You're the sales managers of the BEST Home Textiles Corporation. Your products include towels, bedclothes, tablecloth and curtains. You're now having a talk with an Africa business person about your company, the scope of business and the products, trying to persuade him to buy your products.

Your partner's role:

You're a newcomer at the foreign trade area. This is your first visit to China. You're not sure whether you can close a deal or not. The goods you want to purchase are curtains. After going over the catalogue, you find some items very attractive, so you ask a lot of questions.

Terms and Phrases

skillful manufacture	beautiful in colors	sophisticated technology
finely processed	pretty and colorful	modern design
excellent quality	reliable quality	elegant styles
wide varieties	fashionable patterns	durable in use
world-wide renown	reliable reputation	to have a long history

Relative Expressions

1. What company do you work for?
2. The name of company is...
3. Our company is located in...
4. Our headquarter is in...
5. What line of business do you do?
6. Our major products are...
7. We're in the insurance business.
8. What can you tell me about (this product)?
9. Could you please give me some information /details about this?
10. What is special/unique about this?
11. This is one of our latest design/products.
12. Tell me about this one/model.
13. This is one of our top brands.
14. This one is the best in its class.
15. We're really pleased with its performance.
16. I highly recommend this one.
17. This model comes with several features.

Task 2

Background

Your role:

Jeff Chen, the sales representative from Hunan Senan Industries and Trade Imp. & Exp. Co., Ltd., You've met Nissim Picker at the Canton Fair. And he was very keen on your latest products of hardware. You invited him to visit your factory and hoped his company could establish business relationship with you.

Your partner's role:

Nissim Picker, a sales manager from British Royal Co., Ltd. And you met Jeff Chen at the Canton Fair and were interested in their products. He invited you to visit his factory. After visiting and making some investigation, you decided to establish business relationship with him and place a trial order.

Terms and Phrases	
enter into/establish business relation with	be available for supply
bottom/favorable price	have extensive connections with
in charge of	mutual understanding
as is known	open an account with
be in this line of business	up to date

Relative Expressions

1. In order to acquaint you with our latest product, we take pleasure in...
2. We're willing to enter into business relations with your firm.
3. Your firm has been introduced/recommended to us by...
4. Our mutual understanding and cooperation will certainly result in important business.
5. We express our desire to establish business relations with your firm.
6. We specialize in...
7. Your desire to establish business relations coincides with ours.
8. Our lines are...
9. We have been in this line of business for...
10. It would be very helpful if you could...
11. We would like to ask you...

Chapter 2

Composition, Classification and Basic Procedure of International Business Negotiation

Work Objective

After studying this chapter, you will be able to:

- master the components of international business negotiation;
- understand and apply various components in international business negotiation;
- familiarize with the types of international business negotiation;
- apply different types of international business negotiation under different circumstances;
- familiarize with the basic procedure of international business negotiation;
- understand the different negotiation modes of international business negotiation.

Case Guide-Reading

Party A of a certain company in Country A and Party B of a certain urban construction company in Country B formally signed a contract on May 18, 2015 after a number of rounds of negotiations. Party B is responsible for the construction of a restaurant. The contract stipulates: The total construction area of the project is 1,140 square meters, and the total budget cost is 12.47 million yuan. According to Party A's construction engineering design drawings, the quality specifications shall be in accordance with the conditions used in the earthquake zone of magnitude 8. When the first phase of the project was completed on September 25 of the same year, Party A found that the quality of the completed part was unqualified, so there was a serious dispute with Party B about the quality of the project, and then Party A was forced to sue in the local court. After accepting the case, the local court investigated the credit of Party B with the assistance of a law firm in Country B. It found that Party B was indeed a company registered in Country B, but its registered capital was only \$2,000. According to the law, the limited liability company's ability to assume responsibility is limited to its registered capital. This means that even if Party A wins the case, no matter how much damage Party B causes to Party A, the maximum amount of compensation is limited to \$2,000. After Party A learned of the details, it had to abandon the claim for compensation and instead requested to terminate the contract. Finally, in accordance with the requirements of Party A, the court terminated the contract on the grounds that the defendant's rights and abilities were insufficient. Party A only recovered all the deposits paid to Party B. Other losses were only borne by itself. We can see from this case that the fundamental reason for Party A's damage is that it did not find out the qualifications of Party B before the negotiation. Although the contract has stipulated the project cost and quality clause, it cannot avoid its own losses.

Source: Wan Chenglin, Shu Ping. *Marketing Business Negotiation Skills*. Tianjin: Tianjin University Press, 2003.

Module Ⅰ Text

Ⅰ Components of International Business Negotiation (国际商务谈判的构成要素)

International business negotiation as a responsible and rigorous business activity is a process in which different elements interact. Only by systematically understanding various elements that constitute the negotiation, the negotiators can grasp the initiative of the negotiation from the overall situation, so that you can move forward and retreat freely in the process of negotiation, and finally achieve the expected purpose of the negotiation. The components of the negotiation include the negotiating subject, the negotiating object, the negotiation information, the negotiation environment, the negotiation time, the negotiation place, and the negotition result, etc.

国际商务谈判作为一项负责而严密的商务活动，是由不同的要素相互作用的一个过程。谈判人员只有从整体上系统地认识构成谈判的各个要素，才能从全局把握谈判的主动权，使己方在谈判的过程中进退自如、攻防有度，最终达到谈判的预期目的。谈判的构成要素包括谈判主体、谈判客体、谈判信息、谈判环境、谈判时间、谈判地点、谈判结果等。

1. Negotiating Subject (谈判主体)

Negotiating subject, that is, the parties involved in the negotiation, refers to those who participate in business negotiation and actively understand and influence the counter-party so that the counter-party understands or accepts its own views, interests or behaviors. The negotiating subject can be a natural person or a group; the negotiating subject can represent the interests of the negotiators, and can also represent the interests of an organization, a region or a country. It should be noted that the negotiating subject must bear legal responsibility for its words and deeds, otherwise the completed negotiations are also invalid.

商务谈判的主体即谈判的当事人，指参加商务谈判活动、主动了解并影响对方，从而使对方理解或接受己方观点、利益或行为方式的人员。谈判主体可以是自然人，也可以是一个团体；谈判主体可以代表谈判人员的自身利益，也可以代表一个组织、一个地区或一个国家的利益。需要注意的是，谈判主体必须对自己的言行承担法律责任，否则已经完成的谈判也是无效的。

Negotiating subject consists of the subject of behavior and the subject of relationship. The subject of behavior is the persons who actually participate in the negotiation. In the business negotiation, subject of negotiation is the main factor, which plays a vital role in the whole negotiation process. The effectiveness of business negotiation depends to a large extent on the subjective initiative and creativity of the negotiation subject. The subject of relationship is the natural person, social organization and other entities that have the right to participate in the negotiation and bear the consequences in the business negotiation, and other entities that can enjoy rights and assume obligations in the negotiation or in the performance of contract.

商务谈判的主体由行为主体和关系主体构成。行为主体是实际参与谈判的人。在商务谈判活动中，谈判主体是主要因素，在整个谈判过程中起着至关重要的作用，商务谈判活动的成效在很大程度上取决于谈判主体的主观能动性和创造性。关系主体是在商务谈判中有权参加谈判并承担谈判后果的自然人、社会组织以及其他能够在谈判或履约中享有权利、承担义务的各种实体。

In order to ensure the smooth progress of the negotiations and avoid mistakes, the following aspects about the subject must be reviewed before the negotiation. First of all, whether the negotiating subject has the right to participate in the negotiations, and is able to successfully complete the negotiating task through his actions. Secondly, review the qualifications of the counter-party's negotiating subject, which may require the counter-party, directly or indirectly to provide relevant authorization documents and materials for the verification of the negotiation eligibility. In the negotiation process with the counter-party, it is necessary to require it to provide proof of various equipment and technologies, and to investigate the counter-party' ability to perform the contract, so as to ensure the authenticity and effectiveness of the counter-party's subject qualification.

为了保证谈判的顺利进行，避免出现失误，在谈判之前必须对谈判主体就以下几个方面进行审核。首先，谈判主体是否有权参加谈判，并能够通过自己的行为很好地完成谈判任务。其次，审查对方的谈判主体资格，可以通过直接或间接的途径要求对方提供谈判资格审定的相关授权文件、资料等。在与对方谈判的过程中，需要对方提供各种设备、技术的证明材料，并对对方的履约能力进行调查，从而确保对方主体资格的真实有效。

2. Negotiating Object（谈判客体）

Negotiating object is the combination of negotiating issues and various material elements.

In business negotiations, the contents of negotiating issues are very broad and there are almost no restrictions. Any tangible and intangible item that can be bought and sold can be used as the issue of business negotiation. There are funds, such as price and payment methods; there are technical cooperation, such as technical standards; there are commodities, such as the quality, quantity, warehousing, shipment, insurance, inspection and quarantine. The negotiating issue is the cause of the negotiation and the center of the negotiation activities. Without negotiating issues, the negotiation activities cannot be carried out, so the negotiators need to have a full understanding and analysis of the negotiating issues, so as to grasp the initiative of the negotiations.

商务谈判的客体，是谈判的议题和各种物质要素结合而成的内容。在商务谈判中，谈判议题的对象非常广泛，几乎没有限制。任何可以买卖的有形的、无形的物品都可以作为商务谈判的议题。有资金方面的，如价格和付款方式；有技术合作方面的，如技术标准方面的问题；有商品方面的，如商品的质量、数量、仓储、装运、保险和检验检疫等。谈判议题是谈判的起因，是谈判活动的中心。没有谈判议题，谈判活动就无从开展，所以谈判人员需要对谈判议题有充分的了解和分析，从而掌握谈判的主动权。

But to truly be the negotiating object, the following three basic conditions must be met:

但要真正作为商务谈判的客体，还需要满足以下三个基本条件：

(1) Commonality (共同性)

The issue of business negotiation must involve the relationship between the two parties. It is the common concern of both parties and what both parties hope to resolve. Otherwise, it cannot be the issue of negotiations.

商务谈判的议题必须涉及双方的利害关系，是谈判双方共同关心并且希望得到解决的，否则不能成为谈判的议题。

(2) Talkability (可谈性)

The negotiation time must be right for both parties. If the timing of the negotiation is not right, even the issues are concerned and hoped to be resolved by both parties, they cannot sit at the negotiating table. Choosing a right time to negotiate is the prerequisite for the parties to communicate, and the right negotiation time is gradually reached by the parties through their efforts. For example, the Iran-Iraq war broke out in 1980, during which time many countries called for the two sides to resolve disputes through peaceful negotiations, but it was not until eight years after the war that two sides actually sat at the negotiating table.

对谈判双方来说谈判时机要成熟。如果谈判时机不成熟，即使是双方都关心并希望得到解决的问题，双方也不能坐到谈判桌前。谈判时机的成熟是谈判各方得以沟通的前提，而成熟的谈判时机是各方通过努力而逐步达成的。例如两伊战争于1980年爆发，其间许多国家都呼吁双方通过和平谈判的方式来解决争端，但直到交战8年后，双方才真正坐到谈判桌前。

(3) Legitimacy (合法性)

Negotiating issues must comply with the relevant laws. Some trade activities are expressly prohibited by national laws, such as smuggled ammunition, drugs, and national protected cultural relics. Therefore, the negotiating issues must be within the legal limits of the countries where the negotiating parties are located.

谈判议题必须符合相关法律的规定。有些贸易活动是各国法律明文禁止的，如走私弹药、毒品以及国家保护文物等。所以，谈判议题必须在谈判各方所在国家的法律允许范围内。

3. Other Elements（其他要素）

（1）Negotiation Information（谈判信息）

Negotiation information refers to terms, conditions, etc. that are closely related to negotiating activities, and is a special kind of artificial information. Without comprehensive, accurate and timely information, the negotiator cannot specify the negotiation strategy, and the main speaker cannot accurately find the entry point of the negotiation, and the negotiation is difficult to succeed. Therefore, the information on which the negotiation decision is based should be accurate and true. For example, in the 1990s, the United States received intelligence that the Chinese "Yinhe" ship was loaded with chemical weapons precursors (raw materials) to Iran, so it required the Chinese government to order the "Yinhe" ship to return to the place of departure, or to accept the boarding cargo inspection by the United States. China had negotiated with the United States for many times, and then a third country sent people to board the ship for inspection, but did not find any chemicals accused by the United States, which made the United States lose face in this negotiation.

谈判信息是指那些与谈判活动有密切联系的条件、情况等，是一种特殊的人工信息。离开了全面、准确、及时的信息，谈判人员便无法指定谈判策略，主谈人便无法准确找到谈判切入点，谈判就很难取得成功。因此，谈判决策所依据的信息应该是准确的、真实的。例如，20 世纪 90 年代，美国得到情报称中国“银河”号轮船当时装载着化学武器前体（原料）运往伊朗，要求中国政府命令“银河”号返回出发地点，或由美国登船检查货物。中国为此与美国进行多次谈判交涉，后由第三国派人登船检查，但没有发现任何美国所指控的化学物品，这使美国在这场交涉中大失颜面。

（2）Negotiation Environment（谈判环境）

The negotiation environment refers to the background of the negotiation and the objective conditions for conducting business negotiations. The background here includes both the macro-background, that is, the external environment, such as political envioronment, economic envioronment, legal envioronment, religious beliefs, social customs, and cultural background and so on. It also includes the micro-background, that is, the small environment of the negotiation, such as the time and place of the negotiation and so on.

谈判环境是指谈判所处的背景，也是进行商务谈判的客观条件。这里的背景既包括宏观背景，即外部大环境，例如政治环境、经济环境、法律环境、宗教信仰、社会风俗和文化背景等，也包括微观背景，即谈判的小环境，如谈判的时间和地点等。

a. Political Environment（政治环境）

In international business negotiations, excellent negotiators will attach great importance to the analysis of the political negotiating environment, especially making in-depth and detailed analysis of the changes in the international situation toward the political situation of the counter-party's country, and the status and trends of bilateral relations between the two governments which can ensure the negotiation to proceed smoothly in the context of a harmonious political atmosphere.

在国际商务谈判中，优秀的谈判人员都会非常重视对政治谈判环境的分析，特别是对国际形势的走向、谈判对手所在国家的政治局势的变化以及双方政府之间的双边关系的现状和变化趋势进行深入详细的分析，从而确保谈判能在和谐的政治氛围这个大背景下顺利进行。

b. Economic Environment（经济环境）

Economic environment is an important environmental factor affecting international business negotiations. Because international business negotiations are different from domestic business negotiations, they occur between different countries, and the economic environment of each country is different. Therefore, negotiators should always pay attention to changes in the economic situation of the country where the counter-party is located, especially in-depth exploration of changes in the economic situation that are closely related to the content of the negotiation, and adjust the negotiation plan based on the prejudgment result, thereby reducing their own risks. Generally speaking, the analysis of the economic environment includes national infrastructure construction, economic cycles, balance of payments, international trade policies, and financial policies.

经济环境是影响国际商务谈判的一个重要环境因素。由于国际商务谈判有别于国内商务谈判，它们发生在不同国家之间，各国的经济环境又各不相同，因此，谈判人员应该随时关注谈判对手所在国家的经济形势变化，特别是对与谈判内容密切关联的经济形势的变化进行深入探究，并且对这些变化可能会对此次谈判所产生的影响进行预判，根据预判的结果来调整谈判计划，从而降低己方的风险。一般来讲，对经济环境的分析包括国家基础设施建设、经济周期、国际收支、国际贸易政策、金融政策等。

c. Legal Environment（法律环境）

The legal environment is generally confirmed in the form of negotiated agreements or contracts, and only contracts that meet legal requirements can be protected by law. Because contracts in international business negotiations involve the laws of different countries, negotiators must understand the national law, counter-party's law, international laws, regulations and international practices related to the content of the negotiation before negotiation, and analyze the impact of these laws that will affect this negotiation, then make sure that the terms of the final contract are in accordance with the laws of the countries of the negotiating parties and international regulations to avoid unnecessary trouble in the performance of the contract.

法律环境一般都是通过谈判达成的协议或合同的形式加以确认，只有符合法律约定的合同才能受到法律的保护。由于国际商务谈判的合同会涉及不同国家的法律，因此，谈判人员在谈判前必须对与此次谈判内容相关的本国法律、对方国家法律、国际法律法规和国际惯例进行了解，并就各项法律有可能对此次谈判产生的影响进行分析，保证最终合同中的各项条款符合谈判双方国家的法律和国际法规，避免在合同的履行中引起不必要的麻烦。

d. Religious Beliefs, Social Customs, Cultural Background（宗教信仰、社会风俗、文化背景）

In international business negotiations, negotiators come from different countries, who have their own cultural background and religious beliefs, so their values, moral norms, religious beliefs and customs will be different. For example, the values of Americans are advocating freedom, being self-centered, and pursuing the maximization of personal value, while the Chinese are emphasizing collective and team spirit. For another example, the Arabs have no concept of time. If they do not arrive at the place of negotiation according to the agreed time, you should understand their concept for time. The Germans advocate "time is money". The Germans attach great importance to punctuality in the negotiations. Because they think punctuality is the basic courtesy.

在国际商务谈判中，谈判人员来自不同的国家，各自都有自己国家的文化背景和宗教信仰，所以他们的价值观、道德规范、宗教信仰以及风俗习惯就会有所不同。例如，美国人的价值观就是崇尚自由，以自我为中心，追求个人价值最大化；而中国人则是讲究集体和团队精神。又例如，阿拉伯人不讲究时间观念，如果他们没有按谈判约定时间抵达谈判地点，作为谈判对手应该要理解；而德国人崇尚"时间就是金钱"，德国人在谈判中非常注重准时，他们认为这是最基本的礼貌。

Negotiators should have an understanding of counter-party's religious beliefs, customs, and cultural background before negotiations, and respect counter-party's religious beliefs and customs during the negotiation. This will not only help to understand the negotiating style of the counter-party, promote the communication between both parties, but also help the negotiators to formulate different negotiation strategies and adopt different negotiation techniques for different negotiators.

谈判人员在进行谈判之前应对对方的宗教信仰、风俗习惯、文化背景有所了解，在谈判中尊重对方的宗教信仰和风俗习惯。这样既有助于了解对手的谈判风格，促进谈判人员彼此沟通，也有助于谈判人员针对不同的谈判对手制定不同的谈判策略，采用不同的谈判技巧。

(3) Negotiation Time（谈判时间）

Whether there is time limit for negotiations or not, the psychological impact on negotiators is different. If negotiations are required to be completed in a short period of time, it will bring great psychological pressure to the negotiators. Then the appropriate negotiators will be arranged and the proper negotiation strategy will be selected according to the negotiation time. In addition, the negotiation time also involves the choice of favorable timing for negotiation. If the timing is chosen right, the negotiation will take the initiative. If the timing is not properly chosen, the original advantage will be lost and the counter-party will take the initiative. For example, the 8th round of the GATT negotiations (Uruguay Round), which began in September 1986, was originally planned to end by the end of 1990, but due to the contradiction between developed countries, especially the United States and the European Community in agricultural subsidies and tariff negotiations, there are great differences between the developing countries and the developed countries in terms of safeguards clauses and textile negotiations. Many of the parties have been mutually restrained in the case of specific concerns in bilateral negotiations. As a result, there was no result until the fall of 1993. Under this circumstance, the new Director General of the GATT, Sutherland, proposed a package of final agreement, announcing that the Uruguay Round negotiations must end on December 15, 1993. Once the negotiation period was announced, the US and European negotiators changed their procrastination and ended the most comprehensive trade agreement negotiations in the history of the world in less than a week.

谈判有无时间限制，对谈判人员来说造成的心理影响是不同的。如果要求谈判在短时间内完成，就会给谈判人员带来巨大的心理压力，那么双方就会根据谈判时间来安排恰当的谈判人员，选择合适的谈判策略。此外，谈判时间还涉及有利谈判时机的选择。时机选得好，在谈判中就会占据主动；时机选择不当，则会丧失原有的优势，让对方占据主动。例如，从1986年9月开始的关贸总协定第八轮谈判（乌拉圭回合）原计划到1990年底结束，但因发达国家尤其是美国和欧共体在农产品补贴和关税谈判方面的矛盾，发展中国家与发达国家之间在保障条款和纺织品谈判方面分歧很大，不少缔约方在双边谈判中涉及具体利害关系时相互牵制，结果直到1993年秋天仍没有结果。在此情况下，上任不久的关贸总协定新任总干事萨瑟兰提出了一个一揽子最终协议方案，宣布乌拉圭回合谈判务必在1993年12月15日结束。该谈判期限一经宣布，美欧谈判代表一改拖拉态度，在不到一个星期的时间里给这个世界历史上最全面的贸易协定谈判画上了句号。

(4) Negotiation Place（谈判地点）

The choice of negotiation place will have an impact on the psychology of the negotiators, and will also have a certain impact on the effectiveness of the negotiations. The location and the place that are beneficial to you can enhance your negotiating position and negotiation power. Therefore, negotiators should have a good understanding and application of this factor.

谈判地点的选择对于谈判人员的心理会产生影响，对谈判效果也有一定的影响。有利于己方的地点、场所能够增强己方的谈判地位和谈判力量。所以，谈判人员应当很好地理解和运用这一要素。

The choice of negotiation place is more tactical. There are generally four options: host field negotiation, guest field negotiation, host-guest field negotiation and the neutral field negotiation. Each of these four options has its own advantages and disadvantages and needs to be negotiated and determined by the negotiating parties. In general, the location of business negotiations is best to hold at your own location, so the chances of success in the negotiations will be even greater. Experienced negotiators will try to invite the counter-party to the local and treat them with hospitality in order to strive for the best negotiation results. For example, in the negotiation that Japan purchased coal and steel from Australia, the Japanese side invited Australian negotiators to negotiate in Japan. As Australians used to live comfortably, Australian representatives rushed back to their hometown after spending a few days in Japan. Therefore, the negotiators of Australia showed irritable emotions during the negotiation process. Furthermore, as the host of the negotiation, the Japanese side took control of the initiative and bargained unhurriedly. As a result, the Japanese won the success of the negotiation at a lower hospitality cost.

谈判地点的选择比较讲究策略，一般有四种方案可供选择：主座、客座、主客座轮流和中立的第三地。这四种方案各有利弊，需要谈判各方根据具体情况协商确定。一般来说，商务谈判最好争取在己方地点进行，这样谈判取得成功的概率会更大。有经验的谈判者都会设法将对方邀请到本地并热情款待，从而争取最佳的谈判效果。例如，在日本向澳大利亚采购煤和钢铁的谈判中，日方将澳大利亚的谈判代表请到了日本谈判。由于澳大利亚人过惯了舒适的生活，澳方的代表在日本待了几天后就急于回国，因此在谈判过程中就表现出急躁的情绪。此外，作为东道主的日本谈判代表掌握了谈判主动权，不慌不忙地讨价还价，结果日方仅用较低的招待成本就赢得了谈判的成功。

(5) Negotiation Result (谈判结果)

The ultimate purpose of business negotiation is to have a negotiation result, which is also one of the signs of a complete negotiation activity. The outcome of the negotiation may or may not have achieved its purpose. Business negotiations that have achieved their goals are successful, while those that have not achieved their goals have failed. However, regardless of whether the negotiation is successful or not, as an interpersonal communications activity has a result, it marks the end of the negotiation. As a negotiator, you cannot just be satisfied with the outcome of the negotiations, but you must make every effort to achieve the desired results of the negotiations. Otherwise, the benefits have not been finally reached, and it is likely that the next round of new negotiations will be held.

商务谈判的最终目的就是要有一个谈判结果，这也是一个完整的谈判活动的标志之一。谈判的结果可能达到了目的，也有可能没有达到目的。达到了目的的商务谈判就是成功的，而没有达到目的的商务谈判则是失败的。但无论谈判是否成功，作为一次人际交往活动，有了结果就标志着谈判活动的结束。作为谈判人员，不能仅仅满足于谈判有了结果，而应该竭尽全力让谈判结果符合己方的理想目标，这样的谈判才算是圆满的谈判。否则，利益没有最终实现，很有可能要进行下一轮新的谈判。

Ⅱ Classification of International Business Negotiation (国际商务谈判的类型)

Negotiation is the most common form of social interaction. Almost every person in the world is involved in negotiations in one way or another. Negotiation is a very important component in international business activities, a process between the buyers and the sellers. International business negotiation can be divided into different classification according to different standards. The purpose of the division is to organize negotiations according to various types of different characteristics and requirements, adopt effective negotiation strategies, reduce blindness, and strive for the initiative of negotiation.

谈判是社会互动最常见的形式。世界上几乎每个人都是以某种方式参与到谈判中。谈判是国际商务活动中非常重要的组成部分，是买卖双方达成交易的一个过程。国际商务谈判根据不同的标准可以分为不同的类型。划分的目的在于根据各种类型的不同特征和要求组织谈判，采取有效的谈判策略，减少盲目性，争取谈判的主动权。

1. Individual Negotiation and Collective Negotiation（个体谈判和集体谈判）

According to the number of people participating in the negotiations, the negotiations can be divided into one-on-one individual negotiations and collective negotiations composed of multiple people.

按照参加谈判的人数，谈判可以被划分为一对一的个体谈判和由多人组成的集体谈判。

One-on-one individual negotiation refers to the way in which a negotiating party sends a representative to negotiate, which is mainly suitable for informal or non-important occasions, such as simple business negotiations. The one-on-one individual negotiation is flexible and can be carried out in formal and informal situations, thus contributing to the creation of a relaxed and harmonious atmosphere of negotiation. In the one-on-one individual negotiation, the negotiators have greater decision-making power, and can cope with various situations that arise in the negotiation according to the situation. At the same time, it also puts forward higher requirements for the negotiators. They need to be able to stand on their own and have a strong comprehensive ability to deal with aspects of business, law, technology.

一对一的个体谈判是指由谈判各方各派一位代表出面谈判的方式。主要适合于非正式或不重要的场合，比如简单的业务洽谈。一对一的个体谈判形式比较灵活，可以在正式场合与非正式场合进行，因此有利于营造轻松融洽的谈判氛围。在一对一的个体谈判中，谈判人员拥有较大的决策权，可以根据情况独自应付谈判中出现的各种情况，但同时对谈判人员也提出了较高的要求，需要能独当一面，同时具备较强的处理商务、法律、技术等方面问题的综合能力。

Multi-person collective negotiation refers to the negotiation in which all negotiating parties send two or more people to participate in the negotiation which applies to more formal and larger occasions. In the collective negotiation, the participating parties mainly rely on the composed negotiating team to complete the mutual communication. In the negotiating team, each member has a clear division of labor, and each has his own duties: there are people who are responsible for bargaining, who assist to the main speaker; there are people who are responsible for business, technology, finance, and law, as well as professional translators. The negotiating team can help members overcome the shortcomings of limited personal ability and inability to cope with complex situations, and exert power of teamwork to great extent. Large-scale business negotiations in the world, including the World Trade Organization negotiations, trade negotiations between countries and countries, such as the 2019 Sino-US trade negotiations, are conducted in the form of collective negotiation.

多人参加的集体谈判是指谈判各方都是由两个或以上的人员参加协商的谈判形式。适用于比较正式且规模也比较大的场合。在集体谈判中，参与各方主要依靠组成的谈判小组来完成相互之间的协调沟通。在谈判小组中，各个成员分工明确，各司其职：有主谈人，有辅谈人；有负责商务、技术、财务、法律的人员，也有专职的翻译人员。这样有助于克服个人能力有限、无法应对复杂局面的弊端，在更大程度上发挥团队协作的力量。世界上较大规模的商务谈判，包括世界贸易组织谈判、国家与国家之间的贸易谈判，如 2019 年中美贸易谈判，都是以集体谈判的形式进行。

2. Bilateral Negotiations and Multilateral Negotiations（双边谈判和多边谈判）

According to the number of stakeholders participating in the negotiations, the negotiations are divided into bilateral negotiations and multilateral negotiations.

根据参加谈判的利益主体的数量不同，谈判可以分为双边谈判和多边谈判。

The number of stakeholders participating in bilateral negotiations is two, such as trade negotiations between two countries or trade negotiations between two companies. In bilateral negotiations, the interests of both parties are clear and specific, so it is easy to reach an agreement.

在双边谈判中参与的利益主体的数量为两个，比如两个国家或两个公司之间的贸易谈判。在双边谈判中，双方的利益关系明确、具体，因此容易达成一致。

Multilateral negotiation refers to the participation of more than two interest parties, such as trade negotiations between multiple countries and trade joint ventures and trade negotiations between multiple companies. With the development of global economic integration, the scope of exchanges between countries has become more extensive, and multilateral negotiations are also increasing. Since in the multilateral negotiations, the interest relationship between the parties is more complex and it is difficult to coordinate, therefore, in many multilateral negotiations, certain specific issues require specific solutions, and bilateral negotiations are often required.

多边谈判是指参与的利益主体的数量在两个以上，比如多国之间的贸易谈判以及多个公司之间的贸易合资、贸易谈判等。随着全球经济一体化的发展，各国之间的交流范围也越来越广泛，多边谈判也越来越多。由于在多边谈判中，各方之间的利益关系比较复杂，难以协调一致，因此，在很多多边谈判中，某些特定的问题需要特定的解决方式，常常需要进行双边谈判。

3. Direct Negotiation and Indirect Negotiation（直接谈判和间接谈判）

Negotiations can be divided into direct negotiations and indirect negotiations according to the different ways of contact between the negotiating parties.

按照谈判各方接触的方式不同，谈判可以分为直接谈判和间接谈判。

Direct negotiation means that the negotiating parties directly exchange information and negotiate conditions in a face-to-face manner. Generally, the company sends negotiators to negotiate at the counter-party's location, invites customers to negotiate with the company, or to third parties. Direct negotiation is one of the most used forms of negotiation. Through face-to-face communication, the two parties can observe the counter-party's facial expressions and body language, master the counter-party's psychological conditions, check the counter-party's honesty and reliability, and also help deepen understanding, enforce feelings, and promote the smooth progress of negotiations.

直接谈判是指谈判各方面对面地直接用语言交流信息、协商条件。一般包括企业派出谈判人员到对方所在处谈判、邀请客户到本企业谈判或到第三方谈判等。直接谈判是各种谈判中运用得最多的一种形式。谈判双方通过面对面的交流，可以观察到对方的面部表情和肢体语言，掌握对方的心理，借此来考察对方的诚实度和可靠性，并且有利于加深了解，增进感情，促进谈判顺利进行。

Indirect negotiations are conditions in which the negotiating parties use written language, such as writing words, television, telephone, and Internet, to exchange information and negotiate terms.

间接谈判是谈判各方利用文字等书面语言或电视、电话、网络等进行信息交流、协商条件。

(1) Written Negotiation (书面谈判)

The negotiating parties used letters, telegrams, telexes, faxes and other communication tools to negotiate on relevant issues. This type is suitable for the case where the trading conditions are relatively standardized, clear, the content is relatively simple, and the parties to the negotiating parties are more familiar with each other.

谈判各方利用信函、电报、电传、传真等通信工具就有关问题进行磋商。这种类型适合于交易条件比较规范、明确，内容比较简单，谈判各方对彼此比较了解的情况。

(2) TV/Telephone Negotiation (电视/电话谈判)

This type of negotiation is a verbal consultation on a transaction in the form of a video and telephone. Because of the distance between the two parties, this kind of negotiation is generally used between negotiating parties who know each other very well or have cooperated with each other before. In this way, the process of negotiations are quick, avoiding long-distance travel and saving money, but sometimes telephone negotiations are prone to misunderstandings and disputes due to rush.

这类谈判是通过电视、电话的形式对某项交易进行口头磋商。这种谈判由于双方距离相隔较远，一般多用于谈判各方对彼此非常了解或曾经合作过的客户之间。采用这种方式，谈判迅速，可以避免长途旅行和节省开支，但有时电话谈判因对答仓促，容易引起误解和纠纷。

(3) Network Negotiation (网络谈判)

This type of negotiation refers to negotiating activities conducted by the negotiating parties through various Internet services and technologies. With the continuous advancement of Internet technology, including online conferences, online telephone, and online audiovisual systems, Internet-based transactions have grown rapidly. However, the network identity authentication, network security, network regulations and other aspects are still not well established. It may take some time to truly become the main negotiation tool, especially when it comes to network contract negotiations and the resolution of disputes.

这种类型的谈判是指谈判各方依靠各种网络服务和技术，通过互联网进行的谈判活动。互联网技术的不断进步，包括网络会议、网络电话、网上视听系统，使得基于互联网的交易飞速增长。但网络身份认证、网络安全、网络法规等方面还不健全，网络要真正成为主要的谈判工具，可能还需要一定的时间，尤其是涉及网络合同谈判及其争端解决。

4. Host Field Negotiation, Guest Field Negotiation and Neutral Field Negotiation（主场谈判、客场谈判和中立地谈判）

Negotiations can be divided into host field negotiation, guest field negotiation and neutral field negotiation depending on the location of the negotiation.

根据谈判地点的不同，谈判可以分为主场谈判、客场谈判和中立地谈判。

Host field negotiation, also known as the home field negotiation, means that for one negotiating party, the negotiation is conducted at their place and they are the host. Then for the counter-party of the negotiation, it is the guest field negotiation. Neutral field negotiation refers to negotiation in a third country or region outside the negotiating parties, and there is no distinction between the negotiating parties. The host field negotiation brings a lot of convenience to the host, such as language, climate, diet, culture, negotiation schedule, preparation of various negotiating materials, and it is more convenient to ask for instructions from superiors in case of encountering some unexpectation during the negotiation. As a host, you must show your politeness in invitation, welcoming, reception, consultation, organization, etc. On the contrary, for the guest, there may be many problems and difficulties, which require them to have better adaptability and resilience to deal with various emergencies in the guest field.

主场谈判，又称主座谈判，是指对谈判的某一方来讲谈判是在其所在地进行，其是东道主。那么对于谈判的另一方而言就是客场谈判。而中立地谈判是指在谈判各方所在地以外的第三国或地区进行谈判，对谈判各方而言无主宾之分。主场谈判给东道主带来了不少便利，从语言、气候、饮食、文化到谈判时间表、各种谈判资料的准备；在谈判中遇到突发情况向上级请示也比较方便。作为东道主，必须礼貌待客，包括邀请、迎送、接待、洽谈、组织等。相反，对于客方来说，可能会遇到很多问题和困难，这就要求客方谈判人员具有较好的适应能力和应变能力，来应对客场的各种突发情况。

5. Soft-typed Negotiation, Hard-typed Negotiation, Principle-based Negotiation（软式谈判、硬式谈判、原则式谈判）

According to the attitudes and guidelines adopted by the parties in the negotiation, the negotiation can be divided into soft-typed negotiation (concession negotiation), hard-typed negotiation (position-based negotiation), and principle-based negotiation (value-based negotiation).

根据谈判中各方采取的态度和方针，谈判可以分为软式谈判（让步型谈判）、硬式谈判（立场型谈判）、原则式谈判（价值型谈判）。

（1）Soft-typed Negotiation（软式谈判）

Soft-typed negotiation, also known as concession negotiation and friendly negotiation, means that negotiators hope to avoid conflicts and contradictions in the negotiation, and are ready to make concessions in order to reach an agreement. They hope to negotiate an agreement that is satisfactory to all parties. Using this type of negotiation does not treat counter-parties as enemies, but treats them as friends, advocates concessions, trusts counter-parties, stays friendly, and even succumbs to counter-parties in order to avoid conflicts. If all negotiating parties adopt a friendly attitude, then soft-typed negotiation will help promote the relationship between the parties and achieve satisfactory results. But if any one of parties is in an absolute advantage and adopts hard-typed negotiation, then the party who adopts soft-typed negotiation will sacrifice their own interests for compromise.

软式谈判，也称让步型谈判、友好型谈判，是指谈判者希望在谈判中尽量避免冲突和矛盾，随时准备为了达成协议而做出让步，希望通过谈判签订一个谈判各方都满意的协议。采用软式谈判不把对方当敌人，而是以朋友相待，提倡让步、信任对方、保持友善，甚至会为了避免冲突而屈服于对方。如果谈判各方都采取友善的态度，那么软式谈判有利于促进各方的关系并能取得各方都满意的结果。但是如果一方处于绝对优势，并且采用硬式谈判，那么采取软式谈判就是牺牲己方利益以求妥协。

（2）Hard-typed Negotiation（硬式谈判）

Hard-typed negotiation is also called position-based negotiation. In this type of negotiation, the negotiator regards the negotiation as a willpower competition. The stronger the position in the negotiation, the more the gains will be. Negotiators believe that they have sufficient strength, so they put forward their own conditions in the negotiation, emphasize their own negotiating position, and refuse to make any concessions. Such negotiations often lead to fierce conflicts between two parties and even lead to the breakdown of negotiation.

硬式谈判也称立场型谈判。在这种类型的谈判中，谈判者将谈判看成是一场意志力的竞争，在谈判中立场越强硬，收获就越多。谈判者认为己方具备足够的实力，因此在谈判中提出自己的条件，强调己方的谈判立场，不肯做出任何让步，这样的谈判往往会造成双方的激烈冲突，甚至导致谈判破裂。

（3）Principle-based Negotiation（原则式谈判）

Principle-based negotiation, also known as value-based negotiation, means that the negotiating parties regard counter-party as partners of cooperation rather than enemies, and the attitude is between soft-typed negotiation and hard-typed negotiation. The principle-based negotiation emphasizes four aspects: advocating that negotiation is tough on issues, being gentle on people, and separating people from issues; advocating openness and honesty, and pursuing benefits without losing grace; advocating reaching an agreement in accordance with the principle of objective fairness and fair value instead of simply relying on bargaining on specific issues; advocating common interests, giving up respective positions, trying to find common ground, eliminating differences, and striving for a mutually satisfactory negotiation result.

原则式谈判也称价值型谈判，是指谈判各方将对方看作合作的伙伴而不是敌人，态度介于软式谈判和硬式谈判之间。原则式谈判强调四个方面：主张谈判对事强硬，对人温和，把人和事区分开；主张开诚布公，追求利益而又不失风度；主张按照客观公正的原则和公平价值来达成协议，而不是简单地依靠具体问题讨价还价；主张谋求共同的利益，放弃立场，努力寻找共同点、消除分歧，争取共同满意的谈判结果。

The value obtained through principle-based negotiation includes both economic value and the value of interpersonal relationships, and is therefore highly recommended by negotiators around the world.

原则式谈判通过谈判所取得的价值既包括经济价值，又包括人际关系的价值，因此为世界各国的谈判人员所推崇。

Ⅲ Basic Procedure of International Business Negotiation（国际商务谈判的基本程序）

The basic procedure of international business negotiations generally includes the phases of preparation, the opening, the bargaining and the contract signing (See Figure 2.1).

国际商务谈判的基本程序一般包括准备阶段、开局阶段、实质性磋商阶段和签约阶段（见图 2.1）。

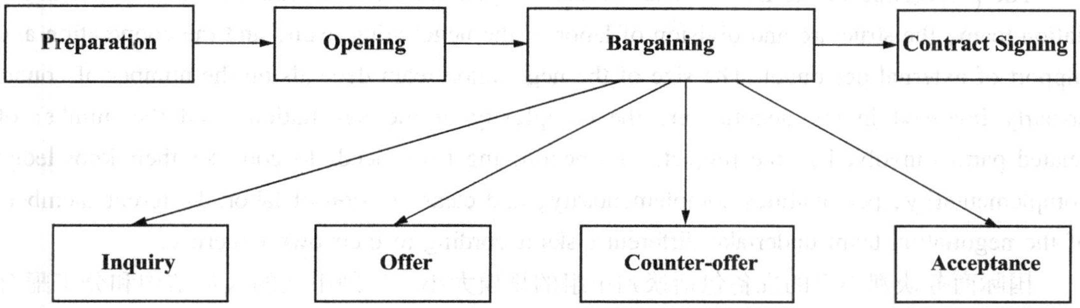

Figure 2.1 Basic Procedure of International Business Negotiation

（1） Preparation（准备阶段）

The successful outcome of international business negotiations depends not only on the use of relevant strategies and negotiation skills in the formal negotiation process, but also on whether sufficient and detailed preparations are made before the negotiation. The better preparation you make before the negotiations, the better the results will be. Therefore, the adequacy of pre-negotiation preparations will directly affect the outcome of the negotiations.

国际商务谈判能否取得圆满的结果，不仅取决于正式谈判过程中相关策略和谈判技巧的使用，也和谈判前是否做好充分细致的准备工作密切相关。谈判前准备得越充分，谈判结果就会越好。因此，谈判前的准备工作是否充分会直接影响谈判结果。

The preparations before international business negotiations mainly include the following aspects:

国际商务谈判前的准备工作主要包括以下几个方面：

a. Information Collection（信息收集）

Information collection refers to intelligence collection and screening. It is the first work to be done in the preparation phase of international business negotiations. Collect, screen and analyze information and materials on counter-party, project uses, market conditions and related laws in a timely and comprehensive manner. Having accurate and detailed information on counter-party can master the negotiation initiative and formulate relevant countermeasures, which will greatly be beneficial to the success of the negotiation. The use of inaccurate or one-sided information may cause you to stuck in a passive position, or even lead to the break-down of negotiations. The information that should be collected mainly includes the information of the counter-party, the information of the negotiating representatives, market conditions, laws, and culture.

信息收集是指情报收集和筛选。它是国际商务谈判准备阶段首先要做的工作。及时和尽可能全面地收集、筛选和分析有关谈判对手、项目用途、市场行情和相关法律等方面的信息和资料。拥有准确、详尽的对手信息，就可以掌握谈判主动权，有针对性地制定相关对策，对谈判取得成功会有很大帮助；而运用不准确或片面的信息，可能会使己方陷入被动，甚至导致谈判破裂。需要收集的信息主要包括谈判对手公司信息、谈判代表信息、市场行情、法律、文化等。

b. Preparation for Negotiation Team（谈判小组的准备）

The preparation of the international business negotiation team includes the size of the negotiation team, the structure and division of labor of the negotiating team, and the cooperation and support of external personnel. The size of the negotiation team depends on the number of counter-party involved in the negotiation, the complexity of the negotiation, and the number of related parties involved in the project. The negotiating team needs to consider their knowledge complementarity, personalities complementarity, and clear division of labor. Different members of the negotiation team undertake different tasks according to their own expertise.

国际商务谈判小组的准备包括谈判小组的规模大小、谈判小组的人员结构和分工配合以及外围人员的配合与支持。谈判小组的规模大小会根据对方参与谈判的人数、谈判的复杂程度、项目涉及的关联方数量而定。在谈判小组人员结构上需要考虑他们的知识互补、性格互补并且有明确的分工。谈判小组不同的人员根据自身的特长承担不同的任务。

c. Formulation for Business Negotiation Plan（谈判方案的制订）

Business negotiation plan is a program to guide the negotiators' actions, and to make arrangements for the goals, agenda, strategy and division of labor in advance of the negotiations. When formulating a negotiation plan, it is necessary to clarify what is the key content and what is the secondary content of the negotiation, formulate ideal goals, acceptable goals, and minimum goals, and pay attention to grasping the negotiation time and atmosphere.

谈判方案是指导谈判人员行动的纲领，是在开始谈判前对谈判目标、谈判议程、谈判策略和人员分工提前做好安排。在制订谈判方案时，需要明确哪些是谈判的重点内容，哪些是次要内容，制定理想目标、可接受目标和最低目标，同时注意对谈判时间和谈判氛围的把握。

d. Other Preparation（其他准备工作）

Other preparation includes the selection of main negotiation place, selection and arrangement of negotiation place. The choice of negotiation place is mainly based on the negotiation between the negotiating parties to determine whether to negotiate at home field, guest field or at a neutral place. The selection of the negotiation venue is based on factors such as the content of the negotiation, the personal character preferences of the counter-party's representatives, the negotiation strategy, and expenditure. In formal international business negotiations, the proper arrangement of the venue can reflect the management level of the negotiators at the home.

其他准备工作包括主要谈判地点的选择、谈判场地的选择与布置。谈判地点的选择主要根据谈判双方协商确定是在主场谈判、客场谈判还是中立地点谈判。谈判场地的选择是根据谈判内容、谈判对手个人性格偏好、谈判策略以及经费等因素来进行。在正式的国际商务谈判中，会场布置是否得当可以反映出主场谈判方的管理水平。

e. Simulated Negotiation（模拟谈判）

Hypothetical reasoning and preliminary practice can be performed on formal negotiations through simulated negotiations. Simulate various performances and reactions of counter-party on a given occasion to detect various problems that may arise during the implementation of the negotiation plan, so as to further correct and improve, while training and improving the resilience of your own negotiators.

通过模拟谈判可以对正式谈判进行假设推理和预备练习。模拟对手在既定场合下的种种表现和反应，来检测已制订的谈判方案在实施过程中可能出现的种种问题，从而进一步修正和完善，同时训练和提高己方谈判人员的应变能力。

(2) Opening（开局阶段）

The so-called "opening" refers to the greetings and expression of each party's attitude between the negotiating parties and the detection of the counter-party's detailed information at the beginning of a negotiation, thereby laying a foundation for influencing the control of the negotiation process. The opening phase is a phase in which the negotiating parties clarify their positions, and the negotiation pattern is determined within several minutes after the opening. In the opening phase, the personal status and roles of both parties in the negotiation will be fully exposed, and at the same time, the temperament, personality and the attitude of the counter-party's negotiators, the attitude towards the negotiation and the strategies to be adopted will be initially felt.

所谓开局是指一场谈判开始时，谈判各方之间的寒暄和表态以及探测对手的底细，从而为影响控制谈判过程奠定基础。开局阶段是谈判双方摆明各自立场的阶段，谈判格局在开局后几分钟内就确定下来。在开局阶段，谈判双方阵容中的个人地位以及所承担的角色会充分暴露出来，同时也可以初步感受到对方谈判人员的气质、个性和对本次谈判的态度以及准备采取的策略。

The opening of negotiations also involves the establishment of a negotiating atmosphere.

Different types of negotiations will create different negotiating atmosphere. Some negotiating parties attend the negotiation with a spirit of mutual understanding whose purpose is to sign a mutually satisfactory agreement through the joint efforts of both parties. In this case, it is necessary to create a positive and friendly negotiating atmosphere. While with the attitude of refusing to make concessions and competing for profits, the negotiating atmosphere is cold and antagonistic. However, most of the negotiating atmosphere is between the above two. With the gradual deepening of the negotiations, the atmosphere will be serious and friendly.

谈判开局也涉及谈判氛围的营造。谈判类型不同，营造的谈判氛围也会不一样。有的谈判双方是本着相互体谅的心态进行谈判，目的是通过双方的共同努力签订令双方都满意的协议，在这种情况下，就需要制造积极、友好的谈判氛围；而有的谈判双方是本着寸步不让、寸利必争的态度，那么这种情况的谈判氛围就是冷淡、对立的。而现实中的谈判氛围大部分都是介于以上两种氛围之间，随着谈判的逐渐深入，谈判氛围在友好中也会有严肃。

In a word, the main task of the opening phase is to arouse the interest of the negotiating counter-party, attract the counter-party's attention, do a good job of constructive basic work, pave the way for subsequent negotiations. Furthermore, make a judgement after communication with counter-party for the first time, and create an appropriate negotiating atmosphere according to the goals and strategies as well as the situation of negotiators.

简而言之，开局阶段的主要任务就是要引起谈判对手的兴趣，吸引对方的注意力，做好建设性的基础工作，为后续谈判做好铺垫。此外，通过初步交流对谈判对手的基本情况做出判断，并根据谈判的目标策略及谈判者的情况，选择营造恰当的谈判氛围。

(3) Bargaining（实质性磋商阶段）

This phase is also known as the substantive negotiation phase. It is the core phase of international commerce and business negotiation. It is the process of exchanging opinions on various provisions, and the process to eliminate differences, resolve conflicts, clarify their respective positions and interests, and adjust interests and needs. The bargaining phase includes four stages: inquiry, offer, counter-offer, and acceptance. Inquiry and counter-offer are not necessary stages. Buyers and sellers can make offers directly without inquiry according to the actual situation. For example, the two sides have been customers for many years and are very familiar with each other's trade habits and trading conditions. Acceptance can also be made directly without a counter-offer, but this is relatively rare in actual international business negotiations. Because both buyers and sellers hope to win more benefits for themselves, they will definitely go through a bargaining process. This is a counter-offer. The offer and acceptance are two indispensable stages for successful business negotiation and contract signing.

这个阶段又称实质性谈判阶段，是国际商务谈判的核心阶段，是谈判双方就谈判议事日程的各项条款交换意见、消除差异、化解冲突、明确各自立场和利益、调节利益和需求的过程。磋商阶段包括询盘、发盘、还盘、接受这四个环节。其中询盘和还盘不是必备环节。买卖双方根据实际情况，可以不经过询盘直接发盘。比如，双方已经是交往多年的老客户，对各自的贸易习惯和交易条件非常熟悉。也可以不经过还盘而直接接受，但这在实际的国际商务谈判中是比较少见的，因为买卖双方都希望为自己争取更多的利益，这样必定会经历一个讨价还价的过程，这就是还盘。发盘和接受是商务谈判获得成功和签订合同必不可少的两个环节。

a. Inquiry（询盘）

Inquiry is that one party of the transaction is prepared to buy or sell a certain product, and asks the other party about the relevant transaction conditions for buying and selling the product, such as price, specifications, quality, quantity, packaging, and payment methods, etc. Most inquiries are asking about prices. Therefore, inquires are often regarded as price inquiry. Inquiries can be made by the buyer, for example, if the buyer actively asks foreign manufacturers for the goods he needs, or by the seller, for example, the exporter or manufacturer asks the domestic importer whether it purchases its products. In practice, inquiries are usually issued by buyers to sellers. Inquiries can be oral or written; prices can be inquired, or other trading conditions can be inquired. Because the inquiry is a tentative contact, one party of the inquiry is not responsible for whether an agreement can be reached, so the inquiry is not binding on both parties.

询盘，是交易一方准备购买或出售某种商品，向对方询问买卖该商品的有关交易条件，例如价格、规格、品质、数量、包装、支付方式等。多数询盘都是询问价格，所以，业务上常把询盘称为询价。询盘既可以由买方做出，如买方主动向国外厂商询购所需要的货物，又可以由卖方做出，如出口商或厂商向国内进口商询问其是否购买其产品。在实际业务中，询盘一般多由买方向卖方发出。询盘既可以采用口头方式，也可以采用书面方式；既可以询问价格，又可以询问其他交易条件。由于询盘属于试探性接触，询盘的一方对能否达成协议不承担任何责任，因此询盘对双方都没有约束力。

b. Offer（发盘）

In international trade, an offer is also called a quotation, legally called an "pollicitation". It is the behavior of one party of a transaction that wants to buy or sell a certain commodity and proposes the transaction conditions to the other party and expresses willingness to conclude the transaction according to these conditions. An offer may be issued in response to a request from the counter-party, or directly to the counter-party without an inquiry. An offer is usually issued by the seller, but it can also be issued by the buyer and is called a "bid". The offer is divided into a firm offer and a non-firm offer. Once the offer is accepted by the offeree within the validity period, the transaction is concluded. Therefore, the firm offer is binding on the buyer and the seller. Non-firm offer makes no promises and has no validity period, so it is not binding on buyers and sellers. A valid offer must have the corresponding conditions, which will be described in detail in Chapter 5.

在国际贸易中，发盘也被称为报盘、报价，在法律上被称为“要约”。是交易一方欲购买或出售某种商品而向对方提出交易条件，表示愿意按此条件达成交易的行为。发盘可以是应对方询盘的要求发出，也可以是在没有询盘的情况下直接向对方发出。发盘一般由卖方发出，但也可以由买方发出，被称为“递盘”。发盘有实盘和虚盘之分。实盘在有效期内一旦被受盘人表示接受，交易即达成，因此实盘对买卖双方都具有约束力。虚盘不做出任何承诺，也没有有效期，因此对买卖双方没有约束力。一项有效的发盘必须具备相应的条件，在第5章中会详细介绍。

c. Counter-offer（还盘）

The act that the offeree does not agree with the trading conditions in the offer and proposes to modify or change the terms and conditions is called a counter-offer, legally known as "counter-pollicitation." The counter-pollicitaition is actually a new offer made by the offeree as the new offeror. The original offeror is called the new offeree. The counter-offer is also the offeror's rejection of the original offer. The offer is invalidated by the original offeree's counter-offer, and the original offeror is no longer bound by it. Counter-offer can be repeated between buyers and sellers, which is what we commonly call "bargaining". The content of a counter-offer generally only states the trading conditions that need to be changed or added, and there is no need to repeat the trading conditions that the two parties have agreed on.

受盘人不同意发盘中的交易条件而提出修改或变更的意见被称为还盘，在法律上被称为“反要约”。还盘实际上是受盘人以发盘人的身份发出的一个新的发盘，原发盘人被称为新的受盘人。还盘也是受盘人对原发盘的拒绝，发盘因对方还盘而失去效力，原发盘人不再受其约束。还盘可以在买卖双方之间反复进行，也就是我们俗称的“讨价还价”。还盘的内容一般仅陈述需要变更或增添的交易条件，对双方已经达成一致的交易条件无须重复。

d. Acceptance（接受）

The acceptance means that after receiving an offer or counter-offer from the counter-party, the party expresses its consent to the counter-party by way of statement or action, legally known as "commitment". Acceptance is generally expressed in terms of "agreement" and "confirmation". Acceptance and offer are both commercial and legal acts. There are corresponding conditions to constitute an effective acceptance, which will be described in detail in Chapter 5.

所谓接受，就是交易的一方在接到对方的发盘或还盘后，以声明或行为的方式向对方表示同意，法律上称为“承诺”。一般用“同意”和“确认”等术语表示接受。接受和发盘一样，既属于商业行为，也属于法律行为。构成一项有效的接受应该具备相应的条件，在第5章中会详细介绍。

(4) Contract Signing（签约阶段）

The signing phase is also the end of international business negotiations. After active and serious negotiations, the two parties finally conclude a deal. In this regard, it is necessary to form a written document for the negotiated terms and conditions and give legal recognition to further clarify the rights and obligations of both parties. Therefore, the content of the contract must be completely consistent with the transaction conditions negotiated by the two parties, especially the main transaction conditions need to be clearly established.

签约阶段也是国际商务谈判的结束阶段，双方经过积极认真的磋商，交易最终得以达成。对此，需要对谈判达成的交易条件形成书面文件，给予法律上的认可，从而进一步明确双方的权利和义务。因此，合同内容必须与双方谈妥的交易条件完全一致，特别是主要的交易条件都需要明确订立。

In international business negotiations, the names and contents of written agreements are often different. For example, in international negotiations for the sale of goods, the written agreement documents are often referred to as purchase and sales contracts or sales confirmations; agreements, contracts and articles of association need to be signed in joint venture negotiations. Common written contracts generally take the form of formal contracts, transaction confirmations, agreements, memo, etc., usually the former two are the main ones. The contents of different types of contracts have different composition. For example, the international contract for the sale of goods is mainly composed of the head, the body, the end of the contract, and the appendix; the international technology trade contract is composed of the preamble, the body, and the appendix.

在国际商务谈判中，书面协议的名称和内容往往有区别。比如，在国际货物买卖谈判中，书面协议文件大多被称为购销合同或销货确认书；在合资企业谈判中需要签订协议、合同和章程三种文件。常见的书面合同一般采用正式合同、成交确认书、协议、备忘录等形式，通常以前两种为主。不同类型合同其内容的构成也有所不同。例如，国际货物买卖合同主要由约首、正文、约尾、附件构成；国际技术贸易合同则由序言、合同正文、合同附件三部分构成。

Ⅳ Different Negotiation Modes of International Business Negotiation（国际商务谈判的模式）

During the development of international business negotiations, many negotiation modes have emerged. Different negotiation modes predict the final outcome of the negotiations to a certain extent. Therefore, it is very important to choose and apply a reasonable negotiation mode. There are three most commonly used modes: traditional position negotiation mode, modern rational negotiation mode, and PRAM negotiation mode. In international business negotiations practice, it is often not just one negotiation mode that is used, but there are more flexible changes and comprehensive use according to the environment at the time, in order to achieve a multiplier effect.

在国际商务谈判的发展过程中，出现了很多谈判模式。不同的谈判模式在一定程度上预示了谈判的最终结果，因此，选择和运用合理的谈判模式就非常重要。其中最常用的模式有三种：传统阵地谈判模式、现代理性谈判模式、PRAM 谈判模式。在实际的国际商务谈判中，往往不是单纯地运用哪一种谈判模式，更多的是根据当时的环境进行灵活的变动和综合运用，才能达到事半功倍的效果。

(1) Traditional Position Negotiation Mode（传统阵地谈判模式）

a. Definition（定义）

The traditional position negotiation mode refers to the idea that both parties of the negotiation establish their own positions at the beginning of the negotiation, and both endeavor to maintain their positions throughout the negotiation process, forcing the counter-party to give up its position, make concessions and change its insistence position, and finally compromise and reach an agreement (See Figure 2. 2). If the consultation fails, the negotiations will break down.

传统阵地谈判模式是指谈判的双方在谈判之初都确立自己的立场，并且都竭力维护自己立场的这种理念贯穿整个谈判过程中，迫使对方放弃自己的立场、做出让步并改变其坚持的立场，最后进行妥协并达成协议（见图 2. 2）。若协商不成，则谈判随之破裂。

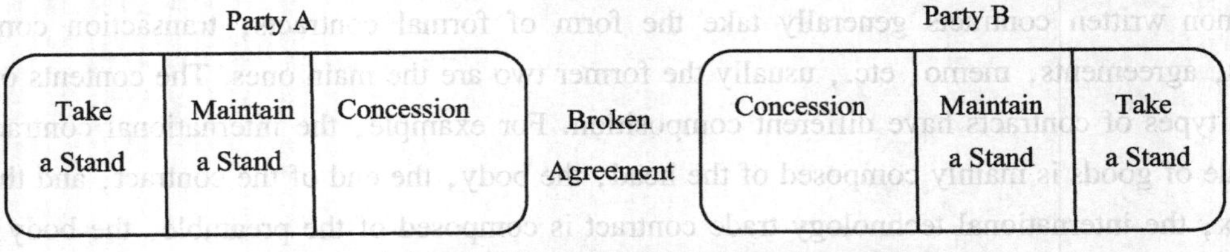

Figure 2. 2　Traditional Position Negotiation Mode

In this negotiation mode, if one party makes concessions, the agreement between the two parties can be reached. But if both parties insist and maintain their positions and refuse to make concessions, the negotiations will break down and the cooperative relationship will collapse. It should be noted that in this mode, compromises are often unilateral. Both negotiating parties make concessions at the same time does not belong to this mode. This mode cannot achieve a win-win. It is a typical "zero-sum game" which means one party makes a profit and the counter-party must suffer.

在这种谈判模式中，如果有一方会做出让步，那么双方之间的协议是可以达成的。但如果双方都坚持并且维护自己的立场，都不肯做出让步，那么谈判就会破裂，合作关系也会随之瓦解。需要注意的是，在这种模式下，做出让步妥协往往是单方面的，谈判双方同时做出让步不属于这种模式。这种模式无法实现双赢，是典型的“零和博弈”：一方获利，另一方必定利益受损。

The advantages of this mode are as follows: the entire negotiation process is simple, so the content of the negotiation is not complicated, the coverage is not extensive, and it does not require too much efforts; the requirements for the quality of the negotiators is not high, which can effectively save manpower costs; the negotiations do not last long, and have low requirements on venues and the negotiation environments, and often do not need to consider subsequent cooperation matters. The shortcomings of this mode are more prominent. If the negotiation result is not ideal, the final result of negotiation often ends in breakdown; the negotiation atmosphere will be relatively depressed; the progress of the entire negotiation is slower and the negotiation efficiency would be lower; interpersonal relationship is difficult to maintain; etc.

这种模式的优点如下：整个谈判过程简单，因此谈判的内容并不复杂、涉及面并不广，不需要消耗太多的精力；对于谈判人员的素质要求不高，能有效节省人力成本；谈判持续时间不长，对场地以及谈判环境要求低，往往不需要考虑后续合作事宜。这种模式的缺点比较突出，如果谈判结果不理想，最终谈判往往以破裂告终；谈判氛围会比较压抑；整个谈判的进度会比较慢，谈判效率低；人际关系难以维护；等等。

b. Negotiation Style（谈判风格）

The traditional position negotiation mode belongs to the control type, that is, you lose and I win. In order to ensure the realization of your own interests, putting your own negotiation goals first, and ignore the relationship between the two parties and the interests of the counter-party, often using extreme methods, and ways of confrontation and conflict to impose a tough attitude on the counter-party. Pressure causes psychological panic and thus achieves your own negotiation goals. This negotiation style is easy to form a tense negotiating atmosphere. Once the negotiation is deadlocked, the negotiation is difficult to continue, so it is generally not recommended.

传统阵地谈判模式属于控制型，即你输我赢型。在谈判中为了确保己方利益的实现，把己方的谈判目标放在第一位，而置双方的关系和对方的利益于不顾，常常采用极端的手段及对抗、冲突的方式，以强硬的姿态向对方施加压力，造成心理恐慌，从而实现己方的谈判目标。这种谈判风格很容易形成紧张的谈判氛围，一旦谈判陷入僵局，谈判就很难进行下去，所以一般情况下不主张采用。

c. Choice and Application（选择与运用）

This mode is essentially a one-time transaction, which is commonly called "one hammer transaction". There are generally several situations in which this mode is adopted: firstly, the negotiating parties do not want to have business dealings in the future; secondly, the counter-parties do not know much about the supply and demand of the goods negotiated in this negotiation, otherwise they will not accept the conditions that are unfavorable to themselves; thirdly, the strength of the two parties is quite different, and you're in an absolute advantageous position, the counter-party is asking for more than your own, and it is entirely possible to adopt a tough attitude at the negotiation. The above three situations are not common in actual negotiations. For negotiators, this mode can be omitted but needs to be understood. At the same time, as negotiators, you need to master and identify some anti-traditional-position-mode measures to prevent the counter-party to use it to minimize your own losses.

这种模式本质上来讲就是一次性买卖，即我们俗称的"一锤子交易"。采用这种模式一般有几种情况：第一，谈判双方以后不想再有业务往来。第二，谈判对手对于本次谈判所交易商品的供求行情不太了解，否则不会接受不利于己方的条件。第三，双方的实力悬殊，己方处于绝对优势。对方有求于己方，且己方在谈判桌上完全可以采用强硬态度。以上三种情况在实际谈判中并不常见。对于谈判人员而言，可以不用这种模式但需要了解，同时还需要具备识别和掌握一定的反传统阵地模式的措施，以阻止对方在谈判中采用这种模式，尽力将己方损失降到最低。

(2) Modern Rational Negotiation Mode（现代理性谈判模式）

a. Definition（定义）

The modern rational negotiation mode is that both parties, while understanding their own needs, also strive to find each other's needs. Based on this, the two parties continue to explore and break in, and work together to explore various feasible ways and solutions to meet the needs of the two parties, then finally decide whether to take one or more of these approaches to reach an agreement that can maximize the interests of both parties. The biggest feature of this mode is "rational". After clarifying each party's needs, both parties analyze the needs of counter-party more rationally, instead of asking for it without paying "reciprocation". It is conducted on the basis of communication and understanding. Even if the negotiation is inconclusive, it will not affect the relationship between the two parties. Through this negotiation mode, negotiating parties can find common ground that can maximize the benefits of them, thereby facilitating the conclusion of the transaction and laying the foundation for future transactions between them (See Figure 2. 3).

现代理性谈判模式是谈判双方在了解自身需求的同时，也努力寻找对方的需求，双方在此基础上不断进行探讨和磨合，与对方一起共同探寻满足双方需要的各种可行途径和方案，最后决定是否采取其中一个或数个途径，达成可能能实现双方利益最大化的协议。这种模式最大的特点在于“理性”。双方在明确了自己的需求后，比较理性地分析对方的需求，而不是一味索取却不付出“回报”，是在沟通理解的基础上进行的，即使谈判没有结果，也不会影响双方之间的关系。通过这种谈判模式，能找到实现双方利益最大化的共同点，从而促成交易的达成，也为双方今后的交易奠定基础（见图2.3）。

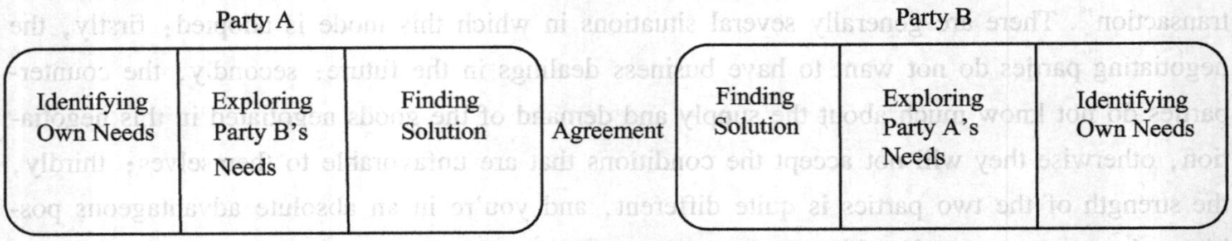

Figure 2. 3 Modern Rational Negotiation Mode

Under this negotiation mode, both parties seek each other's needs to a certain extent, the atmosphere of the entire negotiation will be relatively relaxed, and the success rate of the negotiation will greatly increase. Even if the negotiation fails due to some unreachable consensus, it will not affect the negotiators' evaluation on the counter-party, and can lay a good foundation for the future cooperation. In addition, negotiators can also leave a better impression on the counter-party. Of course, the cost to be paid under this mode will be relatively high, and high-quality negotiators need to be chosen in the selection of negotiators, and simulations should be performed in advance if conditions permit. This mode is also inconsistent with the actual behavior of people. In most cases, the actions of both parties cannot maximize their respective potential benefits. Only a few negotiators choose the goal of maximizing the benefits of both parties. Without long-term training, It is difficult to achieve such a win-win result.

在这种谈判模式下，谈判双方都在一定程度上探求对方的需求，整个谈判的氛围会比较轻松，而且谈判的成功率会大大提高。即使因为一些无法达成的共识导致谈判失败，也不会影响谈判方对对方的评价，能为今后双方开展合作奠定良好的基础。此外，谈判人员个人也能给对方留下比较好的印象。当然，这种模式下要付出的成本会比较高，在谈判人员的选择上需要派出高素质的谈判人员，在条件允许的情况下要进行事先模拟。这种模式也与人的实际行为不符，在大多数情况下，双方的行为都不能最大化各自的潜在收益，只有很小部分谈判人员会选择双方收益最大化的目标。如果没有经过长期培训，很难达到这种双赢的结果。

b. Negotiation Style（谈判风格）

The modern rational negotiation mode is a compromise type, which is a win-win concept. The negotiator's stance on negotiating in this mode is to consider both the negotiation goals of his own party and the interests of the counter-party. The negotiators pay great attention to persuasion and communication and the use of negotiation skills. The goal of the negotiation is to find an expedient solution that is acceptable to both parties so that the interests of both parties can be met. Negotiators will take a low starting point for negotiating with a small win or a small loss. The entire negotiation process was conducted on the basis of communication and understanding between the two parties, creating a harmonious atmosphere for negotiation and also establishing good interpersonal relationships. In negotiating skills, strategies are often used to make the best decisions, so as to determine targeted negotiation plans and details that are both economically reasonable and more conducive to their own.

现代理性谈判模式属于妥协型，即双赢理念。采用这种模式的谈判人员对待谈判的立场是既考虑己方的谈判目标，又考虑对方的利益。非常注重说服沟通的各个环节，注重谈判技巧的运用。所追求的谈判目标是找出某种权宜性的、双方都能接受的方案，从而使双方的利益都能得到满足。谈判人员会采取微赢或微输的低起点的谈判立场。整个谈判过程都是在双方沟通和理解的基础上进行的，营造的是和谐的谈判氛围，同时也建立了良好的人际关系。在谈判技巧上往往会采用将计就计、投其所好的策略，从而有针对性地确定出既经济合理又更利于自身的谈判方案和谈判细节。

c. Choice and Application（选择与运用）

This is an idealized negotiation mode. It needs to meet the interests of both parties and maximize the benefits when it is used. This result is not easy to achieve in negotiation practice. While satisfying the best interests of one party, it is bound to harm the interests of the other party to a certain extent. When your own party's expectations for the negotiation are not high or you know that the counter-party's expectations are not high, this mode can be considered, but it needs to be applied properly to achieve good results.

这是一种比较理想化的谈判模式，在运用时需要满足双方利益，并实现利益最大化，而在现实谈判中这种结果并不容易实现。在满足一方最大利益的同时势必在一定程度上损害对方的利益。在己方对此次谈判的期望结果不高或是了解到对方对谈判的期望结果不高的情况下，可以考虑采用这种模式，但需要恰当运用才会有好的结果。

(3) PRAM Negotiation Mode（PRAM 谈判模式）

a. Definition（定义）

The goal of the PRAM negotiation mode is to pursue a win-win result, that is, one party should treat the negotiation like its own business, and both parties involved in the negotiation are working hard to reach an agreement. It includes four steps: formulating a negotiation plan (P), establishing and developing friendly relations between the two parties (R), reaching an agreement acceptable to both parties (A), implementing the agreement, and maintaining the relationship (M), which refers to as the PRAM mode (See Figure 2.4).

PRAM 谈判模式的目标是追求双赢的结果，即要让谈判的对方像己方一样看待谈判工作，参与谈判的双方都在为达成一致而努力。它包括四个步骤：制订谈判计划（PLAN）、建立和发展双方的友好关系（RELATIONSHIP）、达成双方都能接受的协议（AGREEMENT）、协议的履行和关系的维持（MAINTENANCE），简称 PRAM 模式（见图 2.4）。

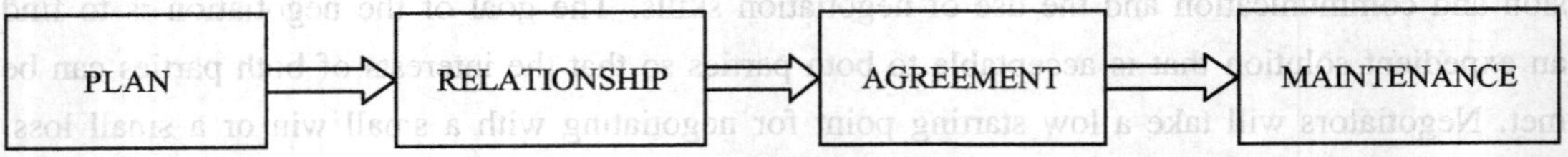

Figure 2.4 PRAM Negotiation Mode

This negotiation mode is a negotiation process based on mutual assistance and cooperation between the two parties. During the negotiation, not only the beneficial relationship but also the interpersonal relationship exist. The interpersonal relationship is the basis and guarantee for the realization of the beneficial relationship; the negotiating parties should not only focus on the negotiation, but also consider future business. In this mode, the goal of the negotiation is to satisfy the common interests of both parties, not limited to sacrifice the interests of the counter-party to meet your own interests, and this kind of interest needs can be reconciled; the process of negotiations is to fully understand each other's interests requirements. The result of the negotiations is that the interests of both parties can be well met, and both parties can find the most common ground for both parties' interests. Under the premise that both parties' interests are valued and met, the two parties have established a good interpersonal relationship, and this relationship can be constantly consolidated and strengthened. But in this negotiation mode, the above four steps are indispensable and they are interconnected. If any one of the steps fails, the negotiation result will be greatly reduced.

这种谈判模式是在双方互助合作关系基础上的协商过程，在谈判中不仅存在效益关系，还存在人际关系，人际关系是实现效益关系的基础和保障；谈判各方不仅要着眼于本次谈判，而且要考虑今后的业务往来。在这种模式下，谈判的目标是满足双方共同的利益，不局限于牺牲对方利益来满足自身利益，而且这种利益需要是可以调和的；谈判的过程是双方充分地理解彼此的利益要求的过程，而谈判的结果是使双方的利益要求都能够得到很好的满足，双方都能找到最大的利益共同点；在双方利益都得到重视和满足的前提下，双方建立起一种良好的人际关系，并且这种人际关系能不断地得到巩固和加强。但在这种谈判模式中，四个步骤缺一不可，它们之间是相互联系的。如果其中任何一个环节出现问题，都会使谈判结果大打折扣。

b. Constituent Elements（构成）

• Formulating a Negotiation Plan（制订谈判计划）

When formulating a negotiation plan, firstly you must define your own negotiation goals, and then try to understand and clarify the negotiation goals of the counter-party. After both parties' goals are determined, it is necessary to compare the two parties' goals to find out what are the common interests of both parties in this negotiation. The common interests of both parties shall be first put forward in the formal negotiation and confirmed by both parties. Regarding the issue that the interests of both parties are inconsistent, both parties should exert their creativity on the basis of the principle called "successful negotiations should satisfy the interests of both parties", and acti-vely seek ways to satisfy both parties.

在制订谈判计划时，首先要明确己方的谈判目标，然后要尽力去理解和弄清楚对方的谈判目标。在双方的目标都确定之后，就需要把双方的目标进行比较，找出本次谈判中双方利益一致的地方。对于双方利益的共同点，要在正式谈判中首先提出来，并由双方确认。对于双方利益不一致的问题，要通过双方发挥创造力根据"成功的谈判应该使双方的利益需要都得到满足"的原则，积极寻找使双方都满意的方法。

• Establishing and Developing Friendly Relations Between the Two Parties（建立并发展友好关系）

Before the formal negotiation begins, a good relationship with the counter-party should be established. This relationship should be a conscious, trustworthy, comfortable, open and harmonious relationship that can be felt by both parties during the negotiation process. How to build a trusting relationship with the negotiating parties who have never met? The first thing to do is to make the counter-party believe in your own beliefs, which includes your care for the negotiator's personal issues, thoughtful etiquette, and diligence at work. Second, show your sincerity. For exam-ple, you can introduce some examples of sincere dealings with others in the past transactions. Third, get the counter-party's ultimate trust through actions. This requires you to keep promises and do what you said. It must always be kept in mind that no matter how strong the trust between you and the counter-party is, if there is a default, the trust between each other will be broken, and once it is broken, it will be difficult to resume.

在正式谈判开始之前，要与谈判对手建立良好的关系，这种关系应该是一种有意识地形成的、能使谈判双方的当事人在协商过程中感受到的信任、舒适、开放、融洽的关系。如何与素未谋面的谈判对手建立起彼此信任的关系？首先要坚持使对方相信己方的信念，包括对对方谈判人员的关心、周到的礼仪、工作上的勤勉等；其次要表现出己方的诚意，例如可以向对方介绍一些在过去的交易中己方与他人真诚相待的例子；最后通过行动取得对方最终的信任。这需要己方信守承诺，言出必行。必须时刻牢记，不论己方与对方之间的信赖感有多强，只要有一次失约，彼此之间的信赖感就会崩溃，一旦崩溃就很难修复。

• Reach an Agreement Acceptable to Both Parties（达成双方能接受的协议）

After the two parties have established a full trustworthy relationship, substantive negotiations can proceed. First of all, it is necessary to further verify the negotiation objectives of the counter-party. The ultimate goal of the negotiation should make sure the content of the agreement can be successfully implemented. No matter how beneficial the content of the agreement is for your party, if the counter-party feels that it is at a disadvantage in the agreement, there is likely an incentive for it to fail to fulfill the terms of the agreement. Once the counter-party does not comply with the agreement, the agreement is meaningless.

在双方建立了充分的信任关系后，就可以进行实质性的谈判了。首先要进一步核实对方的谈判目标，谈判的终极目标应该是使协议的内容能得到圆满贯彻执行。不管协议内容对己方多有利，如果对方感到自己在协议中处于不利位置，很可能就有不履行协议条款的动机。一旦对方不遵守协议，那么协议就毫无意义。

• Implementing the Agreement, and Maintaining the Relationship（协议的履行与关系维持）

In negotiations, people often think that once they have reached an agreement that is satisfactory to them, they are done. Then they celebrate the success of the negotiations. In fact, although the negotiations have ended up, the implementation of the terms of the agreement has just begun. Do not assume that the counter-party who signed the agreement will fully perform its obligations and responsibilities. It is important to sign an agreement, but it is even more important to implement and maintain the agreement to ensure its implementation. How to ensure that the counter-party can fulfill the agreement? You, as one party of the negotiation, must first give an appropriate and good emotional response to the counter-party's compliance with the agreement, such as expressing gratitude and greetings in person, or expressing it by letter or phone. Second, you must firstly abide by the agreement yourself. The basic method of maintaining the relationship with the counter-party is to maintain and contact with it, especially personal contacts, which can avoid wasting time and energy to re-cultivate the relationship with the counter-party when dealing with it in the future.

在谈判中，人们往往会认为一旦达成令己方满意的协议就大功告成了，然后欢呼雀跃，举杯庆祝谈判的成功。其实虽然谈判结束了，但协议中的条款的履行才刚刚开始，千万不要认为签订了协议对方就会完全履行其义务和责任。签订协议固然重要，但履行和维持协议，确保其能得到贯彻实施更加重要。如何确保对方能履行协议呢？作为己方首先要对对方遵守协议约定的行为做出适当的、良好的情感反馈，例如亲自上门拜访表示感谢和问候，也可以通过书信、电话等方式来表达；其次，己方自己首先应做到信守协议。维持与对方关系的基本做法就是保持与对方的接触和联系，特别是个人之间的接触，避免以后与对方进行交易时，再花费时间、精力重新培养与对方的关系。

In all, in order to maintain the win-win relationship, the negotiating parties need to pay attention to the following two aspects. Firstly, in the maintenance of agreement, a positive response should be made to the efforts of the counter-party to achieve the final success of the negotiation, and at the same time, perform your own obligations of the contract. Secondly, in the maintenance of relationship, you need to actively maintain the contact with the counter-party, and reaffirm the trustworthiness between the two parties.

归纳起来，谈判各方为了维持这种双赢关系，需要做到两点：第一，在"协议维持"中，对于对方为这次谈判获得最终的成功所付出的努力应该做出积极的回应，同时要履行己方在合同中的各项职责；第二，在"关系维持"中，要积极与对方保持联系和接触，同时再次肯定双方之间的信任关系。

c. Negotiation Style（谈判风格）

• Cooperative Type（合作型）

Negotiators who adopt this negotiating style rely mainly on maintaining good interpersonal relationships in the negotiations, and seek to negotiate in a harmonious and open negotiation atmosphere. Adopting this negotiating style requires all negotiating parties to follow the basic principle of equality and mutual benefit. In the spirit of friendly consultation, the negotiating parties will benefit from it, so as to achieve a win-win result, and the relationship between them will become better and better, so that they could become each other's regular customer.

采用这种谈判风格的谈判人员，在谈判中主要立足于维持良好的人际关系，追求在和谐、开放的谈判氛围中进行磋商。采用这种谈判风格要求谈判各方都要遵循平等互利这一基本原则，本着友好磋商的精神使谈判各方从中获益，从而实现双赢的结果。双方的关系也会日趋良好，从而使对方成为自己的稳定客户。

• Accommodating Type（通融型）

Negotiators who adopt this negotiating style put the maintenance of good negotiating relations first in their negotiations. Their attitude towards negotiations is to try their best to maintain interpersonal relationships, and they have little or no interest in their negotiation goals. In order to avoid conflicts, concessions and appeasement are often made. This is a concession-type negotiation style. It adopts concessions and tolerance to the conflicts to promote the success of the negotiations.

采用这种谈判风格的谈判人员在谈判中把保持良好的谈判关系放在第一位，对待谈判的态度是竭力维护人际关系，很少或不关心己方的谈判目标。为了避免冲突，经常会向对方做出退让或安抚对方。这是一种退让型谈判风格，对谈判中的冲突采取退让和容忍从而促成谈判的成功。

In the PRAM negotiation mode, no matter what negotiation type is adopted, establishing and developing a good relationship between the two parties is very important, which is not only related to the progress of this negotiation, but also to future business between two parties. This mode is generally applied to regular customers who have specific and clear trading conditions which tend to be fixed or have established a cooperative relationship which tend to be stabilized after multiple contacts between them.

在 PRAM 谈判模式中，不管采用哪种谈判风格，建立和发展双方的友好关系都是一个非常重要的环节，既关系到此次谈判的进展，又关系到今后的业务往来。这种模式一般会运用在双方经过多次交往之后，交易条件比较清楚明确且趋于固定或者是已经建立合作关系且趋于稳定的固定客户之间。

d. Prerequisites for Implementation（实施的前提）

The implementation of the PRAM negotiation mode requires a very important prerequisite, that is, the negotiating parties need to establish a correct sense of negotiation. This correct sense of negotiation mainly includes the following points. Firstly, keep in mind that negotiation is consultation not competition. The competition needs to be won or lost. There is only one winner, but the negotiation is different. During the negotiation, the two parities continuously adjust their needs based on fully understanding the current and future environmental factors that can be judged to form a way to meet the needs of both parties. Secondly, it is clear that the relationship between the negotiating parties is a cooperative one and not a hostile one. Of course, there is also competition at the same time of cooperation. It is a competitive relationship based on cooperation. Thirdly, it is clear that in addition to the interest relationship, the two parties also have interpersonal relationships. Interpersonal relationships are the basis and guarantee for the realization of interest relationships. Any transaction is risky and requires costs. In order to control transaction risks, the negotiating parties must evaluate and select various aspects of the counter-party, and establish a good interpersonal relationship by goodwill and trust with each other. Fourthly, negotiators must not only focus on immediate interests, but also see the long-term interests and future business between them. Each negotiation is actually not isolated. The performance of the company's strength and the establishment of its corporate image are gradually formed through several activities. Finding a long-term trading partner comes at a price, and the implementation of the negotiation plan requires the joint efforts of both parties. Therefore, in the negotiation process, we must look to the future.

PRAM 谈判模式的实施需要具备一个很重要的前提条件，那就是谈判双方需要树立正确的谈判意识。这个正确的谈判意识主要包括以下几点：第一，牢记谈判是协商，而不是比赛。比赛需要分输赢，赢家只有一个，而谈判不同，谈判时通过信息沟通，使双方在充分认识当前和未来可判断的环境因素基础上不断调整自身的需要，从而形成能同时满足双方需要的方式。第二，明确谈判双方之间的关系是合作互助关系而非敌对关系。当然，在合作的同时也有竞争，是合作基础上的竞争关系。第三，清楚双方除了利益关系外还有人际关系，人际关系是实现利益关系的基础和保障。任何交易都是有风险的，是需要付出成本的。为了控制交易风险，谈判双方必须对谈判对手的各方面情况做出评估和选择，通过建立对彼此的好感和信任感从而建立良好的人际关系。第四，谈判者不能仅仅着眼于眼前的利益，更要看到长远的利益和双方今后的业务往来。每一次的谈判其实都不是孤立的，企业实力的表现、企业形象的树立是通过一次次的活动逐步形成的。寻找一个长期的贸易伙伴是需要付出代价的，谈判方案的执行需要双方共同努力，因此，在谈判过程中必须着眼未来。

e. Choice and Application（选择与运用）

Compared with the previous two modes, this mode is more practical. It differs from the traditional model in that the guiding ideology of winning and losing and a strong negotiation style run through the entire negotiation process. Instead, it insists that the two parties are winners as the guiding ideology of the negotiation. At the same time, the PRAM negotiation mode weakens the idealization of the negotiation that is valued in the modern rational negotiation mode. The idea is more operable, which makes the feasibility of the negotiation mode operation greatly improved. It is a more scientific negotiation mode. Although this mode may not meet all the needs of both parties, it can be achieved to the maximum extent, and at the same time, it can improve the efficiency of negotiations, so that the two parties can establish a good cooperative relationship and lay a solid foundation for further cooperation.

和之前两种模式相比，PRAM 模式更实用。它不同于传统模式以论输赢的指导思想和强硬的谈判风格贯穿整个谈判过程，而是坚持以双方都是赢家作为谈判的指导思想。同时，PRAM 模式削弱了现代理性谈判模式中重视的谈判理想化的思想，更具有可操作性，使得谈判模式运行的可行性也大大提高，是一种比较科学的谈判模式。虽然这种模式可能无法满足双方的所有需求，但可以最大限度地得以实现，同时还可以提高谈判效率，使得双方能建立起良好的合作关系，为将来的进一步合作奠定坚实的基础。

In short, with the deepening of globalization, international business nego-tiation activities have become more frequent, and the requirements for negotiation modes have become higher and higher, and they have become more perfect and reasonable. In the future, there will be more new negotiation modes in line with modern business negotiation concepts. But as far as the three main negotiation modes are concerned, the traditional position negotiation mode has a lot of disadvantages, which is not conducive to the negotiation, and will inevitably gradually withdraw from the current negotiation activities. Modern national negotiation mode is not applicable in daily negotiating activities, and it will not be a negotiating mode preferred by negotiators. Since PRAM negotiation mode has many advantage, it has been widely used in negotiation practice and occupies a dominant position in the negotiation.

总之，随着全球化的深入，国际商务谈判活动也越来越频繁，对谈判模式的要求也越来越高，也更趋于完善合理。今后还会出现更多符合现代商务谈判理念的新的谈判模式。但就目前这三种主要的谈判模式而言，传统阵地谈判模式存在很多弊端，不利于谈判的进行，必将逐渐退出谈判活动的舞台；现代理性谈判模式又过于追求完美和理想化，在日常的谈判活动中也不适用，不会成为谈判者优先考虑选择的谈判模式。而 PRAM 谈判模式因为具备很多优势，在现实的谈判活动中已经被广泛采用，在谈判活动中占据主导地位。

Summary

International business negotiations are mainly composed of the negotiating subject and the negotiating object. Negotiating objects need to have three basic conditions of commonality, negotiability, and legitimacy. In addition, international business negotiations also include other elements, such as negotiation information, negotiation environment, negotiation time and negotiation place. International business negotiations are divided into different types according to different standards. The procedure of international business negotiations includes the preparation phase, the opening phase, the bargaining phase and the contract signing phase. The main modes of international business negotiation consist of traditional position negotiation mode, modern rational negotiation mode and PRAM negotiation mode. This chapter focuses on the content of PRAM negotiation mode.

国际商务谈判主要由谈判主体和谈判客体构成。谈判客体需要具备共同性、可谈性和合法性这三个基本条件。除此之外，国际商务谈判还包括其他要素，比如谈判信息、谈判环境、谈判时间和谈判地点。国际商务谈判根据不同的标准可分为不同的类型。国际商务谈判的流程包括准备阶段、开局阶段、实质性磋商阶段和签约阶段。国际商务谈判的主要模式有传统阵地谈判模式、现代理性谈判模式和PRAM谈判模式，本章重点讲解了PRAM谈判模式的内容。

Module Ⅱ Terminology Practice

1. Natural Person: It means one single person, not an organization or company. It's a term used in law.

2. National Law: The symmetry of "international law". It refers to the classification of law from the perspective of the creation and application of the law. It refers to laws created by a particular country and applicable to the scope of national sovereignty, such as criminal law, civil law, and administrative law.

3. International Practice: It's the general term for international custom and international common law. The world-wide practice is a quasi-mandatory mix of arbitrariness in effectiveness. It is an unwritten legal norm that is gradually formed in international exchanges.

4. Negotiation Strategy: It is a general term for various methods, measures, techniques, tactics and means used by negotiators to achieve the goal of negotiating in the process of business negotiation. It is generated by the development of economy and technology. Due to its practicability, specialization and pertinence, the negotiation strategy has been widely used in business negotiation.

5. Main Speaker: It refers to a person who elaborates on position and viewpoint on behalf of his own party at a certain stage of the negotiation or on a topic or aspect. At this time, the others are in an auxiliary position, called the assistant speakers. Generally speaking, there should be a technical main speaker and a business main speaker in the negotiating team.

6. A third Country: It refers to any other country in which the parties involved in the negotiation is also known as neutral countries.

7. GATT: The full name is General Agreement on Tariffs and Trade. It is a multilateral international agreement on tariffs and trade rules concluded between governments. Its purpose is to eliminate tariffs and other trade barriers, eliminate differential treatment in international trade, promote international trade liberalization, and make full use of world resources to expand the production and circulation of goods. The GATT was signed in Geneva on October 30, 1947, and was temporarily applied on January 1, 1948.

8. Uruguay Round: In September 1986, the GATT ministerial meeting was held in Punta del Este, Uruguay, and a new round of negotiations aiming at comprehensively reforming the multilateral trading system was decided. It was named the "Uruguay Round Negotiation". This is the largest round of trade negotiations up to date, which lasted seven and a half years and ended in Marrakech, Morocco, in April 1994. Negotiations involve almost all trade, including toothbrushes, yachts, banks, telecommunications, wild rice genes and AIDS treatment.

9. Safeguard Clauses: In the case of a trade agreement, the state party may revoke the concession when it imposes obligations such as tariff reduction on a certain product, resulting in an increase in imports and damage to the producers of the same kind of products in the country. In the past such clause has always been called the exemption clause, which has often been called the safeguard clause in recent years. The former is exempt from the obligation and responsibility of the concession and the latter is to protect the domestic industry from damage.

10. Joint Venture: It is generally defined as an association of two or more entities combining property and expertise to carry out a single business enterprise. The entities can be corporate, governmental, or individual. The joint venture may be established for only one project or plan, or it may continue to operate in the form of a joint venture like Sony Ericsson.

11. Economic Integration: It is the economic union between the state and the state. Economic integration is not only a peculiar phenomenon of the world economy, but also a peculiar phenomenon of the contemporary world economy. It reflects an important feature of the contemporary world economy. According to the degree and level of development, economic integration can be divided into four types: free trade zone, customs union, common market, and economic union. Generally speaking, economic integration can only be achieved between countries of the same type, and similar economic mechanisms and economic systems form the basis of a new economy.

Module Ⅲ New Words

1. authenticity *n.* 真实性，确实性，可靠性
2. effectiveness *n.* 效率；有效性
3. qualification *n.* （通过考试或学习课程取得的）资格；（胜任某一工作或职位所需的）技能条件，资历；合格，达到标准
4. avoid *v.* 避免，防止；躲避，避开；逃避
5. entity *n.* 实体
6. restriction *n.* 限制，规定；（对大小、数量或范围的）限制
7. talkative *adj.* 爱说话的，健谈的
8. fund *n.* 基金；专款；基金会 *v.* 为（活动、组织、事件等）提供资金，资助
9. quarantine *n.* 检疫 *v.* 对（动物或人）进行检疫隔离
10. initiative *n.* 主动性；计划，措施；主动权
11. mature *adj.* 成熟的，理智的；成年的；发酵成熟的；不再年轻的，老练的 *v.* 变成熟；变理智；（债券保单等）到期；（使）酿成
12. dispute *n.* 争论；争端，纠纷 *v.* 对（某事）表示异议；争执；争夺
13. legitimacy *n.* 合法性；正统性；嫡系
14. comprehensive *adj.* 详尽的；全面的；彻底的
15. appropriate *adj.* 恰当的；合适的 *v.* 挪用；占用；盗用；拨（款）
16. contradiction *n.* （说法、信念、观点等的相互）矛盾，不一致
17. reliability *adj.* 可靠性
18. verbal *adj.* 口头的，非书面的；文字上

的；动词的

19. advancement *n.* 进步；进展

20. unexpected *adj.* 意外的，突然的

21. adaptability *n.* 适应性；可用性；灵活性；适应能力

22. conflict *n.*（意见等的）抵触，冲突，矛盾；武装冲突；战斗；（在对立的需要或影响之间做选择的）矛盾，冲突 *v.* 矛盾，冲突，抵触

23. advocate *v.* 主张，拥护，鼓吹 *n.* 提倡者，拥护者，鼓吹者

24. abandon *v.* 抛弃，遗弃（某人）*n.* 放任；尽情

25. succumb *v.* 屈服，屈从；不再抵抗；患重病；死于（某疾病）

26. compromise *v.* 妥协，让步；在……方面妥协 *n.* 折中，妥协；折中办法

27. eliminate *v.* 消除，根除；（在比赛中）淘汰；消灭，铲除

28. breakdown *n.*（关系的）破裂；（体系的）崩溃；失败

29. pursue *v.* 追求，继续进行；追究某件事，继续争论；追捕，追击；追求（某人）

30. propose *v.* 提议，建议；（在会议上）正式提议；提出（某观点、方法）；（正式地向某人）求婚

31. procrastination *n.* 拖延；延期

32. enhance *v.* 提高；改进；增强

33. representative *n.* 代表，代理人；（美国）众议院议员 *adj.* 典型的；有代表性的；代表各类事物的

34. harmonious *adj.*（关系）和谐的，融洽的；（声音）和谐的，悦耳的；（颜色）协调的

Module Ⅳ Useful Expressions

1. participate in 参与，参加
2. comply with 服从，遵从
3. be related to 与……有关
4. lose face 丢脸，丢面子
5. time limit 时限
6. due to 由于，因为
7. take initiative 积极主动，采取主动
8. in the case of 至于，在……情况下
9. under the circumstance 在此情况下
10. a package of 一揽子，一包
11. be beneficial to 有利于，有益
12. be involved in 被卷入
13. strive for 争取；奋发图强；收下
14. compose of 组成，构成
15. contribute to 捐助；给……投稿
16. cope with 应对；处理
17. put forward 提出（计划、建议、名字）；推荐
18. deal with 处理；应付；与……打交道；论述；讨论；涉及；与……做买卖
19. treat... as 把……看作
20. face-to-face 面对面的

Module Ⅴ Exercise

Ⅰ. Answer the following questions according to the text.

1. What are the components of international business negotiation? What is the most impor-

tant component?

2. What's the subject of business negotiation? What are the components of negotiation subject?

3. In order to ensure the smooth progress of the negotiations, what are the requirements for the negotiation subject?

4. As the object of negotiation, which three basic conditions need to be met?

5. Please give an example of the importance of the negotiation time provisions for negotiations.

6. How many choices can be made for the places of negotiation? And what are the pros and cons for each choice?

7. Under what circumstances should individual negotiation and group negotiation apply?

8. What are the forms of indirect negotiations? Which form is currently most used?

9. What types of negotiations are based on the location of the negotiation?

10. What are the characteristics of principle-based negotiations?

Ⅱ. Match the words in Column A with their definitions in Column B.

Column A	Column B
1. initiative	A. to publicly support a particular way of doing something
2. breakdown	B. to reach an agreement less than what they wanted at first
3. dispute	C. to stop opposing someone or something stronger than you
4. eliminate	D. to delay doing something that you should do
5. compromise	E. a difference between two statements, beliefs or ideas
6. verbal	F. the failure of a relationship or system
7. procrastination	G. you are in a position to control a situation
8. succumb	H. spoken rather than written
9. contradiction	I. a serious argument or disagreement
10. advocate	J. to completely get rid of something that is unnecessary or unwanted

Ⅲ. Translate the following terms and phrases into Chinese.

1. facial expression
2. Sino-U. S. trade negotiation
3. separate... from
4. network contract
5. common interest
6. subject language
7. regard... as
8. rely on
9. be prone to
10. decision-making
11. collective bargain
12. group negotiation
13. legal limits
14. peaceful negotiation
15. resolve disputes
16. technical cooperation
17. subject qualification
18. vital role

19. assume obligation 20. number of participator

Ⅳ. Please determine whether the following statements are True or False.

1. The components of international business negotiation mainly include negotiating subject and negotiating object. (　　)

2. Negotiation object is the combination of the topics of negotiation and various material elements. (　　)

3. The choice for negotiating time and place has little influence on negotiation result. (　　)

4. In general, the location of business negotiations is best to hold at neutral place, so the chances of success in the negotiations will be even greater. (　　)

5. One-on-one individual negotiation refers to the way in which a negotiating party sends a representative to negotiate, which is mainly suitable for formal or important occasions. (　　)

6. Multilateral negotiation means that the number of participators is more than two parties, such as trade negotiations between multiple countries and trade joint ventures and trade negotiations between multiple companies. (　　)

7. Direct negotiation is a means for the parties to negotiate to facilitate the exchange of information and negotiation of written language such as words or television, telephone, and network. (　　)

8. Network negotiation is becoming the most commonly used method of international business negotiations. (　　)

9. Soft-typed negotiation, also known as concession negotiation and friendly negotiation, means that negotiators hope to avoid conflicts and contradictions in the negotiation, and are ready to make concessions in order to reach an agreement. (　　)

10. Principle-based negotiation means that the negotiating parties regard each other as enemies rather than cooperative partners. (　　)

Ⅴ. Translate the following sentences into Chinese.

1. In essence, international business negotiation is the process in which different stakeholders in international business activities negotiate the terms of the transaction in order to close a deal.

2. In this kind of negotiation, negotiators relatively have greater rights to decide, and to deal with various situations independently.

3. The team members have clear distinctive responsibilities. Some are the main negotiators, and some deal with legal aspects.

4. The contents of business negotiations are complex and various, which can be mainly classified as investment, goods purchase, technology trade, labor cooperation and loan business negotiations.

5. Successful multinational business encounters depend to a large extent on a properly

chosen form of communication.

Ⅵ. Translate the following sentences into English.

1. 根据谈判地点的不同，谈判可以分为主场谈判、客场谈判和中立地谈判。

2. 原则型谈判认为在谈判双方对立立场的背后，存在着某种共同利益和冲突性利益。

3. 在国际商务谈判的构成要素中，谈判主体、谈判客体和谈判议题是三个最基本的要素。

4. 我很高兴贵方来续签今年进口我们丝绸产品的订单。

5. 在国际商务谈判中不存在“要么拥有，要么舍弃”的事物。

6. 中立谈判对于谈判双方来说都是客场谈判。选择双方都可以接受的中立地点，有助于营造一个客观、理性的谈判气氛。

7. 如果一方想与另一方保持长期的业务关系，并且具有这样的可能性，那么就不能采取立场型谈判。

8. 在国际商务谈判中，凡是以小组形式进行的谈判，多属于比较正式的谈判，特别是涉及金额巨大或内容比较复杂的谈判。

Ⅶ. Case Study

Case 1: Claim Negotiation in International Business Negotiations

Case Source: The website of *Japan Economic News*, 2003.

Preface

Time: 2001

Key Point: Japan's Mitsubishi Motors Corporation successfully solved the problem of automobile pipeline through compensation scheme.

Background

Industry: Automobile

Subject: Japan's Mitsubishi Motors Corporation and Chinese Consumers

Issue: Japan's Mitsubishi Motors Corporation compensates Chinese consumers for the Pajero V31 and V33 vehicle pipeline problems.

In March 2001, in response to the update of some Mitsubishi off-road vehicles and some users on the oil pipeline, the responsible person of Mitsubishi Motors Corporation of Japan submitted to the China Consumers Association "Mitsubishi Motors recalled the problem car in China—compensation for consumers". This is the final compensation plan made by Mitsubishi.

The "Proposal" compensated Chinese Mitsubishi Motors users and consumers for the recall of the Pajero V31 and V33 vehicles: providing the rear brake tubing to the Pajero V31 and V33 vehicles purchased through regular channels or other channels; free repair, including manual repair and material costs; warranty period for all vehicle repair and replacement parts, recalculated from the date of replacement; related expenses incurred for the vehicle involved in this recall (household accommodation, rental of alternative vehicles or traffic charges, such as petrol fees, highway fees, etc.). Mitsubishi would compensate within reasonable limits. If the repair shop determined that the vehicle couldn't be repaired within 3 hours after inspection, the consumer had the right to request a replacement car, and Mitsubishi would make compensation for the rental fee. The "Proposal" stated that Mitsubishi will conduct a thorough investigation of the requirements of relevant consumers. If it is confirmed that personal injury is caused by vehicle technical problems, Mitsubishi will be in accordance with the provisions of Article 41 of the Consumer Protection Law of the People's Republic of China, and Article 42 to fulfill the liability for compensation to consumers. Regarding the issue of return, the "Proposal" proposes: "If necessary, for the individual who needs to purchase the above two vehicles (ie. consumers) through formal channels, they can contact the direct seller."

The "Solution" considers the interests of buyers through formal channels and informal channels, as well as the special circumstances of the Chinese market, and satisfactorily solves the oil pipeline turmoil of Mitsubishi off-road vehicles.

Questions

1. What types of international business negotiations can be divided according to the content of the negotiations?

2. What type of negotiations are involved in the case? What issues should you pay attention to when conducting this type of business negotiation?

Appendix

The recall of the Pajero refers to the recall of the Pajero car produced by Mitsubishi Motors Corporation of Japan, which occurred three times from 2001 to 2008. Ten years ago, because of two car accidents, the design flaws of the Pajero brake system were revealed, which prompted Mitsubishi to make the first recall of the domestic Pajero in 2001. In 2004, the Pajero was recalled for the second time due to the engine hood problem. Later, in July 2008, due to defects in the brake system, Mitsubishi again recalled Pajero.

Case 2: Subject and Object in International Business Negotiations

Case Source: Zhang Zhi. *International Business Negotiation*. Dalian: Dalian University of Technology Press, 2008.

Preface

Time: 2004-2005

Key Point: Negotiations between China's A Import and Export Corporation and Milano of Milan, Italy

Background

Industry: Clothes

Subject: China's A Import and Export Corporation and Milano of Milan, Italy

Issue: Li Gang, a salesman at A Import and Export Corporation, and Di Pieer from Milano of Milan, Italy, negotiated on Men's Suits.

Li Gang is a salesman of the clothing department of A Import and Export Corporation. In

October 2004, he was appointed by the company to negotiate with Mr. Di Pieer of Milano on the export business of men's suits. After several rounds of negotiations, the following agreement was reached: A Import and Export Corporation sold 1,000 pieces of men's clothing to Milano at a price of CIF Genova USD100. 00 per piece, with a total value of USD 100,000. The payment method was an irrevocable letter of credit at sight, the delivery date was May 2005, and the goods were covered against All Risks and War Risks at 110% of the invoice value.

Questions

1. What is the subject of negotiation? What is the object of negotiation?

2. Who is the subject of the negotiation in this case? Who is the object?

Appendix

The topics of negotiation have three characteristics. First, they have commonality for both parties to the negotiation. Second, they are talkative about the negotiation process. Third, the topics of negotiation involve the interests of two or more parties.

Case 3: Fully Understand the Subject Matter of the Negotiations and Reach a Deal

Case Source: Wang Chao. *Negotiation Analytics*. Beijing: University of International Business and Economics, 1999.

Preface

Time: In the 1990s

Key Point: Negotiation between a Chemical Factory in China and a Factory in Country E on the Trade about Chemical Raw Materials

Background

Industry: Chemistry

Subject: A Chemical Factory in China and a Factory in Country E

Issue: In the 1990s, when a chemical delegation from China visited Country E in Southeast Asia, it was found that a factory in the country had complaints about the use of Country S's chemical raw materials N2121.

In the 1990s, a chemical delegation from China visited Country E in Southeast Asia and found that a factory in the country had complaints about the use of Country S's chemical raw materials N2121. Mr. Li of the delegation is the director of the N2121 chemical plant in China. After returning to China, he made a further understanding of this issue. The enterprise group that produces N2121 in Country S is a large internationally renowned enterprise. Its N2121 production accounts for more than 50% of the world's total output, the product purity is high (purity is above 98%), and the quality is stable. The disadvantage is that only large packaged products are supplied (50kg per bag), while Country E needs a small package. Although Country E has repeatedly requested, the problem has not been solved. After Country E has imported N2121, it will be packed into 10kg per bag at the factory and then will be sent to the workshop. This will not only delay production time, but also increase the cost of the final product. In addition, Country E's factory does not need 98% high purity, as long as the purity reaches 95%. And the price of 95%-purity products is lower.

The factory in Country E needs to purchase about 200,000 tons per year. This amount is only a small business for the chemical industry group in Country S. Therefore, in the process of dealing with Country E's factory, its attitude is very arrogant, and the requirements for changing the packaging specifications of Country E's factory are not considered at all. In normal interactions, it also doesn't pay attention to the customs and habits of Country E, and acts as a representative of big countries. But 200, 000 tons is a big business for Mr. Li's factory, accounting for one-third of the factory's annual output. It is a contract that must be tried. It is not a problem for Mr. Li's factory to produce small packages, 95% purity can also meet the purity requirements of Country E for N2121 products.

After fully understanding the needs of Country E's factory, Mr. Li issued an invitation to the general manager of the factory to visit China. After the general manager came to China, he was warmly received by Mr. Li's factory. During the visit, the delegation also arranged a three-day visit to Beijing's historical sites, indicating that there are many common languages between the two ancient civilizations. After visiting the factory, the general manager was very satisfied with Mr. Li's factory product quality, operation status and respecting the customer and treating people equally. After returning home, he sent a delegation to Mr. Li's factory to negotiate the purchase of N2121 products. In the negotiations, the Chinese representative said:

• The Chinese side can provide small packages of 10kg per bag;

• The purity is 95%, and the price is $40 per metric ton lower than the 98%-purity product in the international market;

• Compared with Country S, China is closer to Country E, and it can save an expense in transportation costs.

After careful weighing, the representative of Country E signed a two-year contract with Mr. Li's factory.

Questions

1. How did Mr. Li win the negotiation?

2. What's the subject matter of the negotiation between the factory in Country E and Mr. Li's factory?

Appendix

Negotiation preparation includes understanding the situation of the subject matter of negotiation.

Ⅷ. Role plays practice. Work in pair and converse according to the given information.

Task 1

Background

You represent a cosmetics company. You are selling fat-reducing soap that is very popular in China. A businessman from the United States heard about your soap and wants to place an order. You start from inquiry and proceed to offer. Your offer is $12 per dozen CIF New York.

Terms and Phrases

quotation	FOB Shanghai	enjoy fast sales
prevailing market price	strike a deal	place an order
rock bottom price	competitive	do everything possible
sample	specialize in	shipment
get in touch with someone	delivery	out of date

Relative Expressions

1. We need to discuss...
2. Let's start with...
3. Next, it's turn to...
4. Let's move on to...
5. I'd like to know your opinion about...
6. What do you think/feel?
7. What do you think about/of...
8. Do we agree (on that)?
9. What should we do about it?
10. What are we going to do about it?
11. Does it fit in with your objectives?
12. Is that compatible with what you would like to see?
13. Is there anything you'd like to change?
14. May I ask what your proposal is in connection with our company?
15. What in general terms are you looking for here?
16. May we leave that till later and first look at...

Task 2

Background

You, the representative from Guangdong Textile Imp. & Exp. Corp., are talking with Mr. Mike, a Canadian businessman, who is interested in Chinese cotton piece goods. Mr. Mike is not quite satisfied with your design and asks you to produce patterns provided by him. You agree to make him an offer provided he increases the quantity for each design to 1,000 yards. As to packing methods, you succeed in persuading him to accept your usual practice.

Terms and Phrases

quotation	without engagement	commission
employ all possible means	afford to do sth.	get down to do sth.
to begin with	subject to	count on
withdraw	firm offer	make an offer
counter-offer	make a bid	unacceptable

Relative Expressions

1. I think that...
2. In my opinion,...
3. I believe that...
4. From my point of view,...
5. Now, I'd like to talk about...
6. As far as I concerned,...
7. It seems to me that...
8. Don't hold me to this, but...
9. I'm not sure, but...
10. I really think that...
11. Sorry to interrupt, but...
12. Here's a question for you. What does...
13. Do you mind if I ask a question?
14. Just a moment, please.
15. Let me make my point first.
16. Pardon me, I'm not through. Just give me a few seconds to finish my point.
17. I'd like to add something here.

Chapter 3

Preparation for International Business Negotiation

Work Objective

After studying this chapter, you will be able to:

- master the staffing and structure of negotiation team;
- understand and apply the division and collaboration of negotiators within a team;
- familiarize with the quality that negotiators should have;
- apply different methods to collect information;
- master the contents of information that should be collected;
- know the contents of negotiation plan and the ways of making negotiation plan;
- understand other issues that should be prepared before negotiation;
- know the importance of simulated negotiation.

1 Case Guide-Reading

In 1967, the Japanese made a fortune in food business. In 1967, Japanese business personnel based in Moscow (actually market information intelligence personnel) had not seen the familiar officials of the Ministry of Foreign Trade of the Soviet Union in public for more than two weeks. They sent this information back to Tokyo. Tokyo sent a report to all overseas market information personnel asking them to look for the whereabouts of senior officials of the Ministry of Foreign Trade of the Soviet Union, and found them to be conducting secret food trade negotiations in the United States. Japan analyzes this information. So many people in the Soviet Union are negotiating. It is not a small business. It must be bought in large quantities. If this is the case, it will inevitably lead to an increase in food prices on the international market. As a result, Japan has preemptively "eaten" a large amount of food. When the Soviet Union and the United

States reached an agreement and started trading, Japan had already mastered a large amount of food. As a result, food prices have risen sharply in the international market. When the Japanese saw the time was ripe, they immediately threw them at high prices and gained huge profits.

Source: Liu Xiangli. *International Business Negotiation*. Beijing: Mechanical Industry Press, 2009.

Module Ⅰ Text

International business negotiations are planned, targeted, and organized economic activities. It is important to adhere to principles, choose appropriate negotiation strategies, and use negotiating skills flexibly in the negotiations. But if there are no smart and competent negotiators, the negotiations will not proceed smoothly, not to mention that it can achieve the expected purpose. Because the content involved in international business negotiations is more complicated than domestic business negotiations, the required knowledge is also very broad, and often not one person's knowledge, energy, and time can be afforded. Generally, a negotiation team is required to complete.

国际商务谈判是有计划、有目标、有组织的经济活动。在谈判中坚持原则、选择适当的谈判策略、灵活运用谈判技巧固然重要，但如果没有精明能干的谈判人员，谈判也不会顺利进行，更别提能达到预期的目的。在国际商务谈判中由于涉及的内容比国内商务谈判复杂，所需要的知识面也很广，往往不是一个人的知识、精力、时间能承担下来的，所以一般都需要组建谈判小组来完成。

Ⅰ Preparation for Negotiation Team（国际商务谈判前谈判队伍的准备）

1. Staffing of Negotiation Team（谈判小组人员的配备）

There is no uniform standard on how to determine the specific number of negotiation teams. However, there are generally three factors that should be considered when determining the scale of negotiations: Firstly, the difficulty of negotiations. Usually the number of people involved in a negotiation is directly proportional to the complexity of the negotiation. Therefore, the more complex the negotiation is, the wider the knowledge and experience involved, the more people will participate in the negotiation. Negotiations sometimes require a large number of professional and technical personnel. For example, when dealing with high-tech products or know-how, technical experts in the field must be involved; if the negotiations involve a large number of laws and regulations in your own country or the counter-party's country, and for international or regional trade agreements, relevant legal experts must be included. Secondly, the number of counter-party. In order to reflect the basic principles of fairness in international business negotiations, the number of your own party's negotiators can be adjusted to be approximately equal to or slightly more than the counter-party, but it should not be too wide, otherwise it will cause an unequal impression and be detrimental to the smooth development of the negotiation. Thirdly, the number of related departments. If the negotiation only involves the interests of one or two departments, the number of negotiators can be appropriately reduced, but if the interests of multiple departments are involved, then representatives from multiple departments need to be involved in the negotiation.

至于如何确定谈判队伍的具体人数，没有一个统一的标准。但是在确定谈判规模时一般应考虑三个因素：第一，谈判难度。通常参与谈判的人数与谈判的复杂程度成正比。因此，谈判的项目越复杂，所涉及的知识面和经验越广，参与谈判的人数就会越多。谈判有时需要大量的专业技术人员，例如，当涉及高科技产品或专有技术的交易时，必须有该领域的技术专家参与其中；又如，如果谈判涉及本国或对方国家的大量法律、法规，以及涉及国际或地区贸易协定，则必须有相关法律专家参与。第二，对方的人数。国际商务谈判时为了体现公平的基本原则，可以将谈判人数调整为与对方大致相等或比对方稍多，但不宜悬殊太大，否则会造成不平等的印象，不利于谈判的顺利开展。第三，关联方的数量。如果谈判只涉及一个或两个部门的利益，参与谈判的人数可以适当减少，但如果关系到多个部门的利益，那么就需要派出多个部门的代表参与。

In fact, only three or four negotiators are required in general business negotiations. If the content of the negotiation is complex, it can be divided into several groups, and the number of negotiators can be appropriately increased, but it cannot exceed eight. According to the experience of domestic and foreign business negotiations, the best leadership benefit of a team leader is three to four people. On this scale, the negotiating team members are easiest to reach agreement and easiest to control, which is also easiest to use the collective power of the negotiating team members. In addition, in order to control the size of the negotiating team, sometimes personnel rotation can be adopted. When some negotiators complete a certain part of the negotiation task and then need to change the issues of the negotiation, one or more negotiators can be replaced, but the total number of negotiating team has not changed, so that more excellent negotiators can play their role, so as to play the role of "external brain". This method is generally used in international business negotiations where there are many negotiation items, the content is complex, and the negotiation time is relatively long.

其实，在一般的商务谈判只需要三四个谈判人员。如果谈判内容复杂，可以分若干小组进行谈判，适当增加谈判人员，但最多不能超过八个人。根据国内外商务谈判的经验，一个谈判小组组长，最佳的领导效益是三到四个人。在这样的规模下，谈判小组成员之间是最容易达成一致的，成员最容易控制，也最容易发挥谈判小组成员的集体力量。另外，为了控制谈判小组的规模，有时也可以采取人员轮换的方法。当某几个人完成某部分的谈判任务，接下来需要转换谈判内容时，可以调换一名或几名谈判人员，但谈判人员总数没有变化，这样可以使更多优秀的谈判人员发挥其作用，从而起到“外脑”的作用。这种方式一般会运用在谈判项目比较多、内容比较复杂、谈判时间比较长的国际商务谈判中。

So for some small-scale negotiations, the negotiators can take on two or three positions. In other words, such negotiation only requires three or four or even two negotiators, but it cannot be reduced to one, because no matter how savvy, knowledgeable, and energetic this negotiator is, it is impossible for one negotiator to fully and properly handle various situations that arise during the negotiation process. In short, the size of the negotiating team should be determined according to the complexity and nature of the specific circumstances of the negotiations.

所以，对于一些规模较小的谈判，参加谈判的人员可以身兼两职或三职。也就是说，这样的谈判只需要三个人、四个人甚至两个人，但不能减少至一个人，因为无论这个人多么精明，知识多么渊博，精力多么旺盛，在谈判桌上要一个人完全独立地妥善处理谈判过程中出现的各种情况都是不可能的。总之，应当根据谈判的具体情况的复杂程度和性质来决定谈判小组人员的规模。

Personnel Structure of Negotiation Team（谈判小组的人员结构）

The personnel structure of negotiation team refers to the professional background level of the negotiators involved and the role they play in the negotiation. Several principles should be considered when selecting negotiators to form a negotiating team. Firstly, the division of labor should be clear. In the negotiation, each negotiator has a clear role positioning, and the protagonist and supporting role must not be offside. Each negotiator should help each other and cooperate in division of labor under strict discipline. Secondly, the knowledge complementarity. The negotiators within a negotiating team can deal with problems in different areas according to their own knowledge and expertise, forming an overall advantage. Finally, the personality complementarity. The complementarity and coordination between the members of the team will help to give play to the advantages of different personalities, make up for their respective deficiencies, and maximize the team's strengths.

谈判小组的人员结构是指参与谈判人员的专业背景层次和在谈判中所起作用的情况。在选择谈判人员构成谈判小组时应考虑几个原则。首先，分工明确。在谈判中每个谈判人员都有明确的角色定位，切忌主角与配角的角色越位。要在严格的纪律下相互提携，分工协作。其次，知识互补。谈判小组人员根据各自擅长的知识和专长能分别处理不同领域的问题，形成整体优势。最后，性格互补。谈判小组成员在性格上的互补和协调关系，有助于发挥不同性格的优势，弥补各自的不足，将团队优势发挥到最大限度。

Therefore, when selecting the personnel of the negotiation team, it is not only necessary to include a business operator or a senior manager who could handle the overall situation, it is but also necessary to consider the needs of various professional knowledge and consider the structure of the personnel. The most important thing is to determine the person in charge of the negotiation team, the chief negotiator and professional assistant negotiators (including business personnel, legal personnel, technical personnel, etc.). The person in charge of the negotiation is generally with authority at a higher level and with greater power who should focus on promoting the overall strength of the negotiation team with strong organizational ability, comprehensive knowledge, and decision-making power. The main speaker should be proficient in business, have good strategic skills in business negotiation, be knowledgeable, have agile thinking, have a strong ability to express, and be good at handling emergencies. As to the supporting personnel, besides their expertise, they also should be good at working closely in ideology and behavior, have a strong sense of teamwork, and ensure coordination within the negotiation team.

所以，在选择谈判小组人员时，既要有掌握全局情况的企业经营者或高级管理人员，又应当考虑各种专业知识的需要，考虑人员的层次结构。最重要的是要确定谈判队伍的主要负责人、主谈人及专业辅助人员（包括商务人员、法律人员、技术人员等）。谈判负责人一般由处于较高级别和具有较大权力的权威人士担任，具有较强的组织能力、全面的知识、果断的决策力，其工作重点应放在促进谈判小组整体力量的发挥上。谈判的主谈人应精通商务，有娴熟的商务谈判的策略技能，知识渊博，思维敏捷，表达能力强，善于随机应变。辅助人员在具备各自专业领域的特长基础上，应善于从思想上、行为上紧密配合，具有较强的团队合作意识，确保谈判小组内部的协调一致。

2. Division and Collaboration of Negotiation Team's Personnel（谈判小组人员的分工与协作）

(1) Division of Labor（分工）

The division of labor refers to the nature and professional division of labor participating in the negotiations. Division of labor requires that each negotiator have the authority of status and professionalism. At the same time, the division of labor must give play to and respect the specialties of each negotiator. In general international business negotiations, the required professional knowledge can be roughly summarized into the following aspects: firstly, the knowledge about product technology; secondly, the business knowledge that is related to contractual rights and obligations, such as price, delivery, payment method, risk division; thirdly, legal knowledge related to contractual rights and obligations; fourthly, language translation knowledge. Personnel of the negotiation team generally include the following categories according to the needs of the above expertise.

分工是指参加谈判的人员工作性质和专业的分工。分工既要求每个谈判人员在谈判中拥有地位与专业的权威，又要求能够发挥与尊重每个谈判人员的特长。在一般的国际商务谈判中，所需要的专业知识大致可以概括为以下几个方面：一是有关产品技术方面的知识；二是有关价格、交货、支付方式、风险划分等与合同条款相关的商务方面的知识；三是与合同权利、义务相关的法律方面的知识；四是语言翻译方面的知识。根据以上专业知识的需要，一般谈判小组成员包括以下几类：

a. Technical Personnel（技术人员）

It is usually a technician, engineer or chief engineer who is very familiar with production technology, product performance and technological development trends. In the negotiations, this kind of personnel will be responsible for negotiating issues related to product performance, technical quality standards, product inspection, and technical services and can also work closely with business personnel to make technical references for price decisions.

一般是由对生产技术、产品性能和技术发展动态及趋势非常熟悉的技术员、工程师或总工程师来担任。在谈判中负责对有关产品的性能、技术质量标准、产品验收、技术服务等问题的谈判，也可以与商务人员密切合作为价格决策提供技术参考。

b. Business Personnel（商务人员）

Business personnel are experienced salespersons or factory directors and managers who are familiar with international trade practices and the terms and conditions of international trade contracts, and understand the international market transactions.

商务人员是由熟悉国际贸易惯例和国际贸易合同条款、了解国际市场交易行情的有经验的业务员或厂长、经理担任。

c. Legal Personnel（法律人员）

They are usually professional lawyers, corporate legal advisers who are familiar with the provisions of international trade laws, regulations and international trade practices, or personnel who are familiar with the domestic legislation of the parties involved in the negotiations. They are mainly responsible for drafting legal documents such as contracts and agreements, and legally demonstrating and explaining the terms of contracts and agreements.

通常由熟悉国际贸易法律法规、国际贸易惯例条款的专职律师、企业法律顾问或熟悉谈判各方国内立法的人员担任。主要负责起草合同、协议等法律文件，对合同、协议条款进行法律论证和解释。

d. Finance Personnel（财务人员）

Generally, it is an accountant who is familiar with the company's cost, payment methods and financial knowledge with strong financial accounting capabilities. In the negotiation, this kind of personnel is mainly responsible for calculating transaction costs and cooperating with other negotiators to make reasonable quotation strategies.

一般是由熟悉公司成本情况、支付方式以及金融知识，具有较强的财务核算能力的会计人员担任。在谈判中主要负责核算交易成本，与其他谈判人员配合做出合理的报价策略。

e. Translators（翻译人员）

It is a full-time or part-time person who is very familiar with business and proficient in foreign languages. A translator is mainly responsible for oral and text translation, accurately conveying the meaning of the negotiator, and using the negotiation language strategy. Sometimes, he can also correct his own mistakes through translation.

是由熟悉业务、精通外语的专职或兼职人员担任。在谈判中主要负责口头与文字翻译工作，准确传达谈判者的意思，配合谈判语言策略的运用，有时还可以通过翻译更正己方的失误。

The above negotiators can be more or less according to the complexity of the negotiation, and one negotiator can hold several positions by himself. Most of time a dozen people were divided into several groups, such as the business group, the technical group, and the legal group. Each group is responsible for its own business in the negotiations. Two pairs of negotiating teams can be organized, one is on-site negotiation team and another is off-site negotiation team. The former is mainly responsible for responding to on-site negotiations and analyzing the technical and price information temporarily provided by the counter-party. The latter is responsible for collecting and sorting out the relevant information which occurs from new situation during the negotiation, and provides the basis for technical and price negotiations for the on-site negotiation team.

以上参加谈判的人员，按谈判复杂程度可多可少，可一人身兼几职。多数将十几人分成几个小组，如商务小组、技术小组、法律小组等，各自负责自己的专业领域的谈判。还可以组织谈判桌上和谈判桌下两个谈判小组。谈判桌上的谈判小组人员主要负责应对现场谈判以及分析对手临时提供的技术、价格资料，谈判桌下的谈判小组人员负责根据谈判中不断出现的新情况去收集整理有关资料，为现场谈判小组提供技术和价格谈判的依据。

It is worth noting that translators play an indispensable role in international business negotiations. Even if the negotiators have a high level of foreign language who can understand the meaning of written documents and grasp the dexterity of oral expressions, and even judge the response of the counter-party, however, from the practical experience, it is still necessary to equip the negotiation team with a competent translator. International business negotiation is a time-consuming and energy-intensive activity. During the negotiation process, you must constantly adjust thinking based on new information that may appear at any time. Although relatively adequate preparations have been made before the negotiations, it is impossible to accurately predict all the problems that may arise during the negotiations, and to fully consider the counter-measures in advance. Negotiators can make full use of the translation time to observe the reaction of the counter-party, and get more time for their own in order to think carefully about their own strategy.

其中值得注意的是，在国际商务谈判中，翻译人员发挥着不可或缺的作用。就算谈判人员本身具备较高的外语水平，能够理解书面文件的含义和掌握口头表达的分寸，甚至可以判断对方的反应，但是，从实践经验来看，仍然要为谈判小组配备一名得力的翻译人员。国际商务谈判是一项耗时间、耗精力的活动，在谈判的过程中需要不断根据随时可能出现的新信息来调整思路。尽管在谈判前已经做了比较充分的准备，但毕竟不可能准确地预见到谈判中可能会出现的所有问题，并事先都充分考虑好应对方法。谈判人员可以充分利用翻译人员翻译的时间，观察对方的反应，缜密思考己方下一步的对策，为己方争取更多的思考时间。

(2) Collaboration（协作）

Division of labor and collaboration are the basic abilities and qualities that negotiation team members should possess. Without division of labor, there will be no good collaboration, and division of labor will lose its purpose and basis for existence.

分工与协作是谈判小组成员应具备的基本能力与素养。没有分工就没有良好的配合，分工就会失去其目的性和存在的基础。

a. Cooperation Between the Chief Negotiator and the Assistant Negotiators（主谈人与辅谈人之间的配合）

The chief negotiator is the leader or chief representative of the negotiating team. The chief negotiator should be an experienced, ethical and talented person with both superb leadership skills and the ability to cope with the unpredictable negotiation environment. Professionals and supporting personnel are assistant negotiators. The close cooperation between the chief negotiator and the assistant negotiators plays a vital role in the success of the negotiation. Generally, when the chief negotiator makes a speech, the assistant negotiators should always agree with what he or she said by oral or body language, and provide support and cooperation. When the counterparty sets up a situation in the negotiation that puts the chief negotiator of your party in trouble, the assistant negotiators of yours should try to get the chief negotiator out of the predicament. When the chief negotiator needs to modify his opinion but cannot speak out because of various reasons, the assistant negotiators can be the bearer of the fault and maintain the reputation of the chief negotiator. The tacit cooperation between the chief negotiator and the assistant negotiators cannot be achieved overnight on the contrary, it requires long-term practice and running-in. And this kind of cooperation does not just mean cooperation during the negotiation process, it has actually begun from the first meeting. In short, the personnel of an efficient negotiation team should tacitly coordinate with each other.

主谈人是谈判小组的领导人或首席代表。主谈人应该经验丰富、德才兼备，既具有高超的领导能力，又能应付变幻莫测的谈判环境。主谈人以外的其他专业人员、辅助人员都是辅谈人。主谈人与辅谈人之间的密切配合对谈判取得成功起到至关重要的作用。一般在主谈人发言时，辅谈人自始至终都应通过口头语言或肢体语言对主谈人表示赞同，并给予支持和配合。当对方在谈判中设局使己方主谈人陷入困境时，辅谈人应设法使主谈人脱离困境。当主谈人需要改变意见却因各种原因无法开口时，辅谈人可以作为过错的承担者，维护主谈人的声誉。主谈人与辅谈人之间的默契配合不是一朝一夕能够实现的，相反，需要长期的实践和磨合。而这种配合并不仅仅是指谈判过程中的配合，其实是从初次见面时就已经开始了。总之，高效的谈判小组，其人员应该是相互协调、默契配合的。

b. Cooperation between On-site Personnel and Off-site Personnel（台前幕后人员的配合）

In order to improve the effectiveness of negotiations, relevant professional and technical personnel will be organized as the off-site negotiators to cooperate with the on-site negotiators. They will not participate in the negotiations directly, but they can provide the on-site negotiators with the materials and information they need at any time and make some creative suggestions.

为了提高谈判效果，会组织相关专业技术人员作为幕后人员配合台前谈判人员的工作。他们虽然不直接参与谈判，但能够为台前谈判人员提供随时需要的资料和信息，并且出谋划策。

c. Cooperation among Negotiators with Different Personalities（不同性格的谈判人员之间的配合）

The ancient Greek doctor Hippocrates gave four types of temperament: bilious, sanguineous, lymphatic, and melancholic. People with different types of personalities behave differently in thinking and action. In the business negotiation, the strengths and advantages of each negotiator should be brought into full play to form complementarity, thereby enhancing the cohesive force and fighting capacity of the negotiation team.

古希腊医生希波克拉底给出了气质的四种类型，有胆汁质、多血质、黏液质、抑郁质。不同类型性格的人在思维和行动上表现不同。在商务谈判中，应充分发挥每名谈判人员的特长和优势，形成互补，从而增强谈判小组的凝聚力和战斗力。

3. Selection of the Personnel of Negotiation Team（谈判小组人员的选择）

When selecting negotiators, in addition to considering that they should have rich professional knowledge and skills, whether they are suitable as negotiators for the negotiation project should also be considered. Generally speaking, a negotiator should possess the following knowledge and capabilities:

在为组建谈判小组挑选谈判人员时，除了考虑其应具有丰富的专业知识和技能外，还应考虑其作为谈判项目的谈判人员是否合适。一般来说，一名谈判人员应具备以下学识和能力：

(1) Personal Qualities（谈判人员的个人素质）

a. Temperament and Personality（气质与性格）

Negotiators should have a good temperament and personality to adapt to the negotiations which can win the respect of the counter-party and it is a favorable factor for the success of the negotiations. Some personalities are not conducive to negotiation, for example, introverted personality, loneliness and suspiciousness, poor expression, indifference, irritablity, narrow-mindedness, and jealousy. The temperament that is beneficial to negotiation should be generous but not frivolous, easy but not impatient, strong but not stubborn, decisive but not arbitrary, modest but not hypocritical, lively but not skittish, serious but not rigid, experienced but not sophisticated, and humorous but not vulgar.

谈判人员应该具备适应谈判的良好的气质和性格，这样可以赢得对方的尊重，是获得谈判成功的有利因素。有些性格特征是不利于谈判的，比如，性格内向、孤僻多疑、不善于表达、冷漠刻薄、急躁粗暴、心胸狭隘、嫉妒心强。有利于谈判的气质与性格应该是大方而不轻佻、爽快而不急躁、坚强而不固执、果断而不武断、谦虚而不虚伪、活泼而不轻浮、严肃而不呆板、老练而不世故、幽默而不庸俗。

b. Psychological Quality（心理素质）

①Reasoning Skills and Self-control Ability（推理能力与自制力）

During the negotiation process, conflicts of interest and positions of the two parties often occur. Negotiators will be under tremendous psychological pressure, so they need to accurately analyze and judge the specific content and nature of a certain negotiation item at any time. Under pressure, negotiators still need to make analysis, judgment, and reasoning based on their own knowledge and experience. At the same time, they also need to identify the counter-party's strategies during the negotiation. When the drastic changes occur in the negotiation, even in fierce bargaining, negotiators should learn to restrain their emotions and behaviors. If excessive emotional fluctuation occurs, the atmosphere of the negotiations will be destroyed, and the negotiations may not be able to proceed. Negotiators should have good self-control ability, which means they do not light up with pleasure when the negotiation is smooth and they do not feel depressed when the negotiations are deadlocked. Negotiators can also restrain their words and deeds when they encounter impolite behaviors and actions.

在谈判过程中经常会出现双方利益冲突和立场对立的情况，谈判人员会在心理上承受巨大的压力，因此需要随时就某个谈判事项的具体内容和性质进行准确的分析和判断。谈判人员在承受压力的情况下，依然需要根据自身的知识、经验进行分析、判断和推理，同时在分析的过程中识别对方的计谋。在谈判局势发生急剧变化时，甚至在激烈的争辩中，要学会克制自己的情绪和行为。如果出现过分的情绪波动，就会破坏谈判的氛围，可能导致谈判无法进行。谈判人员应具备良好的自制力：在谈判顺利时不喜形于色；在谈判陷入僵局时不灰心丧气；在遇到不礼貌的言行时也能克制自己的言行。

②Self-confidence and Determination（自信心与决心）

The most important psychological quality of a negotiator is self-confidence. A negotiator's self-confidence refers to believing in the strength and advantages of one's own company and the wisdom and power of the negotiation team, believing in the willingness of cooperation and bright prospects of the negotiating parties. The establishment of self-confidence needs to be based on a full investigation at the early stage and based on an analysis of the objective's strengths of negotiating parties rather than a blind confidence, nor look down upon the counter-party. Business negotiation is a very tough task, so once you accept this task, you must go all out in accordance with your own goals and principles. At the negotiating table, the interests of the negotiating parities are your advance and our retreat. Therefore, no matter what kind of difficulties and pressures you encounter, you must have the self-confidence and determination to fight to the end of the negotiation.

自信心是谈判人员最重要的心理素质。谈判者的自信心是指相信己方企业的实力与优势，相信谈判小组这个团队的智慧与力量，相信谈判各方的合作意愿与光明前景。自信心需要建立在前期充分调研的基础上，建立在对谈判各方实力的客观分析的基础上，并非盲目的自信，更不是藐视对方。商务谈判是一项十分艰苦的工作，所以一旦接受了谈判任务，就要依照己方既定的目标与原则全力以赴。在谈判桌上，谈判各方的利益是你进我退，因此在谈判中，不管遇到什么样的困难和压力，都要有奋战到底的自信和决心。

③Insight and Resilience（洞察力与应变力）

In international business negotiations, it is necessary to interact with various people, and the negotiation environment is complex and changeable. Many unexpected issues may happen at any time. Therefore, negotiators are required to be adept at detecting and responding to situations. A qualified negotiator should look at the essence through the phenomenon at any time based on the changes in the negotiations and relevant information, then quickly analyze and make a judgment, and decisively propose a solution.

在国际商务谈判中需要与各种各样的人交往，而且谈判环境复杂多变，很多意想不到的事情随时都有可能会发生。因此，要求谈判人员善于察言观色，随机应变。合格的谈判人员要随时根据谈判中的情况变化以及有关信息，透过现象看本质，迅速分析并做出判断，果断地提出解决方案。

c. Political Quality（政治素质）

Negotiators need strong convictions to safeguard the interests of the country, nation and enterprise, and work hard for it. Especially in international business negotiations, negotiators must be loyal to the motherland, resolutely safeguard the sovereignty and benefits of the motherland, and firmly safeguard the state dignity. In negotiating activities, you must consciously abide by organizational discipline, adhere to principles, and do your best to strive for the success of negotiations. At the same time, it is an important moral principle that international business negotiators should follow in the face of material temptation to be honest in performing your duties, and not trying to obtain profit for yourself.

谈判人员需要有维护国家、民族和本企业利益以及为此努力的强烈信念。特别是在国际商务谈判中，谈判人员更要忠于祖国，坚决维护祖国的主权和利益，坚决维护民族尊严。在谈判活动中，要自觉遵守组织纪律，坚持原则，尽最大努力争取谈判的成功。同时，在物质诱惑面前要廉洁奉公、不谋取私利，这是国际商务谈判人员应遵循的一个重要道德原则。

d. Team Spirit（团队精神）

International business negotiations are generally organized by collective way. Each party is a team of several people, one of whom is the chief negotiator who heads the entire negotiation team to complete the on-site negotiations. Those who participate in the negotiation, whether as the team's chief negotiator or other professionals or assistant negotiators, must have a team and collective spirit. In addition to being responsible for the work within their own area, they must also coordinate with other negotiators within the team in order to win more benefits for themselves in the negotiations.

国际商务谈判一般都是集体谈判，每一方都是由几个人组成的团队，其中一人为主谈人，主持领导整个谈判小组完成现场的谈判工作。参加谈判的人员，无论是作为团队的主谈人还是其他专业人员或辅谈人，都必须具有团队意识和集体主义精神。除了负责好分内的工作以外，还要同小组其他谈判人员协调配合，以争取己方在谈判中获得更大的利益。

e. Physical Quality（身体素质）

International business negotiation is an activity that consumes both mental and physical energy. Many negotiations are hard and time-consuming. Without a healthy body, it is difficult to do the negotiation work. So when selecting a negotiator, an appropriate age span should be considered. The selected negotiators should have sufficient energy, generally aged 30-55 years. The negotiators at this stage are active, energetic, and have accumulated rich negotiation experience, which is also a period of strong professionalism, responsibility and initiative. The age structure of the negotiators can also be adjusted flexibly according to the content and requirements of the negotiations.

国际商务谈判是一项既消耗脑力又消耗体力的活动，很多谈判时间紧、任务重。没有健康的身体是很难胜任谈判工作的，所以在选择谈判人员时应该考虑适当的年龄跨度。选择的谈判人员应该具有充沛的精力，年龄一般在30~55岁，这个阶段的谈判人员思维活跃，精力旺盛，并且积累了比较丰富的谈判经验，也是事业心、责任心和进取心较强的阶段。根据谈判内容、要求的不同，谈判人员的年龄结构也可以灵活调整。

(2) Basic Knowledge of Negotiators（谈判人员的基本知识）

An international business negotiator should have two aspects of knowledge: basic knowledge and professional knowledge. Basic knowledge is the cornerstone of wisdom and talent, and professional knowledge determines the depth of a person's knowledge and ability to perform his own duty. As a modern international business negotiator, the broader the knowledge, the stronger the adaptability, and the deeper the professional knowledge, the more able to adapt to the needs of the negotiation. An experienced international business negotiator must have a wealth of basic knowledge in a variety of disciplines, such as economics, folklore, ethology, geography, and psychology as well as the knowledge of business theory, economic theory, negotiation theory; be familiar with commodity science, marketing, business strategy, commodity transportation, trade knowledge, financial management knowledge, etc.; be familiar with and understand the professional knowledge of product performance, maintenance services, cost accounting, etc.; be proficient in cultural customs of various countries and the negotiating styles of negotiators in different countries; be proficient in WTO rules and international trade practices, can resolve trade disputes and be good at organizing international business negotiations.

作为一名国际商务谈判人员，应当具备两方面的基本知识：基础知识和专业知识。基础知识是智慧和才能的基石，专业知识决定一个人知识的深度和从事本职工作的能力。作为现代国际商务谈判人员，知识面越宽，应变能力就越强，专业知识越深，就越能适应谈判的需求。一名成熟的国际商务谈判人员必须掌握经济学、民俗学、行为学、地理学、心理学等多种学科丰富的基础知识；具备必要的商贸理论和经济理论知识，掌握谈判理论；熟悉商品学、市场营销学、经营策略、商品运输、贸易知识、财务经营管理知识等；熟悉并了解本行业范围内产品的性能、维修服务、成本核算等专业知识；精通各国文化习俗和不同国家谈判者的风格；精通WTO规则和国际贸易惯例，能够解决贸易争端，善于组织国际商务谈判。

(3) Comprehensive Capabilities（谈判人员的综合能力）

Negotiators need to achieve a combination of knowledge and ability, be able to cooperate closely with other negotiators during the negotiation process, coordinate relationships with other negotiators, be good at dealing with different people and various social occasions; be expert in using language to express their attitudes and opinions clearly, and at the same time have a strong ability to express, be proficient in the writing of various official documents, agreement contracts, reports related to negotiations, including the ability to understand and independently draft written documents and contracts. Generally speaking, agreements and contracts that are concluded are always beneficial to the party who drafted them.

谈判人员需要做到知识与能力的有机结合，在谈判过程中能够密切配合谈判小组其他成员，协调好与其他成员之间的关系，善于与不同的人打交道，也要善于应对各种社交场合；善于运用语言清晰明了地表达己方的态度和观点，同时要具备较强的文字表达能力，要精通与谈判相关的各种公文、协议合同、报告书的写作，包括对书面文件的理解能力，以及独立起草协议、合同的能力。一般来说，谈判中起草出来的协议、合同草案总是对起草的一方有利。

Ⅱ Preparation for Information（国际商务谈判前的信息准备）

It refers to the planned, organized, and purposeful collection, analysis, and organization of environmental information, market information, scientific and technological information, and negotiating objects that are closely related to the negotiation activities before international business negotiations. It is also a process of objective description for the collected related information and its attributes.

国际商务谈判前的信息准备是指在国际商务谈判前对与谈判活动有密切联系的环境信息、市场信息、科技信息、谈判对象等情况进行有计划、有组织、有目的的收集、分析和整理，是对收集的相关信息及其属性的客观描述的过程。

In international business negotiations, negotiators must obtain the negotiation information as much as possible before the negotiation begins, if they want to achieve final success. The more information they have, the better the analysis, and the more likely the negotiation is successful. Accurate information and scientific methods of processing information can help negotiators gain an advantage in negotiations.

在国际商务谈判中，如果想取得最后的成功，必须在谈判开始前尽可能地掌握与本次谈判有关的信息资料。掌握的信息越多，分析就越充分，谈判成功的可能性就会越大。准确的信息和科学处理信息的方法能帮助谈判人员在谈判中占据优势。

1. Channels for Information Collection（信息收集的途径）

There are two ways to collect information before international business negotiations: direct collection and indirect collection.

国际商务谈判前的信息收集有两种途径：直接收集和间接收集。

Direct collection is the way in which corporate negotiators seek friendship and cooperation from potential partners abroad in various ways under their own name. It mainly reflects as following methods. For international trade contracts, it can be the seller's offer or the buyer's inquiry; for technology contracts, the technology introducer can go abroad for investigation and research; for joint venture projects, the counter-party can be required to provide relevant information directly, such as the registration certificate of the company, balance sheet, patent specifications, product catalogue, laws of relevant countries, etc. In addition, the enterprise can also send personnel directly to the counter-party's country or region to conduct inspections and collect information. When using this method, the relevant information of the counter-party should be collected before going abroad. Analyze the true and untrue information, reliable and unreliable content in the existing data with a clear purpose for investigation. The cost of this approach is relatively high, but because the enterprise sends persons to visit the site, the information and materials they obtained are more reliable and authentic.

直接收集是企业谈判人员以自己的名义采用各种方式向国外的潜在伙伴寻求友谊和合作，主要表现为：对于国际贸易合同来说，可以是卖方的报盘或买方的询盘；对于技术合同来说，引进技术方可以出国考察、研究；对于合资经营项目来说，可以要求对方直接提供有关资料，如企业的注册证明、公司资产负债表、专利说明书、产品介绍资料、有关国家的法律等。此外，本企业也可以直接派人员到对方国家或地区进行考察，收集资料。在采用这种途径时，在出国前应尽量收集对方的有关资料，在已有的资料中分析其真实和不真实之处、可靠和不可靠的内容，带着明确的目的去考察。这种途径成本比较高，但因为是本企业自己去现场考察，获得的信息和资料的可靠性和真实性更高。

Indirect collection refers to entrusting an agent or institution to seek friendship and cooperation from foreign merchants. Different intermediaries or agencies have different capabilities and business scopes. Therefore, when collecting information, choosing the appropriate intermediary channel should be based on its characteristics. For general information, it can be collected through the following channels:

间接收集是指委托中间人或机构向国外的客商寻求友谊和合作。不同的中间人或中间机构有不同的能力和业务范围，因此，在收集信息时要根据其特点来选择恰当的中间渠道。对于一般信息，可以通过以下渠道来收集：

(1) Media（传播媒介）

a. In order to improve the market competitiveness of the product and expand the company's own reputation, the company will promote itself through various channels, such as newspapers, magazines, internal publications, books, pictures, etc., which can become sources of information collection. At present, more than 95% of the information can be obtained directly from various published journals and magazines.

企业为了提高产品的市场竞争力和扩大企业自身的知名度，会通过各种途径进行宣传，例如报纸、杂志、内部刊物以及书籍、图片等，这些都可以成为获得资料和信息的来源。目前有95%以上的情报可以从公开发表的各种期刊、杂志上直接获得。

b. The Internet has become one of the most important ways to obtain information. On the Internet, it is very convenient to check the information of domestic and foreign companies, including market information, product information, and company updates.

网络已经成为获取信息的最重要途径之一，在网上可以非常便捷地查阅国内外公司的信息，包括市场信息、产品信息和公司最新动态。

c. Learn about the materials and information required for the negotiation through radio broadcasts of domestic and foreign news, economic information, financial developments, market conditions, various press conferences, and various advertisements.

通过电台广播播放的有关国内外新闻、经济资讯、金融动态、市场行情、各类记者招待会以及各类广告来了解收集谈判所需要的资料和信息。

(2) Statistics (统计资料)

This kind of material is mainly from public information released by various domestic departments and enterprises, such as the Ministry of Commerce, the Foreign Economic and Trade Promotion Commission and its branches in various places; various statistical yearbooks or monthly publications of countries and national organizations, relevant local governments, and social organizations, statistical data released by international statistical organizations, industry data released by industry associations, survey reports provided by research institutions and statistical data and various statements from major banks or international organizations and domestic consulting companies. In this way, more detailed data can be obtained, providing a basis for accurate data analysis.

主要来自国内各部门、各企业发布的公开资料，如商务部、对外经济贸易促进委员会及其在各地的分支机构；各国及各国组织、有关地方政府、社会组织的各类统计年鉴或月刊；国际统计组织发布的统计资料；行业协会发布的行业资料；研究机构提供的调查报告；各大银行或国际组织和国内咨询公司的统计数据和各类报表。通过这种方式，可以获得比较详尽的数据，为准确的数据分析提供依据。

(3) Overseas Agencies (驻外机构)

This kind of organization includes the local commercial ambassador's embassy or consulate's commercial agency, the local branches of the Bank of China and other domestic financial institutions, local branches of the industry group or company, local agents of the company, and the local Chamber of Commerce.

这类组织包括：本国驻当地的大使馆、领事馆、商务代表处，中国银行及国内其他金融机构在当地的分支机构；本行业集团或本企业在当地开设的营业分支机构；本公司在当地的代理人；当地的商会组织。

(4) Insiders (知情人员)

The related information can be obtained by old friends, loyal customers, international students, overseas Chinese, overseas visitors, visiting inspectors and other insiders. Since these people take field trips, the information obtained will be more reliable.

可以通过老朋友、老客户、留学生、华侨及出国访问者、参观考察者等知情人士去了解并获悉所需要的资料。由于这些人都是采取实地考察方式，所以获得的资料会更可靠。

There are many other ways to obtain pre-negotiation business information. Participating in various international conferences, such as trade fairs, exhibitions, and other targeted investigations into the production, distribution, transportation, and sales of goods, as well as the status of competition and development prospects. The sales information and production information of the counter-party can also be obtained from the correspondence and business cards exchanged with the counter-party. When collecting information, negotiators should adopt methods as many as possible to collect more information and materials to make full preparations for negotiations.

获取谈判前商务信息的途径还有很多，可以通过参加各种国际会议，如交易会、展览会等有的放矢地调查商品的生产、流通、运输、销售以及竞争现状和发展前景等；还可以从与对方来往的函电、交换的名片中获取对方的销售信息、生产信息。谈判人员在收集信息时要根据实际情况，采取尽可能多的途径去收集更多的信息和资料，为谈判做好充分的准备。

2. Methods for Information Collection（信息收集的方法）

Due to the influence of socioeconomic and corporate system management, access to information in international business negotiations is restricted by the confidentiality system, the principle of confidentiality, and commercial competition that makes it difficult to collect information. According to the methods of information acquisition, negotiation information can be divided into primary data and secondary data. The former is obtained through direct collection, and the latter is usually obtained through indirect collection.

由于社会经济和企业制度管理等因素的影响，国际商务谈判的信息获取受到保密制度、保密原则和商业竞争的限制，使得信息收集起来非常困难。按照信息获取的途径，我们可以把谈判信息分为一手资料和二手资料，前者通过直接收集的途径获得，后者一般通过间接收集的途径获得。

(1) Method for Obtaining Primary Data（获取一手资料的方法）

a. Field Survey（实地调查）

Field survey is a method for negotiators to collect and organize information through direct contact. The negotiators can get the information from the people who have been keeping in touch with from the inside of the counter-party, and can also contact the counter-party through correspondence, etc. For more important negotiations, an informal preliminary negotiation can be organized. This kind of prior negotiation is very helpful for information collection.

实地调查是由谈判人员通过直接接触来收集、整理信息的方法。谈判人员可向企业内部与对方有接触的人员进行了解，也可以通过函电等与对方联系。对于比较重要的谈判，则可以安排非正式的初步洽淡。这种事先的洽谈非常有利于信息的收集。

b. Observation（观察法）

The investigator should observe the behaviors and characteristics of the targeted objects being surveyed so as to collect various information. For example, you can visit the factory to understand the counter-party's actual situation; you can also conduct informal negotiations to understand the counter-party's attitude and intentions; you can also analyze the performance of the counter-party's products to determine the production costs by purchasing its products. Relatively authentic information can be obtained through above-mentioned methods.

调查者要对被调查事物及被调查对象的行为和特点进行观察，从而收集各种信息。例如，可以参观对方的工厂，了解对方的实际情况；也可以进行非正式的洽谈，当面了解对方的态度，观察对方的意图；还可以通过购买对方的产品来分析其性能，以确定生产成本。通过这些方法，可以获得比较真实可靠的信息。

c. Business Spies（商业间谍）

Due to the complexity of modern business information and intelligence collection systems and methods, commercial espionage has become a profession with low risks and high payoffs.

由于现代商务信息情报的收集系统和收集手段十分复杂，商业间谍已经成为一种职业，其风险低，但报酬高。

(2) Method for Obtaining Secondary Data（获取二手资料的方法）

a. The Interview Method（访谈法）

Interviewer selects the interviewees to conduct face-to-face interviews around the questions to be investigated, either in the form of individual interviews or in the form of forums attended by many people. Hear the interviewees' opinions on related products or cooperative projects and understand the market situation at home and abroad.

调查者围绕所要调查的问题选择访问对象进行面对面的访问，既可以是个别对象的访问，也可以是众多人参与的座谈会的形式，听取被访问者对相关产品或合作项目的意见，了解国内外市场行情。

b. Expert Adviser Method（专家顾问法）

Solicit expert opinions by sending relevant materials to experts; or discuss the investigation reports of each expert by meeting and then put forward opinions for reference; assist the data investigation and analysis by employing consultants to reasonably "borrow" information from consultants.

可以通过发给专家有关资料来征求专家的意见；也可以通过开会，讨论各个专家的调查报告，然后进行汇总，提出参考意见；还可以通过聘请顾问的方式协助资料调查和分析，合理"借用"顾问的信息资料。

c. Questionnaire（问卷法）

Investigators need to formulate the questions to be investigated in advance, and then send them to relevant persons online or in the field in the form of questionnaires. After they are filled out, they will be collected and analyzed. This method can collect a wide range of information, but the accuracy may be relatively low.

调查者需要事先拟定好所要调查的问题，然后以问卷的形式在网上或实地发给相关人士，待其填好后收集上来进行整理分析。这种方法可以收集到较为广泛的信息，但准确性可能比较低。

d. Purchase Information（购买信息）

At present, banks, market research companies and consulting companies are all conducting research and consulting services. These institutions have specialized market investigators and experts. When the enterprise has insufficient strength, it can purchase the information or entrust an institution to make an investigation.

目前，银行、市场调查公司和咨询企业都在开展调查研究及咨询业务，这些机构拥有专门的市场调查员和专家。企业在自身力量不足时，可以购买其信息或委托调查。

3. Contents for Information Collection（信息收集的内容）

Information collection before international business negotiations mainly includes market information, information of counter-party, information on science and technology, information on policies and regulations, information on finance.

国际商务谈判前的信息收集主要包括市场信息、谈判对手信息、科技信息、政策法规信息和金融信息几个方面。

(1) Market Information (市场信息)

The subject of the negotiation is the core of the negotiation. It is very important to collect information about the domestic market, the international market and the target market. Generally speaking, market information is a general term for various messages, materials, data, and information that reflect the characteristics of market economic activities and their development and changes. The content of market information is extensive, and can be summarized in the following aspects:

谈判的标的物是谈判的核心，收集与之相关的国内市场、国际市场以及目标市场的信息非常重要。一般来说，市场信息是反映市场经济活动特征及其发展变化的各种消息、资料、数据、情报的总称。市场信息的内容很广泛，归纳起来主要有以下几个方面：

a. Information of Domestic and Foreign Markets Distribution (有关国内外市场分布的信息)

It mainly includes the market distribution, geographical location, transportation conditions, political and economic conditions, market potential, market capacity and economic relations with other markets. With the continuous development and expansion of global integration, a country's market is more closely linked to the world market. By collecting market distribution information, companies can clearly understand the market regions and scopes where their products can be sold, so as to determine long-term, medium-term and short-term sales plans, and then establish scientific negotiation goals.

主要包括市场分布情况、地理位置、运输条件、政治经济条件、市场潜力和容量以及与其他市场的经济联系等。随着全球一体化的不断发展和扩大，一国市场与世界市场的联系更加紧密。通过收集市场分布信息，可以帮助企业清楚地了解其产品适于销售的市场区域和范围，从而确定长期、中期和短期的销售计划，进而建立科学的谈判目标。

b. Information on Consumers' Demand (消费需求方面的信息)

This type of information includes the periods and reasons for consumer loyalty to a particular brand; the relationship between users and buyers; the number and composition of consumers; the reasons and motivations for purchasing; the multiple uses of the product; the potential demand for the product, consumption trends; product life cycle; market coverage and market share of the product; influence of market competitors on the company's products; etc.

这类信息包括：消费者忠于某一特定品牌的期限和原因；使用者与购买者之间的关系；消费者数量及构成；购买的原因和动机；产品的多种用途；产品潜在的需求量以及消费趋势；产品的使用周期；产品的市场覆盖率和市场占有率；市场竞争对手对本企业产品的影响；等等。

c. Information on Product Sales (产品销售方面的信息)

As a seller, you should investigate the sales of your company's products; as a buyer, you should investigate your company's purchases. It includes the product's sales volume, total sales and price changes in the past few years, the long-term development trend of the product and the market life cycle, consumer's evaluations and requirements for trusted products and consumer's views on the enterprise, etc.

作为卖方，应调查本企业产品的销售情况；作为买方，应调查本企业购买产品的情况。包括：产品过去几年的销售量、销售总额以及价格变动情况；产品的长远发展趋势及市场生命周期；消费者对信赖产品的评价及要求；消费者对企业的看法；等等。

d. Information on Product Competition（产品竞争方面的信息）

It includes the number, scale, and product types of competitors who produce or purchase similar products; the market share and future trends of major manufacturers producing similar products; the form and price range of each brand's product launch; consumer preferred brands and prices level; after-sales service; dealer's gross profit level; advertising investment; etc.

包括：生产或购买同类产品的竞争者数量、规模以及产品种类；生产同类产品的主要生产厂家的市场占有率及未来变动趋势；各品牌产品推出的形式及售价幅度；消费者偏爱的品牌与价格水平；售后服务情况；经销商的毛利水平；广告投入；等等。

e. Information on Product Sales Channels（产品销售渠道信息）

It contains the distribution routes adopted by major competitors; the availability of storage equipment for various types of intermediaries; the number of wholesalers and retailers; sales promotion and after-sales service; etc.

包括：主要竞争对手采用的经销路线；各种类型的中间商有无仓储设备；批发商与零售商的数量；销售推广和售后服务情况；等等。

(2) Information of Counter-party（谈判对手信息）

In international business negotiations, the situation of counter-party is complicated. If you negotiate with a counter-party who you totally don't know beforehand, the degree of difficulty and risk priority number will be very high, and the success rate of the negotiation will be reduced. So before starting business negotiations, negotiators need to "know yourself and know your enemy", and collecting information of the counter-party is the process of "knowing your enemy".

在国际商务谈判中，对手的情况纷繁复杂。如果同一个事先毫不了解的对手进行谈判，难度和风险会非常大，谈判的成功率也会降低。所以在开始商务谈判之前，我们需要做到"知己知彼"，而收集对方信息就是"知彼"的过程。

a. Types of Merchants（贸易客商的类型）

Firstly, the world-renowned and prestigious multinational companies. This type of merchants adhere to credibility, principles and efficiency who can get accurate business information and have high requirements for the counter-party's information. They have strong capital with complete institutions which are generally supported by consortia. Secondly, merchants who enjoy a certain reputation. This type of merchants has relatively strong capital and their products have a certain competitiveness and market share in foreign markets. They are anxious to occupy the counter-party's market and the offers they made are relatively favorable, so they can be good partners. Thirdly, Merchants who have no reputation but can provide notarial certificates, copies of members of the board of directors, etc. that could prove their registered capital, legal management locations. This kind of merchants' identities must be investigated clearly, and they can also become good partners after authentication. Fourthly, bogus merchants. They are trade intermediaries who have no corporate capacity and do not have the right to sign contracts. They only serve as intermediary to collect commissions to help the two parties conclude the transaction. For such merchants, it is necessary to know their credit standing thoroughly to prevent being deceived. Fifthly, merchants that are subsidiaries of well-known parent companies who make use of great trees for shade. They often do business under the name of the parent company, and you should be cautious in dealing with them. Sixthly, merchants who use their own identity to engage in illegal trading business. Although such merchants serve in a company, they should be carefully aware of when conducting business in their personal capacity. Seventhly, fraud. This kind of merchants use unauthorized official seals, fake business cards, fake certificates, and fake addresses to engage in fraud activities.

第一，世界上享有盛誉和声望的跨国公司。这类贸易商讲信誉、讲原则、效率高、掌握商情准确、对己方提供资料要求高。这类客商资本雄厚，机构完备，一般有财团支持。第二，享有一定知名度的客商。这类客商资本比较雄厚，产品在国外市场拥有一定的销量，产品有一定的竞争力，急于占领对方市场、相关条件比较优惠，因此是很好的合作伙伴。第三，没有知名度但能够提供公证书、董事会成员的副本等足以证明其注册资本、法定营业场所的客商。这类客商一定要明确其身份，认证后也可以成为很好的合作伙伴。第四，皮包公司。它们是交易的中间商，无法人资格，无权签订合同，只为收取佣金而为交易双方牵线搭桥。对于这类客商一定要详细了解其资信情况，防止上当受骗。第五，借树乘凉的客商，属于知名母公司的下属机构，往往会打着母公司的旗号谈生意，应谨慎交往。第六，利用本人身份从事非法经营贸易业务的客商。这类客商虽然在某公司任职，但以个人身份进行商业活动，应严加提防。第七，骗子客商。这类客商私刻公章，利用假名片、假证明、假地址从事诈骗活动。

Therefore, before starting business negotiations, it is necessary to verify the creditworthiness, reputation, registered capital, legal mangement location and legal person of the merchants, and ask the merchants to present a notarial certificate to prove the authenticity of these information, which is the basis for the negotiation between the two parties.

因此，在开始商务谈判前，必须对客商的资信、信誉、注册资本、法定经营地点和法人的情况进行核实，并请客商出示公证书来加以证明，这些信息的真伪是双方谈判的基础。

b. Censor on Credit Standing of the Counter-party（谈判对手资信情况审查）

The investigation of the credit standing of the counter-party is an important part of negotiation preparations which is the prerequisite for determining the negotiation. The investigation of the credit standing of the counter-party includes a censor of the legal qualifications, the capital credit and performance capabilities, the nature and funding status, an analysis of the operating status and financial status as well as the business reputation.

对谈判对手资信情况的审查是谈判前准备工作中的重要内容，是决定谈判的前提条件。对谈判对手资信情况的调查包括对客商合法资格的审查，对前来谈判的客商的资本信用和履约能力的审查，对谈判对手性质和资金状况的审查，对谈判对手的运营状况和财务状况的审查，对谈判对手商业信誉等情况的审查。

(3) Information on Science and Technology (科技信息)

Scientific and technological information is very important for international business negotiations, especially the introduction of technological equipment. It is a prerequisite for technology selection and accurate negotiation. Scientific and technological information mainly includes the comparison of the product with other products in terms of performance, quality, standards, specifications, life cycle, competitiveness, etc.; information on patent transfer or application of similar products; the technical strength of the production unit and the quality of workers as well as the information on its equipment status; information on the production and supply of supporting equipment and parts of the product; information on after-sales service; information on product development prospects and development costs; important indicators for appraisal of product performance and quality, and information on appraisal institution. This kind of information can be obtained by consulting patents, contacting and consulting with relevant organiza-tions, participating in various trade fairs and expositions, and referring to newspapers and ma-gazines.

科技信息对于国际商务谈判特别是引进技术设备的谈判非常重要，它是技术选择和准确谈判的前提条件。科技信息主要包括：本产品与其他产品在性能、质量、标准、规格、生命周期、竞争力等方面的对比；同类产品在专利转让或应用方面的资料；产品的生产单位的技术力量和工人素质及其设备状态方面的资料；产品的配套设备和零部件的生产与供给状况和售后服务方面的资料；产品开发前景和开发费用方面的资料；鉴定产品性能、品质的重要指标和鉴定机构等资料。这类信息可通过查阅专利、与有关机构联系和咨询、参加各种交易会和博览会、查阅报纸杂志等获得。

(4) Information on Policies and Regulations (政策法规信息)

Before the international business negotiations, the laws, regulations, and policies that may be involved in the negotiations should be fully understood, so as to avoid errors due to unfamiliarity with related content and bring unnecessary trouble to yourself. It mainly includes the following aspects:

在国际商务谈判前，应当对谈判可能会涉及的法律、法规、政策、法令进行详细了解，从而避免因不熟悉相关内容而出现失误，给己方带来不必要的麻烦。主要包括以下几个方面：

a. Political Situations of the Country or Region Concerned (有关国家或地区的政治状况)

Politics and the economy have always been closely connected, which means economy and trade cannot be separated from politics. Especially in international business negotiations, negotiators must be completely familiar with laws, regulations, decree regarding the relevant economic policies and economic cooperation of country or region where the counter-party locates as well as the state practice system for enterprises, etc.

政治与经济从来都是紧密联系的，经济和贸易离不开政治。特别是在国际商务谈判中，必须充分了解对方国家或地区的相关经济政策，经济合作方面的法律、法规、法令，以及国家对企业的惯例制度，等等。

b. Rules on the Content of Negotiations（有关谈判内容的法规规定）

China's existing laws related to international cooperation include the Civil Code of the People's Republic of China, the Patent Law of the People's Republic of China, the Trademark Law of the People's Republic of China, the Foreign Investment Law of the People's Republic of China. As a Chinese business negotiator, you should be familiar with the above-mentioned laws and fully understand the relevant international trade practices. In international trade, the commonly used international practices are mainly the United Nations Convention on Contracts for the International Sale of Goods (the Convention), General Principles of Interpretation of International Trade Terms (referred to as Incoterms 2020), Warsaw-Oxford Rules of 1932, 1914 Revision of the Definition of the United States Foreign Trade, Uniform Practice of Documentary Information Certificate (referred to as UPC600). It should be noted that international practice is not universally binding, and its adoption is entirely up to the parties to the contract. Only when the parties to a contract signing an international contract for the sale of goods agree to adopt certain international trade practices to determine their respective rights and obligations, will this international practice be applicable to the contract and be legally binding on the parties to the contract.

我国现有涉及国际合作方面的法律有《中华人民共和国民法典》《中华人民共和国专利法》《中华人民共和国商标法》《中华人民共和国外商投资法》。作为我国的商务谈判人员，对以上法律都应熟知，同时还应充分了解相关的国际贸易惯例。在国际贸易中，常用的国际惯例主要有《联合国国际货物销售合同公约》（简称《公约》）、《国际贸易术语解释通则》（简称《通则 2020》）、《1932 年华沙-牛津规则》、《1914 年美国对外贸易定义修订本》、《跟单信息用证统一惯例》（简称 UPC600）。需要注意的是，国际惯例并不具备普遍的约束力，是否采用完全取决于合同当事人。只有当合同当事人在订立的国际货物买卖合同中一致表示同意采用某种国际贸易惯例来确定各自的权利和义务时，这项国际惯例才适用于该合同并且对合同当事人均产生法律约束力。

c. Various Tariff Policies of Relevant Countries or Regions（有关国家或地区的各种关税政策）

Before international business negotiations, negotiators need to know the tax rates and taxation methods of various tariffs in relevant countries or regions, including import tax, export tax, variable levies, import surcharge, transit tax, transit fee, etc., as well as the situation of countries which have signed trade agreements or reciprocal tariff agreements with China.

在国际商务谈判前需要了解相关国家或地区的各种关税的税率、征税方法等方面的资料，包括进口税、出口税、差价税、进口附加税、过境税、过境费等，以及与我国签订贸易协定或互惠关税协定的国家的情况。

d. Status of Import/Export Quotas and License of Relevant Countries or Regions（有关国家或地区进出口配额与进出口许可证制度的状况）

Under the import quota system, the number of all imported goods must be within the specified quantity or amount, otherwise they are only allowed to be imported with high-level tariffs or even a fine. The import quota system is often closely linked to import licenses. If a government adopts an import quota system, it will definitely adopt an import license system. At present, most countries in the world have adopted import quota systems on varying degrees, so negotiators must understand the relevant content before business negotiations.

在进口配额制度下，凡是进口的商品均必须在规定的数量或金额范围内，否则进口会被征收高额关税乃至罚款。而进口配额制度往往又和进口许可证紧密联系。一国政府如果采取了进口配额制度，就一定会采取进口许可证制度。目前，世界上大部分国家都在不同程度上采取了进口配额制度，所以谈判人员在开始商务谈判前必须了解相关的内容。

e. Foreign Exchange Control Policies of Relevant Countries or Regions（有关国家或地区的外汇管制政策）

Some countries or regions will issue import and export licenses to strengthen foreign exchange control in order to ensure their own foreign exchange reserves and prevent tax evasion, arbitrage, and black market foreign exchange transactions. As business negotiators, you should also have some understanding of these policies.

有些国家或地区为了保证本国的外汇储备，防止逃税、套汇、黑市外汇交易，会颁布进出口许可证等来加强外汇管制。作为商务谈判人员，对这方面的政策也应该有所了解。

(5) Information on Finance（金融信息）

It mainly includes the status and trends of convertible currencies and exchange rates; the operating status of banks where importer and exporter respectively located; relevant regulations on L/C issuance, negotiation, documents against acceptance (D/A) or collections, especially the procedure fees and obligations assumed by banks, etc.

主要包括：可兑换货币、汇率变化状况和趋势；进出口地银行的运营状况；有关银行对开证、议付、承兑赎单或托收方面的有关规定，特别是手续费和银行所承担的义务等。

4. Sorting and Analysis of Information（信息的整理与分析）

After obtaining data through various channels, negotiators should sort and analyze them. There are three main purposes. Firstly, identify authenticity and reliability. Due to various subjective and objective reasons, some data may have been one-sided, incomplete, or even false or forged. Therefore, it must be sorted out and analyzed before the use of negotiation. Secondly, analyze the relationship between these data, information and the negotiation project in combination with the specific content of the negotiation project on the basis of the complete, authentic and reliable data, and then sort these information according to the importance and impact. Thirdly, make a detailed negotiation plan and countermeasures through the analysis of the information.

通过各种渠道获得资料后，必须对这些资料进行整理和分析。主要有三方面的目的：首先是鉴别真实性和可靠性。由于各种主观和客观的原因，在收集的过程中某些资料可能会比较片面、不完全，有的甚至是虚假、伪造的，因此必须进行整理和分析才能为谈判所用。其次是在资料完备、真实、可靠的基础上，结合谈判项目的具体内容，分析这些资料和信息与谈判项目的关系，并根据其对谈判的重要性和影响程度进行排序。最后，通过对信息的分析制定出具体的谈判方案和对策。

The analysis of negotiation information generally has four steps: evaluating, screening, classifying and filing. Evaluating is to discard the useless data collected, and to classify and save the useful data. Screening of data is mainly to delete duplicate data to sort the data by time and to find the most time-efficient data. Classifying and filing the data is to classify the filtered information according to the purpose of use or the content of the data, and finally file these data.

对谈判信息的整理分析一般有四个阶段：评价、筛选、分类和保存。所谓评价就是舍弃收集来的没有用的资料，对有用的进行分类和保存。对资料的筛选主要是删除重复的资料，将资料按时间排序，找出最有时效性的资料；资料的分类和保存就是对筛选后的信息根据使用的目的或资料的内容进行分门别类，最后将资料保存。

Ⅲ Formulation for Business Negotiation Plan（国际商务谈判方案的制订）

The negotiation plan refers to the pre-arrangements made by the negotiators on the negotiation objectives, agenda, and negotiation strategies during the preparation phase of the negotiation. It is the negotiator's program of action and overall analysis and research on the negotiation information, the overall assumptions and specific implementation steps formulated for the negotiation based on the conditions of negotiating parties. Generally speaking, the negotiation plan mainly includes the following aspects: firstly, determining the topics and objectives of the negotiations; secondly, determining the negotiation deadline; thirdly, the arrangement of the negotiation agenda; fourthly, defining the basic strategies for the negotiations.

谈判方案是指谈判人员在谈判准备阶段对谈判目标、议程、谈判策略等预先所做的安排，是谈判人员在对谈判信息进行全面分析和研究的基础上，根据谈判双方的情况，为此次谈判制定的总体设想和具体实施步骤，是谈判人员行动的纲领。一般来说，谈判方案主要包括以下几个方面的内容：第一，确定谈判主题和目标；第二，确定谈判期限；第三，谈判议程的安排；第四，确定谈判基本策略。

When making negotiation plan, the following aspects should be paid attention to. Firstly, the negotiation plan should be concise. Try to make it easy for negotiators to remember their main contents and basic principles. When it comes to concepts and numbers, the content must be clear to avoid misunderstanding. Secondly, the negotiation plan must be concrete. Concreteness is to refine the negotiation objectives into small sub-objectives which cannot be vague and abstract so that it is difficult to understand. Finally, the negotiation plan needs to be flexible. During the negotiation process, unexpected situations may occur at any time, so the negotiation plan is just a general idea before the negotiation, and it is impossible to take all the circumstances into consideration. Therefore, negotiators should apply and master the negotiation plan flexibly according to emergencies during the negotiation. For example, some routine affairs and controllable factors can be planned in details, while some irregular matters can be arranged crudely.

在制订谈判方案时应注意以下几个方面：首先，谈判方案应简明扼要。要尽量让谈判人员能容易地记住其主要内容和基本原则。凡涉及概念、数字，内容一定要明确，避免引起误会。其次，谈判方案要具体。所谓具体就是要将谈判目标细化或各个小的分目标，不能空泛和抽象，从而让人难以理解。最后，谈判方案要灵活。在谈判过程中，随时都可能会发生意想不到的情况，所以谈判方案仅仅是谈判前的一个总体设想，不可能把所有情况都考虑进去。谈判人员要根据谈判中的突发情况灵活运用和把握谈判方案。例如，对于常规性事务和可控因素可以规定得详细一些，而对于无规律的事项可以安排得粗一些。

1. Theme and Goals（谈判主题和目标）

(1) Negotiation Theme（谈判主题）

The theme of negotiations is the purpose of participating in the negotiations as well as the expectations and desired value. Generally, there is only one negotiation theme in a negotiation, and it is always carried out when you are formulating negotiation plans. The theme of the negotiation should be an opinion that can be made public and not confidential. Negotiation theme should be simple and clear which can be summarized in one sentence. For example, *closing a transaction at the lowest price*. As to what kind of price is the lowest price is the issue need to be solved in the negotiation goal.

谈判主题是参加谈判的目的、对谈判的期望值和期望水平。一般一次谈判只有一个谈判主题，在制订谈判方案时都是围绕这个主题展开。谈判主题应是己方可以公开的观点，不具有保密性。谈判主题必须简单明确，一般可用一句话来概括。例如：“以最低的价格达成交易”。至于什么样的价格才是最低价格就是谈判目标要解决的问题了。

After the negotiation theme is determined, the theme needs to be concrete, that is, to set specific negotiation goals. The entire negotiation will be carried out closely around this specific goal, and all efforts will be made to achieve this goal. Therefore, the determination of the negotiation goals requires serious and careful consideration. The following principles need to be observed in determining the negotiation goals:

在谈判主题确定下来后，接下来就需要把主题具体化，即制定出具体的谈判目标。整个谈判活动都会紧紧围绕这个具体的目标进行，都要为了实现这个目标而努力，因此谈判目标的确定需要认真而慎重的考虑。在确定谈判目标时需要遵守以下几个原则：

a. Practicality（实用性）

The negotiating parties should set the negotiation goals according to their own strength and power which can be finally achieved and create more benefits for yourself. If the goals are set and the actual situation do not match, negotiations may not be carried out smoothly, and even huge losses may be brought to the enterprise.

谈判各方要根据自己的实力和水平制定谈判目标并且最终可以实现这些目标，从而为己方创造更多的利益。如果制定的目标和实际情况不符，可能会导致谈判无法顺利开展，甚至会给企业带来巨大的损失。

b. Rationality（合理性）

It means reasonable in space and time. The prices of the international market are changing at any time, and the reasonableness of the same goal in different time and space is different. The negotiating parties should analyze their own goals from aspects of space and time, and the goals determined should be beneficial to both parties, so as to achieve win-win.

是指空间和时间上具有合理性。国际市场的行情随时都在发生变化，同样的目标在不同的时间和空间范围内的合理程度是不同的。谈判双方应该对己方的目标在空间和时间上进行分析，确定的目标应该是对双方都有利的，这样才能实现“双赢”。

c. Legality（合法性）

Both the content of the negotiations and the objectives of the negotiations must be in compliance with the laws and regulations. Negotiating parties could not use unscrupulous methods in order to pursue their own interests, such as bribery, threats, providing false information, etc.

不管是谈判的内容还是谈判的目标都要符合法律法规的规定。谈判双方不能为了追求己方的利益不择手段，采用违法的方式来获取利益，如贿赂、威胁、提供虚假信息等。

（2）Negotiating Goals（谈判目标）

The degree to which the negotiation goals are achieved can be expressed in the level of negotiation goals. It is reasonable to choose different levels of goals according to the actual situation of the negotiations. The goals of negotiations are usually divided into three levels.

谈判目标的实现程度可以用谈判的目标层次来表示，根据谈判的实际情况的变化选择不同层次的目标是比较合理的。通常谈判的目标分为三级。

a. Primary Goal（一级目标）

This is a goal that must be achieved, also known as a minimum goal. For negotiators, the minimum goal is the last line of defense that must be adhered to and the goal that must be achieved. It is the minimum requirement for negotiations. If this goal is not reached, it is preferred to break down the negotiation rather than lower the goal. There is no room for bargaining on this goal. It is an absolute confidential internal secret that concerns the main or all economic interests of one of the negotiating parties. Therefore, it is generally only proposed at a certain phase of the negotiation process.

这是必须达到的目标，也称最低目标。对于谈判人员来说，最低目标是必须坚守的最后一道防线，也是必须实现的目标，是谈判的最低要求。如果达不到这个目标，宁愿谈判破裂也不能降低这个标准。这个目标没有任何讨价还价的余地。它是绝对保密的内部机密，关系到谈判一方主要或全部的经济利益。所以，一般只在谈判过程的某个阶段才提出。

b. Secondary Goal（二级目标）

It is also called an acceptable goal. If the primary goal is represented by a point, then the secondary goal is an interval and a range. It is a range in which you can strive for or make concessions during negotiations, and can meet part of the needs of one party in the negotiation to realize part of the economic benefits. Therefore, it is not only the focus for bargaining between the negotiating parties, but also the range where the negotiation is easiest to reach an agreement.

即可以接受的目标。如果一级目标用一个点来表示，那么二级目标是一个区间和范围。它是在谈判中可以努力争取或做出让步的范围，可以满足谈判一方的部分需求，实现部分经济利益。所以它既是谈判双方讨价还价的焦点区域，也是谈判最容易达成协议的范围。

c. Tertiary Goal（三级目标）

It is the ideal goal, which is the highest goal that one party pursues in business negotiations. If one party achieves this goal, the interests will be maximized. However, this is also the most unacceptable goal for the counter-party. Although this goal is difficult to achieve, it is not absolutely impossible. It is entirely possible for the negotiations between a highly reputable enterprise and a well-funded and reputable bank to achieve this kind of goal. Therefore, it is necessary to determine the ideal goal which can motivate the negotiators to do their best to achieve the highest expectations. It can also clearly evaluate the gap between the final result of the negotiation and the reasonable goal.

即理想目标，它是己方在商务谈判中追求的最高目标。实现了这个目标，己方的利益将实现最大化，但这同时也是对方最不愿意接受的目标。虽然这个目标一般很难实现，但并不是绝对不可能达到的。一个信誉极高的企业和一家资金雄厚、信誉良好的银行之间的谈判，达到理想目标是完全有可能的。所以确定理想目标是非常有必要的，它可以激励谈判人员尽最大努力去实现最高的期望值，也可以清楚地评价谈判最终结果与理性目标之间的差距。

According to the above-mentioned level of the negotiation objectives and the principles set out, the negotiators need to work out the minimum and maximum goals for the negotiation based on the actual situation, and then control the acceptable range between the highest and lowest goals that both parties can accept. In negotiation practice, negotiators need to ensure that they are not far bellow the minimum goal and work towards the ideal goal.

根据以上谈判目标的层次和制定的原则，谈判人员需要根据实际情况制定出谈判的最低目标和最高目标，然后将双方可以接受的范围控制在最高目标和最低目标之间。在实际谈判中要确保不低于最低目标，向理想目标努力。

It should be noted that it is rare that there is only one kind of goals in business negotiation. There are usually many kinds of negotiation goals. In this case, it is necessary to sort the negotiation goals according to their importance, determine whether to achieve all the goals, and determine which goals can be discarded, which goals need to be achieved, and which goals cannot be lowered.

需要注意的是，商务谈判中只有一个目标的情形是很罕见的，一般都会存在多个谈判目标，这种情况需要根据其重要性对谈判目标进行排序，确定是否要达到所有目标，确定哪些目标是可以舍弃的、哪些目标务必争取达到、哪些目标是绝对不能降低的。

2. Negotiation Deadline（谈判期限）

The negotiation deadline refers to the period from the preparation phase to the final phase of the negotiation. The deadline of negotiations in international trade generally means the time when the negotiator prepares for the negotiation to the end of the validity period of the offer. For modern international business negotiations, efficiency has become an important indicator to measure the success of negotiations, and the deadline of negotiations directly affects the efficiency. Therefore, the negotiation deadline should be taken into account when negotiating parties are formulating the negotiation plan.

谈判期限是指从谈判准备阶段到谈判终局阶段的这段时间。在国际贸易中谈判的期限一般是指从谈判人员着手准备谈判到报价的有效期结束为止。对于现代国际商务谈判而言，效率已经成为衡量谈判成功与否的一个重要指标，而谈判期限会直接影响到效率问题。所以谈判双方在制订谈判方案时应该将谈判期限考虑进去。

The length of the negotiation deadline is mainly determined by the adequacy of the time of the negotiating parties and the time required for normal negotiation. It can be long or short, but it must be concrete and specific, and it must be flexible so that it is able to adapt to unexpected events. Generally speaking, the topics of international business negotiations are relatively time-sensitive, especially for seasonal products which will suffer losses if they exceed the prescribed period. So the negotiating parties must make accurate calculations of the negotiation deadline. For example, the price of mooncakes will plummet after the Mid-Autumn Festival, so they must be sold before the Mid-Autumn Festival.

谈判期限的长短主要是根据谈判双方时间的充裕程度和正常谈判所需要的时间来确定，可长可短，但一定要具体、明确，同时要有伸缩性，能够适应谈判过程中的突发情况。通常来讲，国际商务谈判议题的时效性比较强，特别是时令商品和季节性产品，如果超过了规定的期限就会遭受损失，所以谈判双方一定要对谈判的时限做出精确计算。例如，月饼在中秋节后的价格会大跌，因此必须在中秋节前销售。

3. Arrangement for the Negotiation Agenda（谈判议程的安排）

After determining the negotiation theme, negotiation goals and negotiation deadline, the negotiation agenda can be set. The negotiation agenda is simply the schedule for the negotiation which mainly describes the final negotiation time, negotiation topics, general agenda and detailed agenda. The negotiation agenda is very important for negotiating parties and it can be prepared and consulted by one party or both parties.

在确定了谈判主题、谈判目标和谈判期限后，就可以制定谈判议程。所谓谈判议程，简单说就是谈判的议事日程，主要是说明最后确定的谈判时间、谈判议题、通则议程与细则议程。谈判议程对谈判双方非常重要，谈判议程可以由一方准备，也可以双方一起准备、协商确定。

(1) Arrangement of the Negotiation Time（谈判时间的安排）

The arrangement of the negotiation time means to determine when and how long the negotiation will be held. If it is a phased negotiation, it is necessary to divide the negotiation into several stages and determine the time required for each stage. Whether the negotiation schedule is appropriate will have a great impact on the outcome of the negotiations. So negotiators should pay enough attention to the arrangement of negotiation time. Generally speaking, when scheduling or selecting negotiation time, negotiators need to consider the following factors.

谈判时间的安排是指要确定谈判在何时举行，持续多久。如果是分阶段的谈判，还需要将谈判分成几个阶段，确定每个阶段所需要的时间。谈判时间安排是否恰当，会对谈判结果产生很大的影响。所以谈判人员应对谈判时间的安排给予足够的重视，一般来说，在安排或选择谈判时间时，需要考虑以下几个方面的因素：

a. Physical and Emotional Status of Negotiators（谈判人员的身体和情绪状况）

When arranging the negotiation time, remember to leave sufficient preparation time for the negotiators, especially when the negotiators travel long distances. Especially when negotiators need to adjust jet lag, do not arrange for immediate negotiations, as this will lead to the trap which the counter-party set beforehand because of poor mental state, difficulty in concentration, and loss of memory and thinking ability.

在安排谈判时间时要注意给谈判人员留有充分的准备时间，特别是在谈判人员长途跋涉时。尤其是在谈判人员需要调整时差时，不要安排他们马上进行谈判，在这种情况下他们会因为精神状态不佳、注意力难以集中、记忆力和思维能力下降而误入对方的圈套。

b. Timing of Negotiation（谈判时机的选择）

The timing of negotiations may also have a significant impact on negotiations. For example, exporters may be panic when the backlog of inventory is very serious and sales are not good, so negotiators should try to avoid negotiating against themselves.

谈判时机的选择也可能对谈判产生重大影响。例如，出口商在库存积压很严重而销路不畅时，可能会慌不择价，所以，谈判人员应尽量避免在对自己不利的情况下进行谈判。

c. Situation of the Counter-party（谈判对方的情况）

Negotiation is the beginning of the cooperation between the two parties. Achieving a successful negotiation is the common goal for both parties. Therefore, do not arrange the negotiation in a time that is obviously unfavorable to the counter-party that will arise the resentment from the counter-party and in conducive to the smooth progress of negotiations.

谈判是双方合作的开始，取得谈判成功是双方共同的目标，因此不要为了己方的利益将谈判安排在对对方明显不利的时间内进行，这样会引起对方反感，不利于谈判的顺利进行。

(2) Determination of Negotiation Topics（谈判议题的确定）

It means to determine the content, items and the order of negotiations and the time that each part will occupy. All issues related to this negotiation that need to be discussed by the negotiating parties are all the topics of negotiation. When determining the topics of negotiation, firstly, list all the issues related to the negotiation; secondly, classify the issues listed, determine the importance of these issues and their advantages and disadvantages; and finally, list the issues that are beneficial to you, discuss the key issues and avoid the disadvantages of yourself as much as possible, which will help you to be in an active position, but you also need to consider your countermeasures when the counter-party raises similar issues.

谈判议题的确定主要是指要确定进行谈判的内容、项目以及各谈判事项的先后顺序和分别占用的时间。凡是与本次谈判有关的、需要谈判双方展开讨论的问题都是谈判的议题。在确定谈判议题时，首先应将与本次谈判有关的所有问题罗列出来；其次，将罗列出来的问题进行分类，确定问题的重要性以及与己方的利弊关系；最后，将对己方有利的问题列为重点问题加以讨论，对己方不利的问题尽量回避，有助于己方处于主动地位，但同时也要考虑当对方提出类似问题时，己方应采取的应对策略。

There are many ways to arrange the order of negotiation topics, appropriate method should be chosen according to the specific situation. For example, general, non-principle, and easy-to-solve issues can be discussed first, which will create a good atmosphere for negotiation, and lay the foundation for discussing difficult issues. However, time and energy could also be focused on discussing specific, principled, and disagreeing issues. After resolving the most important issues, and minor issues could be handled. All issues could be put forward to discuss regardless of the major issues and minor issues.

安排谈判议题先后顺序的方法有很多，应根据具体情况选择合适的方法。例如，可以讨论一般性、非原则性、容易解决的问题，创造良好的谈判氛围，为讨论困难的问题打下基础；也可以先集中时间和精力讨论具体的、原则性的和有分歧的问题，待重要问题解决后再处理次要的问题；也可以不分重要问题和次要问题，把所有要解决的问题全部提出来讨论。

How much time needs to be arranged for discussing every issue is appropriate depends on the importance, complexity of the issue, and the size of the differences between both parties. Generally speaking, important, complicated issues, and issues with very different opinions between the negotiating parties should be arranged more time to discuss. Experienced negotiators can estimate which issues will lead to major differences before negotiations, and which issues are easy to make agreement. Controversial issues are better not to be placed at the beginning of the negotiations, as these issues may take up a plenty of time and may affect the mood of negotiators and the negotiation atmosphere. Nor is it apropriate to put it to the end, because the negotiation time is too short for both parties to discuss in depth and complete the negotiation. Controversial issues are better to be placed after the two parties have reached an agreement and before the last one or two issues are going to be discussed, that is, the most controversial issues should be discussed at the middle of negotiation.

每个问题需要安排多少时间来讨论才合适，应该根据问题的重要性、复杂程度和双方分歧的大小来确定。一般来说，重要的、复杂的、双方意见分歧很大的问题，应安排多一些时间，以便让双方能有充裕的时间对这些问题展开讨论。有经验的谈判人员在谈判开始前就能估计到哪些问题双方会产生较大分歧，哪些问题容易达成一致。有争议的问题最好不要放在谈判开始，这样可能会占用较多的时间，也可能会影响双方的情绪和谈判氛围。也不要放到最后，这样有可能因为谈判时间不够导致双方无法深入讨论而无法完成谈判。有争议的问题最好放在双方达成一致的问题之后、谈最后一两个问题之前，也就是在谈判的中间阶段讨论分歧较大的问题。

(3) General Agenda and Detailed Agenda (通则议程与细则议程)

The general agenda is a schedule for two parties to observe and use which generally takes effect only after the two parties negotiate and agree. In the general agenda, the following contents should be determined: the arrangement for overall time and period time of the negotiations; the central issues and its order for discussion; the arrangement for various personnel; the place of negotiations and entertainment.

通则议程是谈判双方共同遵守和使用的日程安排，一般要经过双方协商同意后才能正式生效。在通则议程中，应确定以下内容：谈判总体时间及分段时间安排；双方谈判讨论的中心议题和问题讨论的顺序；谈判中各种人员的安排；谈判地点及招待事宜。

The detailed agenda is a specific arrangement of your own strategy for participating in the negotiation which is only used by your own personnel and confidential. It generally includes several aspects such as a unified word to counter-party, like opinions, data, documents, etc.; how to respond to the situation; how to ask your questions (eg: When to ask questions? What kind of questions to ask? Ask whom questions? Who is responsible for asking questions? Who will supplement questions? Who will answer counter-party's questions? Who will refute counter-party's point of view? Under what circumstances is it necessary to suspend negotiations?); advance arrangements for the replacement of negotiators; strategic arrangements for your own negotiation time and negotiation deadline.

细则议程是己方参加谈判的策略的具体安排，只供己方人员使用，具有保密性，其内容一般包括几个方面：对外统一口径，例如发言的观点、数据、文件资料等；对谈判中可能出现情况的对策；己方的发言策略（如何时提出问题？提哪些问题？向谁提出问题？由谁来提问题？谁来补充问题？谁来回答对方的问题？谁来反驳对方的观点？什么情况下要求暂停谈判?）；谈判人员更换的预先安排；己方谈判时间的策略安排、谈判时间期限。

The agenda is just an ex ante plan, not a contract. If any party is dissatisfied with its form after the negotiation, it is necessary to be frankly informed of the amendment, otherwise neither party can bear the losses caused by neglecting the agenda.

议程只是一个事前计划，并不是合同。如果任何一方在谈判开始后对它的形式不满意，就需要坦诚地告知进行修改，否则双方都无法承担因为忽视议程而造成的损失。

4. Selection of Negotiation Strategy (谈判对策的选择)

During the negotiation process, the situation for two parties is complex and changing rapidly. However, the negotiation is time-limited. It is impossible to delay the negotiation schedule indefinitely. In order to ensure the smooth progress of the negotiations and achieve the set goals under a complex situation within a limited time, it is necessary for negotiators to review the situation and select the corresponding negotiation countermeasures when making the negotiation plan. The following factors should be considered when negotiators are choosing a negotiation strategy: the strength of the two parties; the negotiation goals of the two parties and the personality of the main speaker; the previous trade relations between the two parties; the respective advantages of the two parties; the importance of the transaction itself; time constraints for the negotiation; whether there is a necessity to build friendly long-term relationships.

谈判双方在谈判过程中，形势错综复杂、瞬息万变，而谈判又是有时间限制的，不可能无限期地拖延谈判日程。要想在复杂的形势下、在有限的时间里保证谈判顺利进行并实现既定目标，就需要谈判人员在制订谈判方案时审时度势，选择相应的谈判对策。在选择谈判对策时应考虑以下几个因素：双方实力的大小；双方的谈判目的和主谈人的性格特点；谈判双方以往的贸易关系；谈判双方各自的优势；交易本身的重要性；谈判的时间限制；是否有建立持久、友好关系的必要性。

Firstly, determine the basic strategy for negotiation, means to determine the ideal goal and minimum goal that need to be reached in the negotiations as well as the methods that can be used to achieve these goals. Secondly, determine the terms and conditions of contract and transaction conditions. When you are making a negotiation plan, the focus is to analyze and study the transaction conditions or contract terms one by one, to weigh the advantages and disadvantages from the perspective of policy, legal and economic benefits, and to distinguish which terms are acceptable and which terms can be agreed upon by negotiations and which terms are absolutely unacceptable by your party, and then you can put forward specific amendments to facilitate their implementation in the negotiations. Finally, determine the price range. In the international trade practice, price is always the core issue of negotiations, and it is also the one that most easily causes conflicts between the two parties. When you are making a negotiation plan, it is necessary to have clear ideas and opinions on the price range, and to determine the most beneficial strategy and specific measure for your own party.

首先，确定谈判的基本策略。就是要确定谈判要达到的理想目标和最低目标，以及为了实现这些目标所能采用的方法。其次，要确定合同条款或交易条件的内容。在制订谈判方案时，重点就是要对交易条件或合同条款逐一进行分析和研究，要从政策、法律、经济效益等角度来权衡利弊，分辨出哪些条款是可以接受的、哪些条款是可以通过双方协商达成一致的、哪些条款是己方坚决不能接受的，然后己方再提出具体的修改意见，便于在谈判中得以实施。最后，确定谈判价格的幅度。在国际贸易实践中，价格始终是谈判的核心问题，也是最容易引起双方分歧的。在制订谈判方案时，要对价格的幅度有明确的想法和意见，并要确定对己方最有利的策略和具体措施。

Of course, the negotiation plan made before the negotiation is not always completely implemented intact during the negotiation. This requires the negotiators to observe the counter-party's behavior during the negotiation process, analyze the negotiation situation and make proper judgments, make some amendments to the original negotiation strategy, and use them flexibly according to the specific situation.

当然，对于谈判前制订的谈判方案在谈判中并不是总能原封不动地完全执行，这就需要谈判人员在谈判过程中观察对方，对谈判形势进行分析并做出判断，对原定的谈判对策进行修正，根据具体情况灵活运用。

Ⅳ Other Preparation Items（国际商务谈判前的其他准备）

1. Determination of the Negotiation Location（谈判地点的确定）

The determination of the negotiation location is very important for the negotiating parties because it will directly affect the use of negotiation strategies and tactics in the negotiation. When you are selecting a negotiation location, the strength of the negotiating parties, the relationship between the two parties, and the cost of the negotiation are generally considered. Chapter 2 has introduced the types of negotiations in detail which are divided into host field negotiations, guest field negotiations and neutral field negotiations according to the differences in the negotiation location, whose advantages and disadvantages are not to be discussed here. Regardless of where the negotiation is held, the specific negotiation location provided in general include: office, reception room, meeting room and other daily office places. It basically depends on the scale of the negotiations and the number of negotiators.

谈判地点的确定对谈判方而言是非常重要的，因为它会直接影响谈判中谈判策略和战术的运用。在选择谈判地点时一般会考虑谈判双方力量的对比、双方的关系和谈判的费用等。在第2章讲到谈判类型时详细介绍了根据谈判地点的不同，可将谈判分为主场谈判、客场谈判和中立场谈判。这三种谈判各有利弊，这里就不再介绍。不管是主场谈判还是客场谈判，一般情况下提供的具体谈判地点有：办公室、会客厅、会议室等日常办公场所。基本上是按照谈判的规模、谈判人员的数量来选择。

(1) Negotiation in Office（谈判地点选择在办公室）

The office as negotiation venue is extremely beneficial to the host of the negotiations. The host is very familiar with the office environment and has a psychological advantage, while the counter-party sitting in the host's office will always have a psychological hint for paying a visit. For the negotiation issues, the division of the negotiation benefits will have an adverse effect. Another problem is that the seat height of any office prepared for guests will be lower than the table and chairs of the host. In this case, there is a visual difference between the host and the guest, and the host will have a sense of supremacy unconsciously while the client will feel inferior to the host, which will affect the psychological balance between the two parties in the negotiation. Due to the limited office space, it cannot meet the negotiations with a large number of people. At the same time, the office is not quiet enough, telephone, fax, and staff access will adversely affect the negotiations.

办公室作为谈判场所对于谈判的东道主一方是极为有利的。东道主方对办公室环境非常熟悉，在心理上就占据了优势，而对方坐在东道主方的办公室中，始终会有登门拜访的心理暗示。对于谈判问题的提出，谈判利益的分割会产生不利的影响。还有一个问题就是任何一间办公室给客人准备的座位高度都会低于主人的桌椅，在这种情况下，东道主方与客方在视觉上就存在落差，东道主方会不自觉地产生居高临下的感觉，而客方则会产生低人一等的感觉，这样会影响到谈判双方的心理平衡。由于办公室空间有限，无法满足人员数量较多的谈判；同时办公室也不够安静，电话、传真以及工作人员的出入等都会对谈判造成不良的影响。

（2）Negotiation in Reception Room or Conference Room（谈判地点选择在会客厅或会议室）

A reception room is a space that is relatively comfortable and has a large space that is relatively closed to the outside world. A conference room is a room with a ring or a conference table that can be regarded as a ring, not a conference venue with a podium. In fact, many small and medium-sized enterprises integrate small conference rooms and reception rooms together. Firstly, the host will use the conference room or the reception room as a place for negotiation that means the advantages and disadvantages are more balanced for both parties, and there will be no big psychological gap. Secondly, the conference room or the reception room is more comfortable with enough space which can accommodate more negotiators. The facilities are also more suitable for negotiation. A round table can be placed, which can greatly reduce the psychological distance between the two parties and is more suitable for them to exchange opinions. The conference room or reception room is relatively quiet in which there is no extra office equipment. And the interference will be relatively small, which will help the negotiating parties to focus on the negotiation issues.

会客厅是指条件比较舒适、空间比较宽敞的与外界相对封闭的空间；会议室是指具备环形或是可以视为环形摆设的会议桌的会议室，而不是开大会的具备主席台的会场。实际上很多中小型企业是将小型会议室和会客厅融为一体的。首先，东道主方将会议室或会客厅作为谈判的地点，对于双方而言优劣势比较均衡，在心理上都不会产生过大的落差。其次，会议室或会客厅比较舒适，有足够大的空间，可以容纳较多的谈判人员。设施也比较适合谈判，可以放圆桌，这样在很大程度上可以拉近双方的心理距离，更适合双方交换意见。会议室或会客厅相对比较安静，没有多余的办公器材，受到的干扰会比较小，有利于谈判双方将精力集中于谈判议题。

Regarding the selection of negotiation location, the selection of the counter-party should be respected as much as possible. Respecting the counter-party is the most basic quality and etiquette requirements of the negotiators. Firstly, the host should take full account of the needs of the guests and try to avoid making them unhappy. Under the premise that the guests did not make a clear request, try to provide an equal occasion for both parties so that the two parties can psychologically balance. In particular, it is necessary to take into consideration the number of people, the positions, gender of the counter-party, and even cultural customs. Secondly, if the guests think that the location provided by the host is not beneficial to them, they should frankly put it forward.

关于谈判地点的选择，应该尽量尊重对方的选择。尊重对方是谈判人员最基本的素质和礼仪的要求。首先，东道主方应当充分考虑到客方的需求，尽力避免令对方产生不愉快的情绪。在客方没有提出明确要求的前提下，尽量提供双方平等的场合，从而使双方能够在心理上趋于平衡。尤其是要考虑到对方的人员数量、级别高低、性别差异甚至文化风俗的差异。其次，如果谈判的客方认为东道主方提供的地点不利于己方的谈判，应该坦诚地提出。

2. Preparation for the Negotiation Site（谈判现场的准备）

The arrangement of the negotiation site will directly affect the atmosphere of the negotiation opening. Generally speaking, it is better to arrange three rooms as the negotiation venue, one room for negotiation, one room for private discussion, and one room for resting. The layout of the negotiation room should be comfortable and have sufficient lighting. Both natural light and artificial light can be used. When natural light is used, window screens should be provided to prevent excessive glare, which can make it difficult to see the facial expression of the counter-party and lead to misjudgment of the situation. If you use artificial light, you should equip the room with lamps properly to make the light as soft as possible; do not choose the location of the room near the street and the construction site; doors and windows should be soundproofed to ensure that there is no interference. In order to make the counter-party face pressure and uncomfortable, thereby affecting their mood and established thinking, sometimes you can also create some interference factors. Although it does not conform to the negotiating conventions, it is difficult for the counter-party to detect when it is set subtly. However, the boundary needs to be mastered. The negotiation room also needs to be equipped with electronic equipment that can display video materials, such as network cables, notebooks, whiteboards, projectors, etc. The negotiation room generally does not require recording equipment unless negotiating parties agreed mutually. The private room is a separate room that can be used by both parties. It can be used for internal negotiation by one party's negotiating group or for private discussions between the two parties. Therefore, the private room should be reliable and applicable, equipped with facilities and comfortable chairs but without recording equipment, and close to the negotiation room. The layout of the room for resting should make negotiators feel relaxed and pleasant, so as to relieve nervousness of both parties during the negotiation, and ease the tense atmosphere. It is better to place some potted plants or flowers in the room and play some soft music to relax and adjust the tension.

谈判现场布置的好坏会直接影响谈判开局的氛围。一般来说，谈判场地最好能安排三个房间：一间作为主谈室，一间作为密谈室，一间作为休息室。主谈室的布置应当舒适、光线充足，可以利用自然光源，也可以采用人造光源。利用自然光源时应配备窗纱，以防光线过于刺眼，看不清对方的表情，从而对情况有误判；如果采用人造光源，要合理配置灯具，使光线尽量柔和；在房间位置的选择上不要临街和靠近施工现场；门窗隔音效果要好，确保周围没有其他声音的干扰。为了让对方感到压力和不适从而影响谈判的情绪和既定的思路，有时也可以制造一些干扰因素。尽管不符合谈判的常规，但做得微妙时，对方也很难察觉，但一定要把握度。主谈室还需要配备能进行视频资料展示的相关电子设备，例如网线、笔记本、白板、投影仪等。主谈室一般不要求有录音设备，除非双方同意才能安装。密谈室是一个双方都可以使用的单独房间，既可以供某一方谈判小组内部协商，也可以供双方进行私下讨论，因此密谈室应该可靠、适用。位置要靠近主谈室，室内应配备相关的设施设备和比较舒适的座椅，密谈室不应配备录音设备。休息室的布置应该轻松，让人感觉愉悦，便于放松谈判双方紧张的神经，缓和双方紧张的氛围。室内最好能摆放一些绿色植物或鲜花，播放一些轻柔的音乐来放松和调节紧张的情绪。

3. Arrangement for Negotiating Table and Seating（谈判桌和座位的安排）

Material preparations, such as the arrangement of negotiation rooms, the selection of negotiating tables, the arrangement of negotiating seating are important objective factors influencing the atmosphere of negotiations. There are three main options for negotiating tables: square negotiating tables, round negotiating tables, and no negotiating tables.

物质方面的准备工作，如谈判房间的布置、谈判桌的选择、谈判座位的安排都是影响谈判氛围的重要客观因素。谈判桌的选择主要有三种：方形谈判桌、圆形谈判桌和不设置谈判桌。

(1) Arrangement for Negotiating Table（谈判桌的安排）

Negotiating at the square negotiating table, the negotiating parties will have a sense of security and strength psychologically. At the same time, it is also convenient for one party to exchange information internally. However, because the negotiators of both parties will sit face to face, it may give people a sense of formality, seriousness and unliveliness, and even an opposite feeling. In general, sitting on one side of the table will make the atmosphere of negotiation become tense. It is mainly used for formal bilateral negotiations and also the most commonly used method in international business negotiations. It is divided into two categories: horizontal table and vertical table, as shown in Figure 3.1 and Figure 3.2.

在方形谈判桌上进行谈判，各方谈判人员在心理上会有安全感和实力感，同时便于己方交流信息；但由于双方谈判人员会面对面而坐，会给人以正规、过于严肃而不太活泼的感觉，甚至还会有对立面的感觉。总体上来说，各居一方而坐，会使谈判氛围变得紧张。该安排主要适用于正式的双边谈判，也是国际商务谈判中最常用的一种方式，具体又分为横桌式和竖桌式两种，如图 3.1 和图 3.2 所示。

Figure 3.1 Horizontal Table

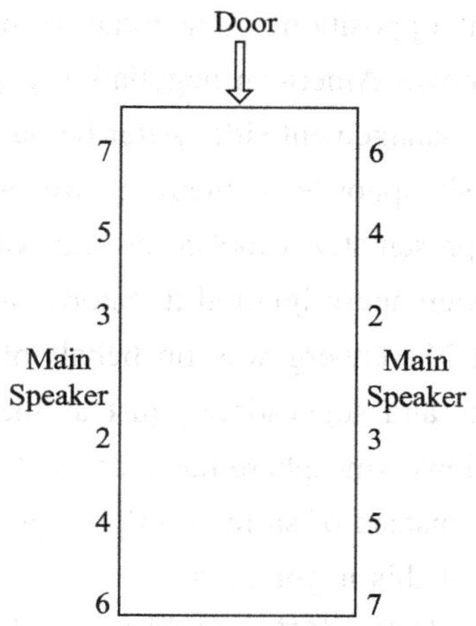

Figure 3.2 Vertical Table

If a round negotiating table is used for negotiation, the negotiators of both parties will form a circle and can effectively eliminate contradictory emotions, and discussion with each other becomes convenient and easy and it helps create a harmonious atmosphere for negotiation. It is mainly applicable to formal multilateral negotiations.

如果采用圆形谈判桌进行谈判，双方谈判人员坐成一个圆圈，能有效地消除对立情绪，而且彼此交谈变得方便和容易，还有助于创造一种和谐一致的谈判氛围。主要适用于正式的多边谈判。

For the case where no negotiating table is set up, it is mainly applicable to informal negotiations or fewer negotiators.

不设置谈判桌的情形，主要适用于非正式谈判或谈判人员较少的情况。

(2) Arrangement of Negotiating Seat（谈判座位的安排）

The arrangement of negotiating seat is also very important for large and medium-sized negotiations which can reflect the basic qualities and working style of the negotiating team. However, it can be used by some immoral people as an interference or affect the counter-party's ways of thinking and working efficiency. The arrangement for negotiating seat needs to be paid particular attention which means the different seating will have an impact on the atmosphere of the negotiation, internal communication and control during the negotiation process.

谈判座位的安排对于大中型谈判来说也是非常值得重视的，它可以从侧面反映出谈判队伍的基本素质和工作作风。但有时还可能会被一些不道德的人利用，作为其干扰或影响对方思路及工作效率的手段。谈判座位的安排是很有讲究的，不同的座位安排对谈判的氛围、谈判各方在谈判过程中的内部交流与控制都是有影响的。

There are three main ways to arrange negotiating seat: negotiators from each party sit together; negotiators from each party sit corss-over; negotiators from each party sit at random. This first way is convenient for negotiators' information exchange from each party. However, it is easy to form a negotiating atmosphere that two parties will fight each other. The second way is conducive to more in-depth exchanges and discussions between the two parties, but it is not easy to form an atmosphere of mutual opposition. A negotiation between the union and managers atended by Nierenberg, a well-known American negotiating expert, is a typical example. Nierenberg was the negotiator on the management side. After he had been introduced, the union representatives asked Nierenberg to sit opposite to them. However, Nierenberg sat with the union representatives, and the union representatives looked at him with wired eyes, indicating that he was in the wrong position, but Nierenberg ignored it. Shortly after the negotiation began, union representatives almost forgot that Nierenberg was on behalf of the management. They listened carefully to his analysis, opinions and suggestions, just as they listened to their own opinions and suggestions. And the harmonious atmosphere has increased dramatically. Nierenberg chose to sit with the negotiating opponents instead of sitting on their opposites, which has played a crucial role in the successful conclusion of this negotiation.

谈判座位的安排主要有三种方式：各方的谈判人员各自坐在一起；各方的谈判人员交叉而坐；各方的谈判人员任意就座。各方的谈判人员各自坐在一起便于谈判小组成员相互交流，同时无形中双方形成各自为战的谈判氛围。各方的谈判人员交叉而坐，有利于双方之间更深入地交流和讨论，同时不容易形成相互对立的氛围。美国著名的谈判权威尼尔伦伯格参加工会与管理人之间的谈判就是一个典型的例子。在介绍了作为管理人一方谈判代表的尼尔伦伯格之后，工会代表请尼尔伦伯格坐在他们的对面。但是，尼尔伦伯格却和工会代表同坐在一起，工会代表们都用奇怪的眼光看着尼尔伦伯格，示意他坐错了位置，可尼尔伦伯格却不予理会。谈判开始后不久，工会代表们几乎忘记了尼尔伦伯格是代表管理者一方，他们仔细倾听他的分析、意见和建议，就像是在听己方的意见和建议一样。对抗的氛围锐减，而融洽的氛围陡增。尼尔伦伯格选择与谈判对手坐在一起而非坐在他们的对立面，可以说为这次谈判的圆满成功起到了至关重要的作用。

V Simulated Negotiation（模拟谈判）

Simulated negotiation means that the negotiating parties organize relevant negotiators to preview or rehearse the upcoming negotiations before the formal negotiation. By simulating the various attitudes and reactions of the counter-party on a given occasion, one party can check the possible effects of the negotiating plan formulated by the party in the implementation in order to amend and improve in a timely manner. In modern international business negotiations, it can be said that whoever carefully simulates before the negotiation, whoever has the opportunity, initiative and advantageous position in the negotiation. For some particularly important or difficult negotiations, simulated negotiations can play a vital role in the success of the entire negotiation.

模拟谈判是指在正式谈判开始之前，谈判方组织相关谈判人员对将要进行的谈判进行预演或彩排。通过模拟谈判对手在既定场合下的各种态度和反应，来检查己方制订的谈判方案在实施过程中可能会产生的效果，以便及时修正和完善。在现代国际商务谈判中，可以说谁在谈判前认真地进行了模拟，谁就掌握了先机和主动权，就有可能在谈判中处于优势地位。对于一些特别重大的谈判或难度较大的谈判，模拟谈判能够对整个谈判的成败起到至关重要的作用。

1. Functions of Simulated Negotiation（模拟谈判的作用）

（1）Negotiators can find problems in the negotiation plan and make up for them in time.（通过模拟谈判，谈判人员可以及时发现谈判方案中的问题并及时弥补。）

The negotiation plan is formulated by the negotiators based on the information collected and mastered and the negotiators' experience, assumptions and judgments before starting formal negotiations. Whether these assumptions and judgments are correct needs to be tested in simulated negotiations. At the same time, the objective factors that affect business negotiation are always changing. These changes may cause some new problems. By simulating the objective scene at the time and simulating various reactions of the counter-party, one party can simulate the countermeasures of its own negotiators. To predict various objective situations as early as possible and make the negotiation plan more objective and practical can improve the negotiation plan's instructiveness and operability for the negotiation.

谈判方案是谈判人员在开始正式谈判前根据所收集和掌握的信息以及谈判人员的经验、假设和判断而制订的。而这些假设和判断是否正确就需要在模拟谈判中得到检验。同时，影响商务谈判的客观因素总是在发生变化，这些变化可能会引发一些新的问题。通过模拟当时的客观情景，模拟对手可能有的各种反应，模拟己方谈判人员的对策，尽可能提前预测各种客观情况，使谈判方案更客观和实际，从而提高谈判方案对谈判的指导性和可操作性。

（2）The best solution can be selected from various negotiation plans.（通过模拟谈判可以从众多方案中选择最佳方案。）

Before the formal start of negotiations, there are often more than one negotiation plan formulated. As to which negotiation plan is the most appropriate one to choose during the negotiation, simulated negotiation can help the negotiators to make the correct choice. For example, Company A and Company B are going to negotiate the purchase of equipment. For Company A, the quotation from 20,000 yuan/set to 25,000 yuan/set will have objective profits. Therefore, Company A formulated two negotiation plans. The first plan made offer at 20,000 yuan/set, and it was determined not to budge in the negotiations. The second plan made offer at 25,000 yuan/set firstly, and then gradually reduce the price according to the response of the counter-party, but the bottom line was 20,000 yuan/set. In order to show sincerity and leave a good impression on the counter-party, Company A decided to choose the first plan in the simulated negotiation. However, during the re-simulation negotiation, the counter-party repeatedly requested to lower the price, and the price was already the lowest price. If the price was lowered, the profit level would be greatly affected. After summarizing the simulated negotiation later, Company A found that the counter-party insisted on lowering the price was a kind of negotiation psychology. The counter-party always thinks that accepting the offer from the beginning, feels like losing in momentum, but also can not reflect the ability to negotiate, so they will try their best to reduce the price, and are even willing to risk the breakdown of the negotiations. Therefore, the first plan is defective. In the end, Company A decided to use the second plan in the formal negotiations. Although the offer is higher, the two parties will bargain during the negotiation. As long as Company A keeps the bottom line, it can give the counter-party a sense of satisfaction in the process of concessions. This is the role of selecting and optimizing the negotiation plan through simulated negotiation.

在谈判正式开始之前，制订的谈判方案往往不止一个，那么在谈判时究竟选择哪个谈判方案最合适，这就需要通过模拟谈判帮助谈判人员做出正确的选择。例如，A公司与B公司准备就购买仪器设备进行谈判。对于A公司而言，报价从20 000元/台到25 000元/台都会有可观的利润，所以A公司制订了两个谈判方案：方案一是报20 000元/台，在谈判中坚决不让步；方案二是先报25 000元/台，根据对方的反应再逐步降价，但底线是20 000元/台。A公司为了显示诚意，给对方留下好印象，决定在模拟谈判中选用方案一。但是在模拟谈判中对方却一再要求己方将价格降低，而己方已经是底价，如果再降价，利润水平会受到较大影响，所以不愿意再降价，谈判陷入僵局。在事后总结时才发现对方坚持压低价格是由于谈判心理在作怪。对方总是认为一开始就接受报价，感觉在气势上就输了，同时也无法体现自己的谈判能力，因此，会想尽办法压低价格，甚至愿意冒谈判破裂的风险，因此方案一就是有缺陷的。最后A公司决定在正式谈判时采用方案二。虽然谈判报价高一些，但在谈判过程中双方会讨价还价，只要守住底线，在己方让步过程中反而能让对方产生一种满足感。这就是通过模拟谈判对谈判方案进行选择和优化的作用。

(3) Negotiators can improve the actual practical ability.（通过模拟谈判可以提高谈判人员的实战能力。）

In practice, many enterprises in China have not realized the importance of simulated negotiations, and have regarded taking part in formal negotiations as an opportunity to exercise and improve the ability and level of negotiators, and this approach often brings huge losses to enterprises. If negotiators are not proficient in negotiating skills and cannot respond to opponents in a timely and efficient manner, it is easy for the negotiators to fall into a situation of being overwhelmed, nervous and prone to mistakes, thus giving the other party a chance to take good use of the weaknesses and disadvantages of their own side and take the opportunity to take the initiative to negotiate, causing unnecessary losses to their own side. Through the simulation of highly realistic negotiation exercises, the negotiators can relax in a relaxed mood and adapt to the atmosphere of the negotiation. By playing their roles and the other party over and over again, they can continuously find problems and correct them in time to achieve the goal of training and improving their negotiation ability and level. If conditions permit, you can record the entire process of simulated negotiations with a camera, so that the negotiators can find and correct their own language, expressions and movements in replay in order to better shape decent talk and behavior, establish a good image for the enterprise.

在实践中，我国很多企业都没有意识到模拟谈判的重要性，而把参加正式谈判作为锻炼和提高谈判人员能力和水平的机会，而这种方式常常会给企业带来巨大的损失。如果谈判人员对谈判技巧不熟练，对对手的反应不能及时做出高效的反馈，很容易使谈判人员陷入不知所措、精神高度紧张而容易出现失误的局面，从而给对方可乘之机，抓住己方弱点和劣势趁机取得谈判主动权，给己方造成不必要的损失。通过模拟谈判高度逼真的演练，谈判人员可以放松心情并适应谈判氛围，通过一次次地扮演己方和对方的角色，不断地发现问题并及时纠正，从而达到训练和提高自己的谈判能力和水平的目的。如果有条件的话，可以将模拟谈判的全过程用摄像机记录下来，以便谈判人员从回放中发现并改正自己在语言、表情和动作方面的不当之处，以便更好地塑造得体大方的言谈举止，为企业树立良好的形象。

2. Methods of Simulated Negotiation（模拟谈判的方式）

There are two methods of simulated negotiation: one is conference simulated negotiation, and the other is dramatic simulated negotiation.

模拟谈判一般有两种方式：一种是会议式模拟谈判，另一种是戏剧式模拟谈判。

(1) Conference Simulated Negotiation（会议式模拟谈判）

The conference simulated negotiation is also called a salon simulated negotiation. It is to gather negotiators together, to discuss fully, to express opinions freely, and to imagine the whole process of negotiations together. The characteristic of this kind of simulated negotiation is to make use of people's competitive mentality, so that the negotiators can fully express their opinions, inspire each other, and jointly improve the level of negotiation.

会议式模拟谈判也称沙龙式模拟谈判。就是把谈判者聚集在一起，充分讨论，自由发表意见，共同想象谈判全过程。这种模拟谈判的特点是利用人的竞争心理，使谈判人员充分发表意见，互相启发，共同提高谈判水平。

(2) Dramatic Simulated Negotiation（戏剧式模拟谈判）

Dramatic simulated negotiation means that each negotiator simulates the specific role played in the negotiation according to different assumptions and different negotiation scenarios, thereby enriching the practical experience of the negotiator. Through dramatic simulated negotiations, the preparations for negotiations can be made more fully and accurately, and each negotiator can accurately determine his position and role in the negotiation, and provide a good opportunity for his party to analyze the negotiation motivation and negotiation objectives, and improve the negotiation strategy.

戏剧式模拟谈判指每名谈判人员根据不同的假设、不同的谈判场景，模拟谈判中所扮演的特定角色，从而丰富谈判人员的实战经验。戏剧式模拟谈判能使谈判的准备更加充分和准确，能使每名谈判人员准确定位自己在谈判中的位置和角色，为己方分析谈判动机、谈判目标和改进谈判策略提供一次很好的机会。

Regardless of whether a conference simulated negotiation or a dramatic simulated negotiation is used, it must be carried out in accordance with the order of negotiations. The entire process of face-to-face negotiation between the party and the other party includes the establishment of the atmosphere during the negotiation, facial expressions, body language, issues that may be involved in the negotiation, the other party's possible objections, your own responses, and the selection and use of various negotiation strategies and techniques. Only in this way can simulated negotiations be more targeted and practical, and can they really play their role.

不论是采用会议式模拟谈判还是戏剧式模拟谈判，一定要按照谈判顺序来进行，演练己方与对方面对面谈判的全过程，包括谈判时氛围的营造、面部表情、肢体语言、谈判中可能会涉及的问题、对方可能会提出的反对意见、己方的答复以及各种谈判策略和技巧的选择与运用。只有这样才能使模拟谈判更具有针对性和实战性，才能真正发挥模拟谈判的作用。

3. Summary of Simulated Negotiation（模拟谈判总结）

The purpose of simulated negotiations is to allow negotiators to discover problems, correct problems, propose countermeasures, and improve the negotiation plan. Therefore, the summary of simulated negotiations is essential. The main contents of the summary of the simulated negotiation include the other party's views and negotiation styles; the other party's objections and countermeasures; their own advantages and use of their advantages; their own disadvantages and improvement measures; compromised conditions for both parties and mutually acceptable conditions; the handling of deadlocked negotiations. Only by summing up the simulated negotiations can we accumulate experience, make targeted corrections to problems, and improve the preparations for negotiations.

模拟谈判的目的在于让谈判人员发现问题、纠正问题、提出对策、完善谈判方案，因此，模拟谈判的总结是必不可少的。模拟谈判总结的主要内容包括对方的观点、谈判风格；对方的反对意见以及对策；己方的优势以及优势的运用情况；己方的劣势和改进措施；谈判所需的资料是否完善；双方的妥协条件以及共同可接受的条件；谈判陷入僵局的处理方式。模拟谈判只有通过总结，才能积累经验，有的放矢地对问题进行纠正，完善谈判的准备工作。

Ⅵ The Business Etiquette（谈判准备阶段的商务礼仪）

1. The Arrangement of Negotiation Seat（谈判座次的安排）

In international business negotiations, rectangular or oval negotiation tables are generally used. The negotiating parties are seated face-to-face, and the host and the guest should sit on both sides of the table. If the table is placed horizontally, the side facing the entrance is the upper position and belongs to the guest; the side facing away from the entrance is lower position and should belong to the host. If the table is laid vertically, the direction of entering the door shall prevail, the right side is the upper position and belongs to the guest; the left side is lower position and belongs to the host.

在国际商务谈判中，一般会采用长方形或椭圆形的谈判桌。谈判双方面对面入座，主宾应分坐于桌子两侧。若桌子横放，面对正门的一方为上方，属于客方；背对正门的一方为下方，属于主方。若桌子横放，则应以进门的方向为准，右为上，属于客方；左为下，属于主方。

When negotiating, the chief negotiators of all parties should sit in the middle of their negotiating team. The rest of the staff should follow the principle that right side is upper, left side is lower, and sit on both sides of the chief negotiator from near to far according to the position. If an interpreter is needed, he or she should be seated on the right side of the chief negotiators.

进行谈判时，各方的主谈人应在己方谈判人员中居中而坐。其余人员应遵循右高左低的原则，根据职位高低由近及远分别坐在主谈人的两侧。如果需要翻译人员，则应该安排其就座于主谈人的右侧。

When holding multilateral negotiations, in order to avoid rudeness, round tables are generally chosen to negotiate according to the international practice, which can downplay the status.

在举行多边谈判时，为了避免失礼，按照国际惯例，一般会选择圆桌来进行谈判，从而淡化地位高低。

2. Reception Etiquette（接待礼仪）

(1) Greet Etiquette（迎接礼仪）

As the host, there should be careful arrangements when welcoming guests. First of all, the host should know the train number and flight number that the guests take in advance, and arrange someone with the same position to meet the guests. If for some reason, the person with the corresponding position cannot go, a polite explanation should be made. Secondly, the greeting staff should arrive at the station and airport ahead of time, and must not be late to let the guests wait, otherwise, it will leave an impression of dereliction of duty and untrustworthiness. Thirdly, after receiving the guests, the greeting staff should make a greeting to the guests first, and then make a simple self-introduction. Finally, the greeting staff should prepare transportation in advance, and do not wait to prepare the transportation in a hurry after the guests arrive, which will make the guests feel insincere.

作为东道主，在迎接来访者时应该有周密的安排。首先应该了解对方到达的车次、航班，安排与对方身份、职务相当的人员去迎接。如果因为某种原因，相应身份的人员不能前往，应该向对方做出礼貌的解释。其次，迎接人员应提前到达车站、机场，绝不能迟到让对方等待。若迎接迟到，必定会给对方留下失职和不守信誉的印象。再次，接到对方后，应首先问候对方，然后做简单的自我介绍。最后，迎接人员应提前准备好交通工具，不要等对方到达后才匆匆忙忙地准备交通工具，那样会让对方觉得没有诚意。

(2) Guide Etiquette（引导礼仪）

In the aisles and corridors, the host should walk two or three steps in front of the guest, and cooperate with the guest's pace to let him walk inside. When ascending the stairs, the guest should be allowed to walk in the front. When descending the stairs, the host should walk in the front. When taking the elevator, the host should enter the elevator first, and then close the elevator door after the guest enters. When exiting the elevator, the guest should be allowed to walk out of the elevator first.

在过道、走廊处，东道主应该走在对方前面两三步的位置，配合对方的步调，让客人走在内侧。在上楼梯时，应该让客人走在前面；在下楼梯时，东道主应该走在客人的前面。当乘坐电梯时，东道主应先进入电梯，等客人进入后再关闭电梯门；当出电梯时，应让客人先走出电梯。

3. Accommodation（食宿安排）

（1）Hotel Arrangement（住宿安排）

Whether the location of international business negotiations is arranged at the host or the guest, it is necessary to arrange food and accommodation for all guests in advance. If guests pay for their own room and board, the host needs to confirm with the guests the standard or class of the hotel in advance. If the host is responsible for the hotel expenses, the investment return and other factors should be considered when determining the hotel standard. International business negotiations value time and efficiency, so the principle of choosing a hotel does not emphasize luxury, but the transportation should be convenient, as close to the negotiating place as possible, and close to the central business district for shopping.

国际商务谈判的地点不论是安排在主方还是客方，都需要为客人提前安排好食宿。如果客人自己支付食宿费用，需要事先与对方确认下榻酒店的标准或等级。如果是东道主承担酒店费用，在确定酒店标准时主要考虑投资回报等因素。国际商务谈判重视时间和效率，因此选择酒店的原则是不强调奢华，但交通要便利，尽可能靠近谈判地点，距离商圈近以便购物。

After receiving the guests, the welcoming staff should help the guests to go through all the procedures and lead the guests into the room. At the same time, the guests will be introduced to the services, facilities, negotiation schedule, and the local customs, natural scenery, special products, etc. Considering that the guests are tired during the journey, the welcoming staff should not stay for a long time, so that the guests have sufficient rest time.

接到客人后接待人员应帮客人办理好一切手续并将客人领进房间，同时向客人介绍住处的服务、设施以及谈判的日程安排，同时向客人介绍当地风土人情、自然景观、特产等。考虑到客人旅途劳累，迎接人员不宜久留，让客人有充足的休息时间。

（2）Catering Arrangement（饮食安排）

Customers who participate in international business negotiations are more focused on efficiency and do not like complicated and lengthy hospitality. If the host entertains guests, he only needs to pay attention to nutritional balance, meat and vegetables, and reflect the local characteristics. It is not necessary to entertain every meal. When ordering, it is necessary to know in advance the guests' religious beliefs, whether they have any food to avoid, whether they are vegetarians, etc. The quantity of orders should not be too much or too little, and avoid waste.

参加国际商务谈判的客户都比较注重效率，不喜欢繁杂冗长的款待。东道主如果宴请客人，只需要注重营养均衡，荤素搭配，体现当地特色即可，不需要每一餐都宴请。在点餐时，需要提前了解客人的宗教信仰，是否有忌口，是否为素食主义者等。点餐数量应适可而止，切忌浪费。

4. Visiting Tour (参观旅游)

When time permits, especially when the host wants to establish good relationship with the counter-party and create a good atmosphere for the start of the negotiation, the host will arrange some tours for the guests who visit the negotiating site for the first time. The places to visit can be local scenic spots, or product production lines and industrial chain production bases related to negotiations, which can help deepen the trust of the counter-party. But when arranging visiting tours, be sure to avoid military restricted areas, secret production areas or sensitive areas involving commercial secrets.

在时间允许，特别是东道主希望与对方建立感情，为谈判开局制造良好氛围的情况下，东道主对于首次来访的客人会安排一些参观游览活动。参观游览的地方可以是当地的风景名胜区，也可以是与谈判相关的产品生产线、产业链生产基地等，这样有助于加深对方的信任。但安排参观游览时一定要避开军事禁区、保密生产地或涉及商业机密的敏感区域。

Summary

The preparation for international business negotiations includes preparation of negotiation teams, preparation of negotiation information, formulation of negotiation plans, preparation of other aspects, and simulation of negotiations and the reserve of business etiquette knowledge at this stage. The preparation of the negotiating team includes the selection of members of the negotiating team, the division of labor and collaboration between negotiating members, and the qualities required of negotiators. Negotiation information can be collected on a direct or indirect basis. The content of information collection includes market information, negotiating party information, scientific and technological information, policy and regulatory information, and financial information. After the information is collected, it needs to be sorted and analyzed before it can be used as the basis for formulating the negotiation plan. When formulating a negotiation plan, it is necessary to clarify the topics and objectives of the negotiations, arrange the negotiation agenda, and select appropriate negotiation countermeasures. Simulation negotiations need to be conducted before formal negotiations, and the importance of simulation negotiations is clearly recognized.

国际商务谈判的准备阶段包括谈判队伍的准备、谈判信息的准备、谈判方案的制订、其他方面的准备以及模拟谈判和这个阶段商务礼仪知识的储备。谈判队伍的准备包括谈判小组成员的挑选、谈判成员之间的分工与协作、谈判人员需具备的素养。谈判信息的收集可以通过直接和间接两种途径进行。信息收集的内容包括市场信息、谈判对手信息、科技信息、政策法规信息和金融信息。信息收集后需要经过整理和分析才能作为制订谈判方案的依据。制订谈判方案时需要明确谈判主题和谈判目标，安排好谈判议程，选择恰当的谈判对策。在正式谈判前需要进行模拟谈判，清楚地认识到模拟谈判的重要性。

The business etiquette at the preparation stage mainly involves the seat arrangement during the negotiation, the welcome etiquette, the accommodation and catering, and the arrangement of visiting tours. When arranging the negotiation seat, the principle of respecting the right should be followed. When welcoming the counter-party, you should know the specific situation of the counter-party's negotiators in advance, and put yourself in the counter-party's shoes, such as the arrival time, the number of men and women in the negotiation team, and eating habits, so that the host can make preparation ahead of time.

在准备阶段的商务礼仪主要涉及谈判时座位的确定、迎接礼仪、食宿的安排以及参观旅游的安排。在确定谈判座位时要遵循以右为尊的原则。在迎接款待对方时一定要事先搞清楚对方谈判人员的情况，设身处地地为对方着想，如到达时间、谈判小组男女人数、饮食习惯等，便于东道主提前做准备。

Module Ⅱ Terminology Practice

1. International Trade Practice: It refers to the rules formulated based on some common customary practices gradually formed in long-term international trade practice. Although it does not have universal legal binding force, however, according to the laws of each country, parties are allowed to choose the freedom of applying international trade practices in international trade. Once a party adopts a certain practice in a contract, it will be legally binding on both parties.

2. External Brain: It refers to think tanks with management experience and intelligence outside the company.

3. Body Language: It refers to the communication of the expression through various actions of the body instead of language. In a broad sense, body language also includes facial expressions; in a narrow sense, body language includes only the meaning expressed by the body and limbs.

4. WTO Rule: From the general theory of international treaty law and WTO practice, WTO rules are an effective part of international law. In terms of specific application and normative role, it can also be called WTO agreement and WTO law. It is currently the most important multilateral trade rule in the international economic and trade field, but it has different characteristics from general international law.

5. International Trade Dispute: It refers to disputes arising from various international trade exchanges or various international trade activities. It generally occurs between large international economic organizations and between countries and regions, involving a wide range of industries, large economic scale and trade volume. International trade disputes often include factors such as political interference, trade protection and so on.

6. UCP 600: It is Uniform Customs and Practice for Documentary Credits. It is applicable to all documentary letters of credit whose texts clearly state that they are bound by this practice (to the extent applicable, including standby letters of credit). Unless the letter of credit is specifically modified or excluded, this practice is binding on all parties to the credit. This is the sixth revision of UCP since its inception in 1933.

7. Incoterms 2020: It is the newest version of International Rules for the Interpretation of Trade Terms which is established by the International Chamber of Commerce. It is the basic international general rules for international trade.

8. Bilious Temperament: It is characterized by rapid and intense emotions, as well as intense and powerful movements. Most of the people in this category are enthusiastic, straightforward, energetic, irritable, sentimental and emotional.

9. Sanguineous Temperament: This type of person is lively, active, sensitive, responsive, enjoying interacting with people, easy to shift attention, easy to change interests and emotions, and so on. Such people are suitable for work that requires quick response and flexibility.

10. Lymphatic Temperament: This type of person is easy to develop qualities such as self-control, calmness, and practicality, but also tends to develop coldness, slowness, and stubbornness. Such people have low reactivity, are not prone to emotions, and are not exposed. They have a strong attitude, moderate communication, and strong self-control over their behaviors; they have a slow psychological response, are not easy to be panic when they are in trouble, have poor plasticity, and are not flexible.

11. Melancholic Temperament: This type of person is prone to develop qualities such as sharp thinking, carefulness, rich imagination, and deep emotions; but they also tend to develop suspicion, loneliness, depression, and cowardice. Such people have higher sensibility and lower agility, and they have slower mental reactions, slower movements, and slower speaking. They are sentimental and emotional, but they are weak and persistent.

Module Ⅲ New Words

1. high-tech *adj.* 高科技的；高技术的 *n.* 高科技
2. multiple *adj.* 多重的；多样的 *n.* 倍数
3. rotation *n.* 旋转；循环；轮流
4. savvy *n.* 理解力；洞察力 *v.* 理解 *adj.* 聪慧的；具有实际知识的
5. offside *n.* 越位 *adj.* 越位的
6. complementarity *n.* 互补性；补充；补足
7. coordination *n.* 协调；对等；同等
8. personality *n.* 个性；品格；名人
9. deficiency *n.* 缺陷，缺点；缺乏；不足的数额
10. agile *adj.* 敏捷的；机敏的；活泼的
11. ideology *n.* 意识形态；思想意识
12. status *n.* 地位；状态；情形；重要身份
13. professionalism *n.* 职业化；特性，方法；

专业主义

14. summarize *v.*（做）总结；（做）概述

15. legislation *n.* 立法；法律

16. specialty *n.* 专长，专业；特产；特性；招牌菜 *adj.* 特色的；专门的；独立的

17. on-site *adj.* 现场的

18. indispensable *adj.* 不可或缺的；绝对必要的 *n.* 不可或缺的人（物）

19. dexterity *n.* 灵巧；敏捷；机敏

20. energy-intensive *adj.* 耗能的；耗精力的

21. auxiliary *adj.* 辅助的；附加的 *n.* 辅助者；附属机构

22. predicament *n.* 困境；状态

23. cohesion *n.* 凝聚力；内聚力

24. suspiciousness *n.* 疑心；可疑

25. temperament *n.* 气质；性情；性格

26. sophisticated *adj.* 复杂的；精致的；富有经验的；世故的 *v.* 变得世故；使迷惑

27. hypocritical *adj.* 虚伪的；伪善的

28. perseverance *n.* 坚持不懈；不屈不挠；毅力；耐性

29. impartial *adj.* 公平的，公正的；不偏不倚的

30. folklore *n.* 民俗学；民间传说；民间风俗

Module Ⅳ Useful Expressions

1. be adjusted to 适应
2. detrimental to 对……有害的
3. play role in 在……中扮演角色；在……中起作用
4. in charge of 主管；负责
5. give play to 发挥
6. cope with 处理；应对
7. preside over 主持；负责
8. be convenient to 对……方便
9. access to 接近；有权使用；通向……的入口
10. the former..., the latter... 前者……，后者……
11. put forward 提出；拿出；推举出
12. a wide range of 大范围的；各种不同的
13. regardless of 不管；不顾
14. take effect 生效；起作用
15. ex ante 事前的；采取措施前

Module Ⅴ Exercise

Ⅰ. Answer the following questions according to the text.

1. What preparation should be made before negotiation?

2. What should we notice when choosing negotiation staff?

3. What different kinds of negotiators should be included in negotiation team? What are their responsibilities?

4. What are the basic qualities that negotiators should have?

5. Before negotiation, what kind of information should be collected? How to collect information?

6. What basic contents should be involved when we are making a negotiation plan?

7. What principles should be adhered to when we are making a negotiation plan?

8. How many negotiating goals are there and what are they? How to understand each of them?

9. What elements should we take into account when arranging a negotiation agenda?

10. What other aspects should we consider before negotiation besides negotiators' preparation and information collection?

Ⅱ. Match the words in Column A with their definitions in Column B.

Column A	Column B
1. savvy	A. to give a summary of sth.
2. dexterity	B. having a lot of experience of the world
3. predicament	C. the qualities of a person's character
4. summarize	D. a person's or an animal's nature
5. personality	E. skill in using your hands or your mind
6. sophisticated	F. respected and admired as very important or of very high quality
7. temperament	G. the act of receiving money especially as compensation
8. prestigious	H. complete and not damaged
9. payoff	I. practical knowledge or understanding of sth.
10. intact	J. a difficult or unpleasant situation

Ⅲ. Translate the following terms and phrases into Chinese.

1. collective power
2. division of labor
3. sort out
4. product life cycle
5. market share
6. specific circumstances
7. legal adviser
8. behind-the-scene
9. professional skills
10. make a judgment

Ⅳ. Please determine whether the following statements are True or False.

1. Generally speaking, the number of negotiation team should be proportional to the complexity of the negotiation. (   )

2. The older a person is, the more experience he has. So when you choose negotiator, the older one is better than the younger one. (   )

3. If one of the negotiators is good at the counter-party's language, there's no need to use a translator. (   )

4. There are three goals in negotiation plan: the best goal, the acceptable goal and the lowest goal. (   )

5. Besides considering the negotiation team and information collection before the negotia-

tion, we also need to consider the negotiating time and place. (　　)

Ⅴ. Translate the following sentences into Chinese.

1. There are several important aspects in preparation stage: assessing the situation and the people; organizing negotiation team; information collection; designing negotiation agenda; and making a feasible negotiation plan.

2. From the point of business negotiation nature, knowledge of a particular executive's background, hobbies, and family status can be a great advantage.

3. When collecting your opponent's information, you should size up the probable goal and preferences of the counter-party's analysis of various data using its perspective rather than yours.

4. Technical personnel is responsible for the area concerning specification, program and methods of work.

5. The duties of team leader are to select the remainder team members, prepare the negotiating plan, conduct the negotiations and make final decisions on concessions, selection of trade-off items and so on.

Ⅵ. Translate the following sentences into English.

1. 国际商务谈判是一项团队合作的活动。它需要专业的技能、很强的沟通能力和团队协作能力。

2. 在国际商务谈判小组中，法律人员主要负责起草和审核合同条款以及熟悉本国、对方所在国的法律和国际公约、国际惯例等。

3. 在收集信息时，一定要注意信息传递的保密性，这直接关系到国家安全及公司的谈判能否取得成功。

4. 一般而言，国际商务谈判方案中都会涉及制定理想目标和最低目标。

5. 在国际商务谈判中，谈判的进程、谈判内容都要围绕事先拟定的谈判日程来进行，因此在安排谈判议程时，需要将其与谈判主题、谈判要点紧密结合起来。

Ⅶ. Case Study

Case 1: Method of Collecting Negotiation Information in International Business Negotiation

Case Source: Tang Xiulian. *International Business Negotiation*. Beijing: Tsinghua University Press, 2009.

Preface

Time: 1991

Key Point: A German company steals rival company's intelligence by installing a bug.

Background

Industry: Equipment

Subject: International Business Machinery Company and a German Company

Issue: The owner of the International Business Machinery Company found that the necklace on the neck of his female secretary was sent by the staff of a German company and equipped with monitoring equipment.

In the summer of 1991, the owner of International Business Machinery Company was surprised to discover that an advanced military computer software system that the company had just developed had become a product of a large German company and was negotiated and exported to some Arab countries. After investigation, he found that the beautiful necklace hanging on the neck of his female secretary is different. The buckle of the second necklace is equipped with a high-density bug and radio transmission. The major decisions and secrets within the International Business Machinery Company were almost unfortunately eavesdropped and passed on. The necklace was sent by a Frenchman working in a German company.

Questions

1. What are the methods of information collection in international business negotiations?

2. What kind of information collection method did the German company use in this case? What are the characteristics of this method?

Appendix

The negotiating body can be a natural person or a combined team. In business negotiations, the main body of negotiation is the main factor, with subjective initiative and creativity, playing a vital role in the negotiations. The subject of negotiation can be divided into the subject of the relationship and the subject of the act.

Case 2: Survey of the Company's Own Situation

Case Source: Huang Weiping. *International Business Negotiation*. Beijing: China Renmin University Press, 2011.

Preface

Time: 1982

Key Point: Shijiazhuang No. 3 Printing and Dyeing Factory succeeded in paying the transfer fee at a lower price through the investigation of the patent.

Background

Industry: Equipment

Subject: Shijiazhuang No. 3 Printing and Dyeing Factory and Federal German Carver Company

Issue: Shijiazhuang No. 3 Printing and Dyeing Factory successfully obtained the transfer of key equipment from Federal German Carver Company through a survey of patents.

In 1982, Shijiazhuang No. 3 Printing and Dyeing Factory prepared a 15-year cooperative production with the Federal German Carver Company in the form of compensation trade, and stipulated that the production process and key equipment of bonded interlining should be provided by foreign party. The process contained a large number of patents. During the initial negotiation, the other party asked us to pay a total of 2.4 million marks for the patent transfer fee and trademark fee. Our factory manager immediately sent a patent investigation into these patents.

The investigation found that the main technology of the "Double Point Coating Process" patent will expire in 1989. Therefore, in the second round of negotiations, we put forward this evidence and proposed to reduce the transfer fee. Foreign investors had to reduce the transfer fee to 1.3 million marks.

Questions

1. What is included in the survey of the company's own situation before the international business negotiations?

2. What kind of negotiation materials do you need to prepare before the international business negotiations? What kind of negotiation materials are mainly involved in this case?

Appendix

Product technical data mainly include product catalogue, product samples, product specifications, product specifications, product technical indicators, product performance, product scope, product design points, product inspection standards.

Case 3: Selection of International Business Negotiators

Case Source: Liu Hong. *International Business Negotiation*. Dalian: Northeast University of Finance and Economics Press, 2009.

Preface

Key Point: Chinese negotiators have irretrievable consequences due to lack of professional knowledge.

Background

Industry: Finance

Subject: A Factory in China and a Company in Country Z

Issue: Due to the lack of professional knowledge of Chinese negotiators and the analysis of changes in Country Z's bank interest rates, China's high interest rates have finally led to the collapse of Chinese liabilities.

A factory in China negotiated a contract with a Country Z company. The Country Z company provided loans to the Chinese side. The Chinese side proposed a calculation based on the Bank ABC's most favorable monthly loan interest rate of 8.7%. The contract stated that it was based on Bank ABC of Country Z——the best lending rate calculation. As the relevant negotiators of the factory did not understand the professional knowledge and lacked an analysis of the changes in Country Z's bank interest rates, they agreed. Later, the Country Z company brought the best lending rate of Bank ABC, which was over 20% for seven or eight months. According to this standard, China will pay high interest rates. To this end, the factory requested to amend the contract at a monthly interest rate of 8.7%, but the Country Z side refused to modify the contract on the grounds that the contract had taken effect. After several negotiations, there was no result, and the chinese factory eventually closed down due to debt.

Questions

1. What are the criteria for selecting negotiators before international business negotiations?

2. What are the problems with the negotiators on the factory side in this case?

Appendix

The comprehensive ability that negotiators should have includes coordinating the relationship with other negotiators, being good at using language to clearly express their own attitudes and opinions, being proficient in all kinds of official documents, writing reports, mastering computer technology, being good at calm analysis and thinking, and fast reaction.

Ⅷ. Role plays practice. Work in pair and converse according to the given information.

Task 1

Background

You are going to import a quantity of chemical fertilizers for your end-users. But you find the price quoted by Mr. Jackson of a German firm on the high side compared with the prevailing price in the world market. Taking advantage of a weak market that is unfavorable to sellers, you try your best to persuade Mr. Jackson to reduce his price.

Terms and Phrases

acceptable	superior to	take into consideration
cut down	comply with	in line with
cost price	bottom price	stand no chance
indication of price	insist on	for your information
see one's way to do sth.	meet halfway	to tell the truth
for friendship's sake	on high/low side	impracticable

Relative Expressions

1. I propose that...
2. I have proposal to make...
3. I would like to make a suggestion.
4. Well, don't you think we should...
5. I strongly recommend that...
6. Why don't we...
7. You might consider...
8. I was wondering if you'd ever thought of...
9. The way I see it, you should...
10. We are happy that the price is looking up.
11. The goods are priced too high.
12. Your price is not convincing.
13. The offer is prohibitive.
14. Price has declined.
15. I'm afraid there's no space for any reduction in price.

16. Our price has already been cut down to cost level.

17. Our products are moderately priced.

Task 2

Background

Mr. Brown, an Italian importer discusses with you about an offer on 10,000 sets of cooking utensils. Having bargained for several times, he finally accepts your final price. After going over the payment and other general terms, the business is concluded. Both Mr. Brown and you take one more look before signing the contract.

Terms and Phrases

in the market for	undercut	supervise
revise	to this effect	deserve
a batch of	suitable arrangement	freight charge
a repeat order	overall reduction	be valid for
total amount	a range of	look forward to

Relative Expressions

1. Don't worry. Everything will be okay.
2. I've no doubt...
3. I wouldn't get upset if I were you.
4. I'm quite convinced that...
5. It's just one of those things.
6. Please rest assured there's no danger at all...
7. I assure you that...
8. You will certainly find this perspective more rewarding.
9. We do understand your concern. It's not always easy to...
10. I am sure about...
11. I can promise you that...
12. I am positive about...
13. I have no doubts that we will...

Chapter 4

Opening for International Business Negotiation

Work Objective

After studying this chapter, you will be able to:

- familiarize with the main contents in the opening stage of international business negotiation;
- probe into how to create negotiating atmosphere;
- familiarize with the contents of assessment work;
- identify different types of negotiating atmosphere;
- know various types of strategies in the opening stage of international business negotiation.

Case Guide-Reading

A U. S. company sells a technologically advanced production line to a Japanese company. The two sides sent a strong lineup of negotiating teams to hold formal negotiation in Tokyo. Out of absolute confidence in the technology, the U. S. representatives firmly believe that the negotiation will be a great victory, so they seem very content. At the beginning of the negotiation, the U. S. representatives spoke incessantly about how advanced their technology is, how reasonable the price is, and how perfect the after-sales service is. The Japanese representatives are very dull, just burying their heads and not saying a word. When the representatives of the United States made a successful speech, they found that the Japanese representatives had a stunned look. When the Americans asked, the Japanese said that they did not understand. The U. S. representatives had to repeat it over and over. The previous excitement was gone. The entire negotiation was filled with enthusiasm that was initially led by the Americans, and gradually shifted to a low and cautious state with the attitude of the Japanese. The Japanese representatives saw that the time was ripe, so they pointed out seriously to the U. S. representatives a series of technical defects and price problems which made the U. S. representatives feel very embarrassed. In the end, Japanese company has pushed the price of this line down to the maximum that the U. S. company can afford.

Source: Dou Ran, *International Business Negotiation and Communication Skills*, Shanghai: Fudan University Press, 2009.

Module Ⅰ Text

Ⅰ Main Works in the Opening Stage（开局阶段的工作内容）

In the opening stage, on the one hand, it is necessary to create conditions for the establishment of long-term friendly cooperative relations between negotiating parties; on the other hand, we must actively understand the characteristics, intentions and attitudes of the negotiating opponents. By grasping and analyzing the counter-party's information, we can correct our own negotiation plan, strive to enter the role as soon as possible, and then get the initiative in the negotiation field. In general, the work in the opening stage is mainly to create a negotiating atmosphere and find out the details of the counter-party.

在开局阶段，一方面要为谈判各方建立长期友好合作关系创造条件，另一方面要积极了解谈判对手的特点、意图和态度。通过掌握并分析对方的信息来修正己方的谈判方案，争取早日进入角色，进而取得谈判场上的主动。总的来说，开局阶段的工作主要是营造谈判氛围、摸清对方底细。

1. Creating a Negotiating Atmosphere（营造谈判氛围）

The atmosphere of negotiation affects people's emotions and behaviors, which in turn affects the outcome of behavior. In different negotiating atmospheres, the outcome of the negotiations may be very different with the same negotiators and the same negotiating issues. In order to achieve the desired outcome of the negotiations, efforts should be made to create a positive and friendly atmosphere of negotiation.

谈判氛围会影响人们的情绪和行为方式，进而影响到行为的结果。同样的谈判人员、同样的谈判议题，在不同的谈判氛围中，谈判的结果也可能大相径庭。要想取得理想的谈判结果，就应努力营造积极友好的谈判氛围。

The atmosphere of negotiation is diverse; it can be calm, serious, enthusiastic, positive, tense and antagonistic. The atmosphere is also very subtle. To form a good atmosphere for negotiation, we should start from the following aspects.

谈判氛围多种多样，有平静的、严肃的，也有热烈的、积极的，还有紧张的、对立的。氛围的形成也十分微妙。要形成良好的谈判氛围，应从以下几个方面着手：

(1) Grasp the Key Opportunity for the Formation of Negotiation Atmosphere（把握谈判氛围形成的关键时机）

The factors that influence the atmosphere of negotiation are diverse. During the negotiation process, these factors will also change with the change of the entire negotiation situation. Therefore, the negotiation atmosphere will also change with the progress of the negotiations. However, the key time to form a negotiating atmosphere is very short-lived which is the moment the two sides meet first. The reason for this is mainly the psychological state and mindset of the negotiators at the beginning of the opening. In this short moment, the negotiator gets the first impression and feeling about the counter-party when contacting with it. This impression and feeling will largely determine the negotiator's evaluation of the counter-party throughout the negotiation process, which will largely determine the atmosphere of negotiation. Therefore, it can be said that the contact within this short moment will determine the tone of the entire negotiation atmosphere. All parties to the negotiations should pay attention to this critical opportunity and strive to create a good atmosphere for negotiation. Usually speaking, the negotiation atmosphere in the opening stage is influenced by two factors: subjective factors and objective factors.

影响谈判氛围的因素是多种多样的。在谈判过程中，这些因素也会随着整个谈判形势的变化而不断变化，因此，谈判氛围也会随着谈判的进展而有所变化。但是，形成谈判氛围的关键时刻却是十分短暂的，这个关键时刻就是双方谈判接触的短暂瞬间。之所以如此，主要是由于开局初期谈判者的心理状态和思维定式的作用。在这一短暂瞬间，谈判者在与对方的接触中，获得有关对方的第一印象和感觉，这种印象和感觉将在很大程度上决定谈判者在整个谈判过程中对对方的评价，而谈判各方对对方的印象和评价将在很大程度上决定谈判氛围。因此，也可以说，这一短暂瞬间的接触将确定整个谈判氛围的基调。谈判各方均应注意把握这一关键时机，力争营造良好的谈判氛围。一般来说，开局阶段的谈判氛围受两种因素影响：主观因素和客观因素。

The first impression has the strongest influence on the atmosphere of negotiation. Therefore, in order to create a negotiating atmosphere of good cooperation, negotiators should pay attention to the following points. First, on the clothing and appearance, the negotiator's costumes should be beautiful, generous, and tidy. The color should not be too bright. The style should not be too strange. The size should not be too small or too large. It must not be unkempt, and the clothes are scattered and shaped to suit their own identity. Second, if you visit France, Norway and other more rigorous countries, it is best to wear dark suits; if you visit the United States, Sweden and other relatively open countries, then wearing sweatshirts, casual clothes are also accepted. Third, the negotiators of both sides should walk straight into the venue and appear in front of each other in an open and friendly manner; shoulders should relax, naturally droop, and eye contact should give the counter-party a credible feeling. Fourth, speak easily and pay attention to the conversation content. Fifth, pay attention to gestures and touch behavior. For example, negotiators should not hesitate to shake hands with each other when they meet. Sixth, it is better for stand talking.

第一印象对谈判氛围的影响最为强烈，因此，为了营造良好合作的谈判氛围，谈判人员要注意以下几点内容。第一，在服饰仪表上，谈判人员的服饰要美观、大方、整洁，颜色不要太鲜艳，样式不能太奇异，尺码不能太小或太大，绝不能蓬头垢面，衣着散乱，要塑造出符合自己身份的形象。第二，如果访问法国、挪威等比较严谨的国家，最好穿暗色西装；如果访问美国、瑞典等比较开放的国家，则穿运动衫、便服也未尝不可。第三，双方谈判人员应该径直步入会场，以开诚布公、友好的态度出现在对方面前；双肩要放松，自然下垂，目光的接触要给对方可信可亲的感觉。第四，说话要轻松自如并且注意谈话内容。第五，注意手势和触碰行为，譬如，双方见面时谈判者应该毫不犹豫地与对方握手。第六，洽谈双方最好站着交谈。

(2) Use Neutral Topics to Strengthen Communication（运用中性话题，加强沟通）

The opening of business negotiations is often referred to as the "breaking ice" period. People who don't know each other come together to negotiate, and it's easy to have a pause or a cold spot. If the negotiations get to business at the beginning, it is easier to increase the thickness of the "ice layer". Therefore, business negotiators should set aside some time before entering the negotiating topic to communicate on topics such as climate, sports, and art that are not business and easy to communicate. However, during this period, we need to pay attention to the following questions: First, if all negotiators have set down, after a moment of pause, someone needs to speak first and to avoid the conversation lags. Under normal circumstances, the negotiators at home will start first. Second, do not prematurely involve specific issues before reaching an agreement on the objectives of the negotiation. Third, in order to maintain a good atmosphere for the negotiation to make it proceed smoothly, we should try our best to provide the parties to the negotiation equal opportunities to speak. The negotiation time and listening time are basically equal and the statement should be short and concise. Fourth, in the process of negotiating objectives and formulating the negotiation agenda, negotiating parties should respect each other and negotiate together.

商务谈判开局初期常被称为"破冰"期。素不相识的人走到一起进行谈判，极易出现停顿或冷场，如果谈判一开始就进入正题，更容易增加"冰层"的厚度。因此，商务谈判人员应在进入谈判正题前留出一定的时间，就一些非业务性的、轻松的话题，如气候、体育、艺术等，进行交流。但在这期间需要注意以下问题：第一，如果所有谈判人员均已坐稳，在片刻停顿后，就需要有人先讲话，不要出现冷场的情形。一般情况下，都是主场的谈判人员首先开场。第二，在没有就谈判目标等问题达成一致前，不要过早涉及具体问题。第三，为了保持良好的谈判氛围，使得谈判能顺利进行，要尽力使谈判各方享有均等的发言机会，谈判时间和倾听时间基本相等并且陈述要简短精要。第四，在商谈谈判目标、制定谈判议程的过程中，谈判各方要互相尊重，共同协商，要多用商量的口吻。

(3) Establish an Honest, Credible and Cooperative Spirit of Negotiators（树立诚实、可信、富有合作精神的谈判者形象）

What kind of image the negotiator appears in front of the counter-party has a very obvious impact on the atmosphere of negotiation. The image of the negotiation is reflected in many aspects, such as the negotiator's posture, whether it is energetic or exhausted, proactive or indifferent as whether the eyes are frank and sincere, evasive, or doubting. Another example is whether clothing and appearance are neat and generous or dirty. Negotiators should pay attention to their own image and appear in front of each other in an honest, trustworthy and cooperative spirit, thus influencing and inspiring the counter-party.

谈判者以何种形象出现在对方面前，对谈判氛围有十分明显的影响。谈判形象体现在多个方面：如谈判者的姿势，是精力充沛还是疲惫不堪；是积极主动还是无动于衷；又如目光，是坦荡诚挚还是躲躲闪闪、疑虑重重；再比如服饰仪表，是整洁大方还是肮脏古怪。谈判人员应注重自身的形象，以诚实可信、富有合作精神的形象出现在对方面前，从而感染、鼓舞对方的谈判人员。

(4) Use Off-site Informal Contact before Formal Negotiations（利用正式谈判前的场外非正式接触）

Before the formal start of negotiations, the two sides may have some informal contact opportunities, such as welcoming banquets, courtesy visits, etc. Using these opportunities to fully influence the attitude of the counter-party's negotiations, can help establish a good atmosphere of negotiation during formal negotiations.

在正式开始谈判前，双方可能会有一些非正式接触机会，如欢迎宴会、礼节性拜访等，利用这些机会充分影响对方人员对谈判的态度，有助于在正式谈判时建立良好的谈判氛围。

(5) Proper Organization（合理组织）

The proper organization of the negotiations, including the proper arrangement of the negotiation time and pre-negotiation activities, and the scientific arrangement of the negotiation room, also contributes to the establishment of a positive and friendly negotiation atmosphere.

对谈判的合理组织，包括对谈判时间和谈判前活动的合理安排、谈判室的科学布置等，也有助于积极友好的谈判氛围的建立。

2. Types of Opening Negotiation Atmosphere（开局谈判氛围的类型）

(1) High-profile Atmosphere（高调氛围）

It refers to the atmosphere in which the negotiation situation is more enthusiastic, the parties to the negotiations are positive and active, and the pleasant factors have become the dominant factors in the negotiation situation. In the case that one has a large advantage, and the main terms such as price are extremely beneficial to one's own side and one wishes to reach an agreement as soon as possible to sign a contract with the counter-party, he must strive to create a high-profile opening atmosphere. In a high-profile atmosphere, negotiating opponents often only pay attention to aspects that are beneficial to them, and their views on the prospects of negotiations tend to be optimistic. Therefore, a high-profile atmosphere can promote the agreement. Creating a high-profile atmosphere usually involves approaches of emotional aggression, praise, humor, and question teasing.

高调氛围是指谈判情势比较热烈，谈判各方情绪积极、态度主动，愉快因素成为谈判情势主导因素的谈判开局氛围。在己方占有较大优势，价格等主要条款对己方极为有利且己方希望尽早达成协议与对方签订合同的情况下，谈判一方要极力营造高调的开局氛围。

在高调氛围中，谈判对手往往只注意到对自己有利的方面，而且对谈判前景的看法也倾向于乐观，因此，高调氛围可以促进协议的达成。营造高调氛围通常有感情攻击法、称赞法、幽默法和问题挑逗法。

Emotional aggression method refers to the use of a special event to trigger the emotional factors that commonly exist in people's hearts, so that such feelings can flow in and out, thereby achieving the purpose of creating a high-profile atmosphere.

感情攻击法是指通过某一特殊事件来引发普遍存在于人们心中的感情因素，使这种感情迸发出来，从而达到营造高调氛围的目的。

For example, in September 2017, Client A from the Middle East took his six family members including his parents, wife, and children to Company B in Chongqing to negotiate business. Company B arranged for an appointment with Client A and his family to go to scenic area with a famous 5A class in Chongqing the next day for playing. During the trip, Company B arranged the itinerary for the client's parents, including hot springs and hunting. The client's precise marksmanship won applause from the crowd. His children were very happy riding on the prairie. The beautiful scenery, the careful preparation that Company B arranged, and the happiness of the family made Client A very happy. Next day, he signed a long-term order with Company B. It can be known from this case that the atmosphere of negotiations will affect people's emotions and behaviors, and then the results of negotiations. To achieve the desired negotiation results, it is necessary to actively strive to create a friendly negotiation atmosphere.

例如 2017 年 9 月，中东 A 客户携全家 6 人（客户父母、妻子、两个女儿）来重庆 B 公司洽谈生意，B 公司安排接机后与 A 客户约好第二天去重庆某著名 5A 级风景区游玩。游玩时 B 公司为客户父母安排了行程，包括泡温泉、打猎，客户精准的枪法赢得了围观人群的阵阵掌声，两个女儿在大草原上骑马非常开心。优美的风景、B 公司的精心准备、家人的开心，让 A 客户非常开心，第二天商谈时即与 B 公司签订了一份长期订单。由此可知，谈判氛围会影响人的情绪和行为方式，进而影响谈判结果。要想取得理想的谈判结果，需要积极、努力营造友好的谈判氛围。

The praise method refers to weakening the counter-party's psychological defense line by praising the counter-party, thereby igniting the counter-party's negotiation enthusiasm, mobilizing the counter-party's emotions, and creating a high-profile atmosphere. The following points should be noted when using the praise method:

称赞法是指通过称赞对方来削弱对方的心理防线，从而焕发出对方的谈判热情，调动对方的情绪，营造高调氛围。在采用称赞法时应该注意以下几点：

a. Choose the right compliment target. The basic principle of choosing a goal of praise is to hit on what one likes. That is to choose the goals that the counter-party is most proud of and hopes to pay attention to.

选择恰当的称赞目标。选择称赞目标的基本原则是投其所好。即选择那些对方最引以为豪并希望己方注意的目标。

b. Choose the right time to praise. If the timing is not right, the praise method will often be counterproductive.

选择恰当的称赞时机。如果时机选择得不对，称赞法往往会适得其反。

c. Choose the appropriate way to praise. The way of praise must be natural. Don't let the other person think that you are deliberately flattering him, otherwise it will cause resentment.

选择恰当的称赞方式。称赞方式一定要自然，不要让对方认为你是在刻意奉承他，否则会引起反感。

Humor method refers to the use of humor to eliminate the alert psychology of the negotiating opponents and actively participate in the negotiations, thus creating a high-profile opening negotiation atmosphere.

幽默法是指用幽默的方式来消除谈判对手的戒备心理，使其积极参与到谈判中来，从而营造出高调的开局谈判氛围。

The question teasing method is to ask some sharp questions to induce the counter-party to argue with you, and to gradually push the counter-party into the negotiating role through arguments. This method is usually used when the counter-party's negotiation enthusiasm is not high, similar to the "taunts". However, under this method it is difficult to grasp the degree. When using this method, you need to choose a good way out.

问题挑逗法是指提出一些尖锐问题诱使对方与自己争论，通过争论使对方逐渐进入谈判角色。这种方法通常是在对方谈判热情不高时采用，类似于"激将法"。但是，这种方法很难把握好火候，在使用时应慎重，要选择好退路。

(2) Low-Profile Atmosphere（低调氛围）

The low-profile atmosphere means that the negotiation atmosphere is very serious and low. One negotiating party has a negative mood and a cold attitude. The unhappy factor has become the starting atmosphere for the leading factor of the negotiation situation. If your party has a bargaining power, but does not have an absolute advantage, some of the terms of the contract do not meet your own requirements, but if you put pressure on the counter-party, and the counter-party will make efforts to make concessions on certain issues, under this circumstance, your party should create a low-profile opening atmosphere. A low-profile atmosphere will cause greater psychological pressure on negotiating parties. Under such circumstances, the party with weak psychological endurance will often make compromise. Therefore, when creating a low-profile atmosphere, you must be fully psychologically prepared and have a strong psychological endurance.

低调氛围是指谈判氛围十分严肃、低落，谈判的一方情绪消极，态度冷淡，不快因素成为谈判情势的主导因素的开局氛围。如果己方有讨价还价的砝码，但是并不占有绝对优势，合同中某些条款并未达到己方的要求，但若己方施加压力，对方会在某些问题上做出让步，在这样的情况下己方应该努力去营造低调的开局氛围。低调氛围会给谈判双方都造成较大的心理压力，在这种情况下，哪一方心理承受力弱，哪一方往往就会妥协让步。因此，在营造低调氛围时，己方一定要做好充分的心理准备并要有较强的心理承受力。

Creating a low-profile atmosphere usually involves methods of emotional aggression, silence, fatigue tactics, and accusation.

营造低调氛围通常有感情攻击法、沉默法、疲劳战术和指责法。

The emotional aggression method has the same nature as the emotional aggression method that creates a high-profile atmosphere, that is, it uses emotion-induced as a means of creating an atmosphere, but the roles of the two are opposite. In creating a high-profile atmosphere, it is necessary to arouse each other to generate positive emotions, which makes the negotiation start with a warm atmosphere. When creating a low-profile atmosphere, it is necessary to induce negative emotions, causing a low and serious atmosphere at the opening stage.

感情攻击法与营造高调氛围的感情攻击法性质相同，即都是以情感诱发作为营造氛围的手段，但两者的作用方向相反。在营造高调氛围时，要激起对方产生积极的情感，使得谈判开局充满热烈的氛围；而在营造低调氛围时，要诱发对方产生消极的情感，致使一种低沉、严肃的氛围笼罩在谈判的开始阶段。

The silence method is to cool the atmosphere of negotiation in a silent way, so as to achieve the purpose of exerting psychological pressure on the counter-party. Note that the silence mentioned here is not speaking nothing, but means that the party tries to avoid commenting on the substantive issues of the negotiations. In adopting the silence method, it is necessary to pay attention to the proper reasons for silence, and to have a degree of silence, to counterattack in time, and to force the counter-party to make concessions.

沉默法是以沉默的方式来使谈判氛围降温，从而达到向对方施加心理压力的目的。注意这里所讲的沉默并非一言不发，而是指本方尽量避免对谈判的实质问题发表意见。在采用沉默法时要注意要有恰当的沉默理由，并且沉默要有度，适时进行反击，迫使对方做出让步。

Fatigue tactics refer to repeatedly making a statement on a certain problem or a few issues, physically and psychologically exhausting the opponent, reducing the counter-party's negotiation enthusiasm, thereby achieving the purpose of controlling the counter-party and forcing it to make concessions. Generally speaking, when people are fatigued, the agility of thinking will decrease, they will be prone to errors, their enthusiasm will be lowered, their work mood will be low, and they will easily succumb to others' opinions. If you want to adopt this kind of tactics, you should prepare more questions in advance, and they should be reasonable. Each question should play the role of letting the opponents get tired. At the same time, listen carefully to the other's words, seize the mistakes and record them as the bargaining chip that forces the opponent to give in.

疲劳战术是指对某个问题或某几个问题反复进行陈述，从生理和心理上使对手疲惫不堪，降低对方谈判的热情，从而达到控制对方并迫使其做出让步的目的。一般来讲，人在疲劳的状态下，思维的敏捷程度会下降，容易出现错误，热情降低，工作情绪不高，比较容易屈从于别人的看法。如果要采用这种战术，应提前多准备一些问题，而且问题要合理，每个问题都要能起到让对手疲惫的作用，同时要认真聆听对方的每一句话，抓住错误并记录下来，作为迫使对方做出让步的筹码。

The accusation method refers to the blame for a certain mistake or ceremonial mistake of the counter-party to make it feel guilty, thus achieving the purpose of creating a low-profile atmosphere and forcing the counter-party to give in.

指责法是指对对方的某项错误或礼仪失误严加指责，使其感到内疚，从而达到营造低调氛围，迫使对方做出让步的目的。

(3) Natural Atmosphere (自然氛围)

The natural atmosphere refers to the stable atmosphere of the negotiating parties, neither warm nor depressed. The natural atmosphere does not need to be deliberately created, and many negotiations begin in this atmosphere. Since the information conveyed by the negotiating parties in the natural atmosphere is more accurate and true than the information conveyed in the high-profile atmosphere and the low-profile atmosphere, this kind of negotiation opening atmosphere is more conducive to understanding each other's situation. When the negotiating party knows little about the counter-party's situation and the counter-party's negotiating attitude is not clear, it is more advantageous to seek a dialogue in a calm atmosphere.

自然氛围是指谈判各方情绪平稳，既不热烈，也不消沉的开局氛围。自然氛围无须刻意地去营造，许多谈判都是在这种氛围中开始的。由于谈判双方在自然氛围中传达的信息比在高调氛围和低调氛围中传达的信息要准确、真实，所以这种谈判开局氛围更有利于摸清对方情况。当谈判一方对谈判对手的情况知之甚少，对手的谈判态度不甚明朗时，谋求在平缓的氛围中开始对话是比较有利的。

When creating a natural atmosphere, you need to pay attention to behavior and etiquette. At the same time, you should listen more and remember more. Don't argue with the counter-party about an issue too early. You should prepare a few more questions. The way to ask questions should be natural. For the counter-party's question, if you can make a positive answer, you must answer it positively. If you can't answer it, you should use the appropriate method to avoid it.

营造自然氛围时需要注意行为、礼仪，同时要多听、多记，不要与对方就某一问题过早发生争论，要多准备几个问题，询问方式要自然。对于对方的提问，能做正面回答的一定要正面回答，不能回答的，要采用恰当方式进行回避。

It should be noted that the atmosphere of negotiation is not static. In the beginning of the negotiation, negotiators must create an atmosphere suitable for their own negotiations according to their needs. However, the formation of the negotiation atmosphere is not entirely the result of human factors, and objective conditions will have an important impact on the atmosphere of negotiations, such as holidays, weather conditions, and emergencies. Therefore, when creating a negotiating atmosphere, we must pay attention to the influence of external objective factors.

需要注意的是，谈判氛围并非一成不变的。在谈判开局阶段，谈判人员要根据其需要来营造适于己方的谈判氛围。但是，谈判氛围的形成并非完全是人为因素的结果，客观条件也会对谈判氛围产生重要的影响，如节假日、天气情况、突发事件等。因此，在营造谈判氛围时，一定要注意外界客观因素的影响。

3. Mapping Work（摸底工作）

In addition to understanding the negotiation goals and needs of your own, it is more important to understand and investigate the situation of the counter-party in details, including the strength of the counter-party, the needs and sincerity of the counter-party, the situation of the counter-party's negotiating team and the principles that the counter-party must adhere to in the negotiation.

摸底工作除了了解清楚己方的谈判目标和需求外，更重要的是对谈判对手的情况做详细的了解和调查，包括谈判对手的实力、谈判对手的需求和诚意、对方谈判小组人员的状况以及对方在谈判中必须坚持的原则。

(1) The Strength of the Counter-party（谈判对手的实力）

The strength of the counter-party includes the history, social influence, capital accumulation and investment status, technical equipment level of the company, as well as the variety, quality, quantity of the product.

谈判对手的实力包括其公司的历史、社会影响、资本积累与投资状况、技术装备水平，以及产品的品种、质量、数量等。

(2) The Needs and Sincerity of the Counter-party（谈判对手的需求与诚意）

Your own party could figure out the counter-party's needs and sincerity by understanding the counter-party's cooperative intention, whether its desire for cooperation is sincere or not, how urgent it is to realize the cooperation, how much choice it has for its partners, and whether it has any contacts with other regions or enterprises of your own party. In short, we must understand their needs, sincerity, credibility, ability and style as widely as possible.

己方可以通过了解对方同己方合作的意图、它的合作愿望真诚与否、它对实现这种合作的迫切程度、它对合作伙伴有多大的选择余地以及对方与己方的其他地区或企业是否有过往来等方面来摸清对方的需求和诚意。总之，己方要尽可能广泛地了解对方的需求、诚意、信誉、能力与作风等。

(3) The Situation of the Counter-party's Negotiating Team（对方谈判小组人员的状况）

It includes the composition of the other negotiating team, the respective identities of the team mem-bers, status, traits, hobbies and negotiating experience, the ability, authority, strengths and weaknesses of the chief representative, past successes and failures, and attitudes and inclinations towards the negotiations. Depending on the nature of the negotiations and the requirements, sometimes it is necessary to collect more in-depth, detailed and targeted intelligence information, such as the ideas and plans of the negotiators of the counter-party, the relationship between the negotiating members, the main opponents of the negotiations, and the determination of the object that may be won, the relationship between the person in charge and the person behind the scenes. Sometimes it is necessary to examine the case of the counter-party's previous failures in order to understand the other's thinking habits, behaviors, psychological orientations and its own needs. These will provide clues for you to find out the counter-party.

包括对方谈判小组人员的构成，他们各自的身份、地位、性格、爱好和谈判经验，首席代表的能力、权限、特长、弱点、以往的成功与失败的经历以及对谈判的态度和倾向意见等。根据谈判性质、要求的不同，有时还需要搜集一些更为深入、细致、针对性强的情报信息，如对方各谈判人员的想法和打算、各谈判成员相互之间的关系、谈判的主要对手和可能争取的对象的确定、主谈人与幕后操纵者之间的关系等。有时还必须考察对方以往谈判失败的案例，以便从中了解对方的思维习惯、行为方式、心理倾向和自身需求等情况。这些都会为己方摸清对方情况提供线索。

(4) The Principles That the Counter-party Must Adhere to in the Negotiation（对方在谈判中必须坚持的原则）

The party should try to find out the principles that the counter-party must adhere to in this negotiation and the matters that can make concessions. In this way, in the substantive consultation stage, we can avoid austerity and strive for the best interests of ourselves.

己方应设法探求对方在此次谈判中所必须坚持的原则以及可以做出让步的事项。这样在实质性磋商阶段就可以避重就轻，为己方争取最大利益。

In this way, the negotiating parties will inevitably proceed in a very clever way. When the parties are involved in substantive negotiations, they should make full use of this stage to obtain the counter-party's information. At the same time, you need to pay attention to the negotiators who are honest, candid, and show a tendency to cooperate. Communicate and cooperate with them, you will get more information. At the same time, you should also pay attention to listening to the voice and understand the potential information of the counter-party's conversation. This information may reflect the counter-party's real intentions. By assessment works, you can get a general idea of where the counter-party's interests are. At this time, you should further discover the possibility of mutual profit. The party can make some preliminary initiatives on the purpose, plan, and procedure of the negotiations. Since this is a question that does not involve or rarely involves the interests of both parties, it is often possible to reach an agreement soon after frank exchanges and negotiations with the counter-party. In this way, one can take the sincere and harmonious atmosphere established before to the serious and cooperative working atmosphere.

这种摸底，谈判方必然都会以十分巧妙的方式进行。双方在转入实质性谈判之前，应该充分利用此阶段去获取对方的这些信息。同时，需要留意对方正直、坦诚和表现出合作倾向的谈判人员，与他们沟通合作，会得到更多的信息；同时也要注意听话外音，领会对方谈话的潜在信息，这些信息可能反映了对方的真实意图。通过摸底，可以大致了解对方利益所在，这时己方应该进一步去发现双方共同获利的可能性。己方可以就谈判的目的、计划、进度等提出一些初步的倡议。由于这是一个不涉及或很少涉及双方利益的问题，所以与对方坦率地交流协商，往往很快就可以达成一致。这样，己方就可以顺势将之前建立的诚挚的、融洽的氛围引向认真与合作的工作氛围。

Ⅱ Steps in the Opening Stage（谈判开局阶段的步骤）

1. Dissemination of the Agenda（分发议程）

Prior to the commencement of the negotiations, the owner shall print and bind the corresponding number of copies of the agenda and place it on each negotiator's desktop.

在谈判开始前，主方应打印并装订好相应份数的议程，并放置在每名谈判人员桌面上。

2. Exchanging Opinions among Negotiating Parties（交换意见）

After establishing a good atmosphere for negotiation, the negotiators take seat and officially start negotiations.

在建立了良好的谈判氛围后，谈判人员相继落座并正式开始谈判。

In the opening stage, the negotiators try to focus on the "4P", namely "Purpose", "Plan", "Procedure", "Personality". If the negotiators naturally focus on the "4P" at the beginning of the negotiation, they will get a satisfactory start.

在开局阶段，谈判人员尽量将话题集中在"4P"上，即"Purpose"（目的）、"Plan"（计划）、"Pace"（进度）、"Personality"（人格魅力）。如果谈判人员在开局时把话题很自然地集中在"4P"上，就会得到令人满意的开局结果。

International business negotiators sometimes fall into a deadlock at the beginning because their goals and countermeasures are far apart. At this time, the negotiating parties should strive to reach an agreement on the purpose, plan, procedure and personality of the talks. This is the basic strategy and skill for mastering the start-up process. Practice has proved that this is suitable for various negotiations. Negotiators should consciously create a sense of "consistency" so as not to create a stalemate in the beginning of the negotiation and create conditions for a good opening atmosphere.

国际商务谈判方有时会因为各自的目标、对策相差甚远而在一开局就会陷入僵局。这时，双方应努力先就会谈的目的、计划、进度和人格魅力达成一致意见，这是掌握好开局过程的基本策略和技巧。实践证明，这样做适合于各种谈判。谈判者应有意识地创造出"一致"感，以免造成开局便陷入僵局的局面，为建立良好的开局氛围创造条件。

When meeting for the first time, the negotiators must first introduce each other to the participants in the negotiations, and then further clarify the objectives to be achieved by the negotiations. This goal should be the cooperation goal pursued by negotiating parties. At the same time, they should negotiate the agenda, progress, discipline to be observed and issues such as the obligation to perform together. The most ideal way to lead a negotiating topic in business negotiations is to talk about topics that are easy for both parties to agree on in a relaxed and pleasant tone. For example, "We will first determine the interview process. Do you agree?" "I want to discuss with you about the topics of today's talks, okay?" On the surface, these questions seem to be insignificant, but these requirements are the most likely to cause the counter-party's affirmative reply, and this affirmative response will produce a feeling of "consensus", which in turn creates an atmosphere of "consensus". With this kind of atmosphere, it is easier to reach an agreement and the negotiations will proceed smoothly.

初次见面，谈判人员首先要相互介绍参与谈判的人员，然后进一步明确谈判要达到的目标，这个目标应是共同追求的合作目标；同时，谈判各方要磋商谈判的议程、进度、需要遵守的纪律和共同履行的义务等问题。在商务谈判中最理想的引出谈判话题的方式是以轻松愉快的语气先谈一些双方容易达成一致意见的话题。例如，"我们先把会谈程序确定下来，你同意吗?""我想先与你商量一下今天会谈的议题，好吗?"从表面上看，这些问话似乎无足轻重，但这些要求最容易引起对方肯定的答复，而这种肯定的答复就会产生一种"意见一致"的感觉，进而创造出"意见一致"的氛围。有了这种氛围，就比较容易达成协议，谈判也就会顺利进行了。

3. Opening Statements（开场陈述）

In order to find out the counter-party's principles and attitudes, the opening statement is that the negotiating parties separately clarify their own views and principles on relevant issues, not specific issues, but principled issues, which can be used as opening statements and initiatives. The focus is on the interests of your own side. The time of the statement should be equally divided between the two parties. It is forbidden to monopolize the entire presentation time. One should appropriately express the intention and emotional inclination. In terms of words and attitudes, minimize the possibility of causing anxiety, dissatisfaction and anger. The content of the speech should be as short and focused as possible.

为了摸清对方的原则和态度，开场陈述即谈判各方分别阐明己方对有关问题的看法和原则，不是具体的问题，而是原则性的问题，可做开场陈述和倡议。其重点是己方的利益，陈述的时间双方应尽量平分秋色，切忌独占整个陈述时间，恰如其分地把意图、感情倾向表达出来即可。在用词和态度上，尽可能减少让对方产生忧虑、不满和气愤的可能性。发言内容应尽量简短且重点突出。

For the counter-party's statement, firstly, you must first pay attention to listening, and concentrate on thinking. Don't spend your energy on finding countermeasures. Secondly, know the contents of the counter-party's statement. If you have any questions, you can ask them. The third is to sum up and be good at understanding the counter-party's key issues. After the parties to the negotiations have completed their statements, an initiative is needed, which is a statement that leads the negotiating party to seek common interests.

对于对方的陈述，己方首先要注意倾听，听的时候要思想集中，不要把精力花在寻找对策上；其次要知晓对方陈述的内容，如有疑问，可向对方提问；三是归纳，要善于理解对方的关键问题。谈判各方陈述完毕后，需做出倡议，即一种能把谈判方引向寻求共同利益的陈述。

At the time of the initiative, the negotiators propose various ideas and solutions to the problem, and then set up a bridge to the transaction between the assumption and the reality of meeting the commercial standards.

在做出倡议时，谈判方提出各种设想和解决问题的方案，然后在设想和符合商业标准的现实之间，搭起一座通向成交的桥梁。

The main contents of the opening statement include: first, state your own understanding of the problem, that is, the issue you believe should be covered by the negotiation; second, state the interests of yourself, that is, the interests that you hope to achieve through this negotiation, especially explain which aspects are your own vital interests; third, state the conditions on which you can make concessions to the other, that is, how you can contribute to the mutual interests of the parties involved; and finally, state your own positions, including the result of previous co-operation, the credibility that you have enjoyed in the other market and the opportunities or obstacles that may arise in the future cooperation.

开场陈述的主要内容包括，第一，陈述己方对问题的理解，即己方认为这次谈判应涉及的问题；第二，陈述己方的利益，即希望通过这次谈判己方所要取得的利益，尤其要阐明哪些方面是己方至关重要的利益；第三，陈述己方可向对方做出让步的条件，即己方可以采取何种方式为共同的利益做出贡献；第四，陈述己方的立场，包括双方以前合作的结果、己方在对方市场上所享有的信誉以及今后合作中可能出现的机会或障碍。

The sequence of opening statements includes striving for the first statement or keeping silence. Try to make a statement first, that is, the negotiating party who speaks first can make full use of the opportunity to explain its own views and insinuate the counter-party's goals. To remain silence, the negotiating party can first listen to the counter-party's statement in order to understand its interests and expectations.

开场陈述的顺序包括争取先做陈述和保持沉默两种。争取先做陈述，即首先发言的谈判方可以充分利用机会说明己方的观点，对对方的目标进行影射。保持沉默，即谈判一方可先听取对方的陈述，借以了解对方的利益所在及对方的期望。

The length of the general opening statement is determined by the nature of the negotiation and the length of the negotiation period. In general, it should be appropriate to control within 5% of the total negotiation time. For up to 5 hours of negotiations, 15 minutes can be used for the opening statement.

一般开场陈述的时间长短要根据谈判性质和谈判期限的长短来决定。一般来讲，控制在总的谈判时间的5%之内比较合适。如长达5个小时的谈判，可用15分钟做开场陈述。

Ⅲ Negotiation Strategy in the Opening Stage（谈判开局阶段的策略）

1. Factors to Be Considered in Creating an Atmosphere（营造开局谈判氛围应考虑的因素）

Negotiations of different contents and types require different atmospheres. A high-profile atmosphere will lead to the agreement, and a low-profile atmosphere will cause great psychological pressure on both sides, which requires different starting strategies and skills to correspond. In combination with different negotiating projects, several factors need to be considered when choosing different ways to create an atmosphere for opening negotiations.

不同内容和类型的谈判，需要营造不同的谈判氛围。高调的氛围会促进协议的达成，而低调的氛围则会给双方造成巨大的心理压力，这就要求有不同的开局策略及技巧与之对应。结合不同的谈判项目，在选择不同的营造开局谈判氛围的方法时需要考虑几个因素。

(1) Relationship between the Negotiating Parties (谈判各方之间的关系)

Choose different opening atmosphere, language, posture and content for negotiation according to the relationship between the parties to the negotiation. If the negotiating parties have had business dealings and the relationship is very good, then this kind of friendly relationship should be used as the basis for negotiations between the two parties; if the negotiating parties have had business dealings, but the relationship is just OK, then the goal of the opening is still striving to create a friendly and easy-going atmosphere; if the negotiating parties have had business dealings, but their own impressions of the other parties are not good, then the atmosphere of the opening stage should be serious and dignified; if the negotiating parties have not any business contacts, this is the first business contact, then in the opening stage, the negotiating parties should strive to create a friendly and sincere atmosphere to dilute and eliminate the strangeness of all parties, and the resulting defense and even hostility to lay a good foundation for substantive negotiations.

根据谈判各方之间的关系来选择不同的开局氛围、语言、态度及内容进行谈判。如果谈判各方曾经有业务往来，并且关系很好，那么，就应将这种友好关系作为双方谈判的基础；如果谈判各方虽然曾经有过业务往来，但关系一般，那么开局的目标仍然是要争取营造一个比较友好、随和的氛围；如果谈判各方虽然曾经有过业务往来，但己方对对方的印象不佳，那么开局阶段的氛围应是严肃、凝重的；如果谈判各方在过去没有任何业务往来，本次为第一次业务接触，那么在开局阶段，应力争营造一个友好、真诚的氛围，以淡化和消除各方的陌生感，以及由此带来的防备甚至敌对的心理，从而为实质性谈判奠定良好的基础。

(2) The Relationship between the Individual Negotiators (各谈判人员个人之间的关系)

Business negotiation is an act of exchange of ideas between negotiators, and the personal feelings of negotiators will have a great impact on the process and effect of the entire negotiation. If the negotiators of the parties have had contact in the past and have formed a certain friendship, then they can talk about friendship in the opening stage, and also recall the past interactions, or talk about the experience after the separation, and can also inquire the family's situation to enhance the personal feelings. Practice has proved that once negotiators have established good personal feelings, it is relatively easy to make demands, make concessions, and reach an agreement. It usually also reduces costs and improves negotiation efficiency.

商务谈判是谈判人员相互之间思想交流的一种行为，而谈判人员个人之间的感情会对整个谈判的过程和效果产生很大的影响。如果各方谈判人员过去有过接触，并且结下了一定的友谊，那么在开局阶段即可畅谈友谊，同时也可以回忆过去交往的情景，或讲述离别后的经历，还可以询问对方家庭的情况，以增进双方之间的个人感情。实践证明，一旦谈判人员之间建立了良好的私人感情，那么，提出要求、做出让步、达成协议就相对比较容易了。通常还可降低成本，提高谈判效率。

(3) Negotiating Power of the Parties Involved（谈判各方的实力）

The so-called negotiating strength refers to the comprehensive strength of the negotiators in the negotiation relative to the counter-party, including not only the objective strength of the negotiators (such as the economic strength, technology level, uniqueness, procedures, etc.), but also the psychological strength of the negotiators compared to the counter-party.

所谓谈判实力，是指谈判者在谈判中相对于谈判对手所拥有的综合能力，不仅包括谈判者所拥有的客观实力（如企业经济实力、科技水平、独特性、规程等），而且包括谈判者与对方相比所拥有的心理实力。

When negotiating parties have the same negotiating strength, in order to prevent strengthening the counter-party's alert mentality from the beginning and arousing the hostile sentiment and extending to the substantive stage, causing the two sides to fight for each other's high and low levels, resulting in a losing outcome, in the opening stage, we must strive to create a friendly, relaxed and harmonious atmosphere. If your strength of the negotiation is stronger than the counter-party, in order to enable the counter-party to be aware of this and will not have high expectations in the negotiations to create a deterrent effect without scaring the counter-party, in the opening stage, in terms of language and posture, you must be polite and friendly, and fully demonstrate your self-confidence and momentum. However, if your strength of the negotiation is weaker than the counter-party, in order not to let the counter-party gain the upper hand in the momentum, thus affecting the subsequent substantive negotiations, in the opening stage, it is necessary for you to express friendship and active cooperation on the one hand in language and posture and on the other hand behave calmly, and talk generously with full confidence so that the counter-party will not despise you.

当谈判方谈判实力相当时，为了防止一开始就强化对方的戒备心理和激起对方的敌对情绪，以致这种氛围延伸到实质性阶段而造成双方为了互争高低，造成两败俱伤的结局，在开局阶段，就要力求营造一个友好、轻松、和谐的氛围。如果己方谈判实力明显强于对方，为了使对方能够清醒地意识到这一点，在谈判中不抱过高的期望值，从而产生威慑作用，同时又不至于将对方吓跑，在开局阶段，就要在语言和姿态上，既要表现得礼貌友好，又要充分显示己方的自信和气势。但如果己方谈判实力弱于对方，为了不使对方在气势上占上风，从而影响后面的实质谈判，在开局阶段，就要在语言和姿态上，一方面要表示友好，积极合作，另一方面也要充满信心，举止沉稳，谈吐大方，使对方不至于轻视己方。

2. Common Negotiation Strategy（常用谈判策略）

(1) Listening and Observing（察言观色）

As the saying goes, everything is difficult at the beginning. The same is true for negotiations. When the negotiators take their own interests and the speculation of the other side to sit on the negotiating table, the real negotiations begin. Usually, the negotiators will make all kinds of positive efforts in order to make the negotiation start in a relaxed, harmonious, friendly and sincere atmosphere.

常言道，万事开头难。谈判也是一样，当谈判方带着彼此利益上的需求和对另一方的揣测心理坐在谈判桌前时，真正的谈判就开始了。通常，谈判方都会做出各种积极的努力，以使谈判开局处于一种轻松、和谐、友善、诚恳的氛围之中。

In the opening stage of the negotiations, the negotiators will pay more attention to the other's words and deeds, but also pay more attention to their own words and deeds. Sophisticated negotiators will carefully observe the other's words and deeds, and even each subtle expression on the other's face, because every subtle expression may conveys some kind of information.

在谈判的开局阶段，谈判方都会比较留意对方的言行，同时也更注重自己的一言一行。老练的谈判者会细心地观察对方的一言一行，甚至对方脸部的每一个微妙的表情，因为每一个细微的神情变化都可能传递着某种信息。

Since the subjective attitude of the people influences the atmosphere of negotiation, the atmosphere of the negotiation is not only formed at the moment when the two sides sit on the negotiating table, but also formed during the negotiation process. Therefore, the negotiating party must have a very vigilant attitude, pay attention to the words and deeds of the opponent, and the information transmitted by every move, because every message conveyed by the opponent, whether intentional or not, can be analyzed and used for one's own. Paying attention to and studying the information conveyed by the other's body language is of great significance for the smooth progress of business negotiations.

由于人的主观态度影响着谈判氛围，谈判开局的氛围不只是在双方坐在谈判桌前的瞬间形成的，同时也是在谈判过程中形成的。所以谈判方必须有着十分警惕的心态，注意对手的一言一行、一举一动所传递的信息，因为对手传达出的每一个信息，无论有意或无意，都是可以经过分析而为己方所用的。留意并研究对方的身体语言所传递的信息，对于商务谈判的顺利进行有着非常重要的意义。

If you can negotiate in a relaxed atmosphere, it is naturally ideal, but in fact it is difficult to really do it. In most cases, you must be careful to observe the counter-party and constantly think about how to influence their strategy. Regardless of whether the message conveyed by the counter-party is expressed through words or limbs, one must respond to it.

如果能在轻松的氛围中进行谈判，那自然最理想不过了，但事实上很难真正做到轻松。在大多数情况下，必须时刻谨慎地注意观察对方，并不断地思考如何影响对方的策略。不论对方传达的信息是经由言语还是肢体来表达，己方都必须对此做出反应。

In short, the negotiators should be decent in words and deeds in the opening stage; they should be neither humble nor pushy and emotionally stable; and they should be sincere, talk less and watch more and use suitable way to induce the counter-party.

总之，谈判者在开局阶段应做到言行得体，不卑不亢；情绪平稳，态度真诚，不唯唯诺诺；少说多看，启诱得法。

(2) Consultative Opening Strategy（协商式开局策略）

The consultative opening strategy refers to the way of "consulting" and "affirming" at the beginning of the negotiations to gain a good impression from the counter-party, creating or establishing a feeling of "consistency" in the negotiation, so that the negotiating parties will continue to push the negotiations deep into the core issues in a happy and friendly atmosphere.

协商式开局策略是指在谈判开始时以“协商”和“肯定”的语言获得对方的好感，创造双方“一致”的感觉，从而使谈判各方能在友好、愉快的氛围中继续深入谈判核心问题。

Modern psychology research shows that people usually have a good impression of those who are consistent with their ideas, and are willing to adjust their ideas according to those people's views. This research conclusion is the psychological basis of the consultative opening strategy.

现代心理学研究表明，人通常会对那些与其想法一致的人产生好感，并愿意将自己的想法按照那些人的观点进行调整。这一研究结论正是协商式开局策略的心理学基础。

There are many specific ways to use a consultative opening strategy. For example, in the beginning of the negotiation, seek the counter-party's views in a consultative manner, and then express approval of their views and work in accordance with their views. What should be noted when using this method is that the question used to solicit the opinions of the counter-party should be an insignificant problem, that is, one party's opinion on the question will not affect the specific interests of the counter-party. In addition, in favor of the counter-party's opinions, the attitude should not be too flattering to let the counter-party feel that they are out of respect, not flattery.

运用协商式开局策略的具体方式有很多，例如在谈判开局时，用一种协商的口吻来征求对方的意见，然后，对其意见表示赞同或认可，并按照其意见工作。运用这种方式时应该注意的是，用于征求对方意见的问题应是无关紧要的问题，也就是一方对该问题的意见不会影响到另一方的具体利益。另外，在赞成对方意见时，态度不要过于献媚，要让对方感觉到自己是出于尊重，而不是奉承。

(3) Reserved Opening Strategy（保留式开局策略）

The reserved opening strategy refers to not making a thorough and exact answer to the key questions raised by the counter-party at the beginning of the negotiation, but retaining it, thus creating a mystery to the counter-party to attract the counter-party to negotiate in depth. When adopting a reserved opening strategy, do not violate the basic principle of honesty on business negotiation. The information transmitted to the counter-party may be fuzzy, but it cannot be false. Otherwise, it will lead to a very embarrassing situation.

保留式开局策略是指在谈判开局时，对对方提出的关键问题不做彻底、确切的回答，而是有所保留，从而给对方造成神秘感，以吸引对方深入谈判。在采用保留式开局策略时，不要违反商务谈判的以诚信为本的基本原则。向对方传递的信息可以是模糊信息，但不能是虚假信息，否则，会使己方陷入非常难堪的局面。

The reserved opening strategy applies to a low-profile atmosphere and a natural atmosphere, not to a high-profile atmosphere. It can also transform other negotiating atmosphere into a low-profile atmosphere. For example, there was a Japanese company that wanted to invest in processing oolong tea in China and then sold it back to Japan. To this end, the Japanese company contacted a company in Fujian Province of China, and the two sides exchanged representatives to negotiate on investment issues. At the beginning of the negotiation, the Japanese representative asked: "What is the strength of your company? We are not very familiar with it. Can you please tell us about it to increase our confidence in cooperation?" The Chinese representative replied: "I don't know what aspects of your strength include, but one thing I can tell you clearly is that we can't make a plane, but we are experts in making tea. Our tea making technology is world-class. Fujian Province has rich tea resources. Our company can be said to be of a 'favorable location'. If your company cooperates with us, it will definitely be more satisfied than cooperation with other companies." The Chinese representative adopted a reserved opening strategy for the Japanese issue, without direct answer, but turning to the other side that clearly shows that our tea quality and tea making technology is absolutely first class.

保留式开局策略适用于低调氛围和自然氛围，而不适用于高调氛围。保留式开局策略还可以将其他谈判氛围转换为低调氛围。例如，曾经有一个日本公司想要在中国投资加工乌龙茶，然后返销日本。为此，日本公司与我国福建省的一个公司进行了接触，双方互派代表就投资问题进行了谈判。谈判一开始，日方代表就问道："贵公司的实力到底如何，我们还不是很了解，能否请您向我们介绍一下以增加我方进行合作的信心?"中方代表回答道："不知贵方所指实力包括哪些方面，但有一点我可以明确地告诉您，造飞机我们肯定不行，但是制茶我们是内行，我们的制茶技术是世界一流的。福建省有着丰富的茶叶资源，我公司可以说是'近水楼台'。贵公司如果与我们合作，肯定会比与其他公司合作来得满意。"中方代表对日方问题的回答就采用了保留式开局策略，没有正面直接回答，而是转而向对方明确表明了我方的茶叶质量和制茶技术是绝对一流的。

(4) Candid Opening Strategy (坦诚式开局策略)

The candid opening strategy is to open up the situation for the negotiations by presenting their views or ideas to the counter-party in an open and honest manner. This kind of opening strategy is more suitable for negotiating parties with long-term business cooperation relationship, and the previous cooperation is satisfactory, and they are familiar with each other. They do not need too much polite formula and diplomatic rhetoric, which save time. One party directly and frankly propose its own views and requirements, which in turn can make the counter-party have a sense of trust in one's own side.

坦诚式开局策略是指以开诚布公的方式向谈判对手陈述自己的观点或想法，从而为谈判打开局面。这种开局策略比较适合于有长期业务合作关系的谈判方，并且以往的合作都比较满意，彼此又比较了解，不用太多的客套，减少了许多外交辞令，节省了时间。直接坦率地提出己方的观点、要求，反而更能使对方对己方产生信任感。

When adopting a candid strategy, consider a variety of factors, such as your identity, relationship with the counter-party, and the situation at the time. Negotiators with weaker strengths can also adopt a candid opening strategy. When the strength of your own side is obviously not as good as the other side and both sides are well aware of this, you show your weaknesses frankly and let it be considered. This can also express your sincerity towards the negotiations and also show your confidence and ability in the negotiations..

采用坦诚式开局策略时，要综合考虑各种因素，例如，自己的身份、与对方的关系、当时的谈判形势等。实力较弱的谈判方也可采用坦诚式开局策略。当己方的谈判实力明显不如对方且双方都对此心知肚明时，己方坦率地表明自己的弱点，让对方加以考虑，更能表明己方对谈判的真诚，同时也表明了对谈判的信心和能力。

For example, Company A, a major customer in Indonesia, and Company B in Guangzhou discussed the procurement of motorcycles by the Indonesian government. Company A arrived in Guangzhou with 10 representatives of the Indonesian government on March 2, 2018. Company B asked the representatives of Company A and the Indonesian government sincerely in the meeting room the next day that they planned to arrange the two-day reception arrangement as follows: (1) Have a meeting in the company's meeting room in the morning to watch the promotional video of Company A and Company B, recommend 2-3 motorcycles styles, and introduce the assembly, after-sale service and free accessories of motorcycles exported to Indonesia. (2) In the afternoon, representatives of Company A and Indonesian government visit the motorcycle factory and have a motorcycle trial riding experience. (3) Arrange a one-day trip to famous attractions in Guangzhou. Company A and 10 representatives were very satisfied with it, and had a good first impression on Company B. The negotiation was very smooth, and the government ordered 1,000 motorcycle parts from Company B. In this case, it is the first time that Company B's representative talked with the government representatives. He understood their working habits, and took a slightly lower stance to show respect to government personnel, so that they felt that they were treated with courteousness, thereby breaking through their psychological barrier. Company B knew that government procurement is not very picky about price, but more attention is paid to technical training, after-sales service, and free accessories. Company B's candid opening strategy has won the opportunity at the beginning.

例如，位于印度尼西亚的大客户 A 公司与广州 B 公司商谈印度尼西亚政府采购摩托车事宜，A 公司在 2018 年 3 月 2 日与印度尼西亚政府代表 10 人一同到达了广州。B 公司第二天在会议室商谈时，非常诚恳地询问 A 公司及印度尼西亚政府代表，打算将两天的接待计划安排如下：(1) 上午先到公司会议室座谈：看 A 公司和 B 公司的宣传片，推荐 2~3 款摩托车，介绍出口摩托车到印度尼西亚之后的组装、售后情况、免费配件的情况。(2) 下午安排 A 公司和 10 名代表参观摩托车工厂，并进行摩托车试骑体验。(3) 安排广州著名景点一日游。A 公司和 10 名代表对此非常满意，并对 B 公司的第一印象很好，随后商谈非常顺利，将政府 1 000 台摩托车散件订单给了 B 公司。在此案例中，B 公司的代表第一次和政府代表商谈。他了解政府人员的工作习惯，采取稍低姿态对政府人员以示尊重，让政府人员感受到礼遇，从而突破防备心理。B 公司知道政府采购对价格不是很挑剔，但是对技术培训、售后服务、免费配件关注更多。B 公司采用的坦诚式开局策略使其在一开始就赢得了先机。

(5) Offensive Opening Strategy（进攻式开局策略）

The offensive opening strategy refers to expressing the strong posture of one party through language or behavior, so as to obtain the necessary respect of the counter-party, and to create a psychological advantage, so that the negotiation can proceed smoothly. It is necessary to be cautious in adopting an offensive opening strategy, because trying to show your strength during the start of the negotiations will bring the start of the negotiations into an arrogant atmosphere, which is extremely unfavorable for the further development of the negotiations.

进攻式开局策略是指通过语言或行为来表达己方强硬的姿态，从而获得谈判对手必要的尊重，并借以制造心理优势，使得谈判顺利地进行下去。采用进攻式开局策略一定要谨慎，因为在谈判开局阶段就设法显示自己的实力，会使谈判开局处于剑拔弩张的氛围，对谈判的进一步发展极为不利。

The offensive opening strategy is usually only used in this case, that is, the counter-party is deliberately creating a low-profile atmosphere, which is very unfavorable to your own bargaining. If you do not reverse this atmosphere, it will damage your own tangible interests.

进攻式开局策略通常只在这种情况下使用，即发现对方在刻意制造低调氛围，这种氛围对己方的讨价还价十分不利，如果不把这种氛围扭转过来，将损害己方的切实利益。

The offensive opening strategy can reverse the low-profile atmosphere that is not conducive to one's own, and change it into a natural atmosphere or a high-profile atmosphere. However, an offensive opening strategy may also bring the negotiations into a deadlock.

进攻式开局策略可以扭转不利于己方的低调氛围，使之转变成自然氛围或高调氛围。但是，进攻式开局策略也可能使谈判陷入僵局。

(6) Picky Opening Strategy（挑剔式开局策略）

The picky opening strategy refers to the blame for an opponent's mistake or errors of etiquette when starting to make him feel guilty, thus achieving the purpose of creating a low-profile atmosphere and forcing the counter-party to make concessions. A Brazilian company went to the United States to purchase complete sets of equipment. Members of the Brazilian negotiating team lost time because of shopping on the streets. When they reached the negotiating place, they were 45 minutes later than the scheduled time. The US representatives were extremely dissatisfied with this. It took a long time to accuse the Brazilian representatives of not complying with time and having no credit. They mentioned that if things keep going like this, many jobs will be difficult to cooperate in the future. Waste of time is a waste of resources and a waste of money. The Brazilian representatives felt guilty and had to apologize to the US representatives. After the start of the negotiations, it seems that the US representatives were still worried about the late arrival of the Brazilian representatives. At one time, the Brazilian representatives were helpless, their speeches were passive and they were unwilling to bargain with the US representatives. They did not calm down and seriously considered many demands put forward by the US, and signed the contract in a hurry. After the contract was signed, the Brazilian representatives calmed down when their minds were no longer hot, only to find that they had suffered a great loss, but it was too late. This is a typical picky opening strategy: the US side caught the problem of being late, constantly blamed it, forced the Brazilian side to make concessions and ultimately achieved its goal.

挑剔式开局策略是指开局时，对对手的某项错误或礼仪失误严加指责，使其感到内疚，从而达到营造低调氛围，迫使对方做出让步的目的。巴西的一个公司到美国去采购成套设备。巴西谈判小组成员因为上街购物耽误了时间。当他们到达谈判地点时，比预定时间晚了45分钟。美方代表对此极为不满，花了很长时间来指责巴西代表不遵守时间，没有信用，如果老这样下去的话，以后很多工作很难合作，浪费时间就是浪费资源、浪费金钱。对此巴西代表感到理亏，只好不停地向美方代表道歉。谈判开始以后，美方似乎还对巴西代表来迟一事耿耿于怀，一时间弄得巴西代表手足无措，说话处处被动，无心与美方代表讨价还价，对美方提出的许多要求也没有静下心来认真考虑，匆匆忙忙就签订了合同。等到合同签订以后，巴西代表平静下来、头脑不再发热时才发现自己吃了大亏，上了美方的当，但为时已晚。这就是典型的挑剔式开局策略：美方抓住对方迟到这一问题，不断地指责、挑剔对方的问题，迫使巴西方因愧疚而做出让步，最终达到己方目的。

For another example, during the Canton Fair in 2018, customer NG from African Motorcycle Company talked with Company FLING in Guangdong. As soon as Company NG's representatives entered the meeting room, they began to be picky about the wrong parts and components sent by Company FLING in the previous order. Company NG thought that it was necessary to bring foldable left and right rear pedals. Company FLING stated that the status sheet signed by both parties did not specify that the left and right rear pedals should be foldable, and that all terms and conditions should be subject to written signature. Company NG stated that it would not place further orders without resending parts. Company FLING is worried about losing the customer, saying that the occurrence of this wrong accessory is not wanted by both parties, and also hoped to work with Company NG to find a way to properly resolve this matter. If Company NG can place a certain number of orders in the future, Company FLING can give Company NG some accessories for free and give 20% discount on new orders. Company NG was very satisfied with Company FLING's response and signed a new contract of 2,000 units. Company NG tried to make things difficult for the counter-party by accusing Company FLING for sending the wrong accessories to Company NG in order to achieve the purpose of getting free accessories and preferential prices for new orders, Company FLING did not bother Company NG to make oral or written confirmations. After realizing Company NG's true intentions, they firstly eased the customer's emotions and expressed that they hoped to work with the customer to find a way to solve the problem, so as to take the opportunity to let the customer place a new order and bundle the accessories and the new order to negotiate.

又例如，2018年广交会期间，非洲客户NG摩托车公司与广东FLING公司会谈。NG

公司一进入会议室便开始挑剔上一个订单中FLING公司发错零配件的事情，NG公司认为自己口头说了要带可折叠的左右后脚踏。FLING公司表示双方书面签字的状态表中并没有列明要可折叠的左右后脚踏，而且一切要以书面签字为准。NG公司表示不重新发配件的话，就不再下订单。FLING公司担心失去该客户，表示出现这种发错配件的事情是双方都不想看到的，也希望与客户一起想办法妥善解决这个事情。如果对方后续能够下一定数量的订单，FLING公司可以免费给NG公司一些配件，并给予新订单8折优惠。NG公司对FLING公司的答复非常满意并签订了购买2 000套摩托车配件的新合同。NG公司以FLING公司发错配件一事故意刁难对方，就是为了达到己方拿到免费配件和新订单优惠价格的目的，而FLING公司也不过分纠结NG公司是口头确认还是书面确认。在了解了客户的真实意图后，先缓和客户的情绪，表示希望与客户一起想办法来解决问题，从而借机让客户下新订单，并把配件和新订单捆绑在一起谈判。

Ⅳ The Business Etiquette（谈判开局阶段的商务礼仪）

1. Proper Attire（得体的着装）

Dressing up to participate in the negotiations will convey to the other party information of whether you value the cooperation and whether you are professional and reliable. Therefore, the formal dress should be chosen according to the custom of the negotiator. If you visit more rigorous countries such as France, Japan and other countries, it is best to wear dark suits; if you visit the United States, Sweden and other more open countries, wearing sweatshirts, casual clothes is not impossible.

参加谈判时的穿衣打扮，会向对方传递你是否重视这次合作、为人是否专业可靠的相关信息。因此，应根据谈判对手的习惯来选择着装的正式与否。如果访问法国、日本等比较严谨的国家，最好穿暗色西装；如果访问美国、瑞典等比较开放的国家，则穿运动衫、便服也未尝不可。

The prevailing dress etiquette is conservative, with men wearing dark suits with white or striped shirts, ties, and black lace-up shoes; with women wearing conservative professional suits or skirts with white shirts, flesh-colored stockings and single shoes, with light makeup and jewelry not much. Clothing fabric also reflects the owner's credibility and status, generally recommended to choose silk, wool, cotton and other natural fabric. The best choice is pure wool fabric.

普遍适用的着装礼仪就是保守，男士穿着深色西装配白色或条纹的衬衫、领带、黑色系带皮鞋；女士穿着保守的职业装或套裙，配白衬衫、肉色长筒袜和单鞋，化淡妆，首饰不可太多。服装面料也体现了主人的信誉与地位，一般建议选择丝、毛、棉等天然布料，最佳选择是纯羊毛面料。

2. Appropriate Introduction（恰当的介绍）

An appropriate introduction is good for making a good impression. To negotiate with people who value status, attention should be paid to the order of introduction. Generally introduce the host to the guest or first introduce the low status to the high status.

恰当的介绍有利于给对方留下良好印象。与重视身份地位的人谈判，介绍时应注意顺序。一般先介绍主方给客方，先介绍地位低的给地位高的。

The address of the introduction should follow the other party's habits. Americans and Britons are more casual and can be introduced by their first names. Germans and Japanese are more formal, and prefer to be called by their last names plus titles. Egyptians prefer to be introduced by their first names plus titles. Russians prefer to be called by their full names to show respect.

介绍时的称呼，应遵循对方的习惯。美国人和英国人比较随便，介绍时可以直呼其名。德国人和日本人比较正式，喜欢对方称呼其姓氏加头衔，埃及人则偏爱名字加头衔。俄罗斯人则喜欢被称呼全名以表示尊敬。

3. Handshake Greetings（握手问候）

Handshakes are the most common form of homage. The two sides usually shake hands at the first meeting and farewell, but some countries such as Germany and Russia are used to shaking hands frequently.

握手是最常见的致敬方式。一般在双方初次见面和告别时握手致敬，但有些国家如德国、俄罗斯习惯频繁握手。

Handshakes vary from country to country. Given the left-handed taboo of some countries, it is recommended to extend the right hand. The strength of handshakes varies from country to country, with Americans, Russians and Germans enjoying a strong handshake, while Asians, Britons and Frenchmen enjoy a soft handshake. In India, men do not shake hands with women. Normally the handshake should be moderate, the time should not be too long, while watching each other with a smile. Pay attention to the order of handshake, generally the host, high status, older or female first stretch out the hand, and the guest, low status, young or male greeting first, wait for the other side to reach out before holding.

握手的方式在不同国家有所区别。鉴于有些国家对左手的忌讳，建议伸右手。握手的力度各国也有不同，美国人、俄罗斯人和德国人喜欢用力握手，亚洲人、英国人和法国人则喜欢轻柔的握手。在印度，男人不和女人握手。通常情况下握手力度应适中，时间不宜过长；同时目视对方，微笑致意。注意握手顺序：一般由主人、地位高的、年长的或女性先伸手，客人、地位低的、年轻的或男士先问候，待对方伸出手后再握。

Some countries also express greetings in other ways. The Japanese bowed, the Thais and Indians put the palms together. Russian male friends give each other a big hug after shaking hands. Latin Americans and African women also greet with hugs or kisses.

有些国家也用其他方式表达问候。日本人用鞠躬礼问候，泰国人和印度人用合十礼问候。俄罗斯男性朋友间在握手后会给对方一个大大的拥抱。拉美人和一些非洲女性间也会用拥抱或亲吻作为问候。

4. Exchange of Business Cards（交换名片）

Exchange of business cards is also a common etiquette when meeting for the first time. For some countries, this is not a necessary step. Such as in the United States, Australia and France, exchange business cards only when there's the need to contact later. But in Asian countries, this is an essential part of business activities.

交换名片也是初次见面时的常见礼仪。对有些国家来说，这不是必要步骤。如在美国、澳大利亚和法国，只有在以后需要联系时才交换名片。但在亚洲国家，这是商务活动中必不可少的一环。

When negotiating with foreigners, the contents of the business cards should be printed in English on the one side and in local language on the other. When exchanging business cards, you should approach the other party, with the English side facing up and the text facing the receiver. Do not pass business cards with your left hand to people from Southeast Asia, Africa and the Middle East. Pass it to the Japanese and Koreans with both hands. When accepting business cards, Americans are used to putting them in their pockets at a glance. The Japanese, on the other hand, think it's proper to read and comment carefully before putting it away. When exchanging business cards with identity oriented teams, you should first pass them to the superior or senior members.

与异国人士谈判，名片的内容最好一面用英语印刷，另一面用本国语言印刷。交换名片时应走近对方，将印着英语的一面朝上，文字正对接受者。在东南亚、非洲和中东国家，不要用左手递名片。递给日本人和韩国人应用双手。在接受名片时，美国人习惯扫一眼就放进口袋。而日本人则认为应该仔细阅读并进行评论后再小心收好。与看重身份的团队交换名片，应先递给地位高者或年长者。

Summary

The work content of the opening stage: To create the negotiating atmosphere, we should grasp the key time of the formation of the negotiating atmosphere, use the neutral topic and strengthen the communication, establish the image of the honest, credible and cooperative negotiator, make use of the off-site informal contact before the formal negotiation, and organize reasonably. The main types of the opening negotiation atmosphere are high-profile atmosphere, low-profile atmosphere and natural atmosphere. The methods to create a high-profile atmosphere usually include emotional attack, praise, humor and question-teasing; the methods to create a low-profile atmosphere usually include emotional attack, silence, fatigue tactics and blame. The purpose of the investigation is to understand the strength, needs and sincerity of the negotiation partner, the situation of the negotiation team members of the other party, and the principles that the other party must adhere to in the negotiation.

开局阶段的工作内容：营造谈判氛围应把握谈判氛围形成的关键时机；运用中性话题加强沟通；树立诚实、可信、富有合作精神的谈判者形象；利用正式谈判前的场外非正式接触、合理组织。开局谈判氛围的类型主要有高调氛围、低调氛围、自然氛围。营造高调氛围的方法有感情攻击法、称赞法、幽默法和问题挑逗法；营造低调氛围通常有感情攻击法、沉默法、疲劳战术和指责法。摸底主要是为了了解谈判对手的实力、谈判对手的需求与诚意、对方谈判小组人员的状况、对方在谈判中所必须坚持的原则。

The main steps in the opening phase of the negotiations include the distribution of the agenda, the exchange of views and the opening statements. The main factors to be taken into account in creating an atmosphere for the opening negotiations are the relationship between the parties and between the individual negotiators and strength of the negotiating parties. The main strategies of the opening stage of negotiation are listening and observing, consultative opening strategy, reserved opening strategy, candid opening strategy, offensive opening strategy and picky opening strategy.

谈判开局阶段的步骤主要有分发议程、交换意见、开场陈述。营造开局谈判氛围应考虑的因素主要有谈判各方之间的关系、各谈判人员个人之间的关系、谈判各方的实力。谈判开局阶段的策略主要有察言观色、协商式开局策略、保留式开局策略、坦诚式开局策略、进攻式开局策略、挑剔式开局策略。

Etiquette at the opening stages of the negotiations included proper attire, apropriate introduction, handshake greetings and exchange of business cards.

谈判开局阶段的礼仪包括得体的着装、恰当的介绍、握手问候和交换名片。

Module Ⅱ Terminology Practice

1. The Opening: It is time for the initial presentation in accordance with the terms of the negotiation plan.

2. Negotiating Atmosphere: It generally takes place during the short time of the negotiation's beginning. Different negotiating atmosphere can cause different results.

3. Neutral Topic: It doesn't involve the topics of personal privacy, politics, and religion. It often includes topics of weather, personal interest and entertainment news.

4. Image of Negotiator: It usually refers to all things that the negotiators display and express to the counter-party which not only include language and appearance, but body language, facial expression and gesture.

5. Informal Contact: It refers to the circumstance that is outside of the formal negotiation, like personal contact and dinner.

6. Negotiating Process: It refers to how the parties negotiate, the context of the negotiations, the parties to the negotiations, the tactics used by the parties, and the sequence and stages in which all of these play out.

7. Negotiating Group: It is usually a negotiating team instead of a person. It is often made up of people from different department within a company, such as finance, marketing, management, R&D and legal department.

8. Negotiating Strategy: It is the sum of various actions, methods and means taken by the negotiator in order to effectively achieve the intended purpose during the negotiation process.

Module Ⅲ New Words

1. cooperative *adj.* 合作的；合作社的 *n.* 合作社
2. negotiate *v.* 谈判；磋商
3. characteristics *n.* 特征；特色；特质
4. opponent *n.* 对手；反对者 *adj.* 对立的；敌对的
5. atmosphere *n.* 气氛；大气；空气
6. emotion *n.* 情感；情绪
7. outcome *n.* 结果；结局；成果
8. diverse *adj.* 不同的；多种多样的，形形色色的
9. enthusiastic *adj.* 热情的；热心的；狂热的
10. tense *adj.* 紧张的；拉紧的 *v.* 变得紧张；使拉紧 *n.* 时态
11. antagonistic *adj.* 敌对的；对抗性的；反对的
12. subtle *adj.* 微妙的；精细的；敏感的；狡猾的
13. short-lived *adj.* 短暂的，短期的；短命的；无常的
14. mindset *n.* 心态；倾向；习惯；精神状态
15. scatter *v.* 散开；散布；驱散 *n.* 零星散布的东西；散射
16. costume *v.* 给……穿上衣服 *n.* 服装，装束；戏装，剧装
17. rigorous *adj.* 严格的，严厉的；严密的；严酷的
18. venue *n.* 聚会地点；犯罪地点；发生地点
19. contradictory *adj.* 矛盾的；反对的；反驳的 *n.* 对立物；矛盾因素
20. cross-legged *adj.* 翘着腿的；盘着腿的
21. prematurely *adv.* 过早地；早熟地
22. energetic *adj.* 精力充沛的；积极的；有力的
23. exhausted *adj.* 筋疲力尽的，疲惫不堪的；耗尽的 *v.* 耗尽；用尽；使……筋疲力尽
24. off-site *adj.* 工作场所外的 *adv.* 工作场所之外
25. deadlock *n.* 僵局，停顿 *v.* 停顿；相持不下
26. monopolize *v.* 垄断；独占；拥有……的专卖权
27. inclination *n.* 倾向，爱好；斜坡
28. trait *n.* 特性，特点；品质；少许
29. austerity *n.* 紧缩；朴素；严厉
30. resentment *n.* 愤恨，怨恨
31. flatter *v.* 奉承；献媚；使高兴
32. fatigue *n.* 疲劳，疲乏 *v.* 使疲劳；使心智衰弱 *adj.* 疲劳的
33. agility *n.* 敏捷；灵活；机敏
34. embarrassing *adj.* 使人尴尬的；令人为难的

Module Ⅳ Useful Expressions

1. long-term relation 长期的关系
2. strive to 争取；努力
3. get the initiative 获得主动权
4. in turn 反过来；依次；轮流地
5. make effort 做出努力
6. be influenced by 被……影响

7. casual clothes 便服；休闲服
8. shake hands 握手
9. a sense of security 安全感
10. a sense of formality 正式感；拘谨感
11. applicable to 适用于；应用于
12. at random 随机地；任意地；偶然地
13. divide into... categories 分成……大类
14. fall into 开始（攀谈或讨论问题）
15. far apart 相隔甚远；距离比较远
16. it is forbidden to 禁止做某事
17. in terms of 在……方面；就……而言；根据……来说
18. concentrate on 集中于……；专心于……
19. capital accumulation 资本积累
20. psychological orientation 心理取向；心理定位
21. substantive consultation 实质性协商
22. make use of 使用；利用
23. be beneficial to 有益于……
24. comment on 就（某人某事）发表看法；评论
25. be prone to 易于……的
26. give in 屈从；让步；认输
27. blame for 责怪（某人）；怪罪
28. be unfavorable to 对……不利
29. be aware of 意识到；知道

Module Ⅴ Exercise

Ⅰ. Answer the following questions according to the text.

1. What are the major works at the opening stage?
2. Please list various types of negotiating atmosphere.
3. How to create a good negotiating atmosphere?
4. What is "4P" in the opening stage?
5. What factors would affect negotiating atmosphere?
6. What are the main contents of opening statement?
7. How many negotiating strategies can be used in the opening stage? What are they?
8. Under what circumstance should the reserved opening strategy be adopted?
9. Under what circumstance can the offensive opening strategy be used?
10. Under what circumstance should the picky opening strategy be adopted?

Ⅱ. Match the words in Column A with their definitions in Column B.

Column A	Column B
1. strategy	A. approve of; be behind; give support or one's approval to
2. atmosphere	B. to declare solemnly and formally as true
3. offensive	C. the ratio of the output to the input of any system
4. consultative	D. giving advice
5. endorse	E. a particular environment or surrounding influence
6. affirm	F. a formal charge of wrongdoing brought against a person

7. efficiency — G. showing no care or concern in attitude or action

8. external — H. an elaborate and systematic plan of action

9. accusation — I. violating or tending to violate or offend against

10. indifferent — J. happening or arising or located outside or beyond some limits or especial surface

Ⅲ. Translate the following terms and phrases into Chinese.

1. establishment of friendly relations
2. negotiating parties
3. negotiating opponent
4. exchange opinions
5. negotiating issue
6. desired outcome
7. grasp opportunity
8. key time
9. psychological state
10. first impression
11. eye contact
12. bilateral negotiation
13. negotiation table
14. neutral topics
15. achieve the purpose
16. make concession
17. thorough answer
18. fuzzy information
19. adjust ideas
20. vigilant attitude

Ⅳ. Please determine whether the following statements are True or False.

1. Credit-ability study of the counter-party is done after the negotiation. (　　)

2. The appearance and clothing of negotiators are not important for negotiation. (　　)

3. The parties' attitudes are being formed at the post-negotiation stage. (　　)

4. The final concession should be made at the right time, neither too early nor too late. (　　)

5. In the opening stage, negotiators are getting to know each other and identifying the issues involved. (　　)

6. In order to form good atmosphere of opening stage, negotiating parties can talk about some topics, such as weather, politics, religions and interests. (　　)

7. Generally speaking, in bilateral negotiation, the round table are often used. (　　)

8. The objective at the opening stage of the negotiations may be described as exploration without commitment. (　　)

9. After knowing each other's fundamental information, it is time for the initial presentation in accordance with the terms of the negotiation plan. (　　)

10. If the parties are presenting the initial proposal at the end of the opening stage, the negotiators should know which parts of their offer is likely to be accepted by the opponent. (　　)

Ⅴ. Translate the following sentences into Chinese.

1. In the opening stage, negotiators are getting to know each other and identifying the

issues involved. After that, the review is followed. The negotiators then modify their negotiating plan as necessary to take account of any factors disclosed in the opening of which they had not previously been ware.

2. One party may be in the situation to take the initiative and submit a proposal required by the counter-party or to respond to one already provided by the other.

3. The opening stage is influential because energy and concentration are naturally at a high point at the start of any activity.

4. Before proceeding further with the negotiations, negotiating parties should review the results achieved from the opening stage and then decide whether the negotiations can be placed on a bargain acceptable to both parties.

5. Many relationships in international transactions begin with the formation of personal relationships between the players.

Ⅵ. Translate the following sentences into English.

1. 谈判开局阶段需要营造良好的开局氛围，这样有利于谈判的开展。

2. 从商务谈判的特性而言，能了解对方主谈人的背景、嗜好和家庭状况对谈判是有益处的。

3. 谈判是一种集体项目，需要谈判成员具有专业技能、沟通能力、团队协作精神。

4. 谈判是一个长时间的讨价还价过程，双方均做出让步，从中获利，从而使双方之间的差距缩小到一定程度。

5. 谈判开局阶段应注意传递信息的准确性，紧扣谈判主题同时运用正确的谈判策略。

6. 谈判开局营造氛围时应选择中性话题来进行交流，比如天气，切忌讨论政治、宗教等敏感性话题。

7. 每一场谈判都有独特的气氛，有的是冷淡、对立的；有的是积极、友好的；有的是平静、严谨的。

8. 在谈判开局阶段，谈判人员对于表情、眼神的合理运用能对谈判起到很大的作用。

Ⅶ. Case Study

Case 1: Music Played in the Banquet

Case Source: Liu Yuan, *International Business Negotiation: Theory, Practice, Case*. Beijing: China Business Press, 2008.

Preface

Time: 1972

Key Point: The Welcome Banquet

Background

Industry: Trade

Subject: Premier Zhou Enlai and President Nixon

Issue: To Create a Harmonious Environment and Atmosphere of Negotiations

February 1972, President Nixon visited China, and the two sides launched an international negotiation of great historical significance. In order to create a harmonious environment and negotiation atmosphere, the Chinese party, under the leadership of Premier Zhou Enlai, prepared and organized the negotiation process carefully, and even painstakingly selected the folk music of the two countries to play at the banquet.

At the welcome banquet, President Nixon was simply listening when the military band played skillfully "Beautiful America" selected personally by Premier Zhou. He absolutely did not expect to hear his familiar music in Beijing of China, because this is the favorite of his life, and also the specified music played in his inauguration.

While toasting, he specially went to thank the band, and the state banquet reached a climax at this time, and a harmonious and warm atmosphere also infected with the American guests meanwhile.

Questions

Try to analyze the way to form a harmonious and warm atmosphere.

Appendix

People involved in international business negotiations come from different countries. They are persons who have different personalities and accomplishments, and are also influenced by cultural, conceptual, ethnic, religious, political, educational, and even family and educational backgrounds. The special atmosphere and environment of the negotiations often have a direct impact on people's emotions.

Case 2: The Opening Statement of Siemens

Case Source: Dou Ran. *International Business Negotiation and Communication Skills*. Shanghai: Fudan University Press, 2009.

Preface

Time: In the 1990s

Key Point: South Korea AG was invited to Siemens AG in Germany to negotiate the technology and equipment of the Siemens rail transit control system.

Background

Industry: Manufacture

Subject: South Korea AG and Siemens AG in Germany

Issue: The Opening Steps of Negotiation

South Korea AG was invited to Siemens AG in Germany to negotiate the technology and equipment of the Siemens rail transit control system. In the negotiating room of the spacious and bright Siemens headquarter building, both sides have taken seats. After the witty start of the talks by the German side, the administrative secretary first distributed a list of the agenda of the negotiations to each negotiator. The representatives of both sides then began to exchange views on the negotiating agenda. The representatives of the South Korean side proposed to add two issues related to technical testing. The German side agreed. Next, the chief negotiators of the two sides discuss the significance of the technology transfer, how to ensure their respective interests, the level of the technology in the international counterparts, the supply and demand of the international market, the transfer price of similar technologies, and the transaction of the project. The obstacles are stated separately. During the presentation of the German representative, the Korean staff listened carefully and recorded the main points. Occasionally, they also asked questions about the meaning of a proper noun and the specific technical performance parameters. When the German personnel stated the statement, the German representative explained some of the problems raised by the Korean side and conducted a live demonstration through the projector. Finally, the chief negotiator of Siemens made a general summary, emphasizing the actual benefits brought by the technology transfer to both parties, and sorting out several issues that need to be discussed first.

Questions

1. What are the opening steps of international business negotiations?
2. What kind of opening negotiation atmosphere is created in this case?

Appendix

The beginning of international business negotiations often goes through three stages: providing each delegate with a meeting agenda, exchanging views on the agenda and other related issues, and the chief negotiators of each party making separate statements.

Case 3: Cooperation between *European Business* and *World Market*

Case Source: Dou Ran. *International Business Negotiation and Communication Skills.* Shanghai: Fudan University Press, 2009.

Preface

Time: In the 1970s

Key Point: To Provide a Convenient Negotiation Condition for the German Editor-in-chief

Background

Industry: Journal

Subject: *World Market* and *European Business*

Issue: The Chinese government has some restrictions on the cooperation between domestic media and foreign journals, especially in Shanghai, there is no precedent for Sino-foreign cooperation in business journals.

In order to provide a convenient negotiation condition for the German editor-in-chief who first came to China, and to show them the strength of the *World Market* magazine, and to deepen the vivid impression of Shanghai, the most developed city in China's economy, the Chinese side would specially arrange the negotiation at the Peace Hotel, just a stone's throw from the *World Market* magazine headquarter.

The venue for the negotiation was arranged in the conference room of *World Market* magazine, No. 33, Zhongshan East Road. At the beginning of the negotiations, the two sides first talked about the initial impression of the German president on Shanghai and the European architecture where the *World Market* magazine is located, and then introduced each other in detail the historical background and status quo even though they had preliminary understanding. Then, the editor-in-chief of *World Market* magazine pulled the conversation back to the theme of the talk. Because the Chinese government has some restrictions on the cooperation between domestic media and foreign journals especially in Shanghai, there is no precedent for Sino-foreign cooperation in business journals. Therefore, this negotiation has a taste of ice-breaking.

In order not to violate the relevant policies and regulations of the Chinese government, but also to benefit each other in cooperation, the two sides conducted serious discussions on the specific terms of cooperation in the first round of negotiations, and there were divergent differences of opinion on individual key terms. In order to ease the atmosphere of the talks and to let the German editors know more about the situation of Shanghai and *World Market* magazine in the market, the Chinese editor-in-chief assigned a foreign-language fluent trainee reporter to accompany the German editor-in-chief for half a day to visit the Pudong Jinmao Tower and the Oriental Pearl TV Tower, and to investigate the sale of the latest issue of *World Market* magazine on the streets of the downtown area and the newsstands in the subway station. In the People's Square and Lujiazui subway station, the editor-in-chief of the German side discovered a few large "lightbox" advertisements of *World Market* magazine, which surprised him, so he stopped and used the digital camera to shoot the advertisements several times.

On the evening of the same day, the editor-in-chief of *World Market* magazine set up a banquet for German guests. The location was chosen at Shanghai Longxing Hotel, the old restaurant of Nanjing West Road. Many former international celebrities such as former British Prime Minister Margaret Thatcher and French President Jacques Chirac have visited this place. The Chinese editor-in-chief entertained the German editor-in-chief in the places where many celebrities came in and out, making the guests feel flattered. In addition to what he saw and heard in the afternoon, the doubts of the German editor-in-chief gradually disappeared. With the wonderful Jiangnan silk bamboo music, they tasted the exquisite Shanghai local banquet dishes (actually the price of the dishes is not high, but there are local characteristics) and Zhang Yu red wine, when the Chinese editor-in-chief once again mentioned issues they failed to reach consensus in the morning, the attitude of the German editor-in-chief has changed significantly. The German side made important concessions on the main clauses. The Chinese side also made some adjustments in other clauses. During the opening negotiations of the first day, the two sides reached a preliminary consensus on several major terms of cooperation.

Questions

1. What strategy does *World Market* magazine use in the negotiations with the *European Business* magazine? What is the effect? If you are the editor-in-chief of *World Market* magazine, how would you design the start of the negotiations?

2. What is the impact of different negotiating atmospheres on international business negotiations?

Appendix

The Peace Hotel is one of the first European-style hotels in Shanghai, situated on the bustling East Bund of Nanjing East Road. Looking out from the window of each room of the hotel, you can enjoy the beautiful scenery of the Huangpu River and the two banks. This is a surprise and intimate feeling for the German editor-in-chief of the same port city of Hamburg.

The No. 33 compound was once the British Consulate General in Shanghai. The No. 1 Building of the magazine was the place where the British Consul General was working and meeting guests. It was also the earliest European building on Shanghai Bund, and its history is even longer than the Peace Hotel. Nowadays, it has become the most expensive place in the central city of Shanghai. It can work here, obviously with extraordinary background and strength. Although the floor and door and window facilities in Building No. 1 are somewhat outdated due to age, the large and spacious meeting rooms still reveal the solemn momentum of the living room of the Consulate General.

Case 4: Green Onions Trading Negotiation

Case Source: Ma Chunzi. *International Business Negotiation and Etiquette*. Beijing: Beijing Institute of Technology Press, 2017.

Preface

Time: In the 1990s

Key Point: The Price Conditions

Background

Industry: Agriculture

Subject: A Chinese Company and a Korean Company

Issue: The Korean side said: "Your price is still too high."

A Chinese company has exported green onions to a Korean company for one year. In the second year, the Chinese side quoted the Korean side to continue supply. According to the international market conditions, the Chinese company lowered the price from the previous year's transaction price to $ 80/ton (previous year is 100/ton). The Korean side felt acceptable and recommended that the Chinese sign the contract with it. Two Chinese arrived at the headquarter of Seoul. The two sides talked for less than 20 minutes. The Korean side said: "Your price is still too high. Please look at the price of the Korean market. Let's talk after three days." Chinese personnel felt that they were teased when they returned to the hotel. They were angry, but they had come to Seoul and negotiations must be carried out.

Chinese personnel collected statistics on the importation of Korean onion through the relevant associations and found that imports from Colombia, Belgium, South Africa and other countries were large. There were also many imports from China, and the Chinese share was large. The price level of South Africa was the lowest among the above-mentioned countries but higher than the price of Chinese products. The prices in Colombia and Belgium were higher than those in South Africa. In the Korean market survey, the wholesale and retail prices were higher than the current offer of Chinese companies by 30% to 40%. Although the market price was declining, the Chinese company's offer was the lowest price in the world market.

According to this analysis, after consultation, the Chinese personnel decided to make a fuss about the price conditions. In general, the attitude should be tough (because the counter-party has already agreed to the Chinese offer before coming), and Chinese personel should not be afraid to return empty-handed. In addition, the price conditions will rise back to the market level (e. g. around $120/ton).

Before noon after one and a half days, the Chinese personnel telephoned the Korean side: "The investigation has ended. The conclusion is: the offer before our visit to Seoul is low, and should rise back to the price of last year's transaction, but for the friendship of old friends, we can lower the price by $20/ton. Please let us know if you have any results. If we are not in the hotel, please leave a message." One hour after the Korean staff received the call, they called the Chinese personnel to talk at their company. The Korean side believed that China should not raise the past price. The Chinese side believed that this was the right given by the ROK. The Chinese side conducted a market survey according to the requirements of the ROK, and the result should be an increase in prices. The South Korean side hoped that the Chinese side would drop some of the price. The Chinese side believed that the original offer had been lowered to the end. After several rounds of discussions, the two sides agreed to close the deal according to the offer made by the Chinese side before they came to Seoul. In this way, the Chinese side succeeded in making the Korean side abandon the demand for price reduction and getting back the contract as planned.

Questions

1. What kind of negotiation opening strategy has the ROK adopted?

2. What techniques has China adopted in the international business negotiations to reverse the negotiation situation?

Appendix

The offensive opening strategy means preparing to express the strong position of one party through language or behavior, thus winning the respect of the opponent and forcing the opponent to start negotiations according to the intention of the party.

Ⅷ. Role plays practice. Work in pair and converse according to the given information.

Task 1

Background

You represent Suzhou Arts & Crafts Imp. & Exp. Corp., selling paper umbrellas. An American businessman has ordered a total of USD 30,000 worth of your products. But since this is the first time you are doing business with him, you want to be careful about the details. So you point out that the L/C should be "irrevocable", because L/C without the word "irrevocable" provides no protection for the exporter.

Terms and Phrases

in connection with	in advance	letter of credit
financial standing	documentary collection	installment payment
make a down payment	pay off the rest	cash on delivery
clean payment	deferred payment	dishonor
D/P sight	payment order	payment in full

Relative Expressions

1. Regarding your proposal, our position is...
2. Our basic position is...
3. As far as your proposal is concerned, we think that...
4. We would be willing to..., provided, of course, that...
5. May we offer an alternative? We propose that...
6. From where we stand, a better solution might be...
7. What you don't seem to understand is that...
8. Let me say something about...
9. I'd like to make a comment about...
10. There are other issues/considerations; for example, the price...
11. There are other points to bear in mind. Firstly, we have...
12. To put you in the picture, we are...
13. If you haven't already heard of our products, we are...
14. As you probably know, we are...

Task 2

Background

Suppose you are having a talk with a Finnish merchant about the time of shipment. He asks you to make shipment in November. The reason is that he wants to catch the Christmas demand for plastic decorative lights on the market in time. Since it takes time to find the manufactures locally, you could not promise the shipment. The best you can do is in early of December. If conditions permit, you'll do your best to advance the shipment as he wishes.

Terms and Phrases

shipping space	shipping advice	have a word about
shipping instruction	ship on board	customs
shopping season	back orders on hand	in strict rotation
discharge/unload	cargo freight	load time
to arrange transport	make shipment	take delivery of goods
prompt shipment	to speed up	prompt delivery
transportation cost	way of transportation	over-shipment

Relative Expressions

1. I'm afraid there seems to be a slight misunderstanding...
2. Perhaps I haven't made myself clear...
3. Let me put it in another way...
4. To be more specific, I think the date...
5. Allow me to rephrase that...
6. What I am suggesting is...
7. What I am getting at is...
8. What steps would you suggest to correct that?
9. I'm sure you don't realize it, but...
10. There's a good reason for...
11. I'm sorry. I can't tell you that right now.
12. Can I go back to you on that?
13. We'll come to that later.
14. Let me try to make that clearer.
15. Put simply...

Chapter 5

Consultation for International Business Negotiation

Work Objective

After studying this chapter, you will be able to:

- familiarize with the procedures in the consultation stage;
- probe into the principles and methods of bidding;
- master the strategies of bargaining;
- know the principles and strategies of concession;
- familiarize with the methods of creating and breaking deadlock.

Case Guide-Reading

Harbin Rubber Factory imported 2 million yuan of modern rubber shoes production equipment. Because the raw materials and technical strength could not keep up, the equipment could not be used for three years. Later, the new factory manager decided to resell it to a foreign rubber factory. During the formal negotiations, the director of the Harbin Rubber Factory said: "I have been watching your factory for a whole day and have a detailed understanding of the production situation of your factory. Your management level and technical strength have really made me respectful. If you resell the equipment of our factory to your factory, I can assert that your factory will soon become the star of the rubber industry in the country under the leadership of your young factory director... "The factory director's sincere and not false praise made the other party feel very proud, and did not show off the economic strength and technical strength of his factory. After some words, the Harbin factory finally succeeded in "cultivating" for three years. The equipment was resold.

Source: Liu Yuan. *International Business Negotiation*. Beijing: Capital Economic and

Trade University Press, 2016.

Module Ⅰ Text

Ⅰ Offering Stage of International Business Negotiation（国际商务谈判的报价阶段）

The bargaining stage of business negotiation is also the substantive consultation stage of the negotiation. It refers to the whole process of negotiation between the negotiating parties on substantive matters after the start of the negotiation and before the end of the negotiation. It is the central link of the negotiation. This stage is the practical stage of the negotiation after the completion of the tasks at the beginning stage of the negotiation. It is not only a stage of specific contests of strength, intelligence and technology among the negotiating subjects, but also a stage of seeking common ground while shelving differences and making concessions among the negotiating subjects. The substantive bargaining stage is usually the one that takes the largest proportion of time in the entire negotiation process. The actual bargaining of international business negotiations is mainly based on price, that is, a process of bargaining and counter-offer.

商务谈判的磋商阶段，也是谈判的实质性阶段，它是指谈判开局后到谈判终局之前，谈判双方就实质性事项进行磋商的全过程，是谈判的中心环节。该阶段是继谈判开局阶段的任务完成后，议题不断深入的谈判的实践阶段，它不仅是谈判主体间的实力、智力和技术的具体较量阶段，而且是谈判主体间求同存异、让步妥协的阶段。实质磋商阶段一般也是整个谈判过程中占时间比重最大的一个阶段。国际商务谈判的实质磋商主要是围绕价格展开的，也就是一个报价、讨价、还价的过程。

1. Definition of Offer（报价的含义）

An offer is also called a quotation, which is legally called a pollicitation. Any proposal made by one or more specific persons to enter into a contract constitutes an offer if its content is sufficiently definitive and it indicates that the bidder is bound by the offer once it is accepted.

报价又称报盘或发盘，在法律上称为要约。凡是一个或一个以上的特定的人提出的订立合同的建议，如果其内容十分确定并且表明报价人一旦报价得到接受就受其约束的意思，即构成报价。

An offer can be made by either the seller or the buyer, so there is a distinction between a seller's offer and a buyer's offer.

报价既可由卖方提出，也可由买方提出，因此，有卖方报价和买方报价之分。

The offer (bid) mentioned here is not limited to the price of the commodity, but refers to all the requirements of one party to the counter-party, including the quantity, quality, packaging, price, shipping, insurance, payment, commodity inspection of the commodity, claim, arbitration and other transaction conditions, of which the price clause is the most important, and it is also a clause often disputed by the parties in international business negotiations.

这里所说的报价（报盘），不仅仅局限于商品的价格，而是泛指谈判的一方对另一方提出的所有要求，包括商品的数量、质量、包装、价格、装运、保险、支付、商检、索赔、仲裁等交易条件，其中价格条款最为重要，也是国际商务谈判中谈判各方经常发生争议的条款。

2. Basis and Principles of Offer（报价的依据和原则）

(1) Basis of Offer（报价的依据）

a. Cost（成本因素）

Cost is the most basic factor affecting the offer. The offer of a commodity is based on the cost plus a reasonable profit.

成本是影响报价的最基本因素，商品的报价是在成本的基础上加上合理的利润。

b. Market Conditions（市场行情）

It is the general price and its fluctuation range of the subject matter in the market.

市场行情是指标的物在市场上的一般价格及波动范围。

c. Product（产品因素）

The more complex the structure and performance of a product, the higher and more sophisticated the manufacturing process requirements, the higher the cost, value, and price. Old and new level of the goods, as well as the conditions and services of the product, will also affect the price. Conditions attached to the product and services, such as quality assurance, installation and commissioning, free maintenance, and supply of accessories, can reduce the price level of the product in people's minds and slow down the resistance to price negotiations.

产品的结构和性能越复杂，制造工艺及工艺要求越高和越精细，成本、价值及其价格就会越高。货物的新旧程度以及产品的附带条件和服务也会对价格产生影响。产品的附带条件和服务，如质量保证、安装调试、免费维修、供应配件等能降低产品的价格水平在人们心目中的地位和减缓价格谈判的阻力。

d. Competition（竞争因素）

In addition to considering the cost of goods, market demand and quality, we must also pay attention to competitors' prices, especially competitors' offer strategies and the latest competitors joining the market.

除了考虑商品成本、市场需求及品质外，还必须注重竞争对手的价格，特别是竞争对手的报价策略以及最近加入市场的竞争对手。

e. Policy（政策因素）

Each country has its own economic policy, and there are corresponding restrictions and legal regulations on the level and change of market prices. At the same time, the state also uses production, markets, monetary finance, customs and other economic means to indirectly adjust prices, so it must comply with national policy requirements when quoting.

每个国家都有自己的经济政策，对市场价格的高低和变动都有相应的限制和法律规定。同时，国家还利用生产、市场、货币金融、海关等经济手段间接调节价格，因而在报价时必须遵守国家的政策要求。

（2）Principles of Offer（报价的原则）

The basic principle of offer is: through repeated comparisons and trade-offs, try to find the best combination of the price and its accepted success rate. When quoting to the other, you cannot speak carelessly, but after careful analysis, you must consider not only the benefits that can be obtained, but also whether the offer can be accepted by the counter-party, that is, the probability that the offer will be successful.

报价的基本原则是：通过反复比较和权衡，设法找出价格与其被接受的成功率之间的最佳结合点。一方向另一方报价时，不能信口开河，而要经过仔细分析，不仅要考虑能获得的利益，还要考虑报价能否被对方接受，即报价能够成功的概率。

For the seller, the opening price must be "highest"; for the buyer, the opening price must be "lowest". This is the first principle of offer.

对卖方来讲，开价必须是"最高的"；对买方来说，开价必须是"最低的"。这是报价的首要原则。

The offered price must be reasonable. For the seller, even if the offer is high, it cannot be overpriced or baseless quotation. It must be reasonable. If the offer is too high, but cannot give a reason to convince the counter-party, this will make the counter-party feel insincere and may terminate the negotiation. For the buyer, he should not be bargaining for no reason, which will make the counter-party think that you have no common sense, no negotiation experience and lose confidence. Therefore, both the buyer and the seller must be justified and reasonable when offering.

报价必须合情合理。对于卖方而言，虽然报价要高，但也不能漫天要价，毫无根据地报价，必须合情合理。如果报价过高，但又无法给出让对方信服的理由，这会让对方觉得没有诚意，可能会终止谈判。对于买方而言，也不能毫无理由地乱砍价，这会让对方认为你方毫无常识、没有谈判经验，从而失去信心。所以，无论是买方还是卖方，在报价时一定要有理有据，合乎情理。

The offer target must be clear and the position must be firm. The goal includes two aspects. On the one hand, the content and requirements of offer, bargaining and counter-offer must be concrete, clear and complete. On the other hand, we must correctly judge the expectations of the counter-party, clarify our negotiation goals and the lowest price level that we can accept, and strive to close the transaction with the highest possible trading conditions that are beneficial to our party. At the substantive bargaining stage of international business negotiations, we must be decisive and firm, and put forward our own requirements without hesitation, so as to show our own confidence and leave an honest and serious impression on the counter-party.

报价目标要明确，立场要坚定。目标包括两个方面的内容。一方面，报价、讨价、还价的内容及要求必须明确、清楚且完整。另一方面，要正确判断对方的期望，明确己方的谈判目标以及可以接纳的最低价格水平，争取以有利于己方的尽可能高的交易条件成交。

在国际商务谈判的实质磋商阶段，态度一定要果断而坚定，毫不犹豫地提出己方的要求，这样才能显示出己方的自信，给对方留下诚实、认真的印象。

Give no explanation or description when offering. When offering, you should be very clear without adding too much explanation and description. You should follow the principle of "no question, no answer; can ask, no answer; answer for question". Do not explain and do not answer without being asked for; ask in reply if the counter-party asks questions about the price. For example, the counter-party asks, "Your offer is not reasonable?" You can ask, "Where do you think it is not reasonable?" Push the question to the counter-party to answer.

报价时不解释，不说明。报价时应该非常清楚，不加过多的解释和说明，应遵循“不问不答，能问不答，有问必答”的原则，即报完价格后，如果对方不要求解释，就不要进行解释；如果对方针对价格提出问题，能反问就不要回答。比如，对方在己方报价后问：“您的报价不太合理吧?”己方可以反问：“您觉得哪里不合理呢?”将问题推给对方来回答。

3. Form and Method of Offer（报价的形式和方式）

(1) Form of Offer（报价的形式）

Formally speaking, offer can be divided into two forms: written offers and oral offers.

从形式上来讲，报价可以分为书面报价和口头报价两种形式。

Written offers are usually provided by the negotiating party in advance with more detailed texts, data and charts, etc., and clearly express their obligations in written form, so that the counter-party has time to make adequate preparations for the offer. This form of offer is more formal and serious, which can lay the foundation for good communication between the two sides and make the negotiation process more compact and rigorous. This form of offer is advantageous for stronger negotiators. At the same time, in the case where the subject matter is clear and the price terms are more complicated, the use of this form is helpful to explain the complex terms clearly. However, this kind of offer is relatively rigid and lacks flexibility, which has been rarely used in realistic international business negotiations.

书面报价通常是谈判一方事先提供了比较详尽的文字资料、数据和图表等，将己方愿意承担的义务以书面形式表达清楚，使对方有时间针对报价做充分的准备。这种报价形式比较正规、严肃，能为双方良好的沟通奠定基础，可以使谈判进程更加紧凑和严谨。这种报价形式对于实力比较强的谈判者而言是有利的。同时，在标的物明确且价格条款比较复杂的情况下，采用这种报价形式有利于将复杂的条款解释清楚。但这种报价形式比较死板，缺乏灵活性，在现实的国际商务谈判中已经很少使用了。

Oral offer refers to proposing trading conditions by way of oral notification. Compared with written offer, oral offer has great flexibility; negotiators can adjust their negotiation tactics according to the negotiation process. Oral offer adheres to the principle of obligation after consultation, and does not have the sense of obligation of written offer. However, on the one hand, for some complicated price negotiations, the oral offer cannot clearly explain the main points, which may cause the counter-party's deviations in understanding the terms. On the other hand, the oral offer is likely to deviate from the subject of the negotiation and is not conducive to the smooth progress of the negotiation.

口头报价是指以口头告知的方式提出交易条件。和书面报价相比，口头报价具有很大的灵活性，谈判者可以根据谈判的进程来调整变更己方的谈判战术。口头报价奉行的是先磋商后承担义务的原则，没有书面报价的义务约束感。但是，一方面，对于某些价格条款比较复杂的谈判，口头报价不能很好地把要点表述清楚，可能会使对方对条款的理解出现偏差；另一方面，口头报价很容易偏离谈判的主题，不利于谈判的顺利推进。

(2) Method of Offer（报价方式）

In terms of methods, offers can be divided into European offer and Japanese offer.

从报价方式来讲，报价可以分为欧式报价法和日式报价法。

The European offer method means that the seller first offers a high price, and then after the concession in the bargaining stage, while striving for other favorable conditions, the original price is gradually reduced until it is accepted by the buyer. The European offer method is more common and is more in line with the principle of offer. If your own strength is strong or the strength of both parties is equal, you can use this offer method.

欧式报价法是指卖方先报出一个高价，然后经过讨价还价阶段中的让步，争取其他有利条件的同时，逐渐将原报价降低，直到让买方接受。欧式报价法比较普遍，也比较符合报价的原则。如果己方实力较强或者双方实力相当，都可以使用这种报价法。

The Japanese offer method means that the seller first offers a relatively low price to attract potential trading partners. However, the other trading conditions proposed by the seller in this offer method are beneficial to his own. If the buyer wants the other trading conditions to be beneficial to his own, the seller will increase the price accordingly. Therefore, the final transaction price is often higher than that in the price list. If your own strength is weak, or your negotiation power is weak, or there are many competitors, you can use the Japanese offer method to lure the buyer with a lower price first, which will increase the probability of successful negotiations.

日式报价法是指卖方先报出一个比较低的价格，吸引潜在的交易对象。但是在这种报价法下卖方提出的其他交易条件都是有利于己方的，如果买方想让其他交易条件也有利于己方，卖方就会相应提高价格，因此，最后成交的价格往往高于价格表中的价格。在己方实力较弱，或谈判能力较弱，或在己方竞争对手较多的情况下，可以通过日式报价法，用较低的报价先将买方引诱过来，这样会增加谈判成功的概率。

4. Order of Offer（报价次序）

It is a delicate question which party makes offer first in international business negotiations. The order of offer will, to some extent, have a substantial impact on the outcome of the negotiations. There are advantages and disadvantages to offering first and offering later.

在国际商务谈判中哪方先报价是个很微妙的问题。报价的先后在某种程度上会对谈判的结果产生实质性影响。先报价和后报价各有其利弊。

(1) Advantages of Offering First (先报价的优势)

The impact of offering first on the negotiation is relatively huge, a framework or baseline is drawn for the negotiation, and the terms of the agreement reached in the end are all within this framework. The current offer exceeds the counter-party's imagination, which can often break the counter-party's original plan and deployment and have an unexpected effect. For example, if your own party first offers at $10,000, then it is difficult for the counter-party to expect a counter-offer of $1,000. Of course, you also need to grasp a "degree" before offering, so you can't ask for prices out of the market to make the counter-party disdain negotiation.

先报价对谈判的影响比较大，为谈判划定了一个框架或基准线，最终达成一致的协议条款都位于这个框架内。当先报价超出对方的设想时，往往能打破对方原有的计划和部署，起到出其不意的效果。比如，己方先对商品报价1万美元，那么对方很难奢望还价到1 000美元。当然，先报价也需要掌握一个"度"，不能漫天要价，使对方不屑于谈判。

(2) Disadvantages of Offering First (先报价的劣势)

In fact, you may virtually leak some of your own information from your offer. The counter-party can compare its hidden price with the unquoted price, and then adjust it. If your first offer is too low, the counter-party can modify the prepared price and get unexpected gains. In addition, offering first will also set an attack target for the counter-party, and make it focus on bargaining, forcing the offering party to continue to make concessions, thus putting itself in a passive situation.

己方报价后，其实无形中也泄露了一些己方的情报。对方了解后可以把信息中隐而不报的价格与之比较，然后进行调整。比如，如果己方的报价起点太低，对方就可以修改预先准备的价格，获得意外的收益。除此之外，先报价也会给对方树立一个攻击的目标，集中力量来讨价还价，迫使报价方不得不退让，从而使己方处于被动的局面。

Generally speaking, the negotiating party or the seller will make an offer first according to the usual practice; if you're fully prepared and know your counter-party, you will try to make an offer first; if you're not particularly experienced in the negotiations, and the counter-party is an experienced negotiator, then you need to stay calm, offer later, get more information from the counter-party's offer and correct your own ideas in a timely manner; if the negotiating party has had many pleasant cooperation experiences, then either party can make an offer first.

一般按照惯例由发起谈判方或卖方先报价；如果己方准备充分，知己知彼，就要争取先报价；如果己方在谈判方面经验不是特别丰富，而恰恰对方是谈判老手，那么己方需要沉住气，后报价，从对方的报价中获取更多的信息，及时修正己方的想法；如果谈判方曾经有过多次愉快合作的经历，那么任何一方都可以先报价。

5. Common Used Offer Strategies (常见的报价策略)

(1) High Price Quotation (高价报价策略)

This strategy is based on the highest expected price determined by the seller. In international business negotiations, the negotiators will first increase the price according to their own needs, which will cause certain pressure to the counter-parties during the negotiations. In this case, the counter-parties can reduce the requirements and make concessions in this way, so that the offerer can increase interest. You can choose a high quotation method in the quotation at will, so that the counter-party will adjust requirement, so that the counter-party's psychological expectations are exceeded, so that there is more room for quotation in the negotiation, so that the benefits can be improved to achieve the ultimate goal. This strategy is suitable for one-time, monopolistic or time-relaxed business negotiations.

这种策略是以卖方确定的最高期望价格报出价格的策略。在国际商务谈判中，谈判者会首先根据自身的需求将价格提高，对谈判中的对方施加一定的压力，在这种情况下可以使对方将要求降低，通过这种方式进行退让，从而使己方利益增加。可以随意在报价中选择高报价的方式使对方调整要求，从而使对方的心理预期被超越，使谈判中有更多的报价空间，使利益得以增加从而达到己方的最终目的。这种策略适用于一次性、垄断性或时限比较宽松的商务谈判。

For example, the Maldivian customer Company A purchased motorcycles from Chongqing Company B for the first time. Company B learned that Company A runs a tourism company with relatively strong funds, so the company's favorite motorcycle model 150-5 was quoted at \$360 per set instead of \$340 per set. Company B also explained that this price was luxury configuration with luxury large cargo rack at \$8.00/set (convenient for legs down of the person on the back seat), with voice reminders at \$2.00/set to remind driver when turning direction), with the flaky muffler cover at \$5.00/set to prevent people in the back seat from being scalded by muffler, with Caller ID at \$5.00/set, etc. Company A felt that the price was too high, so it requested that the luxury large shelves should be changed to ordinary rear shelves without electricity display, so it was traded at \$350 per set. In this case, Company A runs a tourism company with relatively strong funds and is not sensitive to the offer of motorcycles. By adopting a method of high allocation and high quotation, Company B needs to reduce the motorcycle configuration if it wants to reduce price of motorcycles.

例如，马尔代夫客户A公司第一次到重庆B公司采购摩托车，B公司了解到A公司在马尔代夫经营一个旅游公司，资金比较雄厚，于是将A公司看中的摩托车150-5从日常报价340美元/台改报为360美元/台，并说明这个价格是豪华配置：带豪华大货架（方便坐摩托车后座的人放下双腿）8.00美元/台，带语音提示器（以便开车的时候提醒左右转）2美元/套，带片状消声器护罩（防止后座的人被消声器高温器烫伤）5.00美元/台，带来电显示5.00美元/台等。A公司觉得价格过高，于是要求将豪华大货架改为普通后货架，不带来电显示，从而以350美元/台的价格成交。在此案例中，A公司在马尔代夫经营一个旅游公司，资金比较雄厚，对摩托车的报价敏感度不高，B公司通过采取高配置、高报价的方式，使得A公司一旦要求降价，就需要降低摩托车的配置。

(2) "Skillful Arrayed Maze"（"巧布迷阵"策略）

The "skillful arrayed maze" is a strategy in which one party deliberately understates the reserve price, enticing the counter-party to enter the maze, and then profit from it. If you are in a disadvantaged position, you urgently need a certain product or you urgently want to sell a certain product, and you are desperately hoping to close the deal which has been perceived by the counter-party and you are likely to be in a disadvantaged position in the negotiation, in this case, if the use of a false reserve price intentionally proposes an unexpected condition to the counter-party, which makes your attitude far from the situation held by the counter-party, it will immediately make the counter-party confused.

"巧布迷阵"策略是谈判一方有意虚报底价，引诱对方步入迷阵，进而从中取利的策略。若己方处于劣势，急需某种商品或急需出卖某种商品并迫切希望成交，而这种情况已被对方察觉，己方在谈判中很可能处于被动挨打的不利地位，那么在这种情况下，如果采用虚报底价方法，故意提出一个令对方意想不到的条件，使己方的态度与对方所掌握的情况相差甚远，就会使对方顿时感到迷惑，乱了方寸。

When the counter-party knows very little about your intentions and refuses to show its cards first, and tries to induce you to report the reserve price first and obtains your information, you can use the intentional misrepresentation of the reserve price to observe the counter-party's reality and increase your asking price level. When the negotiating parties are equal in strength, you can adopt a strategy of falsely quoting low prices to cleverly disguise and shake the counter-party's beliefs.

当对方对己方的意图知之甚少，不肯首先亮出底牌，要想方设法诱使己方先报底价并从中获取己方信息的情况下，己方可以采用故意虚报底价的方法，从中观察对方的虚实，提高己方的要价水平。在谈判方旗鼓相当、实力对等的情况下，己方可以采用虚报低价的策略，巧布迷阵，动摇对方的信念。

(3) Price Changing Midway (中途变价策略)

The price changing midway refers to when the seller makes a quotation based on a product during the international business negotiation process, in order to increase the benefit obtained, he raises or lowers the price in the offer. This change expresses the negotiator's psychology in the negotiations. Adopting this strategy can affect the psychological state of the counter-party, adjust the raised price, and turn the quotation into a downward trend, so that the counter-party's psychology can be disturbed, and the rationality of the price can be reconsidered. By changing the price midway, the price of the downward trend can be adjusted to the upward trend, which can surprise the counter-party, make the offer help the negotiation, and improve the success rate of the negotiation.

中途变价策略是指在国际商务谈判过程中当卖方根据产品进行报价时，为了使获得的效益增加，卖方将报价中的价格提升或降低。这种变化在谈判中表达着谈判者的心理。采用这种策略可以影响对方的心理状态，将提升的价格进行调整，使报价转为下降的趋势，这样可以使对方心理被干扰，并重新考虑价格的合理性。通过中途变价使下降趋势的价格调整为上升的趋势，可以使对方产生惊喜的情绪，使报价为谈判带来帮助，使谈判的成功率提高。

(4) Bait Quotation (鱼饵报价策略)

In international business negotiations, it is necessary to analyze the requirements of the counter-party and then use the conditions of cooperation as bait to protect one's own interests. When adopting this strategy, the scale needs to be clarified. When the attractiveness of the bait is relatively small, effective results cannot be obtained. If there is more bait, although an agreement can be reached, it will cost more and eventually lead to a negotiation result that is under expectations. Therefore, when using the bait quotation strategy, it needs to be performed by someone with more negotiation experience.

在国际商务谈判中，需要结合对方的要求进行分析之后将合作条件作为鱼饵，使己方利益得到保障。在采用这种策略时，需要对尺度进行明确。当鱼饵的吸引力比较小时，不能得到有效的结果；而如果鱼饵较多，虽然可以达成协议，但需要花费更多成本，最终导致谈判的结果没有达到预期。所以，在利用鱼饵报价策略时需要由具有较多谈判经验的人进行。

(5) Psychological Pricing (心理价格策略)

People generally think that \$9.90 is cheaper than \$10, and that the precision of fractional prices is high, giving people a sense of trust and making people feel cheap. A price that is below the decimal place and is considered psychologically smaller is called a psychological price. Therefore, there is a base pricing strategy in marketing. In international business negotiations, we can make good use of this psychological price to make quotations. For example, the list price is \$49.00 instead of \$50.00; the list price is \$19.99 instead of \$20.00. The difference of one cent or one US dollar gives people the feeling of "a real bargain".

人们在心理上一般认为 9.90 美元比 10 美元便宜，而且认为零头价格精确度高，给人以信任感，容易使人产生便宜的感觉。像这种在十进位以下而在心理上被人们认为较小的价格称为心理价格。因此，在营销中有一种基本的定价策略。在国际商务谈判中，我们可以很好地利用这种心理价格来进行报价。例如，标价 49.00 美元而不是 50.00 美元；标价 19.90 美元而不是 20.00 美元。这 1 美分或 1 美元钱之差，给人“大大便宜”的感觉。

Ⅱ Substantive Consultation Stage of International Business Negotiation (国际商务谈判的实质磋商阶段)

At the offering stage, the negotiating parties have proposed trading conditions. After comparing the trading conditions proposed by the counter-party with the trading conditions set in advance, there will often be differences and contradictions which bargaining is made to resolve. This stage is the key stage of the negotiation and the most difficult and tensest stage in the entire negotiation process. This stage includes four phases—bargaining, counter-offer, concession and deadlock breaking.

在报价阶段，谈判方都各自提出了交易条件，在通过对比对方提出的交易条件和己方事先设定的交易条件后常常会存在分歧和矛盾。为了解决这些分歧和矛盾从而进行讨价还价，这个阶段是谈判的关键阶段，也是整个谈判过程中最困难、最紧张的阶段。在这个阶段中包括了讨价、还价、让步和缓解僵局四个阶段。

1. Bargaining Phase（讨价阶段）

（1）Definition of Bargaining（讨价的含义）

Bargaining means the behavior that after one party quotes a price, the other party thinks that the price is far from its expected price, and asks the bidder to improve the quotation. The purpose of bargaining is to force the other party to improve the offer, mislead the other party's judgment of one's price expectations, and change the other party's price expectations in preparation for one's counter-offer.

讨价是指在谈判的一方报价之后，另一方认为该价格距离其预期的价格比较远，从而要求报价方改善报价的行为。讨价的目的是迫使对方改善报价，误导对方对于己方价格期望的判断，并改变对方的价格期望，为己方的还价做准备。

（2）Method of Bargaining（讨价的方式）

In the practice of international business negotiations, bargaining is often divided into overall bargaining and specific bargaining.

在国际商务谈判的实践中，讨价往往可分为总体讨价和具体讨价。

Overall bargaining refers to require re-quoting from the aspect of overall price and content. It is generally used for the first asking price after reviewing or for complex transactions. The negotiating parties proceed from a macro perspective and lower prices based on "attitude". The overall bargaining is a comprehensive intervention, not limited to one time, but no more than three times.

总体讨价即从总体价格和内容方面要求重新报价，一般用于评论之后的第一次要价，或者用于比较复杂交易的第一次要价。谈判方从宏观出发，凭"态度"压价。总体讨价是全面介入，不限于一次，但最多不会超过三次。

The specific bargaining is to require re-quoting according to the items and the specific content of the quotation, which is often used after the counter-party has improved the offer for the first time, or when it is not easy to adopt general bargaining methods. The requirements for specific bargaining are strong accuracy and pertinence instead of telling the whole story. In practice, the specific discussions are classified, such as transportation fees, insurance fees, payment conditions, technical service fees, equipment conditions, training costs, materials costs, etc. When using this method, it should be noted that the bargaining should start from the part with the largest false content, then the part with medium false content, and finally the part with smaller false content.

具体讨价就是依据分项价格和具体报价内容要求重新报价。常常用于对方第一次改善价格之后，或不易采用总体讨价方式时。具体讨价的要求在于准确性和针对性强，而不在于将己方的谈判内容全盘托出，在做法上是将具体的讨论内容进行分类，如运费、保险费、支付条件、技术服务费、设备条件、培训费、资料费等。在采用这种方式时应注意从水分最大的那一部分开始讨价，然后对水分中等的部分讨价，最后对水分较小的部分讨价。

(3) Commonly Used Bargaining Strategy (常用讨价策略)

a. "Throw a Stone to Clear the Road" Strategy (投石问路策略)

It means that after one party makes an offer, the counter-party does not immediately counter offer, but asks the price of the product under various assumptions to observe the response and answer of the counter-party to infer the true intention of the counter-party and the bottom line of the price. This will not only maintain the atmosphere of "equal trust", but also help to better understand the situation of the counter-party before counter-offering. Generally speaking, any "stone" can give the buyer a better understanding of the seller's business habits and motivations, and it is difficult for the counter-party to refuse. For example, you can ask the counter-party, "If we have signed a one-year contract with you, what is the price concession you can give us?" "If we pay in cash or installments, will the price of your product be any differences?"

它是指在一方发盘后，另一方不会马上还盘，而是提出种种假设条件下的商品售价问题，来观察对方的反应和回答，推测对方的真实意图及价格底线。这样既能保持"平等信赖"的氛围，又有利于还价前进一步掌握情况。一般来讲，任何一块"石头"都能使买方进一步了解卖方的商业习惯和动机，而且对方难以拒绝。例如，可以询问对方："如果我们和你方签订了为期一年的合同，你方能够给我们的价格优惠是多少?""如果我们以现金支付或采取分期付款的方式，你方的产品价格会有什么区别?"

If the counter-party adopts this strategy, you must first find out what the counter-party really wants to buy, and at the same time do not immediately evaluate the "if" requirements, and not every question is worth answering. You may ask the counter-party to put forward a "guarantee", which in turn can find out the sincerity of the counter-party.

如果对方采用了这种策略，作为己方而言，首先要找出对方真正想要购买的东西，同时不要对"假如"的要求马上估价，而且并不是每个问题都值得回答。己方可以要求对方提出"保证"，这样可以反过来摸清对方的诚意。

b. Strict Requirement Strategy (严格要求策略)

This strategy is one that all negotiators can use. As far as the buyer is concerned, it is the buyer who strictly inspects the seller's goods from all aspects, raises many issues in the seller's transaction and asks the counter-party to improve the quotation. This is the buyer's strict requirement strategy. The buyer's strict requirements generally include looking for "weak points" in terms of value in use like commodity quality and performance, cost price and transportation.

这个策略是谈判方均可运用的策略。就买方而言，是买方对卖方的商品从各个方面进行严格检查，提出卖方交易中的许多问题并要求对方改善报价，这就是买方的严格要求策略。买方严格要求的范围一般包括从商品质量、性能等使用价值方面和成本价格以及运输方面寻找"弱点"。

If the other party adopts this strategy, you should be patient, look for loopholes and untrue words in the other party's questions, and explain them realistically; for some difficult and controversial issues, you must directly put forward your own views; for questions inconvenient to answer or minor issues, you can appropriately avoid them.

如果对方采用了这种策略，作为己方应该保持耐心，寻找对方提问中的漏洞和不实之词，实事求是地加以解释；对于某些难题、有争议的问题，要直截了当地提出己方看法；对于不便回答或次要的问题，可以适当回避。

c. Fatigue Strategy（疲劳轰炸策略）

Fatigue strategy refers to interrupting the opponent's attention through fatigue tactics, dissolving the opponent's will and seizing the favorable opportunity to reach an agreement with the opponent. The use of this strategy should not be stubborn. Once the opponent's rivalry is stirred up, it will easily lead to the breakdown of negotiations. In international business negotiations, if one party shows a condescending and aggressive attitude, then this strategy can be chosen. If the counter-party adopts this strategy, the leader of your own negotiating group should try his best to complete the negotiation within the stipulated time, and ensure that the members of your negotiating group have sufficient rest time. You must ensure that the time outside the negotiation is arranged by yourself, and must not act according to the plan of others. You must learn to reject the excessive arrangement of the counter-party.

疲劳轰炸策略是指通过疲劳战术来干扰对方的注意力，瓦解对方意志并抓住有利时机与对方达成协议。该策略的运用切忌以硬碰硬，一旦激起对方的对立情绪，就很容易导致谈判破裂。在国际商务谈判中，如果一方表现出居高临下、盛气凌人的态度，那么，可以选择这种策略。如果对方采用这种策略，作为己方谈判小组的领导者应尽量使谈判在规定的时间内完成，确保己方谈判小组成员有足够的休息时间。一定要保证谈判以外的时间由自己来安排，而不能按别人的计划行事。对对方的过度安排要学会拒绝。

2. Counter-offer Phase（还价阶段）

(1) Definition of Counter-offer（还价的含义）

A counter-offer is legally called a counter-pollicitation. Counter-offer refers to the act of one party in international business negotiations to propose its own price requirements based on the counter-party's offer and in combination with its own negotiation goals.

还价又称还盘，在法律上称为反要约。还价是指国际商务谈判的一方根据对方的报价，结合己方的谈判目标，提出己方的价格要求的行为。

If a counter-offer substantially changes the offering conditions, it will constitute a rejection of the counter-party's offer. Its legal consequences negate the original offer to cause the original offer fail, and the original offeror will no longer be bound by it. According to the provisions of the United Nations Convention on Contracts for the International Sale of Goods, any addition or change made by the counter-offeror to the price, payment, quality, quantity, time and place of delivery of the goods, the scope of liability of one party to the counter-party or the method for settling disputes, etc., shall be deemed as a substantial change in terms of quotation.

还价如果在实质上变更了报价条件，就构成对对方报价的拒绝，其法律后果是否定了原报价，原报价即告失败，原报价人就不再受其约束。根据《联合国国际货物销售合同公约》的规定，还盘人对货物的价格、付款、品质、数量、交货时间与地点、一方当事人对另一方当事人的赔偿责任范围或解决争端的办法等条件提出添加或更改，均为实质性变更报价条件。

Conditional acceptance of a quote is also a form of counter-offer. For example, when the offeree responds to the bidder with provisions such as "subject to final confirmation", "not selling valid" or similar additional conditions, which shall only be regarded as a counter-offer or an invitation to quote. The content of the counter-offer is "invitation to quote" if it does not meet the conditions for quotation. If the content of the counter-offeror meets the quotation conditions, it constitutes a new quotation, and the counter-offer becomes the new offeror; the original offeror becomes the new offeree and has the right to accept, reject or re-offer the new quotation.

对报价表示有条件的接受，也是还价的一种形式。例如，受盘人在答复报价人时，附有"以最后确认为准""未售有效"等规定或类似的附加条件，这种答复只能被视作还价或邀请报价。还价的内容，凡不具备报价条件，即为"邀请报价"。如果还价的内容具备报价条件，就构成一个新的报价。还价人成为新报价人；原报价人成为新受盘人，有对新报价做出接受、拒绝或再还价的权利。

(2) Principle of Counter-offer (还价的原则)

Prepare for counter-offer. Before making a counter-offer, we must fully understand the full content of the counter-party's quotation, and accurately understand the real intention of the counter-party's offer. So try to find out the conditions in its offer before the counter-offer, and know which are the key conditions, which are the main conditions, which are the secondary conditions, which are the additional conditions, and even which conditions are only chips for exchange. Only by making these clear can we make a more scientific counter-offer.

做好还价前的准备。在还价前必须充分了解对方报价的全部内容，准确了解对方提出条件的真实意图。因此，要在还价前设法摸清对方报价中的条件，知道哪些是关键条件，哪些是主要条件，哪些是次要条件，哪些是附加条件，甚至哪些条件的提出仅仅是交换性的筹码。只有把这些弄清楚了，才能做出合理的还价。

In most cases, the counter-party does not immediately respond to an offer, but adjusts it to its previous ideas, prepares a proposal, and then makes a counter-offer to "let one's opponent start hitting and then get the better of him".

谈判的一方报价后，在多数情况下，另一方不会马上回答，而是根据对方的报价，再针对自己先前的想法加以调整，准备好一套方案后，再进行还价，以实现"后发制人"。

A counter-offer is not a simple act of lowering prices; it must be based on market research and "comparative shopping". In order to ensure that the counter-offer has a certain scientific basis, for example, the market competition of technical indicators such as the supply and price status of the subject matter market, the quality of the subject matter traded and the development trend.

还价不是一种简单的压低价格的行为，它必须建立在市场调查与"货比三家"的基础之上。例如，掌握标的物市场供应和价格状况、交易标的物的质量以及发展趋势等各项技术指标的市场竞争情况，以确保还价具有一定的科学依据。

(3) Strategies of Counter-offer（还价的策略）

a. Picky Strategy（吹毛求疵策略）

The picky strategy is aimed at the seller's products to try to find faults and pick on them. What was originally satisfactory can be described as dissatisfied, and deliberately put forward requirements that the counter-party could not meet, showing that you have compromised out of consideration for the general interest to make excuses for counter-offer. A large number of facts in commercial transactions prove that it's a good way to force the seller to accept the buyer's counter-offer, thereby enabling the buyer to obtain greater benefits.

吹毛求疵策略就是针对卖方的商品，想方设法寻找缺点，百般挑剔。本来满意之处，也非要说成不满意，并故意提出令对方无法满足的要求，表明自己委曲求全，以此为自己的还价制造借口。商务交易中的大量事实证明，迫使卖方接受买方的还价能够使买方获得较大的利益。

For example, TF, a large Argentine customer, is looking for motorcycle suppliers in Chongqing. The company is very picky about the quality of motorcycle and lists high technical requirements, road test requirements, and after-sales requirements, which have discouraged many companies. HL, a large Chongqing private company, has been in contact with TF for 2 years, and has continuously sent motorcycles that have been improved in accordance with the requirements of TF to Argentina. In August 2019, TF finally stated that it would place an order with HL, which was offered in large quantities at low prices and with picky requirements. And TF proposed many improvements to HL's product quality. In the end, HL and TF reached an agreement at a very low profit. In this case, TF is a big customer and will not worry about the lack of partners, so it is picky about products from various companies, whose purpose is to get the ideal unit price and achieve better profits.

例如，阿根廷大客户 TF 公司在重庆寻找摩托车供货商，该公司对摩托车产品的质量十分挑剔，罗列了很高的技术要求、路试要求、售后要求，让很多公司望而却步。重庆大型民营企业 HL 公司接触 TF 公司已有两年，不断将按照 TF 公司的要求改进的摩托车送往阿根廷。2019 年 8 月，TF 公司终于表态将订单下给 HL 公司，然而量大、价低、要求苛刻，对 HL 公司的产品质量提出了众多改进意见，最终 HL 公司以极低利润的价格达成双方合作。在该案例中，IF 公司是大客户，不会担心没有合作方，对众多公司的产品各种挑剔，其目的就是为了拿到理想的单价，从而实现更好的利润。

b. Maximum Budget Strategy（最大预算策略）

On the one hand, you express interest in the counter-party's offer, and on the other hand, you force the counter-party to make concessions and accept your own offer based on your own maximum budget. For example, after a negotiation, the seller has reduced the price of a certain item from $100,000 to $85,000. The buyer would say, "We want to purchase this batch of goods, but at present our company only has a total purchase price of $78,000. Now, if the transaction can be made at this price, we are willing to maintain a cooperative relationship with you in the future." In this way, the buyer used the "maximum budget" technique to make a counter-offer of $78,000, and the transaction was realized.

一方面，对对方的商品报价表示出兴趣；另一方面，又以自己的最大预算为由来迫使对方做出让步和接受自己的报价。例如，经过讨价，卖方已将某货物的报价由10万美元降至8.5万美元。买方便说："贵方这批货我们很想购买，但是，目前我公司总共只有7.8万美元的购货款了，如果能按这个价格成交，我们愿今后与贵方保持合作关系。"这样，买方采用"最大预算"的技巧做出了7.8万美元的还价，实现了交易。

c. Emotional Investment Strategy（感情投资策略）

When using emotional investment strategies, we must first treat negotiations and opponents correctly. Second, do not over-calculate minor issues and actively cater for counter-party. Third, use the negotiation interval to discuss topics that are of interest to the counter-party outside the scope of business, such as sports competitions, cultural programs, local specialty and places of interest, etc. Finally, if there are previous contacts between the negotiating parties, it is generally necessary to talk about the old days.

在使用感情投资策略时，首先要正确对待谈判，正确对待对手；其次，对于一些较为次要的问题不要过分计较并主动迎合对方；再次，利用谈判间隙谈论业务范围以外让对方感兴趣的话题，如体育比赛、文艺节目、当地土特产、名胜古迹等；最后，如果谈判方之间有过交往，一般要叙旧。

3. Concession Phase（让步阶段）

Concession is a strategy in itself, which embodies the spiritual essence that negotiators take the initiative to meet the needs of the other side in exchange for their own needs. In any international business negotiation, both sides of the negotiation will inevitably make some concessions. It can be said that without concessions, there will be no successful negotiations. Therefore, when to make concessions, how to make concessions, and to what extent, are questions that require careful study.

让步本身就是一种策略，它体现了谈判者用主动满足对方需要的方式来换取己方所需的精神实质。在任何一个国际商务谈判中，谈判双方都难免会做出一些让步，可以说，没有让步，也就没有谈判的成功。所以，何时让步，如何让步，让步到何种程度，是需要仔细研究的问题。

(1) Basic Principle of Concession（让步的基本原则）

a. Target Price Maximization（目标价最大化原则）

First of all, it is necessary to determine what is an important goal, an urgent goal, and not to set too many important goals, so as not to care for this and lose that or even to confuse each other, and leave the opponent an opportunity. After identifying important goals, seek to maximize the value of the goals.

首先要确定什么是重要目标、紧迫目标，不要把重要目标定得太多，以免顾此失彼，甚至自造混乱，留给对手可乘之机。在确定重要目标后，寻求己方目标价值最大化。

b. Clarity Principle（清晰原则）

The object and reason of the concession, the specific content and implementation details of the concession must be very clear to avoid new problems and contradictions caused by the concession.

让步的对象、理由，让步的具体内容和实施细节都要非常清晰、明确，避免因为让步而导致新的问题和矛盾。

c. Rigid Principle（刚性原则）

Concessions come at a price and at a cost. At the same time, it is necessary to clearly recognize that the resources available for concessions are limited, so you must set yourself a bottom line for concessions and slowly make concessions step by step. Furthermore, you must be clear about the number of concessions and the effect of concessions. With so many limitations, the use of concessions is even more prudent.

让步要付出代价和成本，同时要清楚认识到可以使用让步的资源是有限的，因此必须给自己定一条让步底线，一步步慢慢地让；此外，要清楚让步的次数和让步的效果也是有限的。既然有这么多限制，那么对让步的使用就更要慎重。

d. Timing Principle（时机原则）

Make the right concessions at the right time at the right place. Maximize the effect of concessions and achieve the best results.

要在适当的时机、适当的场合做出适当的让步。要使让步的作用发挥到最大，起到最佳效果。

e. Make-up Principle（弥补原则）

If the failure to make a greater concession could lead to the breakdown of the negotiations, a greater concession can be given. But we must find a way to get double or at least equal return from the other side. In international business negotiations, necessary concessions are required in order to reach an agreement. But concessions must be prudent and not to be made rashly. The general principle is to sacrifice small part benefits in exchange for large overall benefits.

在不做出较大让步就有可能导致谈判破裂的情况下，可以做出较大的让步。但一定想办法在另一方面得到对方的加倍的、至少是均等的回报。在国际商务谈判中，为了达成协议，必要的让步是必要的。但是让步一定要慎重，不可轻率行动。总的原则是牺牲局部的小利益换取整体的大利益。

(2) Skills of Concession（让步的技巧）

a. Make a Concession Plan（制订让步计划）

The rate of concession must be reduced, the number of times must be small, and the speed must be slow. Before concessions, it is necessary to know clearly what issues must not be conceded, what issues can be actively conceded, what issues can be conceded passively, and how much you want to make concessions. The concessions of major issues must be required by the other side, and then you consider whether to make concessions. Do not take the initiative.

让步幅度要递减，次数要少，速度要慢。让步前要清楚地知道哪些问题决不可让步，哪些问题可以主动让步，哪些问题可以被动让步，如果要让步让出多少。重大问题一定要由对方先提出让步，再考虑是否让步，己方不可主动提出让步。

b. Leave Room for Negotiation（留出让步的谈判空间）

Concessions take a lot of time and space, and concessions are essentially an extension of bargaining. Before making concessions, you must first seek for a more adequate leeway and time for your most basic interests. For example, the plane landed late, the flight attendant reported from one hour delay to half an hour delay, and then landed immediately after the report. The passenger plane was indeed late, but the passengers showed satisfaction and happiness, because the stewardess reserved themselves an hour for the delay.

让步是要花很多时间与空间的，让步实质上也是讨价还价的延伸。在做出让步之前，要先给自己最基本的利益寻求一个更充分的回旋余地与时间。例如：飞机落地晚点，空姐报时从晚一个小时到晚半个小时，而广播后即刻着陆。客机确实是晚点了，但乘客表现出来的却是满意与庆幸，因为空姐事先给自己晚点留了一个1小时的空间。

(3) Type of Concession（让步的类型）

Concession are classified differently according to different criteria.

让步根据不同的标准有不同的分类。

a. Positive and Negative Concessions（积极让步和消极让步）

This is a classification based on the attitude of concession. Positive concessions, also called active concessions, are concessions that involve compromises in some negotiating clauses in exchange for major or fundamental benefits. Negative concessions, also called passive concessions, are concessions that seek to break the deadlock and reach a deal with pure self-sacrifice and partial concessions.

这是按照让步的姿态进行的分类。积极让步，又称主动让步，是指用某些谈判条款上的妥协换取主要方面或基本方面的利益的让步。消极让步，又称被动让步，是指以单纯的自我牺牲、退让部分利益，求得打破僵局、达成交易的让步。

b. Substantive Concession, Virtual Concession and Symbolic Concession（实质让步、虚置让步和象征让步）

This is a classification according to the nature of concessions. Substantive concessions are real concessions in terms of interests, the purpose of which is to exchange your own concessions for cooperation and concessions from the counter-party. The virtual concession is not a real concession; it is just a form of concession without any substance, that is, without giving up any interests. A symbolic concession usually occurs in a stalemate between two sides, when it is necessary for one side to make concessions. In addition to reducing the benefits, there are also ways to compensate for non-interests, that is, substitute alternatives of the same value in exchange for the looseness of the counter-party's position, so that the counter-party's psychology is satisfied, and the transaction is concluded.

这是按照让步的本质进行的分类。实质让步即利益上的真正让步，目的是以己方的让步换取对方的合作与让步。而虚置让步并不是真正的让步，只不过是有让步的形式，而没有任何实质内容，即并未让出自己的任何利益。象征让步是在双方僵持不下时，一方做出让步是必要的。让步除利益的要求降低以外，还有非利益要求的补偿方式，即以同等价值的替代方案换取对方立场的松动，使对方心理上得到满足，从而达成交易。

(4) Strategy of Active Concession（主动让步的策略）

a. First Concession Strategy（最先让步策略）

The first concession refers to the first step to give up all, and the next three steps to give up little or no profit. Since the first step is to give up all your benefits, it gives people a sense of honesty and frankness. It is easier to impress the counter-party to take reciprocating actions, and it is easier to obtain the counter-party's trust to facilitate an agreement. At the same time, this first major concession will leave a good impression on the counter-party, give the counter-party a sense of cooperation and trust, and may generate a large appeal, which is conducive to obtaining long-term benefits. Because the negotiators make the whole concession at the first step and are honest, the negotiation efficiency is improved, the negotiation cost is reduced, and the negotiation time is saved. However, because this concession is a little too rushed, it will have a strong impact and stimulus on the counter-party, and may send a still profitable message to the counter-party, which will cause the counter-party's expectations to increase greatly and make the counter-party continue to bargain. Because of one-time stride concessions, it is also possible to lose the benefits that could have been obtained. This type of concession applies to negotiations where one side is at a disadvantage or the relations between the parties to the negotiation are friendly.

最先让步是指第一步让出全部，以后三步一点儿不让或无利可让。由于第一步就让出了自己的全部可让利益，给人以坦诚和直率的感觉，比较容易打动对方采取回报行动，容易取得对方的信任，以促成和局。同时这种率先大幅让步会给对方留下好印象，给对方以合作感、信任感，可能产生较大的号召力，有利于获取长远利益。由于谈判者一步让利、坦诚相见，因此提高了谈判效率，降低了谈判成本，节省了谈判时间。但是由于这种让步有点操之过急，对对方会有极强的影响和刺激，可能给对方传递一种尚有利可图的信息，因而导致对方的期望值大大提高，从而继续讨价还价。由于一次性做出大步让利，还有可能失掉本来能够争取到的利益。这种类型的让步方式适用于己方处于劣势或谈判各方之间关系较为友好的谈判。

b. Final Concession Strategy（最后让步策略）

This is a concession that yields all concessions in the final stage of the concession. If you insist on not giving a price three times, you will show your own tough attitude, which will hurt the counter-party's spirit, shake the counter-party's confidence to continue bargaining, and obtain greater benefits for yourself. This way of giving up all at the last time will make the counter-party feel that the concessions obtained are hard to come by, and they are especially grateful and cherished. However, since one has always been reluctant to give up, the counter-party may mistakenly believe that there is no sincerity. Therefore, it is easy to lead to a deadlock in the negotiations and even to a breakdown of the negotiations, which is relatively risky. Generally speaking, this strategy is suitable for the dominant party to employ in the negotiation.

这是一种在让步的最后阶段一步让出全部可让利益的让步方式。如果连续三次坚持不让价，会显出己方强硬的态度，从而挫伤对方的锐气，动摇对方继续讨价还价的信心，为己方获取较大的利益。这种方式在最后一次全部让出，会让对方觉得取得的让步来之不易，并且特别庆幸和珍惜。但由于开始时一直寸步不让，对方可能误认为己方没有诚意，因此容易导致谈判陷入僵局，甚至导致谈判破裂，具有较大的风险性。这种策略一般适合谈判中占据优势的一方使用。

For example, the owner of Iranian company M, Alex's schedule for his stay in Chongqing was 3 days, and arranged to the motorcycle company H to discuss motorcycle prices in the third day morning. Alex selected a motorcycle and requested to reduce it to $400 per set on the basis of the seller's quoted price of $410 per set. The negotiation between Company H and Alex failed for many times. Alex proposed to leave the company to the airport. Company H retained Alex to dine in the meeting room and negotiated the price while eating. Company H closed a deal with Alex at $405 per set.

例如，伊朗客户M公司老板Alex在重庆的时间安排为3天，第三天上午到摩托车公司H商谈摩托车价格事宜。Alex选中了一款摩托车，在卖家报价410美元/台的基础上，要求降低为400美元/台，H公司和Alex多次磋商未果。中午时，Alex提出要离开H公司前往机场，H公司挽留Alex一起在会议室就餐，边吃饭边磋商价格。H公司以405美元/台与Alex成交。

In this case, Alex went to Company H on the last day of the trip. It is certain that he had gone to other companies to make a price comparison in the first 2 days. At the same time, it was seen that Alex wanted to do business with Company H. Why Alex did not leave Company H for the airport was that he had been waiting for Company H's final price. Company H reduced the price while having lunch together, which made Alex feel invaluable, and he quickly signed a contract with Company H.

在本案例中，Alex在行程的最后一天到H公司，可以肯定的是他前两天已经去其他公司对价格进行了摸底，同时可看出Alex想把订单给H公司。Alex之所以迟迟没有离开H公司前往机场，是因为他在等H公司最后的价格。H公司在一起吃午饭的时候降低价格，让Alex觉得难能可贵，从而赶紧与H公司签订了合同。

c. Equal Concession Strategy（均等让步策略）

Equal concession means giving all concessions equally. Since the concessions are equal and the concession time lasts long, it is difficult for the counter-party to gain an advantage. It is more advantageous for both parties to bargain, and it is easy to ensure that the benefits are balanced. We can use concessions to delay time and make it easier to act according to circumstances. If the counter-party is impatient or has no time to talk, one tends to gain the upper hand and weaken the counter-party's bargaining power and make it lose the patience to continue bargaining. However, due to the limited scope of each concession and the slow progress, the negotiations may be dull and tedious, which may easily make people feel tired. At the same time, such concessions are inefficient and usually waste a lot of energy and time, so the negotiation cost is high. Due to the uninterrupted giving of profits, it may give the counter-party the illusion that as long as there is patience, further benefits can be obtained. This strategy is currently commonly used in business negotiations.

均等让步指等额地让出全部可让利益。由于让步幅度均等，让步时间持久，对方很难占到优势，对于双方讨价还价比较有利，便于保证利益均沾。己方可以凭借让步拖延时间，便于见机行事。如果对方性情急躁或无时间长谈，己方往往会占上风，从而削弱对方的议价能力，使对方丧失继续讨价还价的耐心。但是由于每次让步幅度有限，进度缓慢，可能导致谈判平淡无味，容易使人产生疲劳、厌倦之感。同时这种让步效率较低，通常要浪费大量精力和时间，因此谈判成本较高。由于不间断地让利，可能给对方以错觉，认为只要有耐心就可以进一步获得利益。目前在商务谈判中这种策略被普遍采用。

d. More, Less and More Strategy（先高后低再高的策略）

This is a concession strategy that concedes more in the first step, then concedes less in the second step, and next concedes more in the last step. That is, the first concession is much larger, the second concession is the smallest, the third and the fourth concessions continue to increase the margin of concessions. The starting point of this strategy is relatively appropriate and moderate, and it can send cooperative and profitable messages to the other side. The price reduction in the second step may make the counter-party think that it is nearing the end, which is conducive to urging the counter-party to hold its own interests. This concession strategy is full of changes. If an agreement cannot be reached after the slow-down in the second step, then concessions will be increased, which will make it easier to succeed. Because this concession strategy is characterized by small to large instability, the counter-party may be encouraged to continue to bargain. This dramatic change may also disrupt the atmosphere of harmony because the message of the end was passed to the counter-party at the second concession, but later a big concession was made, so that the counter-party felt that you were not honest enough and it was not conducive to establishing a long-term friendly cooperative relationship. This strategy is generally suitable for use by experienced negotiators in highly competitive negotiations. This strategy should not be adopted in some friendly relations and cooperation negotiations.

这是一种先高后低、然后又拔高的让步策略。即第一步让步幅度较大，第二步幅度最小，第三步幅度加大，第四步幅度继续加大。这种策略让步的起点比较恰当、适中，能够向对方传递可以合作并有利可图的信息。第二步的降价幅度，可能使对方认为已接近尾声，有利于促使对方拍板保住己方的较大利益。这种让步策略富有变化，如果不能在第二步的缓速减量之后达成协议，就再大步让利，这样更容易取得成功。由于这种让步策略表现为由小到大不稳定的特点，可能鼓励对方得寸进尺，继续讨价还价。这种戏剧性的变化也可能会破坏和谐的气氛。因为在第二步让步时就已向对方传递了接近尾声的信息，而后来又做了大步让利，这样给对方的感觉是我方不够诚实，不利于建立长期友好的合作关系。这种策略一般适用于竞争性较强的谈判，由有经验的谈判老手来使用。在一些友好关系的合作谈判中，不宜采用此策略。

e. More, More and Less Strategy（先高后高再低的策略）

This is a concession strategy with large concessions in the first two steps and small concession in the third step. This strategy is based on cooperation and supplemented by competition. After two large concessions, the third concession was reduced. If an agreement can be reached on this, a less portion of the benefits can be conceded. If the third step makes a small concession and still cannot reach an agreement, giving up a larger profit at the end will often make the counter-party very satisfied and reach an agreement. However, since this strategy has made a large concession at the beginning, the opponent may think that there is much concession, which will increase the strength of the counter-offer, so it is easy to enhance the opponent's offensiveness. This strategy is generally applicable to cooperation-oriented negotiations.

这是一种从高到低、然后又微高的让步策略。这种策略是以合作为首，以竞争为辅，诚中见虚，柔中带刚。经过两次大幅度的让步之后，第三步让步幅度减小。如果能就此达成协议，则可少让一部分利益。如果第三步做出微小让步仍不能达成协议，再让出最后稍大一点的利润，往往会使对方很满意而达成协议。但是由于这种策略一开始时让步幅度很大，可能会让对方认为大有可让，从而增强还价的力度，因此容易增强对手的进攻性。这种策略一般适用于以合作为主的谈判。

f. Descending Concession Strategy（递减让步策略）

It refers to a large-scale concession as the starting point, and then decreases in order. The fourth step concedes all the rest. It starts with big and then goes small, from large to small, giving people a natural and frank feeling, which makes the counter-party easy to accept and willing to cooperate. Because this strategy adopts a more prudent concession rhythm, it usually does not make mistakes in concessions, which is conducive to the parties to negotiations to reach an agreement under the conditions of equivalent exchange and equal benefits. Since this strategy starts with a high starting point and then gradually decreases, for the counter-party, the more you fight for benefits, the less it will be, it may make the counter-party feel frustrated or affect the speed of reaching an agreement. This strategy is generally suitable for the proactive party or proposer of a negotiation.

它是指以大幅度的让步为起点，然后依次递减，第四步将剩余的部分全部让出。先大后小，由多到少，给人以顺其自然、坦率的感觉，容易使对方接受并愿意合作。这种策略由于采取了一次比一次更为审慎的让步节奏，一般不会出现让步上的失误，有利于谈判各方在等价交换、利益均沾条件下达成协议。由于这种策略刚开始让步时起点较高，随后逐渐递减，对于对方而言，越争取利益越小，可能会使对方感到沮丧，或者影响达成协议的速度。这种策略一般适合谈判的主动方或提议方使用。

g. Intermittent Concession Strategy（间断让步策略）

It refers to a sharp concession at the beginning, the middle two steps do not concede or give up very little, and the last step rebounds to make a larger concession. This strategy is based on the spirit of peace, and most of the benefits are given off at the beginning, so it will get a larger return from the counter-party. The two steps in the middle do not give up or give up very little, which is a kind of strong attitude expression that helps to weaken the counter-party's expectation of asking for interest concessions again. In the end, giving up small profits not only shows your sincerity, but also makes it difficult for the accessible negotiating opponents to refuse to sign the contract, so it often works well. Although there is also a motive for retaining profits, objectively, it still shows a gentle attitude that values peace, which is a more artistic approach. However, a large concession at the beginning may give the counter-party the impression of eagerness that it may become more aggressive. The two-step rejection can sometimes lead to a deadlock in the negotiations or break up. This strategy is suitable for a party that is disadvantaged in the negotiation competition, but is anxious to get a successful negotiation.

它是指一开始大幅度递减，中间两步不让或让得很少，最后一步让步幅度又比较大，出现反弹的让步方式。这种策略是以求和的精神为先，开始就让出多半利益，因此会换得对方较大的回报。中间两步寸步不让或让得很少，是一种态度强硬的表示，有益于削弱对方要求己方再一次让利的期望。最后又让出小利，既显示了己方的诚意，又会使通达的谈判对手难以拒绝签约，因此往往收效不错。尽管其中也藏有留利的动机，但客观上仍表现了以和为贵的温善态度，是比较艺术的做法。但由于一开始大幅度让步，可能给对方留下急于求成的印象，对方可能会变本加厉、得寸进尺。中间两步的拒绝有时可能导致谈判出现僵局或者不欢而散。这种策略适用于在谈判竞争中处于不利境地，但又急于成功达成谈判的一方。

(5) Strategies to Forcing the Counter-party to Concede (迫使对方让步的策略)

a. "Wheel Battle" Strategy ("车轮战"策略)

"Wheel battle" is a military term that refers to one's own dispersal of forces, taking turns to fight the enemy, or adopting a roundabout strategy to physically and intellectually fatigue the enemy and then destroy the enemy. "Wheel battle" is used in international business negotiations, which means that the negotiator takes turns to discuss and negotiate with the counter-party, thereby dragging down the counter-party's energy and forcing the counter-party to compromise. There are certain conditions and principles for the use of this strategy. It is often adopted by a disadvantaged party in the middle or near the end of negotiations. Create and use various "objective" reasons to recall the responsible person or an important member, and replace with another person of equivalent status. This strategy can also be applied to situations where one party is eager to trade or one party begs for the other.

"车轮战"是军事术语，指己方分散兵力，轮流与敌人作战，或者采取迂回战略，在体力上和智力上使敌人疲劳，然后消灭敌人。"车轮战"应用在国际商务谈判中，指谈判一方轮流与对方谈判，借以在精力上拖垮对方，迫使对方妥协让步。该策略的使用有一定的条件和原则。它往往是在谈判中期或接近尾声时，由处于不利形势的一方采用。制造、利用各种"客观"原因召回负责人或某个重要成员，让另一个身份相当的人替代。该策略还可以运用于一方成交心切或一方有求于另一方的场合。

If the counter-party uses this strategy to request a substitution, you must also substitute accordingly. If your side does not change people, don't bother to entangle past disputes. If the newcomer overturns his predecessor's promise, you can reinterpret your concession. You can also use the counter-party to make substitutions and ask the counter-party to explain the reasons and show its sincerity. At the same time, you can also deliberately make it difficult for the counter-party to make the decision to retreat automatically. You can even raise an objection or suspend negotiations.

如果对方采用这种战略要求换人，己方也要相应换人。若己方不换人，则不要费力去纠缠过去的争执。如果新人员推翻前任的承诺，己方可以重新解释自己的让步。己方还可以借口对方换人，要求对方解释原因，表明诚意。同时己方还可以因对方换人故意刁难，使其自动下台。己方甚至可以提出异议，或者暂停谈判。

b. Tactics to Use Competition（利用竞争策略）

In negotiations, one should consciously create and maintain a situation of competition with the other side. Sometimes, the counter-party does not actually have a competitor, but one can cleverly create illusions to confuse the counter-party in order to force the counter-party to yield. For example, when negotiating technology introduction, one can inspect several foreign manufacturers, and invite them to come to negotiate at the same time, and disclose some information about the counter-party's competitors appropriately. Don't end the negotiations with other manufacturers prematurely until one of them is finally negotiated. For face-to-face competition, two opposite countermeasures are taken: one is to participate in such meetings, but only listen without speaking, do not answer any conditions proposed by the other side and still act according to the established conditions; the other is not to participate in such meetings and not to listen to the counter-party's point of view, because the meeting is easily affected by the conditions proposed by the counter-party.

在谈判中，己方应该有意识地制造和保持与对方竞争的局面。有时，对方实际上并没有竞争对手，但己方可以巧妙地制造假象来迷惑对方，以求逼迫对方做出让步。比如，在进行技术引进谈判时，己方可以多考察几个国外的厂商，同时邀请它们前来进行谈判，并且适当地透露一些有关对方竞争对手的情况；在与其中的一个厂商最终谈成协议之前，不要过早地结束与其他厂商的谈判。对于面对面的竞争，可以采取两种相反的对策：一种是参加这种会议，但只倾听而不表态，不答应对方提出的任何条件，仍按照自己的既定条件办事；另一种是不参加这种会议，不听对方的观点，因为在会议上容易受到对方所提条件的影响。

c. Fait Accompli Strategy（既成事实策略）

The fait accompli strategy is also called the act-first and report-afterwards strategy. This can be interpreted in business negotiations as "closing first, then negotiating", that is, the weaker party often makes the deal a reality through some clever methods, and then forces the counter-party to compromise during the held negotiations. The essence of the act first and report afterwards strategy is to allow the counter-party to pay the price first, and use the price as "hostages" to reverse the weak situation of the party, let the counter-party measure the price paid and the degree of losses suffered from the suspension of transactions, and passively accept the fait accompli. For example, the seller first obtains the buyer's advance payment, and then finds a reason to raise the price or defer the delivery; the buyer first obtains the seller's pre-delivered goods, and then proposes to delay the payment. After the buyer obtains the goods, he suddenly asks for a price reduction with plausible reasons. Strictly speaking, this strategy is an unreasonable strategy, but under certain conditions, using it can also produce a certain effect. When you are applying this strategy, it should be noted that there must be a valid reason; otherwise it is considered to be unethical and unsuitable.

既成事实策略也叫先斩后奏策略。这在商务谈判中可以解释为"先成交，后谈判"，即实力较弱的一方往往通过一些巧妙的办法使交易成为既成事实，然后在谈判过程中迫使对方做出让步。既成事实策略的实质是让对方先付出代价，并以这些代价为"人质"扭转己方实力弱的局面，让对方衡量所付出的代价和中止成交所受损失的程度，被动接受既成事实。例如，卖方先取得买方的预付金，然后找理由提价或延期交货；买方先获得卖方的预交商品，然后提出延迟付款。买方在取得货物之后，突然又以堂而皇之的理由要求降价。严格地讲，该策略是一种不讲道理的策略，但在特定的条件下，使用它也可以产生一定的效果。在运用这种策略时应注意，必须有正当理由，否则会被视为缺乏商业道德，而不宜采用。

In order to prevent losses caused by the counter-party's use of established facts, negotiators should try to avoid "hostages" falling into the hands of others in the negotiation, so that the counter-party does not have the opportunity to "act first". Even if a deposit must be paid in the transaction, a credit investigation should be done and the circumstances under which the refund can be made are indicated. Adopt the method of "treating people in their own way" to master the "hostage" of the counter-party as much as possible; once the counter-party uses this measure, you can give tit for tat; once the situation occurs, you should dare to protest to the leader of the counter-party. If you cannot resolve it, you can sue to the local judicial authority.

为了防止出现由于对方采用既成事实策略造成损失的情况，己方谈判人员在谈判中应尽量避免"人质"落入他人之手，从而让对方没有"先斩"的机会。即使交易中必须先付定金或押金，也应做好资信调查，并注明何种情况下才可以退款。采取"以其人之道，还治其人之身"的做法，尽可能相应掌握对方的"人质"；一旦对方使用此计，则可针锋相对；一旦情况发生，要敢于向对方领导抗议。若不能解决，可向当地的司法机关起诉。

d. Ultimatum Strategy（最后通牒策略）

This is a strategy commonly used when the enemy is weak. There are two ways of ultimatum tactics in the negotiation: one is to use the deadline; the other is to confront the stubborn and ambiguous negotiating opponents with tough oral or written language to tell the counter-party the last conditions that must be answered, otherwise you will withdraw from the negotiation or cancel the negotiation, thereby forcing the counter-party to change its attitude and accept the conditions proposed by yourself.

这是一种敌弱我强时惯用的策略。谈判中的最后通牒策略有两种情况：一是利用最后期限；二是面对态度顽固、暧昧不明的谈判对手，以强硬的口头语或书面语向对方最后一次提出必须回答的条件，否则将退出谈判或取消谈判，由此迫使对方改变态度，接受己方提出的条件。

The basis and prerequisite for using this strategy is that the negotiator knows that he is stronger than the other. In particular, the transaction is more important to one party than the counter-party. The ultimatum can only be used at the last stage or at the last moment of the negotiation, because the counter-party has already invested a lot of manpower, material resources, financial resources and time in the negotiation, and it has cost a lot. Once the negotiation breaks down, these costs will be lost. You can use actions outside the negotiating table to cooperate with the ultimatum, such as hotel checkout, booking a return car, ship, or air ticket, let the negotiators have a holiday to visit local attractions and purchase local souvenirs, thus demonstrating to the counter-party the determination of the ultimatum, ready to return home after the negotiation break down. The basis of the ultimatum strategy must be strong. It must be strong in objectivity and irresistible. At the same time, the words should not be too strong.

运用这一策略的基础和必备条件是谈判者知道自身的实力强于对方。特别是该笔交易对对方来讲，要比对己方更为重要。最后通牒只能在谈判的最后阶段或最后关头使用，因为这时对方已在谈判中投入了大量人力、物力、财力和时间，花费了很多成本，一旦谈判破裂，这些成本将付之东流。可以借用谈判桌外的行动来配合最后通牒，如同旅馆结账，预定回程的车、船、机票，让谈判人员放假去游玩当地名胜，购买当地土特产等，从而向对方表明最后通牒的决心，准备谈判破裂后打道回府。最后通牒策略的依据要过硬，要有较强的客观性和不可违抗性，同时言辞不要太强硬。

If the counter-party adopts this strategy, you can ignore the ultimatum, turn to a third party, and pretend to reach an agreement with the third party. It is possible to defeat the ultimatum. If your own side is confident and capable of defeating, you may deal with the counter-party as it deals with you and make an ultimatum. In addition, as long as you understand that the counter-party's ultimatum is only a trick of negotiating, you may interrupt the negotiation and make it clear that the ultimatum means that the negotiation is broken. In this case, the counter-party who does not intend to disrupt the negotiation would consider whether to stop the strategy.

如果对方采用这种策略，己方可以不理会最后通牒，转向第三方，摆出与第三方达成协议的架式，就有可能击败最后通牒。如果己方有把握、有能力击败对方，不妨以其人之道还治其人之身，也来个最后通牒。除此之外，只要了解对方实施最后通牒仅仅是玩弄谈判的技巧，就不妨中断谈判，让其明白最后通牒意味着谈判破裂。在这种情况下，并不打算使谈判破裂的对方该考虑要不要停止该策略。

4. Deadlock Breaking Phase（缓解僵局阶段）

Negotiation deadlock refers to the fact that during the course of international business negotiations, when the negotiating parties have great differences in the interests of the issues being discussed, but they are not willing to make concessions, which leads to the confrontation of the negotiations because of the temporary irreconcilable contradictions, and thus leads to a stalemate in the negotiations. When the deadlock occurs, it must be dealt with promptly, otherwise it will affect the smooth progress of the negotiations. The occurrence of a deadlock does not mean that the negotiations have broken down, but it will seriously affect the negotiation process. If it is not resolved well, it will lead to the breakdown of the negotiations.

谈判僵局指在国际商务谈判过程中，谈判各方对所谈问题的利益要求差异较大，但又都不肯做出让步，导致谈判因暂时不可调和的矛盾而形成对峙局面，从而使谈判出现不进不退的僵持局面。在僵局出现后，必须进行迅速的处理，否则就会对谈判的顺利进行产生影响。出现僵局不等于谈判破裂，但它会严重影响谈判的进程。如不能很好地解决，就会导致谈判破裂。

(1) Reason of Negotiation Deadlock (谈判僵局产生的原因)

Generally speaking, the deadlock in negotiations comes from three aspects: first, the deadlock created by your own; second, the deadlock created by the counter-party; and third, the deadlock caused by the parties to the negotiation.

一般来说，谈判僵局的产生来自三个方面：一是己方制造的僵局；二是对方制造的僵局；三是由于谈判各方的原因产生的僵局。

a. Created by the Negotiating Party (谈判一方故意制造)

This is a highly adventurous and dangerous negotiation strategy. That is, in order to test out the counter-party's determination and strength, you intend to create difficult problems for the counter-party, misleading the counter-party and even cause quarrels, and thus bring the negotiations to an impasse. The purpose is to subdue the counter-party, forcing the counter-party to abandon its negotiation goals and move closer to your own goals, so as to reach a transaction that is beneficial to your own side.

这是一种带有高度冒险性和危险性的谈判策略，即谈判一方为了试探出对方的决心和实力而有意给对方出难题，搅乱视听，甚至引起争吵，使谈判陷入僵局，其目的是使对方屈服，迫使对方放弃自己的谈判目标而向己方目标靠近，从而达成有利于己方的交易。

b. Negotiator Factor (谈判人员的因素)

First of all, it may be because of negotiators' style or lack of knowledge and experience, strategic skills, or mistakes that will lead to a deadlock in the negotiations. Secondly, due to the subjective prejudice and dissatisfaction of the negotiators, starting from their own emotions in the negotiation, even with serious emotional coloring, they put forward some incorrect opinions or views on the counter-party or the negotiation topic, which will lead to the deadlock in the negotiation. There are also negligent words and deeds of negotiators during negotiations, which can hurt the self-esteem and lead to negotiation deadlock, such as careless words and deeds, hurting the feelings of the counter-party, or making the counter-party lose face. If the counter-party feels losing face during the negotiation, the counter-party will fight back to save face and even quit the negotiation.

首先，谈判人员作风方面的原因或知识、经验、策略技巧方面的不足或失误，都可能会导致谈判出现僵局。其次，由于谈判人员存在主观偏见和不满，在谈判中从自身情感出发，甚至带有严重的感情色彩，对对方或谈判议题提出一些不正确的意见或看法，就会导致谈判陷入僵局。此外，在谈判中谈判人员言行不慎、伤人自尊也会导致谈判陷入僵局，例如言行不慎、伤害对方的感情或使对方没有面子等。如果在谈判中让对方感到丢了面子，对方会奋起反击来挽回面子，甚至不惜退出谈判。

c. Cultural Barriers（文化障碍）

In international business negotiations, since the parties to the negotiation are born with different cultures and form a fixed behavior in business activities, once this behavior exceeds the cultural environment in which it is located, it will conflict with the behavior generated under another cultural environment. An entirely reasonable request on one side would also be considered a non-ideal request by the other side, thus creating a barrier to communication between the two sides, which is a cultural barrier. For example, Americans think differently about making collections from Japanese. Japanese businessmen attach great importance to the cost of capital, so they will take interest into account at any time. Therefore, interest is calculated when the product is marketed. In this regard, Americans can't figure it out, because American businessmen determine the price based on the risk of collection, and pay special attention to the payment method during negotiations. Bargaining is an important part of business negotiations, but when negotiating a deal with an Australian businessman, you must be careful not to slowly reduce the price after opening a high price because Australians hate sky-high bargaining and try to avoid wasting time on bargaining. Most purchases are made through bidding to avoid bargaining. When bidding, you can only bid at the lowest price, and once the price is determined, the price issue must never be mentioned again when the conditions of the next stage are negotiated.

在国际商务谈判中，由于谈判各方生来就受着不同文化的熏陶，并在商业活动中形成了固定的行为方式，因此，一旦这种行为方式超出了其所在的文化环境，就会与另一种文化环境下所产生的行为方式发生冲突，在一方看来完全合理的要求也会被对方认为是非分之想，从而使双方的交流产生障碍，这就是文化障碍。例如，美国人对于收款的看法就与日本人不同。日本商人非常重视资金成本，所以随时都会考虑到利息。因此，在推销产品时就计算着利息。对此，美国人是想不通的，因为美国商人是基于收款的风险大小来决定价格的高低，在洽谈中特别注重支付的方式。讨价还价是商务谈判中的重要内容，但在与澳大利亚商人洽谈交易时，就得注意不要在开高价后再慢慢减价，因为澳大利亚人讨厌漫天要价，极力避免在讨价还价上浪费时间。大部分采购都采用招标的方式以避免讨价还价。在投标时，只能以最低的价格竞标，而价格一经确定，在下一阶段的条件洽谈中，就决不能再提及价格问题。

d. Disputes on Positions and Opinions（立场、观点的争执）

Each of the parties to the negotiations insists on its own positions and views, and rejects the positions and views of the counter-party, which will naturally result in a stalemate. For negotiators, disputes over standpoints are the easiest mistakes to make in negotiations, and are therefore the most common type of deadlock.

谈判各方各自坚持自己的立场和观点而排斥对方的立场和观点，自然会形成僵持不下的局面。对于谈判者而言，立场和观点的争执是在谈判中最容易犯的错误，因此也是最常见的一种僵局。

e. Communication Barriers（沟通的障碍）

Communication barriers refer to the obstacles to understanding that may be encountered by the negotiating parties due to subjective or objective reasons in the process of exchanging their respective situations, opinions, cooperation intentions and transaction conditions in the negotiation. The main manifestations are: conceptual barriers, custom barriers, language barriers caused by differences in the cultural background of the negotiators, differences in understanding of issues caused by differences in knowledge structure and educational level, emotional barriers caused by differences in psychology and personality, barriers to communication caused by expressive ability and means. For example, when the president of a multinational company visited a famous Chinese manufacturing company, the Chinese general manager was proud to introduce to the counter-party that "my company is a second-level enterprise in China" and the translators naturally expressed it as "second class enterprise". The president not only became indifferent, but also got up to leave. He complained, "How can we cooperate with a second-class company?"

沟通障碍是指在谈判中谈判各方在交流各自情况、观点、合作意向、交易条件的过程中，所可能遇到的由于主观或客观的原因所造成的理解障碍。主要表现为：由于谈判方文化背景差异所造成的观念障碍、习俗障碍、语言障碍，由于知识结构和教育程度的差异所造成的问题理解的差异，由于心理、性格差异所造成的情感障碍，由于表达能力和表达方式所造成的传播障碍等。例如，某跨国公司总裁访问一个中国著名制造企业时，中方总经理很自豪地向对方介绍说"我公司是中国二级企业"，翻译人员很自然地用"second class enterprise"来表述，结果对方总裁不仅冷淡下来，还起身告辞。他抱怨道："我们怎么能和一个二流企业合作呢？"

f. Other Contingent Factors（其他偶发因素）

During the period of conducting international business negotiations, there are likely to be some other contingent situations. When these situations involve the interests of one party in the negotiation, the negotiation will be bogged down by the disruption of these occasional factors (changes in the external environment).

在进行国际商务谈判的这段时间内很有可能会出现一些其他偶发情况，当这些情况涉及谈判某一方的利益得失时，谈判就会由于这些偶发因素（外部环境的变化）的干扰而陷入僵局。

(2) Principles of Dealing with Negotiation Deadlock（谈判僵局的处理原则）

a. Calm and Rational Thinking（冷静理智思考）

When negotiators are dealing with deadlocks, they must be able to correctly handle the interference caused by over-excited emotions. A good negotiator must have a calm mind and negotiating qualities that can handle matters calmly. Only in this way can he face the stalemate and handle it calmly. Only by calming yourself down and not being controlled by emotions can you sort out your clues and correctly analyze the situation you are facing. Fully consider what the potential interests of the negotiating parties are, and reasonably overcome the blind hoping to "win" the negotiation by insisting on your own positions.

谈判者在处理僵局时，要能正确处理过激情绪带来的干扰。一名优秀的谈判者必须具备冷静的头脑以及遇事能心平气和处理的谈判素养，只有这样才能面对僵局而泰然处之。只有让自己冷静下来，不被情绪所左右，才能理清头绪，正确分析当前所面临的情况。充分考虑到谈判各方潜在的利益到底是什么，从而理智地克服一味地希望通过坚持自己的立场来"赢"得谈判的做法。

b. Avoid Quarrel（避免争吵）

Once the negotiations are deadlocked, don't fall into an endless quarrel, because the quarrel can only intensify the contradictions. Once the two sides of the negotiation have quarrels, it will make the two sides more confrontational, making it difficult to break the deadlock and reach an agreement. Even if one party wins the quarrel, it is difficult for the counter-party to hold the same opinion, emotionally or psychologically, and negotiations will still face various obstacles.

一旦谈判陷入僵局，切忌陷入无止境的争吵中，因为争吵只能激化矛盾。谈判双方一旦出现争吵，就会使双方对立情绪加重，从而很难打破僵局、达成协议。即使一方在争吵中获胜，另一方无论从感情上还是心理上都很难持相同的意见，谈判仍会面临各种障碍。

c. Coordinate the Interests of All Parties（协调好各方的利益）

When the two sides confront each other on the same issue, and their respective reasons are sufficient, they cannot convince the counter-party, nor can they accept each other's conditions, so that the negotiations are at a deadlock, they should carefully analyze their own interests that may break the deadlock. Make adjustments from the respective current and long-term interests, find a balance point that is acceptable to all parties, and finally reach an agreement.

当双方在同一问题上发生对立，并且各自理由充分，都无法说服对方，又无法接受对方的条件，从而使谈判陷入僵局时，应认真分析各自的利益所在，只有平衡好各方的利益才有可能打破僵局。从各自的目前利益和长远利益两个方面来做出调整，寻找各方都能接受的平衡点，最终达成协议。

(3) Use and Creation of Deadlocks（商务谈判中僵局的利用和制造）

In business negotiations, negotiators use the deadlock in the negotiation process for two reasons: first, to change the existing negotiation situation and improve their status in the negotiation; second, to strive for favorable negotiation conditions. When the deadlock arises in the negotiations, there will be two consequences: one is to break the deadlock and continue the negotiations; the other is to break the negotiations which the deadlock maker is unwilling to see. Therefore, creating a deadlock is risky. As long as you show an uncooperative attitude, a deadlock could be simply made in negotiations which will inevitably lead to some unavoidable trouble that both parties are not willing to see. Generally speaking, a higher request is made to the counter-party, which requires the counter-party to fully accept it. However, this request must not be unattainable, because if the request is too high to meet, the counter-party will think that you have no sincerity and exit the negotiation, thus resulting in the breakdown of the negotiation.

在商务谈判中，谈判者在谈判过程中利用谈判僵局，主要出于两种原因：一是改变已有的谈判形势，提高在谈判中的地位；二是争取有利的谈判条件。在谈判僵局出现后，会有两种后果：一是打破僵局继续谈判；二是谈判破裂。第二种后果是僵局制造者不愿意看到的。因此，制造僵局是有风险的。想要制造谈判僵局很简单，只要表现出不合作的态度，必然会产生双方都不愿意看到的"麻烦"，且无法回避。一般来说是向对方提出较高的要求，要求对方全面接受，但这一要求绝不能高不可攀，因为若要求太高，对方会认为你没有谈判诚意而退出谈判，导致谈判破裂。

For example, in February 2020, Shandong Company LF planned to import 1,000 sets of protective suits from Russian Company KK, and Company KK insisted on quoting $50 per set, and Company LF counter-offered $40 per set. Due to the epidemic, the market was in short supply. Company KK stated that the price was the lowest one, and it couldn't make further reduction. Company LF requires that if there is no price reduction, Company KK must be responsible for delivery to the warehouse designated by Company LF. Company KK agreed on the terms and the two parties signed a purchase contract. Due to the epidemic, medical materials like protective clothing and masks are in short supply, which means that as long as the goods are available, the price can be accepted no matter how high it is. Company KK fully understood this and created a deadlock, forcing LF to agree to the counter-party's offer.

例如，2020年2月，山东LF公司拟从俄罗斯KK公司进口防护服1 000套，KK公司坚持报价50美元/套，LF公司还价40美元/套。由于疫情导致市场供不应求，KK公司表示价格一分不少，愿买就买，不买拉倒。LF公司要求如果一分不少，KK公司必须负责送货到指定的仓库。KK公司同意，双方签订了采购合同。因为疫情原因，防护服、口罩等医疗物资供不应求，只要有货可抢，价格再高都可以接受。KK公司充分把握了这一点从而制造了僵局，迫使LF公司同意了对方的报价。

(4) Strategies to Break the Deadlock（打破谈判僵局的策略）

Negotiation itself is the process of the distribution of the interests and bargaining between the two parties which will inevitably lead to deadlock. Therefore, we must correctly understand, treat it carefully, and handle it carefully. Master the strategies and techniques for dealing with the deadlock in negotiations, so as to better fight for the initiative and break the deadlock.

谈判本身就是双方利益的分配，双方讨价还价的过程，僵局的出现也就不可避免。所以必须正确认识、慎重对待并认真处理好。掌握处理谈判僵局的策略与技巧，从而更好地争取主动，打破僵局。

a. Horizontal Negotiations（采用横向式谈判）

Leaving aside the issue of disputes, talk about other issues first, instead of focusing on one issue, and not quitting. For example, on the issue of price, the two sides refused to give in and brought the negotiations to a deadlock. The issue of price could be put on hold temporarily, and other issues such as delivery time and payment methods could be discussed. If the counter-party is satisfied on these issues, and then revisit the price issue, the resistance will be less, and there will be more room for negotiation, thus bridging the differences and bringing about a new turn in negotiations.

撇开争执的问题，先谈其他问题，而不是盯住一个问题不放，不谈妥誓不罢休。例如，在价格问题上双方互不相让使谈判陷入了僵局，可以暂时把价格问题搁置，改谈交货期、付款方式等其他问题。如果在这些议题上对方感到满意了，再重新来谈价格问题，阻力会小一些，商量的余地也就更大些，从而弥合分歧，使谈判出现新的转机。

b. Take Advantage of External Force（借用外力）

When there is a serious confrontation and deadlock, there will be serious obstacles, mistrust, prejudice and even hostility between the two sides. At this time a third party mediation can save face for both sides, so that both sides feel fair, and information exchange can become smooth. The middleman in business negotiations is mainly selected by the negotiators themselves. In the actual negotiation process, the intermediary can be a third party independent of the parties to the negotiation, or a party that has an interest relationship with both parties, and can even choose a key person who has practical influence on the counter-party's team as a breakthrough to persuade the counter-party to withdraw the line of defense set at the negotiating table.

当谈判双方严重对峙并陷入僵局时，双方信息沟通就会发生严重障碍，互不信任，互相存在偏见甚至敌意，此时由第三者出面斡旋，可以为双方保全面子，使双方感到公平，信息交流可以变得畅通起来。商务谈判的中间人主要由谈判者自己挑选。在实际谈判过程中，中间人可以是独立于谈判双方的第三方，也可以是与双方都有利益关系的一方，甚至可以选择一位对对方团队具有实际影响力的关键人物作为突破口，借以劝服对方撤走设置在谈判桌上的防线。

c. Change the Negotiation Environment and Atmosphere（改变谈判环境与氛围）

When the negotiating parties hold their own opinions, refuse to give up, or even frown on the basis of non-speculation, the tense negotiating atmosphere can easily cause people to have a depressed, dull feeling and restlessness. In this case, as the host, you can suggest putting the problem at hand aside and organizing the personnel of both parties to go sightseeing, attend a cold dinner party or participate in cultural activities, etc., to relax the tight nerves. Even during the entertaining process, the two sides may wish to continue to exchange views on some stalemate informally, remove obstacles in a harmonious and relaxed atmosphere, and make a new turn in negotiations.

当谈判各方各执己见、互不相让甚至因话不投机而横眉冷对时，紧张的谈判氛围容易使人产生一种压抑的、沉闷的感觉和烦躁不安的情绪。遇到这种情形，作为东道主的一方，可以建议把手头的问题放一放，组织双方人员共同游览观光、出席冷餐会或参加文娱活动等，让紧绷的神经松弛一下。即使在游乐过程中，双方也不妨不拘形式地就某些僵持的问题继续交换意见，在融洽、轻松的氛围中消除障碍，使谈判出现新的转机。

d. Narrate the Old Story and Emphasizing the Commonalities（叙述旧情，强调双方的共同点）

By reviewing the past history of cooperation between the two sides, emphasizing and highlighting common ground and the results of cooperation, this will weaken each other's rivalry. Once the rivalry's emotions are alleviated, we will take the opportunity to proceed from our current and long-term interests and coordinate our interests. Find a balance, and finally reach a negotiated agreement.

通过回顾双方以往的合作历史，强调和突出共同点和合作的成果，以此来削弱彼此的对立情绪，一旦对方的对立情绪得以缓解，己方趁机从各自目前利益和长远利益出发，协调双方的利益，找到平衡点，最终达成谈判协议。

e. Finding Alternatives（寻找替代法）

Generally, there are many schemes that can satisfy the interests of both parties. Negotiators often simply adopt a certain scheme, but when such a scheme cannot be accepted by both parties at the same time, a deadlock will form. During the negotiation preparation period, if multiple options that are beneficial to each other can be conceived as alternatives, the negotiation will often go smoothly. If the initially selected options in the negotiations encounter obstacles, as long as the alternatives are selected in time, the deadlock can be broken and finally reach an agreement.

谈判中一般存在着多种可以满足双方利益的方案，而谈判人员经常只是简单地采用某种方案，但当这种方案不能为双方同时接受时，僵局就会形成。在谈判准备时期，如果能构思对彼此有利的多种方案作为备选，往往会使谈判如顺水行舟；而如果谈判中最初选择的方案遇到障碍，只要及时选择备选方案，就能打破僵局，最终达成协议。

f. Role Shift（角色移位法）

The role shift is to observe and think about the problem from the perspective of the other party. When one side thinks more from the other side's perspective, or tries to guide the other side to stand on one's own side to think about the issue, they can understand each other a little more. This method is often used especially in international business negotiations. When the negotiations are deadlocked, first check whether the conditions put forward by yourselves are reasonable and conducive to the long-term development of the cooperative relationship, and then see whether the conditions are reasonable from the perspective of the counter-party. If you are good at analyzing the way the other person thinks, you will get more ideas to break the deadlock.

角色移位，就是要设身处地、从对方角度来观察和思考问题。当一方更多地从对方角度来思考问题，或设法引导对方站在己方的立场上来思考问题，彼此就能多一些了解。特别是在国际商务谈判中经常会采用这种方法。当谈判陷入僵局时，先审视己方提出的条件是否合理，是否有利于合作关系的长期发展，然后再从对方的角度看看其所提出的条件是否合理。如果善于用对方思考问题的方式进行分析，就会获得更多突破僵局的思路。

g. Use of Adjournment（运用休会策略）

The adjournment strategy is a basic strategy often used by negotiators to control and adjust the negotiation process, ease the atmosphere of negotiations, and break a deadlock in negotiations. Sometimes when the negotiation reaches a certain stage or encounters certain obstacles, a cold approach can be adopted, that is, summarizing the results obtained, and then deciding to adjourn the meeting, so that the parties to the negotiations can calm down and seriously consider each other's requirements. At the same time, they can further study the market situation and confirm the correctness of their views, while also helping negotiators to recover their strength. When the negotiating parties sit together again at the scheduled time and place, they will propose a revised view of the original point of view. At this time, the deadlock can be easily broken.

休会策略是谈判人员为控制和调节谈判进程，缓和谈判气氛，打破谈判僵局而经常采用的一种基本策略。有时当谈判进行到了一定阶段或遇到某种障碍时，可以采用冷处理的办法，即总结已取得的成果，然后决定休会，使谈判各方冷静下来认真思考对方的要求。同时各方可进一步对市场形势进行研究，以证实自己观点的正确性，同时也能帮助谈判人员恢复体力。当谈判各方再按预定的时间和地点坐在一起时，会对原来的观点提出修正的看法，这时，僵局就很容易被打破了。

For example, in January 2020, Chongqing company MC planned to import 1 million masks from Brazil company EF. Company EF insisted on quoting $0.30 per piece. Company MC requires $0.20 per piece for the reason of large volume. The two parties held their own opinions, and don't want to meet each other halfway, which made the atmosphere extremely tense. Company MC asked Company EF to take a break for a cup of tea. Company EF thought about the requirements of Company MC during the tea break and thought that Company MC is a large company and has experience in selling masks. During the discussion after the tea break, Company EF agreed to a counter-offer at $0.20 per piece from Company MC. Since 1 million masks are not a small number, in order to ensure smooth import clearance, there must be sales after customs clearance. Company EF made an assessment that Company MC has the strength in this area, so the negotiation was more smooth after the adjournment.

例如，2020年1月，重庆MC公司拟从巴西EF公司进口口罩100万个。EF公司坚持报价0.30美元/个，MC公司以量大为由，要求0.20美元/个。双方各持己见，互不相让，气氛异常紧张。MC公司以茶歇名义，请EF公司先休息一下。EF公司在茶歇时思考了一下MC公司的要求，想到MC公司是大公司，并且有口罩销售的经验。在茶歇之后的商谈中，EF公司同意了MC公司0.20美元/个的还价。由于100万个口罩不是个小数目，进口清关时为了确保顺利，清关之后要有销量，EF公司估计MC公司具有这方面的实力，所以在休会后谈判进行得更加顺利。

Ⅲ The Business Etiquette（国际商务谈判磋商阶段的商务礼仪）

The etiquette in the consultation stage mainly involves the negotiator's due performance when listening, questioning and presenting in the negotiation process. It is helpful to show good manners to the counter-party through proper words and behaviors and get the counter-party's appreciation and promote the negotiation.

磋商阶段的礼仪主要涉及在谈判过程中倾听、提问、陈述时，谈判者应有的表现。通过恰当的语言和举止向对方展示自己良好的风度，获得对方的欣赏，有助于推动谈判的进行。

1. The Etiquette of Listening（倾听的礼仪）

（1）Stay Patient and Focused（保持耐心和专注）

When listening to the counter-party's statements, you should show concern for its views. Keep eye contact with the speaker and express your positive reaction with body movements such as nods, smiles or proper records. Don't show absent-mindedness, impatience or contempt, such as looking left and right, tapping the table, shaking the lower limbs, talking to the next person, etc.

在倾听对方发言时，应表现出关注其意见的态度。要与说话者保持目光接触，用点头、微笑等肢体动作或适当记录表达出你的积极反应。切忌摆出心不在焉、不耐烦或轻视的样子，如左顾右盼、敲击桌面、抖动下肢、与旁边人说话等。

（2）Don't Interrupt Counter-Party's Statement at Will（不要随意打断对方的陈述）

Rushing to talk and retorting is rude to people who emphasize patience, which is a sign of disrespect for the narrator, and is prone to aversion.

急于抢话和反驳对强调耐心的人来说是很失礼的行为，是对讲述人不尊重的表现，容易引起对方的反感。

（3）Maintain a Calm Attitude（保持平和的态度）

Even if there are offensive or aggressive words, you'd better not lose control of the mood and not lose the proper demeanor to affect the atmosphere of negotiations.

即使听到冒犯、过激的语言，也不要情绪失控，丧失应有的风度，影响谈判气氛。

2. The Etiquette of Asking Questions（提问的礼仪）

（1）Avoid Causing Objectionable Questions（避免提出引起对方反感的问题）

a. The question of being too private. Individualists don't like to be asked personal questions that have nothing to do with business such as income, family status, age of women, health status, etc.

过于隐私的问题。信奉个人主义的人不喜欢被问及与业务无关的个人问题，如收入、家庭状况、女士年龄、健康状况等。

b. Question of hostility to the counter-party. Asking corresponding questions to people with different political views or religious beliefs can make the person feel hostile and cause unhappiness.

敌视对方的问题。向与自己政治观点、宗教信仰不同的人提相关问题，会让对方感受到提问者的敌对而引起不快。

c. Questions of questioning counter-party's character. This kind of questions can hurt counter-party's self-esteem.

质疑对方人品的问题。这种问题会伤害到对方的自尊。

d. Issues unrelated to the content of the transaction. Efficient negotiators will feel that the questioner is wasting their time and energy.

与交易内容无关的问题。讲究效率的谈判者会觉得提问者在浪费自己的时间、精力。

(2) Pay Attention to the Attitude of Questioning (注意提问的态度)

a. Be honest in asking questions. A sincere attitude sends a positive message to the questioner.

提问时态度应诚恳。诚恳的态度会向对方传递提问者积极合作的信息。

b. Don't be aggressive when asking questions. Negotiation is not a debate. To overwhelm the other side and make the other side feel at a loss by consecutive questions will only have a negative impact on the negotiations.

提问时不应咄咄逼人。谈判不是辩论，以连续的发问压倒对方，让对方不知所措，只会给谈判带来不良影响。

c. Don't stick to the questions the other side won't answer. Insisting on asking a question that the other person is obviously reluctant to answer will embarrass him.

不执着于对方不愿回答的问题。坚持询问对方明显不愿回答的问题，会让其觉得尴尬。

3. The Etiquette of Statement (陈述的礼仪)

(1) Be Polite (注意礼貌用语)

Negotiators should pay attention to use proper words in their statements. Use neutral and polite language even when contradicting the other person so that the other person will not feel physically assaulted.

谈判者在发言时应注意语言得体。即便是在反驳对方的时候也应使用中性和礼貌的措词，让对方不会觉得人身受到攻击。

(2) Peace of Mind (态度平和)

The tone and expression of the statement should be peaceful. Even if you are in an advantageous position, don't be rude and arouse the dislike of others.

陈述的语气和表情应平和。即使己方处于优势地位，也不要态度蛮横，引起别人的反感。

(3) Don't Expose Others' Weaknesses (不揭人短处)

A person who wants to save face hates his weakness being exposed. If the other side feel discriminated against, it may be desperate to fight back to lose the possibility of cooperation.

要面子的人很忌讳被人揭短。如果对方觉得受到了歧视，可能会不顾一切地反击，从而失去合作的可能性。

Summary

The consultation phase of international business negotiations includes an offering phase and a substantive consultation phase. Reasonable quotations need to be made based on factors such as cost, market conditions, product conditions, competition, and policies. The quotation follows the principle of fairness and reasonableness. When offering, the goal must be clear, and the position must be firm without explanation. The offer can be oral or written. The offer can be a European offer from high to low, or a Japanese offer from low to high. There are pros and cons to offer first and offer later. Common quotation strategies include high price quotation, "skillful arrayed maze" strategies, price changing midway, bait quotation, and psychological pricing.

国际商务谈判的磋商阶段包括报价阶段和实质磋商阶段。合理的报价需要根据成本、市场行情、产品情况、竞争状况、政策等因素做出。报价遵循合情合理原则，报价时目标要明确，态度要坚定，不做解释和说明。报价既可以是口头形式的，也可以是书面形式的。报价可以采用由高到低的欧式报价，也可以采用由低到高的的日式报价。不管是先报价还是后报价都有各自的利弊。常见的报价策略包括高价报价策略、“巧布迷阵”策略、中途变价策略、鱼饵报价策略、心理价格策略。

The substantive consultation stage includes bargaining phase, counter-offer phase, concession phase and deadlock breaking phase. According to different situations, bargaining can be divided into overall bargaining and specific bargaining. Commonly used bargaining strategies include "throw a stone to clear the road" strategy, strict requirement strategy, and fatigue strategy. Before the counter-offer, sufficient investigation and preparation shall be made to provide the counter-offer with a reasonable basis. Counter-offering strategies mainly include picky strategy, maximum budget strategy, and emotional investment strategy. In concessions, the target price maximization principle, the clarity principle, the rigid principle, the timing principle, and the make-up principle must be followed. Concessions are divided into different types according to different criteria. Active concession strategies include first concession strategy, final concession strategy, equal concession strategy, and so on. The strategies for forcing the counter-party to concede mainly include the "wheel battle" strategy, tactics to use competition, fait accompli strategy, and the ultimatum strategy.

实质磋商阶段包括讨价阶段、还价阶段、让步阶段和缓解僵局阶段。讨价根据不同的情况可以分为总体讨价和具体讨价。常用的讨价策略包括投石问路策略、严格要求策略、疲劳轰炸策略。还价前需要做好充分的调查和准备，使还价具有合理的依据。还价策略主要包括吹毛求疵策略、最大预算策略、感情投资策略。在让步时要遵循目标价最大化原则、清晰原则、刚性原则、时机原则和弥补原则。让步根据不同的标准可分为不同的类型。主动让步策略包括最先让步策略、最后让步策略、均等让步策略等。迫使对方让步的策略主要包括“车轮战”策略、利用竞争策略、既成事实策略和最后通牒策略。

Negotiation deadlock may come from your own reasons, the counter-party's reasons, or both parties' reasons. Negotiator factors, cultural barriers, antagonisms, communication barriers, and other contingent factors can put negotiations at a standstill. Once the negotiations are deadlocked, you need to think calmly and avoid quarrels with each other, and at the same time coordinate the interests of all parties. If you want to break the deadlock in negotiations, you can use horizontal negotiation, take advantage of external force, change the negotiation atmosphere and environment, narrate the old story, and use adjournment strategy.

谈判僵局的产生可能来自己方的原因、对方的原因或者谈判各方的原因。谈判人员的因素、文化障碍、立场对立、沟通障碍和其他偶发因素都可能使谈判陷入僵局。一旦谈判陷入僵局，需要冷静沉着思考、避免与对方发生争吵，同时还要协调好各方的利益。想要打破谈判僵局可以采用横向式谈判策略、借用外力、改变谈判环境和氛围、与对方叙旧情、运用休会策略等。

Business etiquette at this stage involves three aspects: listening, asking questions, and making statements. Be patient and attentive when listening, don't interrupt the other party at will, and always maintain a calm attitude. Avoid asking offensive questions when asking questions, and pay attention to the attitude of asking questions. Use politeness when making statements, and keep a calm mind.

在这个阶段的商务礼仪主要涉及在谈判中的倾听、提问和陈述三个方面。在倾听时要保持耐心和专注，不要随意打断对方，始终保持平和的态度。在提问时避免提出令对方反感的问题，同时要注意提问的态度。陈述时要使用礼貌用语，保持平和心态。

Module Ⅱ Terminology Practice

1 **Substantial Change**: A change in the subject matter, quantity, quality, price or remuneration, time of performance, place and method of performance, liability for breach of contract and method of dispute resolution, etc., is a substantial change to the offer.

2 **Trading Conditions**: It includes the main trading conditions and general trading conditions. The main trading conditions include quantity, packaging, price, insurance, payment methods, etc. General trading conditions include force majeure, arbitration, application of law, etc.

3 **Offering Strategy**: In the process of international business negotiation, through the skills of quotation sequence, quotation level, etc., the party can finally get the expected benefits.

4 **Bottom Price**: The lowest price that one party can accept in international business negotiations.

5 **Deadlock**: A situation in which no progress can be made or no advancement is possible in the business negotiation.

6 **Bargaining Power**: It is the relative ability of negotiating parties in a situation to exert influence over each other. If both parties are on an equal footing in a business negotiation, then they will have equal bargaining power, such as in a perfectly competitive market, or between an evenly matched monopoly and monopsony.

7. **Conditional Acceptance**: It means that when the original offer is accepted, the content is changed to form a new offer.

8. **Offeree**: It refers to the person receiving the offer, in other words, the offeree is usually the buyer or potential buyer.

9. **Concession Range**: The range of conceding or yielding in the business negotiation.

10. Negotiation Power: It refers to the ability of one party to effectively reach consensus in business negotiations and to maximize and protect its own interests.

11. Dispute: Disagreement or arguments about something important that arise in business negotiation.

12. Mediate: The act between parties with a view to reconcile differences or occupy middle position or form a connecting link or stage between two otherparties.

Module Ⅲ New Words

1. substantive *adj.* 实质的；大量的；真实的；独立存在的 *n.* 独立存在的实体
2. intelligence *n.* 智力；情报工作；理解力；才智；智慧
3. shelve *v.* 搁置；将某事放一旁不予考虑；罢免；（陆地）逐渐倾斜
4. invitation *n.* 邀请；引诱；要约
5. bidder *n.* 投标人；出价人
6. fluctuation *n.* 波动；起伏；变动；动摇
7. indicator *n.* 指标，标志；迹象；指示器
8. sophisticated *adj.* 复杂的；精致的；世故的；富有经验的 *v.* 使变得世故；使迷惑
9. installation *n.* 安装，装置；就职
10. commission *n.* 委员会；佣金；服务费；委任 *v.* 委任；使服役
11. maintenance *n.* 维护，维修；保持；生活费用
12. accessory *n.* 配件；附件 *adj.* 副的；同谋的；附属的
13. monetary *adj.* 货币的；财政的
14. trade-off *n.* 交换，交易；权衡；协定
15. skyrocket *n.* 流行烟火；冲天火箭 *v.*（价格）飞涨，猛涨；（使）……猛然上涨
16. terminate *v.* 使终止；使结束；解雇；结果
17. compact *adj.* 紧凑的；坚实的；简洁的 *n.* 小汽车；契约 *v.* 把……压实；压缩
18. tactics *n.* 策略；战术
19. explode *v.* 爆炸；爆发；激增；推翻
20. deployment *n.* 调度，部署
21. disdain *n.* 藐视 *v.* 鄙弃
22. ultimate *adj.* 最终的；极限的；根本的 *n.* 终极；基本原则
23. monopolistic *adj.* 垄断的；独占性的；专利的
24. deliberately *adv.* 故意地；谨慎地
25. understate *v.* 轻描淡写；避重就轻地说；不充分陈述
26. entice *v.* 诱使；怂恿
27. disguise *v.* 掩饰；假装；隐瞒 *n.* 伪装；假装
28. contradiction *n.* 矛盾；否认；反驳
29. macro *adj.* 巨大的，大量的 *n.* 宏，巨（计算机用语）
30. pertinence *n.* 针对性；有关性；相关性
31. loophole *n.* 漏洞；换气孔；射弹孔
32. controversial *adj.* 有争议的；有争论的
33. constitute *v.* 组成，构成；建立；任命
34. negate *v.* 否定；取消；使无效 *n.* 对立面；反面
35. concede *v.* 承认；让步；给予
36. yield *v.* 出产；屈服；放弃 *n.* 产量；利润
37. cherish *v.* 珍爱；怀有（感情等）；抱有（希望等）
38. tedious *adj.* 沉闷的；冗长乏味的
39. magnitude *n.* 大小；量级；重要

40. summation *n.* 合计

41. fatigue *n.* 疲劳，疲乏 *v.* 使疲劳 *adj.* 疲劳的

42. dispersal *n.* 分散；传播；散布

43. entangle *v.* 使纠缠；卷入；使混乱

44. suspension *n.* 暂停；停职

45. impasse *n.* 僵局；死路

46. subdue *v.* 征服；抑制；减轻

Module Ⅳ Useful Expressions

1. central link 中心环节
2. practical stage 实践阶段
3. negotiating subject 谈判主题
4. common ground 共同基础；一致之处
5. consultation phase 磋商阶段
6. be based on 以……为基础
7. be limited to 限于；局限于；限制到
8. quality assurance 品质保证
9. slow down 放慢速度；使……慢下来
10. corresponding restrictions 相应的限制
11. legal regulations 法律条例；法律规定
12. opening price 开盘价格
13. common sense 常识
14. close a deal 达成交易
15. put forward 提出；放出；拿出
16. deviate from 偏离；脱离
17. set a target 制定目标
18. usual practice 惯例
19. psychological expectation 心理预期
20. reserve price 保留价格；最低价格
21. downward trend 下跌趋势；向下趋势
22. meet expectation 符合预期
23. in advance 提前；预先
24. be classified into 分类为……
25. as far as... be concerned 就……而言
26. be bound by 受……约束；由……联系起来
27. subject to 使服从；取决于……
28. be regarded as... 被认为是，被当作是
29. figure out 解决；想出；算出；理解
30. seek to 追求；争取；力图
31. in exchange for 作为……的交换
32. apply to 适用于；应用于
33. come by 得到；短暂拜访
34. as long as 只要
35. conducive to 有益于
36. reach an agreement 达成协议；达成共识
37. drag down 贬低；向下拖
38. be born with 天生具有……

Module Ⅴ Exercise

Ⅰ. Answer the following questions according to the text.

1. What should we pay attention to in each step of bargaining?
2. How to break the deadlock during the business negotiation?
3. How many methods can you use when you make offer? And what are they?
4. When offering, what basic principles should be adhered to?
5. What are the pros and cons of offering firstly?
6. What are the active concession and passive concession respectively?

7. What factors should be taken into account when you are making concession plan?

8. What reasons would cause the deadlock of business negotiation?

9. Under what circumstance should the ultimatum strategy be adopted?

10. How many bargaining strategies can be used in business negotiation?

Ⅱ. Match the words in Column A with their definitions in Column B.

Column A	Column B
1. substantive	A. furthest or highest in degree or order; utmost or extreme
2. sophisticated	B. opposition between two conflicting forces or ideas
3. ultimate	C. be fond of, be attached to
4. monopolistic	D. temporary loss of strength and energy resulting from hard work
5. contradiction	E. a time interval during which there is a temporary cessation
6. negate	F. having or appealing to those having worldly knowledge
7. cherish	G. end resistance, as under pressure or force
8. fatigue	H. deny the truth of
9. suspension	I. having exclusive control over a commercial activity by possession
10. yield	J. having a firm basis in reality and being therefore important, meaningful, or considerable

Ⅲ. Translate the following terms and phrases into Chinese.

1. consultation stage
2. substantive matter
3. seek common ground
4. make offer
5. definitive contents
6. commodity inspection
7. free maintenance
8. monetary finance
9. adequate preparation
10. stronger negotiator
11. original price
12. hidden price
13. shake belief
14. good manner
15. offensive words
16. objectionable question
17. break deadlock
18. reach an agreement
19. remove obstacles
20. line of defense

Ⅳ. Please determine whether the following statements are True or False.

1. When the seller's goods sell well or when the seller is unaware of the market situation and is not sure whether the buyer is willing to buy, he usually makes the offer first. (   )

2. Once both parities' interests are designed, it is time for negotiators to set forth suggestions and opinions for how to address the issue. (   )

3. Getting to know each other is just confined to the opening stage of business negotiation. (   )

4. Sometimes, when the difference between negotiating parties seems too large to be mentioned, the negotiation is on the verge of breaking down. (　　)

5. The reservation point means the target that negotiators have to achieve for assurance of their basic interest. (　　)

6. As a result of the bargaining between the negotiating parties, it is not possible for each party to modify its original objective. (　　)

7. When responding to statements of goals, positions and offers, it's a good idea to use the reflective listening technique described earlier. (　　)

8. On some minor points, negotiating parties also should strive for their own benefits. (　　)

9. Descending concession strategy is usually applicable to cooperation-oriented negotiations. (　　)

10. Once the negotiation is in deadlock, the third party can be employed to break the deadlock. (　　)

Ⅴ. Translate the following sentences into Chinese.

1. This stage covers a broad period of bargaining in which concessions are made and advantages are gained, so that the gap between the two parties is narrowed to a point.

2. The final concession should be made at the right time. For the purpose of timing, it can be divided into two parts. The major part of concession should be made just before the counterparty is to review and consider the deadline.

3. One minor concession should be held as a final benefit and offered at the very last moment if it is absolutely necessary.

4. As a result of the initial contacts between the two sides, it is probable that each side will modify its original objective, reassess the potential outcomes and the time taken to achieve each of these.

5. When responding to statements of goals, positions, and offers, it's a good idea to use the reflective listening technique described earlier.

Ⅵ. Translate the following sentences into English.

1. 谈判双方在结束非实质性交谈后，就会将话题转向有关交易内容的谈判，即开始报价。

2. 报价需要以市场行情、利益需要、产品属性、交货时间、交易规模以及支付方式为依据做出。

3. 不同的报价顺序对谈判的最终结果也会有不同的影响。

4. 如果在开局阶段已经营造出了友好、合作的氛围，进入磋商阶段后需继续保持这种氛围。

5. 全面讨价一般运用于第一次要价，是买方从总体报价的全局来看要求卖方重新报价。

6. 还价可以按分析成本来进行，也可以按还价项目的多少来进行，需要具体情况具体分析。

7. 出现谈判僵局一般会有两种结果：一是打破僵局继续谈判；二是谈判失败。

8. 当谈判出现僵局时，双方都可以考虑向对方妥协让步。否则谈判永远无法达成协议，双方追求的目标也无法实现。

Ⅶ. Case Study

Case 1: Why Is the Contract Price Higher Than the Original Price?

Case Source: A real case of a large private enterprise in Chongqing.

Preface

Key Point: US company KR and Chongqing company LH negotiated a contract to purchase a batch of motorcycles.

Background

Industry: Manufacturing

Subject: US Company KR and Chongqing Company LH

Issue: When US company KR and Chongqing company LH signed a contract for the purchase of a batch of motorcycles, the total contract price increased due to exchange rate changes.

US company KR and Chongqing company LH signed a contract for the purchase of a batch of motorcycles. The contract amount is 500,000 yuan. Due to the change of the exchange rate of the US dollar against Chinese yuan, the cost increases. Company LH needs to raise the total contract price to 520,000 yuan to avoid losing money.

Questions

As a business manager, how do you pay attention to the loss caused by the change in the contract amount and the amount of the foreign exchange due?

Appendix

In the contract negotiation stage, the contract price of the two parties may also be affected by various factors, such as exchange rate changes, government temporary policies and measures, and changes in international market prices.

Case 2: Negotiating Expert's Successful Counter-offer Strategy

Case Source: Liu Yuan. *International Business Negotiation* (Fourth Edition), Beijing: Capital Econoplic and Trade University Press, 2012.

Preface

Key Point: Negotiating experts receive more compensation than expected from the insurance company by adopting an appropriate counter-offering strategy.

Background

Industry: Insurance

Subject: A Negotiating Expert and an Insurance Company Abroad

Issue: A negotiating expert represented his neighbors and insurance companies in negotiating compensation payments, and ultimately achieved unexpected results.

A negotiator advised his neighbors to negotiate a compensation with an insurance company abroad. The insurer's claimant first commented: "Sir, I know that you are a negotiating expert. I have always been negotiating for huge sums of money. I am afraid I can't afford your asking price. If our company only pays $100 in compensation, what do you think?" The negotiator is serious and silent, because his experience tells him that when the counter-party proposes the first condition, it always implies that the second, the third...

The claimant was really unsettled. He said, "Sorry, please don't mind my proposal. Add some, how about $200?" It was a long silence. Finally, the negotiating expert stated: "Sorry, people can't accept this price order." The claimant went on to say, "Well, what about $300?" The negotiator looked thoughtful and the claimant looked a little confused. He said, "Okay, $400." After a moment, the experts said slowly: "400 dollars?... Hey, I don't know."

"Just $500!" The claimant said with grief.

Finally, the result of the negotiation was that the claim was finally agreed at $950, and the expert's neighbors were only prepared to receive $300 in damages.

Questions

1. In the case, what kind of strategy did the negotiating expert use to allure the counter-party to increase the amount of compensation repeatedly?

2. How is this strategy generally used?

Appendix

In international business negotiations, there are generally two actions to choose from for each other's quotation: one is to ask the counter-party to lower the quotation; the other is to make one's own quotation. In general, the first option is advantageous. Because this is a reflection of the quotation side, if successful, you can win the counter-party's concessions.

Case 3: Volume for Price Strategy

Case Source: A real case of a large private enterprise in Chongqing.

Preface

Time: 2017

Key Point: When Company B in Chongqing negotiated with Company A in Iran to purchase some spare parts for motorcycles, the manager of Company B used the volume for price strategy to sign the contract.

Background

Industry: Manufacturing

Subject: Company B in Chongqing and Company A in Iran

Issue: Company A in Iran negotiated a motorcycle spare parts purchase from Company B in Chongqing. The Iranian side put forward various demanding requirements. After Company B analyzed the Iranian intentions, it used the volume for price strategy to make the two parties finally sign the contract.

Company A and Company B negotiated a motorcycle parts purchase for export to Iran. Company A's purchasing general manager Mike is good at calculating. On September 20, 2017, Company B is required to report the price of HD125-3. Company B reports FOB Chongqing Price: USD415.00/set (margin is 3%). Mike arrived in Chongqing on September 21, 2017, and agreed to meet with Chris, the department manager, at 9:30 a.m. on September 22.

When arriving at Company B's meeting, Mike said that there were 1,010 sets of orders for 5 containers, but the price requirement was FOB Chongqing: $407.00/set, and all the shortcomings in Company B's products and previous cooperation orders were proposed. At noon 11:00 a.m., the two sides were deadlocked, but Mike did not immediately leave Company B, and always asked for price cuts for various reasons. As early as 11:40 a.m., Mike saw that Chris still did not agree, so he planned to take the plane at 3:00 p.m. to Guangzhou.

Chris analyzed Mike's real intention: Why Company A asked Company B to extend the quotation to September 22 from September 20? Chris supposed that Mike must have gone to other manufacturers in Chongqing to make an inquiry on September 21. In addition, Mike spent three hours in Company B, which also indicated that he would like to take Company B as the best supplier to stay in the final negotiation and lower the price.

Chris invited Mike to have lunch with him. Mike said that he could have a simple meal in the office. At dinner, Chris agreed to Mike's offer: $407/set FOB Chongqing, with a profit margin of 1%, for the sake of year-end momentum. However, Chris asked Mike to help him to complete the year-end task and increase the order quantity to 10 cabinets, a total amount of 2,020 sets. Finally, both parties conclude the business immediately.

Questions

1. Is the judgment of Chris correct? Which aspects can show his correctness?

2. What strategy is adopted by Mike and Chris to win the negotiation success?

Appendix

In this case, it is appropriate and desirable to negotiate the psychological understanding of each other. It is a relatively successful negotiation.

Case 4: Fashionable Dressing Stops the Negotiation

Case Source: A real case of a large private enterprise in Chongqing.

Preface

Time: 2016

Key Point: When a business team from a company in Chongqing went to Iran for negotiation, the negotiation was terminated because it did not respect the negotiating etiquette and customs of the other party.

Background

Industry: Manufacturing

Subject: A Company in Chongqing and a Company in Iran

Issue: When a business team from a company in Chongqing was negotiating in Iran, it did not conform to the negotiating etiquette and customs of the other party, resulting in the termination of the negotiation.

When a business team from a company in Chongqing went to Iran to negotiate an engine order, one of the young women in the team wore a business skirt, and the V-neck was low-cut, causing dissatisfaction among the other members. When talking about some substantive terms, the older business negotiators did not give in and did not want to stop negotiation.

Questions

1. What are the main obstacles to communication in the case?
2. What caused this situation in the negotiation?
3. What measures should be taken to overcome these obstacles?
4. From this case, what lessons should Chinese negotiators learn?

Appendix

In the process of international business negotiation, it is necessary to pay attention to the relevant instrument dress etiquette and abide by the relevant dressing principles: (1) the dress should be solemn, generous, elegant and decent; (2) the dress should adapt to its own conditions; (3) the dress should be matched with one's occupation, the occasion, the purpose of the interaction.

Case 5: Meet Each Other Half Way

Case Source: Zhao Limin. *Foreign Trade Negotiation Strategy and Skills*. Beijing: China Customs Press, 2009.

Preface

Key Point: A foreign trade company in Guangzhou negotiated with an electrical appliance company in Singapore about the import of electronic products. The two sides caused a negotiation deadlock due to price problems. Finally, the foreign trade company in Guangzhou made an effective retreat to break the deadlock and make the transaction a smooth conclusion.

Background

Industry: Electrical Equipment

Subject: A Foreign Trade Company in Guangzhou and an Electrical Company in Singapore

Issue: A foreign trade company in Guangzhou negotiated with an electrical appliance company in Singapore about importing electrical goods. Negotiation encountered a deadlock due to the fact that the two sides did not make an agreement on the price. As the Chinese side did a good job in research, the company finally reached a deal with the counter-party by increasing the order quantity.

In 1993, a foreign trade company in Guangzhou negotiated with a Singaporean electrical company to import electrical products. The two sides held negotiations in Guangzhou. Due to the large number and large amount of transactions, both parties attached great importance to this negotiation. Before the negotiations, they had prepared sufficient international market forecasts and investigated the prices of similar products in Japan, South Korea and other countries. After comparison, because the quality of the products of the Singapore company is relatively good, the focus of the negotiations is on the transactions of Singapore companies.

At the beginning of the negotiation, according to international practice, the seller first quoted the price of the offer at a price of US $ 300 per piece. The price actually deviated from the normal price. The seller used this as the basis for bargaining. The Chinese negotiators went straight to the point and clearly pointed out that the price was too high. The Chinese side is absolutely unacceptable. The seller knew that China had investigated the international market, so he said: "We have fully considered the requirements of your company. In order to cooperate with you, we have decided to provide you with the maximum discount, and the price per piece has dropped to US $ 280." Our negotiators did not buy the account and clearly pointed out the situation that the Chinese side had learned, the seller's offer of US $ 280 is still too high, and the Chinese side can only accept the price of US $ 200. The seller's representative took a tough attitude and repeatedly stressed that US $ 280 was the cheapest price and couldn't be lower. He hoped that China could accept this price from the perspective of both the performance and quality of the product.

At the beginning of the second round of negotiations, the attitude of the seller's negotiators has eased. They said if the Chinese side agreed to increase the order quantity, the price reduction issue could be considered. The Chinese negotiators saw the seller's intention, but pretended not to know and replied: "The basis on which we can consider increasing the order is that your company first proposes a price that is easy for us to accept." The seller's negotiators once again cut the price, the unit price is US $ 260. The representative of the Chinese company said: "We welcome your company's concessions, but it is not a reasonable price reduction. Recently we have received invitations from Japan and Korean companies." After the statement, the Chinese negotiators presented the offer of the Japanese and Korean companies to the seller's representatives. The seller's negotiators were shocked and knew that they had encountered a real opponent and requested a temporary suspension of negotiation so as to ask the head office about the price issue. During the recess, the Chinese negotiators carefully analyzed the situation and thought that the result of the seller's representatives' request for instructions would be beneficial to us, however, they would not accept our counter offer of US $ 200 yet, because the price of similar products of Japanese and Korean companies is US $ 200, but the quality and function are not as good as those of Singapore companies. In order to win the initiative, China should take the initiative to give in, in exchange for greater concessions from the other side, and strive to reach an agreement.

Three days later, the third round of negotiation began. The Chinese representatives first spoke and proposed that China agreed to increase orders by 40%, but the seller would reduce the unit price to US $ 220. The seller's negotiators immediately agreed. The negotiation ended successfully.

Questions

1. What strategy is used by the Chinese representatives in this case?

2. How should the strategy be applied?

Appendix

For any party to the negotiations, the purpose of the negotiating table is mainly to successfully reach an agreement, and never come to negotiate with the purpose of failure. Therefore, when the negotiation encounters a deadlock, we should be soberly aware that if the benefits of successful cooperation are greater than the benefits of adhering to the original position and letting the negotiation break down, the effective concession is also a strategy that should be adopted.

Ⅷ. Role plays practice. Work in pair and converse according to the given information.

Task 1

Background

You represent Nanfang Native Produce and Animal By-products Corporation. A businessman from Brazil has ordered a total of USD 20,000 worth of your bamboo ware. He is not sure what kind of packing would be most appropriate for his order. You suggest paper cartons according to different sizes of the products. Now you discuss this issue with him.

Terms and Phrases

standard packing	shockproof packing	eye-catching
dampness protection	to be lined with	breakage-proof
bundle	barrel	cargo in bulk
container	keep away from cold	keep dry
packing cost	nude cargo	kraft paper
seaworthy packing	wooden cases	water-proof

Relative Expressions

1. I really don't think so, because...
2. I'm afraid I can't accept that.
3. I see your point, but...
4. I can't go along with your view.
5. Surely not.
6. I am not sure if I agree...
7. I can't say I share your view on...
8. I feel I must disagree...
9. That might be OK, but...
10. Would it be possible for you to recheck...
11. I'm sorry, but I can't support the proposal.
12. I'm afraid I think that would be a mistake.
13. Quite honestly, I think that would be a big mistake.
14. In general practice, it is buyers who will bear the charges of packing.

15. Normally, packing charge is already included in the contract price.
16. For ocean transportation, the goods are to be packed in strong cases and securely strapped.
17. We will enforce the packing with metal straps.
18. The key point of packing is to protect the goods from moisture.

Task 2

Background

Mr. Michael, a regular customer of yours has done business with you on FOB basis for ages. This time he requests a quotation on CIF basis for a repeat order of 1,000 pieces of Computer Type 350. But he is not very familiar with insurance clauses of the PICC. You try to explain briefly the Ocean Marine Cargo Clause of the PICC in the form of a dialogue and sort out the appropriate coverage for this kind of goods for Mr. Michael.

Terms and Phrases

SRCC	premium	underwriter
open policy	insurance policy	insured amount
marine losses	insurance broker	insurance expense
partial loss	TRND	to provide the insurance

Relative Expressions

1. Could you be a bit more precise?
2. Could you expand on that?
3. Would you mind clarifying that for me?
4. I'm sorry, I didn't catch that.
5. Could you tell me more about...
6. Something else I was wondering about was...
7. Sorry, that's not really what I mean. What I'd like to know is...
8. A WPA covers clients against partial loss in all cases.
9. If you cover an All Risks, it means you have every sort of hazard covered.
10. Marine insurance is much higher than aviation insurance.
11. FPA insurance doesn't cover losses on consumer goods.
12. The premium varies according to the type of goods and the circumstances.
13. The insurance rate for this risk will vary according to the goods.
14. What insurances are you able to provide for this consignment?
15. Could you give an introduction of risks that the PICC is able to cover?

Chapter 6

Closing of International Business Negotiation

Work Objective

After studying this chapter, you will be able to:

- master how to judge the end of the negotiation;
- master how to develop claim negotiation;
- familiarize with strategies to facilitate the transaction;
- familiarize with the drafting and review of the contract;
- familiarize with the process and protocol of signing ceremony;
- familiarize with the banquet etiquette, gift giving and farewell etiquette;
- know ways of ending negotiations.

1 Case Guide-Reading

A western arms merchant and a Middle East buyer for the police department negotiate a batch of anti-riot equipment—thousands of sets of night vision helmet, bulletproof vest, tear gas and its firing gun, wheeled armored vehicles with water cannon. The arms merchant quoted a total price of $81 million, while the buyer's psychological transaction price was ranging from $76 million to $78 million. However, his counter-offer was $70 million. After a bargain, the western arms merchant reduced the total price to $77 million, leaving the terms of the deal to differ only on the delivery time, and the other terms of the deal were largely agreed. At this point, the buyer made a decisive decision to end the negotiation, suggesting that if the other side could adjust the total price down another $1 million, he was willing to make a concession on the delivery time. Eventually, the two parties signed the contract at a total price of $76. 5 million.

Source: Dou Ran. *International Business Negotiation and Communication Skills*. Shanghai: Fudan University Press, 2009.

Module Ⅰ Text

At the end of the negotiation, negotiators are ready to conclude the negotiation after they have reached agreement on the main terms of the transaction through consultation; or after several negotiations, the negotiators are still unable to reach agreement on the key issues and have no choice but to abandon the negotiation.

在谈判的结束阶段，谈判人员通过磋商在就主要交易条件达成一致后，准备成交，结束谈判；或谈判各方几经交涉，仍无法就关键问题达成统一，无奈放弃谈判。

Ⅰ Judgment of the End of the Negotiation（谈判进入尾声的判断）

When to conclude the negotiations is traceable, the negotiator's expression, the questions raised, and the strategies used will reveal their intentions. In the final stage of the negotiation, the tactful negotiator can recognize the transaction signal sent by the other side keenly, fully grasp the time to conclude the negotiation, successfully conclude the transaction or timely suspend the meaningless negotiation, so as to shorten the consultation time, reduce the useless consumption of manpower and material resources of negotiation teams, and improve the negotiation efficiency.

什么时候结束谈判是有迹可循的，谈判者的表情、提出的问题、使用的策略都会泄露其意图。在谈判的最后阶段，机智的谈判者能敏锐地识别对方发出的成交信号，充分把握结束谈判的时机，成功达成交易或及时终止无意义的谈判，从而缩短磋商时间，减少谈判小组无谓的人力、物力消耗，提高谈判效率。

1. Judging from the Conditions of Transaction Achieved（从达成的交易条件判断）

Quantitatively, if most trading terms have been agreed and only a few, or even one or two, are still in dispute, and no matter these terms are primary or secondary, it can be judged that the negotiations have entered an end stage. But more important than the number is whether the key terms of the transaction have been agreed. If all the important terms of the transaction have been agreed, we can confirm that the negotiation has entered the end stage.

在数量上，如果大多数交易条件已经达成一致，只有少数甚至一两个条件还存在分歧，不管这些条件是主要的还是次要的，都可判断谈判已经进入了结束阶段。但与数量相比更重要的是关键的交易条件是否已达成一致。如果重要的交易条件都协商好了，那么我们可以确定谈判已经进入结束阶段。

2. Judging from the Time（从时间上判断）

One of the bases to judge whether the negotiation is coming to an end from time is the arrangement of the negotiation agenda. If the prescribed negotiation completion time is reached, the negotiation enters the completion stage. If there is no negotiating agenda, and one of the parties involved in the negotiation asks for the completion of the negotiation at a specific time for its own reasons, it can also be the time to conclude the negotiation.

从时间上判断谈判是否进入尾声的一种根据是谈判议程的安排。如果到了规定的谈判结束时间，则应该进入谈判结束阶段。如果没有谈判议程，而参与谈判的某方因自身原因，提出在特定时间完成谈判的要求，则该时间也可成为结束谈判的时间。

However, the time limit proposed by one party can be accepted or rejected according to one's own needs. If the other party wants to exert pressure, one should refuse. If the other party's offer can be accepted in exchange for other concessions, it can be accepted. Of course, if the other party really needs to complete the negotiation within the time limit, you should also actively cooperate, otherwise it may lead to negotiation failure. In this case, don't over-coerce the other party to cause resentment and affect the negotiation result.

不过，对于一方提出的时间期限可以根据自身需要接受或拒绝。如果对方想借此施加压力，则应拒绝。如果可以用接受对方提议换取对方在其他方面的让步，则可以接受。当然，如果对方确实需要在期限内完成谈判，也应积极配合，否则可能导致谈判失败。在这种情况下不要过度要挟对方，以免引起反感情绪，影响谈判结果。

3. Judging from the Content of the Consultation of the Other Party（从对方磋商内容上判断）

If the other party begins to mention the delivery time, the price of new and old products and related products, specific requirements for quality and processing, requirements for detailed description of price-related conditions, inquiries about product maintenance, requests for extension of the validity period of quotation, requests for trial products and other topics, it shows that it has the intention to conclude transactions.

如果对方开始提及交货时间、新旧产品及有关产品的价格问题、对质量和加工提出具体要求、要求详细说明与价格相关的条件、询问产品保养问题、要求延长报价有效期、要求试用产品等话题，说明其已经有了成交的意图。

Negotiators from different countries have different negotiation processes, and we can judge the negotiation process according to their negotiation habits. Americans, for example, like to solve all problems that need to be discussed one by one. As a result, when most of the issues are discussed, the negotiations are nearing completion. The French, on the other hand, like to discuss the issues of principle before the details. So if they turn to the details of the discussion, it means they are ready to conclude the negotiations.

不同国家的谈判者有不同的谈判流程，我们也可以根据他们的谈判习惯判断谈判的进程。比如美国人喜欢把所有需要讨论的问题逐一解决。因此，当大部分问题都讨论完后，谈判就接近尾声了。而法国人喜欢先讨论原则性问题，再讨论细节。所以如果他们转向细节问题的讨论，说明其准备结束谈判。

4. Judging from the Scope of the Deal（从是否进入成交范围判断）

This is the basis for determining whether the negotiations have entered the end stage on the terms and conditions adopted by both parties. When the terms of the deal have entered into your own set of the deal, it can be judged that the negotiations have entered the end stage.

这是以双方通过的条件是否进入己方成交范围来判断谈判是否进入结束阶段的依据。当双方达成的交易条件已经进入己方设定的成交范围，则可以判定谈判已经进入结束阶段。

5. Issues That Need to Be Identified Before Concluding Negotiations（结束谈判前需要明确的问题）

（1）Have all the issues on the agenda been discussed?

（2）Have the costs of each link been taken into account?

（3）Have the technical issues involved in the transaction been reviewed?

（4）Have the local and international law relevant to the transaction been studied?

（5）Is the party concerned capable of providing after-sales service?

（6）Is the deadline for this transaction feasible?

（7）Do the parties have consistent understanding of the statements and terminology involved in the transaction?

（8）Is the partner reliable?

（9）Does the negotiator have the authority to make decisions on behalf of the company?

（1）是否讨论了议程中所有的问题?

（2）是否考虑了各环节的费用问题?

（3）是否审核了本交易涉及的技术性问题?

（4）是否研究了与本交易相关的地方法和国际法?

（5）相关方有能力提供售后服务吗?

（6）本交易的最后期限可行吗?

（7）各方对交易中涉及的表述及术语理解一致吗?

（8）合作方可靠吗?

（9）参与谈判人员有代表公司决策的权限吗?

Ⅱ Ways of Ending Negotiations（结束谈判的方式）

There are three main ways to conclude negotiations: concluding a transaction, negotiation suspension or breakdown.

谈判终结的方式主要有三种：成交、谈判中止和谈判破裂。

1. Concluding a Transaction（成交）

If the negotiating parties agree on all terms of the transaction through consultation, they can reach a deal. The main sign of the transaction is that the party concerned signs the contract according to the result of the negotiation. However, the form, binding and complexity of the contract vary from country to country. For example, many cultures in the world attach great importance to oral contracts. The contents of the contract can also be amended again due to subsequent changes in circumstances. In desert countries in the Middle East, it is normal for trading conditions to change depending on the actual situation because of bad weather. For American negotiators accustomed to signing contracts, the concept may be completely unfamiliar. Not only do they have to sign the contract formally, but the contents of the contract set out in great detail the rights and obligations of the buyer and the seller. Once signed, random changes are not allowed. Although the Japanese sign a contract, the content is much simpler than that of the Americans, with only the basic terms, leaving room for possible changes in the future.

如果谈判各方通过磋商就所有交易条件达成一致，则可以达成交易。成交的主要标志是相关方根据商讨的结果签订合同。但合同的形式、约束性、复杂性在不同国家有所差异。例如，世界上许多文化都非常重视口头合同。合同内容因随后情况的变化也可以再次修改。在中东沙漠国家，因气候恶劣，交易条件根据实际情况变化是很正常的事情。而对于习惯于签署合同的美国谈判代表来说，这个概念可能完全陌生。他们不仅要正式签订合同，而且合同会非常详尽地列出买卖双方的权利与义务。合同一旦签署，则不允许随便改动。日本人虽然会签订合同，但内容比美国人的简单得多，只有基础性条款，为今后可能的改动留下了空间。

2. Negotiation Suspension（谈判中止）

In the event that the terms of the transaction are not completely settled, the parties to the negotiations have agreed or one party has to suspend the negotiations for some reason, which we call the negotiation suspension. For example, if one party is restricted by decision-making power, it needs to suspend negotiations and ask the superior to decide whether to accept the current trading conditions; or the political instability in the relevant countries may affect the successful completion of the transaction, and the negotiations have to be suspended and wait for the improvement of the situation; or it may occur serious economic crisis which is not conducive to the completion of the transaction, and the negotiations have to be suspended.

在交易条件没有完全谈妥的情况下，谈判双方约定或一方因某些原因需要暂时停止谈判，我们称为谈判中止。比如一方受决策权限制，需要中止谈判以请示上级决定能否接受当前的交易条件；或相关国家出现政局动荡，可能对顺利完成交易产生影响，只能暂停谈判，等待局势好转；或发生较严重的经济危机，不利于交易的完成，也只有中止谈判。

The suspension is divided into suspension with a fixed resumption date and suspension without a fixed resumption date. If the two parties have strong willingness to conclude business and can determine the time to solve the problem, the specific time to resume negotiations will be agreed upon when they suspend the negotiation. For example, when the two parties consider that the transaction price exceeds the quota plan or the size of the use permit for foreign exchange, or the margin of concession exceeds the predetermined authority, or the administrative approval process has not been completed, and both parties have the will to deal, they agree to suspend the negotiation and agree to contact each other within a certain time to determine the new negotiation time. If the two parties are not sure when they can solve the problem the moment they suspend the negotiation, they will have to put it on hold indefinitely. For example, when it comes to the beyond-the-will, influential and wide-ranging issues such as the ratification of international agreements, sudden changes in national policies, deterioration of the economic situation, etc., it is difficult for the parties to make an appointment. In this case, it is better for the two parties to keep in touch and exchange relevant information and to resume negotiations once the situation improves.

中止分为无约中止和有约中止。如果双方成交意愿较强，能够确定解决问题的时间，则会在中止谈判时约定恢复谈判的具体时间。例如，当双方认为成交价格超过了外汇的额度计划或使用许可规模，或者让步的幅度超过了预定的权限，或者行政审批手续尚未完成，而双方均有成交的意愿，于是一致同意中止谈判，约定在某个时间内再联系确定新的谈判时间。如果中止谈判时，双方不确定什么时候能解决问题，则只有无限期地搁置。例如，在涉及国际协议的批准、国家政策突变、经济形势恶化等超越意志、影响大、涉及面广的事由时，当事方就难以相约了。在这种情况下，双方最好能保持联系，交换相关信息，一旦不利于交易的状况得以改善，就着手恢复谈判。

3. Negotiation Breakdown（谈判破裂）

After several consultations, both parties to the negotiation can not reach an agreement on the terms of the transaction. The result of the negotiation does not enter the transaction range of one party, and the other party refuses to make concessions; or one party finds that the other party has problems with funds, ability and reputation during the communication process, and can not guarantee the completion of the transaction. Under the above circumstances, only the breakdown of the negotiations can be declared. It can be divided into friendly breakdown and indignant breakdown. In the case of a friendly breakdown, although the two sides of the negotiation adhere to their respective trading conditions, they fully show mutual understanding, based on a long-term attitude. So the friendly relationship is not affected, which also brings about the possibility of future cooperation. This is also the way we advocate. In the case of indignant breakdown, the negotiating parties ended the negotiation in a bad mood, which seriously undermines mutual trust and goodwill, and the possibility of future cooperation is negligible. The main reason for the indignant breakdown is that one party's attitude is arrogant and does not take the opponent seriously; or in the treatment of transactions, do not pay attention to the essential gap such as conditions, but pay too much attention to the other party's words, attitudes and practices; in the personality, the self-esteem is too strong, the character is irritable, the handling is too direct and so on.

如果几经磋商，谈判双方都无法就交易条件达成一致，谈判结果没有进入某方的成交范围，而对方又拒绝让步，或在沟通过程中发现对方存在资金、能力、信誉问题，无法保证完成交易，则只能宣告谈判破裂。破裂分为友好破裂和愤然破裂。在友好破裂的情况下，谈判双方虽然坚持各自的交易条件，但充分表现出相互理解、立足长远的态度。友好关系没有受到影响，这也为今后的合作带来了可能，这也是我们推崇的方式。在愤然破裂的情况下，谈判双方在情绪恶劣的氛围中结束谈判，严重破坏了互相的信任和好感，以后合作的可能性微乎其微。造成愤然破裂的原因主要是：一方态度傲慢，不把对手放在眼里；或在对待交易上，不注意条件等本质差别，过多注重对方言语、态度及做法；在个性上，自尊心太强，性情暴躁，处事过于直接等。

The breakdown of negotiations is a common phenomenon in business negotiations and may even exceed the transaction. As the competition grows, the choice between the two sides grows, and the breakdown of negotiations is common. It should be pointed out that the success of negotiations can not be determined by whether a deal is concluded or not. Only when the interests of all negotiating parties are fully satisfied, can the successful negotiation be symbolized. A bad deal, even if it is concluded, is likely to result in greater losses. Sometimes a breakdown of negotiations protects one's interests better than a deal.

谈判破裂是商务谈判中的常见现象，甚至可能超过成交。随着竞争的加剧，双方的选择面越来越大，谈判破裂的情况屡见不鲜。需要指出的是，谈判的成功不能用是否成交来决定。只有谈判各方利益都得到最大满足条件下的交易，才是成功谈判的标志。不利的交易，就算达成，也很有可能会带来更大的损失。有时候谈判破裂比成交更能保护自身利益。

Ⅲ Strategies to Facilitate the Transaction（促成交易的策略）

The purpose of business negotiation is to reach a mutually beneficial transaction. At the final stage of the negotiations, both sides should take concrete actions to facilitate the transaction. There are many strategies to facilitate the transaction. How to choose depends on the relationship between the two parties, the goal of the negotiation and the characteristics of the negotiator.

达成对双方均有利的交易，是商务谈判的目的所在。在谈判的最后阶段，双方都要采取切实行动，促成交易。促成交易的策略多种多样，如何选择取决于谈判双方的关系、谈判的目标以及谈判者的特点。

1. Concession Method（让步法）

In order to show their sincerity, the negotiating party will make some concessions before the final contract is reached, thus effectively inspiring the other party to reach a contract. Using concession before the end of negotiations is a more effective strategy. It should be noted that the margin of concession should not be too large, so as to avoid the misunderstanding of the room for negotiation and further bargaining.

为了显示自己的诚意，谈判方在最终合同达成前再次做出一定让步，从而有效激励对方达成合同。在谈判结束前使用让步法是一种较为有效的策略。需要注意的是，让步幅度不应过大，以免让对方产生还有商量余地的错觉，进一步讨价还价。

2. Compromise Method（折中法）

When the negotiations are nearing the end and the differences between the two sides are already small, the compromise method can be adopted for those conditions that do not have much impact on the overall goal of the negotiations. That is, based on the intermediate conditions of the differences between the two parties, the two sides make roughly equal concessions and facilitate the transaction. The compromise method can be either half of the price difference, or a moderate amount of concession in other conditions. Let the other party feel that the concessions of the two sides are equal, and easy to accept.

当谈判接近尾声、双方分歧已经很小的时候，对那些对谈判总体目标实现没有太大影响的条件，可以采用折中法。即以双方分歧的中间条件为基础，双方做出大致相等的让步，促成交易。折中法既可以是价格分歧的各让一半，也可以是在其他条件下等量的让步。让对方觉得双方的退让是相等的，富有诚意，容易接受。

3. Summarizing Method（总结法）

After the two sides reach an agreement on the main issues, one party can briefly summarize the matters discussed and adopted by both parties. Emphasis is placed on the concessions made during the period, allowing opponents to understand the rights they receive when accepting our advice. Improve their sense of accomplishment and thus facilitate transactions.

通过磋商，双方在主要问题上达成一致后，一方可以对双方讨论通过的事项进行简要总结。重点强调自己在其间所做出的让步，让对手清楚他们在接受我方建议的时候，所获得的权益。提升其成就感，从而促成交易。

4. Ultimatum Method（最后通牒法）

An ultimatum is when one party proposes final trading terms and the other party either accepts them within a limited period of time to conclude the transaction, or refuses them, and the negotiation breaks down when the deadline comes. Usually, the parties involved will not be willing to let the negotiations break down. However, this kind of threatening method should also be used cautiously. If it is not properly grasped, it may result in the other party's resentment and confrontation, leading to the breakdown of the negotiations.

最后通牒法指一方提出最终交易条件，对手要么在限定期限内接受这些条件，达成交易，要么拒绝，期限一到则谈判破裂。通常情况下，参与谈判的各方都不会愿意让谈判破裂。但这种有威胁意味的方法也要谨慎采用，如果把握不当，可能引起对方反感，产生对抗，导致谈判破裂。

After taking over the troubled Chrysler, Mr. Akoka, America's auto giant, felt the need to lower wages for workers. He first cut his senior staff's salary by 10% and cut his salary from

$360,000 to $100,000. Then he told the union leader, "There are plenty of jobs at $17 an hour but none at $20. Now it's like having a pistol to your head, so let it be clear." The union did not agree. The two sides were deadlocked for a year, and finally, the situation forced Akoka to issue an ultimatum. One winter evening, at ten o'clock, Akoka went to the union negotiating committee and said to them," You have to make a decision by tomorrow morning, and if you don't help me, I can't help it, and I can declare the company bankrupt tomorrow morning. You may consider what you do for eight hours, whatever you like." This strategy has worked for 22 years from 1947 to 1969. But in 1969, electrical workers' frustration finally erupted, leading to a strike that transcended economic interests.

美国汽车界巨子艾柯卡在接手陷入困境的克莱斯勒公司后，觉得必须降低工人的工资。他首先将高级职员的工资降低 10%，自己的年薪也从 36 万美元减为 10 万美元。随后，他对工会领导人讲："17 美元一个钟头的活有的是，20 美元的一件也没有。现在好比我用手枪对着你们的脑袋，还是放明白点。"工会并未答应，双方僵持了一年，最后，形势逼迫艾柯卡发出了最后通牒。在一个冬天的晚上 10 点钟，艾柯卡找到工会谈判委员会，对他们说："明天早晨以前你们非做决定不可。如果你们不帮我忙，我叫你们也好受不了，明天上午我就可以宣布公司破产。你们还可以考虑 8 个钟头，怎么办好，随你们便。"在 1947—1969 年的 22 个年头里，这个策略一直很有效。但在 1969 年，电气工人的挫败感终于爆发，促成了一场超越经济利益的罢工。

This method can be applied to situations where the other party is more eager to close a deal. In contrast, the other side is more reluctant to bear the losses caused by the failure of negotiations. If these trading conditions enter their lowest target, they will generally accept them. The second situation is bargaining several times, other methods can not make the opponent make concessions, and the current results can not be concluded at all. In the third case, through bargaining, you have reached the lowest transaction line and it is impossible to let it go. You need to curb the other's pursuit and fierce fighting. When adopting this method, you should be resolute and let the other party realize your determination to withdraw from the negotiations.

这种方法适用于对手更渴望成交的情况。己方处于优势地位，相对而言，对方更不愿承受谈判失败带来的损失。如果这些交易条件达到其最低目标，对方通常都会接受。第二种情况就是经过几番讨价还价，其他方法都无法使对手做出让步，而目前的结果根本无法达成。第三种情况是通过讨价还价，己方已经让到了最低成交线，无法再让，需要遏制对方的穷追猛打。采用这种方法时，要态度坚决，让对方认识到己方可能退出谈判的决心。

5. Deadline-setting Method（设定期限法）

This is a strategy that sets a time frame to force the other party to end the negotiations. People psychologically value what may be lost more than what is readily available. The deadline-setting method makes the other party realize that failure to make a decision as soon as possible will incur the loss of the opportunity to cooperate, thus prompting the hesitant opponent to end the bargain quickly.

这是一种设定时间期限来迫使对方结束磋商的策略。比起容易得到的东西，人们在心理上更珍惜可能会失去的东西。设定期限法使对方认识到不尽快做出决定，将会丧失合作机会，从而促使犹豫不决的对手迅速结束讨价还价。

A seller can force the buyer to make a deal as soon as possible by informing the buyer the possibility that the price of the product will increase over time, the validity of the current preferential offer, the effect of the delayed order on the delivery date, and the choice of other partners after the expiration. A buyer can also tell sellers that other partners will be selected if they do not reduce their price within the set period, there may be no cooperation if the delivery time cannot be determined within the set period, and orders will be refused beyond a certain time to force the seller to deal as soon as possible. This strategy applies to cases where the other party has a strong willingness to deal, otherwise it may directly cause the other party to give up.

卖方可以通过告知买方过段时间产品会涨价的可能性、现在的优惠的有效期、推迟订货对交货期的影响、过期将选择其他合作伙伴等方式迫使买方尽快成交。买方也可以通过告知卖方，如果在设定期限内不降价将选择其他合作伙伴、如果在设定期限内不能确定交货时间将无法合作、超过某个时间会拒绝下单等方式迫使卖方尽快成交。这种策略适用于对方有强烈的成交意愿的情况，否则可能直接导致对方放弃合作。

If the other party uses the deadline-setting method, we should pay attention to following aspects. On the one hand, do not let the other party know your own negotiation deadline. Otherwise, it may use procrastination tactics to get to the point near your deadline, forcing you to accept more disadvantages under time pressure. On the other hand, you should calmly analyze the motivation and purpose of the other party to set the deadline, and judge whether this is the other party's pressure strategy. The decision will be taken after careful analysis of the existing terms of cooperation.

如果对方使用设定期限法，己方在应对时要注意如下方面：一方面，不要让对方知道自己的谈判最后期限，否则对方有可能采用拖延战术，在临近己方的最后期限时才进入正题，让己方在时间压力下不得不接受更多不利条件。另一方面，要冷静分析对方设定期限的动机和目的，判断这是否为对方的施压策略。在仔细分析现有合作条件的优劣之后，再做决定。

6. Package Trading Method（一揽子交易法）

The package trading method is the strategy of making the whole advance and retreat exchange in order to reach the agreement. For example, in the negotiation of a complete set of project transactions, it involves technical patents, trademarks, engineering designs, technical materials, technical training, technical guidance, equipment, spare parts, test raw materials, instrumentation, etc. In addition, it may involve trading methods (such as compensation, barter) and payment issues (such as buyer's credit or seller's credit), etc. After a full range of negotiations on each project and multiple concessions to each other, the remaining differences were not negotiated one by one, but rather classification negotiations, including software (i. e. all technical, service, design issues) and hardware (i. e. all supply issues). Then, the two sides make a "package" compromise on the differences in hardware and software, or make a "package" concession by combining the total differences in hardware and software. It can be seen that the "package deal" embodies the overall and decisive characteristics.

一揽子交易法是以各自坚持的条件做整体的进退交换以求达成协议的策略。例如，成套项目交易谈判涉及技术专利、商标、工程设计、技术资料、技术培训、技术指导、设备、备件、测试原材料、仪器仪表等。此外，还可能涉及交易方式（诸如补偿、易货）和支付问题（如买方信贷、卖方信贷）等。在对各项目均进行了全面交涉、多次相互退让后，对剩余分歧不一一谈判，而是分类谈判，包括软件（即所有的技术、服务、设计类问题）和硬件（即所有供货类问题）。然后，双方就硬件存在的分歧量与软件存在的分歧量进行"一揽子"妥协，或者将软硬件总分歧量合起来做"一揽子"退让。可见，"一揽子交易"体现出了全局性和决定性。

Ⅳ Signing of the Contract（合同的签署）

After the transaction, the relevant contracts are sorted out according to the trading conditions reached by both parties, which is beneficial to both parties to clarify their rights and obligations and ensure the smooth progress of the transaction. Take the contract of sale and purchase of goods as an example. It can be divided into oral contract and written contract by form. Although the oral contract is legal in some countries, it is difficult to prove its existence, and the specific content of the clause is not recorded and is prone to controversy. Therefore, international transaction contracts are in written form.

成交后，根据双方达成的交易条件整理出相关合同，有利于双方明确自身权利与义务，保证交易顺利进行。以商品买卖合同为例，其在形式上可以分为口头合同和书面合同。虽然口头合同在一些国家是合法的，但难以证明其存在，条款的具体内容没有记载也容易出现争议。因此，国际交易合同都采用书面形式。

The main forms of written contract are sales contract and sales confirmation. Most companies have a model format. After the transaction is negotiated, the negotiator only needs to fill in the terms of the transaction as confirmed by both parties and confirm the general terms of the transaction one by one. The use of fixed-form written contracts or confirmations can bring a lot of convenience to negotiators and save the possibility of drafting contracts on an ad hoc basis because of omissions or errors caused by inadequate consideration. Therefore, format contract is preferred in reality. However, the negotiation of joint ventures, the negotiation of international technology trade and the negotiation of international compensation trade seldom use the format contract. Therefore, negotiators should also grasp the relevant issues of contract drafting.

书面合同的形式主要有买卖合同和销售确认书。多数企业会有统一格式的范本。交易谈妥后，谈判者只需按双方确认的交易条件逐项填写，并对一般交易条件逐条加以确认即可。使用固定格式的书面合同或确认书可给谈判者带来许多方便，也省却了临时起草合同可能因考虑不周带来的缺漏或者失误，故在现实中，格式合同受到青睐。但进行合资及合作经营企业的谈判、国际技术贸易的谈判和国际补偿贸易的谈判等很少使用格式合同。因此，谈判者也应该掌握合同起草的相关问题。

1. Drafting of the Contract（合同的起草）

A contract is an instrument that clarifies the rights and obligations of both parties and is binding. It is the main basis for judging disputes arising from the performance of the transaction. Therefore, the contract drafting is very important to ensure the smooth completion of the transaction and to protect the rights of the relevant parties, and must be highly valued.

合同是明确双方权利与义务，具有强制约束力的文书，是交易履行过程中产生争议的主要评判依据。因此，合同起草对于保证交易顺利完成、维护相关方权益非常重要，必须引起高度重视。

（1）Determination of the Drafters（起草方的确定）

Usually, the written contract is drafted by the seller. In view of the importance of contract drafting, you can also seek contract drafting rights or participation rights. Due to the variety of textual expressions, similar meanings may have different understandings. Drafting the contract by yourself can accurately grasp the meaning of the clause and the interpretation of the clause, avoiding the risk of the soft draft clause or the incomplete liability clause of the other party's drafting contract, and avoiding misunderstandings and disputes arising from the differences in interpretation of Chinese and foreign languages or the unclear legal interpretations or conventions of certain words. So in international trade, bilingual texts are recommended and Chinese and foreign language clauses should have the same legal effect. In addition, in the discussion of the terms of the contract, if we draft the contract, when the other party proposed amendments, it will help to strengthen our negotiation weight.

通常情况下，书面合同由卖方起草。鉴于合同起草的重要性，我方也可争取合同起草权或参与权。由于文字表述方式多样，相近的意思可能有不同的理解。自己起草合同，能准确把握条款的含义及对条款的解释，避免对方起草合同可能存在的软条款或对方责任条款不全的风险，以及避免因为中外文字释义差异或不清楚对方某些词的法律释义或约定俗成而产生的误解和争议。因此，在国际贸易中，建议采用双语文本，且中文与外文条款应有同等法律效力。另外，在讨论合同条款时，如果由我方起草合同，当对方提出修改意见时，有利于增强我方的谈判砝码。

If the other party insists on drafting the contract, you should negotiate the general framework of the contract according to the nature of the project, and then draft some of the terms and conditions separately to guarantee that the contract completely and accurately express our intention.

如果对方坚持要由他们起草合同，这时己方应该根据该项目的性质，通过谈判，先确定合同总框架，然后分别起草其中某些条款，最后再合起来通过洽谈确定正式文本，保证合同完整、准确地表达了己方意思。

(2) Determination of Drafting Content (起草内容的确定)

The forms and terms of a contract for the import and export of goods are not static, but the main contents are basically the same. It usually consists of the preface, the text, and the ending. The preface of the contract usually includes the name, number, time and place of the contract, and the names and addresses of the parties to the contract. The text is the main part of the contract, and generally includes the product name and specifications, quantity, packaging, price, transportation, insurance, payment, inspection, claim, force majeure, arbitration and other terms. The product name and specifications mainly include the name of the contracted goods, their specifications, and the method of determining the quality of the goods. The quantity clause is mainly composed of the quantity of goods and the unit of measurement. Packaging terms generally include: packaging materials, the type and nature of the packaging, the size of the packaging, the cost of the packaging, and shipping marks. Price terms mainly include: unit price amount, pricing currency, trade term and total amount. The terms of transportation mainly include: the time of shipment, the method of shipment, the port of shipment and the port of destination. The insurance clauses include: insurance company, insurance value, insurance type and insurance document. Payment terms include: payment amount, payment instrument, payment method, payment time and payment place. The inspection clauses mainly include: inspection right, inspection organization, inspection time, inspection place, inspection method, inspection standard, and inspection verification. The claim clauses mainly include: claim method, claim time and claim basis. These are the main terms of the contract of sale. In addition, there may be force majeure clauses including: the scope of force majeure accidents and their consequences, the organization issuing the accident certificate, the time limit for notifying after the accident and the relief methods and procedures after the accident. The arbitration clauses mainly include: place of arbitration, arbitration institution, rules of arbitration procedure and effect of award. The end of the contract mainly includes the validity of different texts of the contract, the number of contracts, the holder and the parties' signatures.

货物进出口合同的形式和条款不是一成不变的，但其主要内容基本一致。通常由约首、正文和约尾组成。约首一般包括合同的名称、编号、订约时间和地点、订约双方的名称与地址等内容。正文是合同的主要部分，一般来讲包括品名及规格、数量、包装、价格、运输、保险、支付、检验、索赔、不可抗力、仲裁等条款。品名及规格条款主要包括合同货物的名称及其规格和确定货物品质的方法等。数量条款主要由货物数量和计量单位构成。包装条款一般包括包装的材料、包装的种类和性质、包装的尺寸、包装的费用及运输标志等内容。价格条款主要包括单位价格金额、计价货币、贸易术语和总金额等。运输条款主要包括装运时间、装运方式和装运港与目的港等事项。保险条款包括保险公司、保险价值、保险险别和保险单证等内容。支付条款包括支付金额、支付工具、支付方式、支付时间和支付地点等。检验条款主要包括检验权、检验机构、检验时间、检验地点、检验方法、检验标准与检验证。索赔条款主要包括索赔方式、索赔时间和索赔依据等内容。这些都是买卖合同的主要条款。另外还可能有不可抗力条款，包括不可抗力事故的范围及其后果、出具事故证明的机构、发生事故后的通知期限以及发生事故后的救济方法与手续。仲裁条款主要包括仲裁地点、仲裁机构、仲裁程序规则和裁决的效力等。约尾主要包括合同不同文本的效力、合同份数、持有人及当事人签章。

The contract must clearly identify the product or service being purchased and sold, as well as the quantity involved. The written contract should also outline the management of changes and dispute resolution during the execution phase of the transaction. In addition, the law applicable in the contract and the place where the dispute is resolved must be determined. For example, if a device is imported from the United States, is the contract governed by US law or Chinese law? If there is a quality problem with the device, will it be filed in a US or Chinese court or a third party?

合同必须明确标识正在购买和销售的产品或服务，以及涉及的数量。书面合同还应概述在交易的执行阶段管理变更和争议解决的处理。此外，必须确定合同中适用的法律以及争议解决的地点。例如，如果从美国进口设备，合同是否受美国法律或中国法律管辖？如果设备存在质量问题，应该在美国或中国法院还是第三方国家提起诉讼？

In addition to the main terms of the transaction between the parties, the contract should also stipulate liability for breach of contract. Without the clause of liability for breach of contract, it is impossible to effectively supervise the performance of the contract and it may undermine the binding force of the contract. The performing party will not bear any responsibility after the breach of contract, and the loss suffered by the other party will not be compensated. Liability for breach of contract should be clear and easy to implement.

除了双方交易的主要条款，合同还应该规定违约责任。没有违约责任条款，就无法对合同的履行进行有效督促，破坏了合同的约束力，履约方违约后不承担任何责任，对方因此遭受的损失得不到补偿。违约责任应该清晰明了、易于执行。

2. Review of the Contract（合同的审核）

Practice has shown that it is not uncommon for the contract text to be inconsistent with the outcome of the negotiations. Therefore, the review of the contract is indispensable. Special attention should be paid to the existence of textual distortions, the existence of conditions that are not involved or agreed upon in the negotiations, and whether the signatory has the authority to represent the company or obtain relevant authorization.

实践表明，合同文本与谈判结果不符的情况并不少见。因此，合同的审核不可或缺。要特别关注是否存在文字歪曲的问题，是否存在谈判中没有涉及或未达成一致的条件以及签字人是否具有代表公司的权限或获得相关授权。

(1) The Examination of the Content（内容的审核）

a. Is the clause stated clearly?（条款表述是否清楚）

The terms of the contract must be clear and specific, without any ambiguity, otherwise it will bring trouble to the performance of the contract, causing controversy and unnecessary disputes. Take the weight unit “ton” as an example. Some people take it for granted that 1 ton =

1,000kg. In fact, in some countries, the weight of tons may exceed or be less than 1,000kg. For example, in the United Kingdom, 1 ton = 1,016kg; while in the United States, 1 ton = 907.2kg. If the weight on the contract is marked in tons, the dispute may be caused by cognitive differences. Therefore, in international trade contracts, in order to avoid misunderstanding, "metric tons" must be used to express the weight of 1,000kg.

合同的条款必须表述清晰、具体，不产生任何歧义，否则会给合同履行带来麻烦，引起争议和不必要的纠纷。以重量单位“吨”为例，有人想当然地认为1吨=1 000千克。实际上，在有些国家，吨的重量可能超过或不到1 000千克。比如在英国，1吨=1 016千克；而在美国，1吨=907.2千克。如果合同上的重量用吨标注，则可能因为认知差异而引起纠纷。因此，在国际贸易合同中，为了避免误解，必须用“公吨”来表述1 000千克的重量。

Problems often arise due to unclear terms. For example, a businessman bought an old house to be demolished and converted into a new building. The entire contract negotiation was smooth and the seller and the buyer signed it. However, the contract did not specify the deadline for the seller to move out of the old house. As a result, the buyer spent a lot of money in preparing for the construction of the house. However, he couldn't start construction as the seller was reluctant to move out of the old house. The buyer then sued to the court, but the protracted lawsuit did not allow the buyer to see favorable results. In addition, the debtor was repeatedly pressed by the creditors, and the buyer suffered heavy losses. For another example, a company in our country and an American businessman have entered into a dispute settlement clause in their contract. It states that "in the event of a dispute, it is resolved through arbitration or by resorting to the courts". In fact, this kind of wording is not very rigorous. From a legal point of view, this kind of vague wording is inappropriate. Because in accordance with the general principles of international law, the choice of arbitration implies the exclusion of litigation, and if the two are juxtaposed, it is an invalid clause. Moreover, in the execution of the contract, the two sides had another dispute. The American lawyer hired by the US businessman caught this improper statement and filed a lawsuit to the local court, stating that this clause was invalid. In this way, the US businessman took the initiative in the entire litigation process, while ours was quite passive.

因条款不明确出现问题的现象经常发生。例如，有一个商人购买了一栋旧房子准备拆除后改建成新的大楼，整个合同谈判很顺利，买卖双方都签了字。然而合同中却没有对卖主搬出旧房子的最后期限做出明确的规定，结果买主花了一大笔钱做建房的准备，却因卖主迟迟不肯搬出旧房子而不能动工。买主遂向法院起诉，然而旷日持久的诉讼并没有让买主看到有利的结果，再加上债主又连连逼债，买主损失惨重。又例如，我国某地一个公司与美商在合同中订立了有关解决争议的条款，规定：“一旦发生争议，通过仲裁或通过诉诸法院解决。”其实，这种用词很不严谨，从法律的角度来看这种含混的用词是不当的。因为按照国际法的一般原则，选择仲裁就意味着排除了诉讼，如果两者并列，则为无效条款。而且在合同的执行中双方又发生了纠纷，美商聘请的美国律师抓住了这个不当的表述，向当地法院提起了诉讼，指出这个条款是无效的。这样，在整个诉讼过程中美商占据了主动，而我方则相当被动。

b. Is the content of the contract consistent with the outcome of the negotiations? (合同内容与双方协商的结果是否一致)

The content of the contract must be completely consistent with the outcome of the negotiations in order to truly guarantee the outcome of the negotiations. However, in the process of formulating the contract, the parties may intentionally or unintentionally have some clauses that are inconsistent with the outcome of the negotiations. If you take it for granted before signing the contract that the terms are okay and rashly sign it, you may suffer losses in the course of future performance. For example, in a contract signed by a company in Africa with a company in China, an unconfirmed one was added to the dispute clause: If the parties have disputes during performance of the contract, they would need to be tried in a local court in Africa. If we don't notice this, then if we need to deal with the problem by litigation, the distant roads and strange laws will bring us a lot of trouble. Therefore, the contract terms, especially some important time, figures, terminology and negotiating memorandum should be checked and confirmed before signing.

合同内容必须与谈判结果完全一致，才能真正保证谈判的成果。但在对方制定合同的过程中，可能有意无意出现一些与谈判结果不一致的条款。如果己方在签约前想当然地以为条款没有问题，贸然签字，可能在今后的履约过程中遭受损失。例如，非洲一个公司曾在与我国一个企业签订的合同中，在争议条款上加上了未经协商的一条：如果双方在履约过程中产生争议，需要在非洲当地法院起诉审理。如果我方没有注意到这一条款，那么一旦需要通过诉讼处理问题，遥远的路途、陌生的法律将给我方带来很大的麻烦。因此，应在签字前把合同条款，特别是一些重要的时间、数字、术语与谈判备忘录一一对照检查，确认无误。

c. Completeness and Accuracy of the Content (内容是否完整、准确)

The signing place should be written at the head of the contract. In international trade, there are certain differences in the laws and regulations of different countries. In cases where the application of the law is not expressly provided for in the contract, the law of the place of signing is generally followed if a dispute arises. If the place of signing is not indicated, the parties may have a dispute over the application of the law.

约首要注明签约地点。在国际贸易中，各国法律规定有一定差异。在合同中没有明确规定适用法律的情况下，如果产生争议，一般遵循签约地法律。如果不注明签约地点，双方可能会就适用法律产生争议。

In the body of the contract, the method of expressing the quality of the goods shall be clearly stated, and if there is a standard, the name of the standard used and the year in which the standard is formulated shall be clearly stated. If it's on specification, the difference or a fixed quality latitude should be written down. The quantity of goods shall be marked in units of measurement. Goods traded by weight shall be stated by gross weight or net weight; for goods whose actual quantity of delivery is difficult to fully match the contract quantity, the flexible range of the quantity of delivery shall be specified, i. e. the term of more or less, which should include the extent of the overflow, how the overflow portion is priced, and who determines the quantity of the portion. On the price term, it is necessary to clarify the choice of currency, what fees are included, and what costs are not included. In the packing clause, if the buyer requests to determine the shipping mark, the buyer's request should be clearly written in the contract. As to the "fixed brand" packaging, it should be stipulated that the seller shall not be held liable for infringement of the interests of any third party if the trademark or brand number provided by the buyer is infringed upon; and he shall not be held liable under the counterfeit and product liability act. In the terms of payment, for remittance, the time of remittance, the specific method of remittance and the amount of payment, etc. shall be specified in the contract; for the collection method, the terms of delivery, the buyer's payment and acceptance liability and the time limit of payment shall be clearly stipulated in the contract; for the L/C method, the kind of the L/C, the issuing bank, the opening time and the delivery time shall be specified. The inspection clause shall indicate whether the validity of the inspection certificate shall be used as the basis for the receipt of payment or as the final basis for proof of the condition of the goods. The clause on the manner in which the contract is performed shall state whether it is executed in stages.

合同正文部分应写明商品质量的表示方法，有标准的，应当写明所采用的标准名称及该标准的制定年份；按规格表示的，应当写明公差或一定的机动幅度。商品数量要标明计量单位。按重量交易的商品，应说明是按毛重还是净重；对于实际交货数量与合同数量难以完全相符的商品，应列明交货数量的机动幅度，即溢短装条款。溢短装条款中应包含溢短装的幅度，溢短装部分如何计价，以及由谁来判定这部分的数量等内容。在价格方面，要明确货币的选择、包含了哪些费用、不包含哪些费用；在包装条款中，如买方要求决定运输标志，应该在合同中将买方的要求写清楚。对于“定牌”包装，必须在合同中明确规定，如果买方所提供的商标、牌号侵害了任何第三者的利益，卖方不负侵权之责；不承担冒牌及产品责任法中所规定的有关责任。若支付条款中使用汇付方式，应在合同中明确规定汇付的时间、具体的汇付方式和金额等；使用托收方式时，应在合同中明确规定交单条件、买方的付款和承兑责任以及付款期限等；使用信用证方式时，应在合同中规定使用何种信用证，并明确开证行、开证时间和送达时间。检验条款中要注明检验证书的效力，是作为收取货款的依据，还是作为证明货物状况的最终依据。有关合同履行方式的条款，要写明是否分期执行。

d. Fairness and Balance of Contract Terms（合同条款的公平与平衡）

The fairness of the terms of the contract is reflected in the equality of the benefits and obligations of the parties concerned, and there will be no provision for one party to enjoy more rights or to perform obligations that are not comparable to the benefits. Balance is reflected in the size of the responsibilities of the two parties, there will not be provision that only one party's dereliction of duty will be punished. In the terms of the contract, the most common and basic conditions should seek a balance between the two parties. For example, the terms of payment of the buyer shall be equal to the terms of the seller's settlement and shipping documents. The buyer's delivery terms should be balanced with the seller's terms of "guarantee and premise" and "acceptance and conditions". Only if the rights and obligations of both parties are equal, will the contract be performed calmly. Otherwise, it may cause disputes in the execution of the contract.

合同条款的公平体现为相关方权益与义务的平等，不会出现一方享有更多权益或履行与收益不相当的义务的规定。平衡体现为双方责任大小相当，不会出现只有一方失职会受罚的规定。在合同条款中，最普通、最基本的条件都应该谋求双方平衡。例如，买方的支付条款与卖方的结算和运输单据的条件要相当。买方的交货条款与卖方的“保证和前提”、“验收与条件”的条件要平衡。只有双方权利和义务相当，才会心平气和地履行合同。否则，可能会造成合同执行中的纠纷。

For example, in the negotiation of a large hotel jointly set up by a coastal city in China, the rights and obligations of the foreign parties and the Chinese side are not equal in the draft contract. The management fee charged by the foreign party is too high, which is much higher than the joint venture hotel can bear, but the foreign party has few obligations, some parts are also very abstract, it is difficult to reflect the specific responsibility. Furthermore, the review of the draft contract found that the management employed by the hotel was controlled by the same parent company as the foreign investor. In this way, the foreign side may use a variety of financial transfers to embezzle most of the profits of the joint venture hotel and we will be helpless. To this end, our negotiators negotiate directly with the foreign head office to clarify our position, and finally the foreign side accepts our point of view and makes corresponding changes in the terms of the contract, which makes the views of both parties be fully stated and avoids a series of possible disputes in the future.

例如，在我国某沿海城市合资兴办的一家大宾馆的谈判中，在合同草案中外方与中方享有的权利与承担的义务不对等。外方收取的管理费过高，比合资宾馆所能承受的高出了许多，但外方承担的义务却很少，有的部分也十分不明确，难以体现具体的责任。而且在对合同草案的审议中又发现，饭店所聘请的管理方与外方投资方是同一个母公司控制的。这样，外方可能采用多种财务转移手法侵吞合资宾馆的大部分利润，届时我方将对此束手无策。为此，我方谈判者直接与外方总公司进行谈判，阐明我方的立场，最后外方接受了我方的观点，并在合同条款中做了相应的修改，使得双方观点得到了充分阐述，避免了以后可能出现的一系列纠纷。

(2) Audit of the Signatory (签字人的审核)

The qualification of the signatory determines the validity of the contract. Therefore, the identity of the signatory needs to be reviewed before signing the contract. Usually the contract requires the signature of the legal representative of the company to take effect. Furthermore, we must also consider the transaction amount involved in the contract, from the salesman, department manager to the company leader, different posts have different signing authority. Verify the identity certificate of the signatory. If the signatory is not a legal representative of the company, you can ask the other party to issue a relevant power of attorney to prove the identity of the signatory. You can't just recognize the identity of the other party based on the title or acquaintance of the other person's business card, so as not to affect the validity of the contract.

签字人的资质决定了合同的有效性。因此，在签约前，还需要对签字人的身份进行审查。通常合同需要公司法人代表签字才能生效。此外，也要考虑合同涉及的交易金额，从业务员、部门经理到公司领导，不同职务有不同的签字权限。需要核实签字人的身份证明资料。如果签字人不是公司法人代表，可以要求对方出具相关授权书，证明签字人的身份。不能仅凭对方名片上的头衔或熟人介绍就随便认可对方身份，以免影响合同的效力。

V Claim Negotiation（索赔谈判）

Claim negotiation refers to the negotiation between the parties when the contractual obligations cannot be fulfilled or cannot be fully fulfilled. In the process of fulfilling the international trade contract, it is easy to have problems because of the long distance of transportation, the large number of people involved, the more complicated formalities and the deviation of the parties to the contract understanding in different countries. If one party defaults and causes losses to the other party, the injured party will file a claim. The defaulting party will confirm the reasonableness of the claim and the parties shall negotiate the relevant contents.

索赔谈判是指合同义务不能履行或不能完全履行时，当事人双方进行的谈判。在国际贸易合同的履行过程中，由于运输距离遥远、涉及人员较多、手续较复杂、不同国家的交易方对合同理解的偏差，很容易出现问题。如果发生一方违约，给另一方带来损失的情况，受损方就会提起索赔。违约方则会确认索赔的合理性，双方就相关内容进行磋商。

1. Treatment of Contractual Disputes（合同纠纷的处理方式）

The common methods of handling disputes in the course of contract performance are consultation, mediation, arbitration and litigation.

在合同履行过程中发生争议时常见的处理方式有协商、调解、仲裁和诉讼。

(1) Consultation（协商）

Consultation is the way to deal with the dispute directly between the parties to the contract. This approach involves the least number of parties and is conducive to cost savings; it is also easier for parties to communicate face-to-face and to resolve problems while maintaining good relationships between the parties. This is the most economical and quickest way to deal with disputes, so when problems arise, the parties usually consult first. Claim negotiation is also a type of consultation.

协商是合同当事人之间直接交涉处理争议的方式。这种方法牵涉方最少，有利于节约成本；当事人面对面进行沟通，也更容易在维系各方良好关系的情况下解决问题。这是最经济、最快捷的纠纷处理方式，因此出现问题后通常当事人都会先进行协商。索赔谈判也属于协商的一种。

(2) Mediation (调解)

Mediation is a way to resolve contractual disputes through the presence of third parties. A third party may be a natural person approved by both parties, who usually has no direct interest in the parties, but also has a good reputation, a high prestige and a strong ability to solve problems; it may also be an organizational body, such as trade associations, arbitration bodies, local courts, etc. The conciliator may be appointed by both parties or agreed upon in the contract. This approach requires a certain amount of mediation costs, but the procedure is relatively simple.

调解是通过第三方出面协调解决合同争议的方式。第三方可以是双方认可的自然人，这种人通常与当事人无直接利益关系，而又具有良好声誉和较高威望并有较强的解决问题能力；也可以是组织机构，如行业协会、仲裁机构、地方法院等。调解人可以由双方指定，或在合同中约定。这种方式需要支付一定的调解费用，但程序相对简便。

(3) Arbitration (仲裁)

Arbitration is the way of determining the liability and compensation for breach of contract for the parties to a contract dispute through an arbitration institution or a provisional arbitration tribunal. China's arbitration bodies include the arbitration tribunals established by Arbitration Commissions of China International Economic and Trade Arbitration Commission and the local governments. The arbitration tribunal shall conduct arbitration in accordance with the arbitration rules, the arbitration agreement and the arbitration application submitted by the parties. The result of its arbitration is final and mandatory. The award may be applied to the local court for enforcement, or the parties may execute it through consultation. This approach is fair and relatively low-cost.

仲裁是通过仲裁机构或临时组成的仲裁庭，为存在合同纠纷的各方判定违约责任及赔偿的方式。我国的仲裁机构有中国国际经济贸易仲裁委员会和地方政府所设仲裁委员会的仲裁庭。仲裁庭根据当事人提交的仲裁协议和仲裁申请，按照仲裁规则进行仲裁。其仲裁结果是终局的，具有强制性。可凭裁决书到当地法院申请强制执行，或双方协商执行。这种方式较为公正，费用也相对较低。

(4) Litigation (诉讼)

Litigation is the way for the court to hear the party's liability for breach of contract and to judge the damages. This takes a long time, after the first instance judgment, if not satisfied with the result of the judgment, the parties can appeal within the validity period. Second instance judgment is the final judgment, which may take one or two years to have a result. The costs are also high, involving a variety of costs, such as paying courts, lawyers, case trials, sentence enforcement, etc. Usually in the case of litigation, the relationship between the two sides has been very tense, which is not conducive to future cooperation. Thus, the parties are generally reluctant to do so unless they have no choice.

诉讼是由法院对当事方的违约责任进行审理并对损害赔偿进行判决的方式。这种方式耗时较长，一审判决后，如果对判决结果不服，当事人在有效期内都可以提出上诉。二审判决才是终审判决，可能需要一两年才有结果。费用也较高，涉及支付给法院、律师、案件审理、判决执行等的各种费用。通常在诉讼情况下，双方关系已经非常紧张，不利于以后的合作。因此，除非别无选择，当事人一般不愿意采用这种方式。

Choosing which way to settle the contract dispute need to consider the advantages and disadvantages of various ways, such as efficiency and cost, etc. Usually we can refer to the amount involved, the contract agreement, the relationship between the two parties and the difficulty of execution. If the amount involved is small, a low-cost approach should be chosen. If the contract has relevant provisions on dispute handling, it shall be executed in accordance with the provisions. If you want to maintain a good relationship, you should choose a more peaceful approach. If the enforcement of compensation is more difficult, the third party should be selected to assist and have a mandatory way.

选择何种方式解决合同纠纷，需要考虑各种方式的利弊，如效率、成本等。通常我们可以参考涉及金额、合同约定、双方关系和执行的难易。如果涉及金额较小，则应选择成本低的方式。如果合同对纠纷处理方式有相关规定，则应按规定执行。如果想保持双方的良好关系，则应选择比较平和的处理方式。如果赔偿执行难度较大，则应选择有第三方协助和强制性的方式。

2. Preparation before Claims Negotiation（索赔谈判前的准备）

（1） Clear Responsibility（明确责任）

For losses of different causes, the parties responsible for the losses are different and the object of the claim is not the same. The missing goods may be the seller's shipment problem or the shipper's loading and unloading problems. The damage to the goods may be a seller's packing problem or a mistake or accident in the course of transportation. Therefore, once there is a problem, the injured party must identify the responsible person and the cause of the accident so as not to complain about no person or the wrong person.

不同原因造成的损失，责任方不同，索赔对象也不一样。货物缺失，有可能是卖方发货问题；也有可能是运输方装卸问题。货物受损，可能是卖方包装问题，也可能是运输过程中的失误或意外。因此，一旦出现问题，受损方必须明确责任人及事故原因，以免投诉无门或找错责任人而误事。

（2） Collection of Relevant Evidence（收集相关证据）

In filing a claim, relevant evidence is required to justify the claim. For claim to the insurance company, you should provide the original insurance policy; for man-made cause of loss of goods, you should provide transport documents and identification report; for quality issues, you should provide quality inspection certificate. Other persuasive correspondence, witness testimony, live photographs should also be collected. At the same time, a claim list should be prepared showing the items and amounts claimed.

在提出索赔时，需要提供相关证据，证明索赔的合理性。向保险公司索赔，应提供保险单正本；对人为原因造成的货物损失，应提供运输单据和鉴定报告；对质量问题，应提供质量检验证明。还应收集其他有说服力的往来函电、证人证言、现场照片。同时，应制作索赔清单，列明索赔项目和金额。

(3) Determination of Damaged Items and Amounts（确定受损项目和金额）

The damaged items should be checked carefully and there should be no omission. The determination of the amount of compensation should first refer to the relevant provisions of the contract. If the contract has the amount of damages and the method of calculation, the amount of compensation shall be claimed according to the agreed amount or method; if there is no relevant provision in the contract, it shall be equivalent to the loss suffered by the injured party, including the profit. In the case of refusal or rejection of the goods, the amount of compensation shall be calculated on the basis of the difference between the contract price and the market price at the time of the breach.

受损项目要检查仔细，不要有遗漏。赔偿金额的确定，首先要参照合同的相关规定。如果合同有关于损害赔偿的金额及计算方法，则应按约定金额或方法计算出的赔偿金额索赔；如果合同没有相关规定，则应与受损方遭受的包括利润在内的损失相当。如果是拒交或拒收货物，赔偿金额按合同价格与违约行为发生时的市价之差进行计算。

3. Main Contents of Claim Negotiation（索赔谈判的主要内容）

(1) Determination of Breach of Contract（违约行为的认定）

The determination of breach of contract mainly discusses the cause and truth of the breach. In the transaction of goods, if the buyer complains that the quality of the products provided by the seller is not up to standard, the type is wrong, the quantity is not enough, the goods are damaged, and so on, the buyer needs to provide the supporting materials, and the seller needs to determine whether the evidence is reliable or not.

违约行为的认定主要讨论造成违约的原因及属实性。如在货物交易中，买方如果投诉卖方提供的产品质量不达标、种类错误、数量不够、被损坏等，需要提供证明材料，卖方则需要确定这些证据是否可靠。

(2) Determination of Liability for Breach of Contract（违约责任的认定）

The liability for breach of contract should be determined to make sure which party's failure caused the breach. If the buyer complains that the seller sent the wrong goods and the seller considers it a fault by the shipping party, then both parties need to provide relevant evidence for discussion.

违约责任的认定要明确是哪一方的失误造成违约。如买方投诉卖方发错货，卖方却认为是运输方的问题，则双方需要提供相关证据进行讨论。

(3) Determination of the Mode of Compensation（赔偿方式的确定）

The way of compensation mainly determines how to compensate the injured party and the time limit of execution. The common ways are to determine the amount of compensation, to replace the wrong goods, to replace the missing goods, to refund the goods, to refuse payment, to repair the damaged goods, to reduce the price, and so on. Based on the principle of no more compensation and no less demands, the two sides need to discuss different ways of specific implementation standards and execution time, so as to ensure the effective implementation of claims.

赔偿方式主要确定如何对受损方进行赔偿及执行的期限。常见方式有确定赔偿金额、对错发的商品进行换货、补发缺失的货物、退货退款、拒付货款、修复受损货物、减价等。本着不多赔、不少要的原则，双方需要讨论不同方式下具体的执行标准以及执行的时间，从而保证理赔的有效实施。

4. Notes for Claims Negotiation（索赔谈判的注意事项）

(1) Timely Claims（及时索赔）

Claims are time-bound and are generally specified in the contract, usually within 15 to 45 days after the arrival of the goods. After finding the problem, collect the evidence in time and file the claim with the other party within the validity period. Don't lose because you're out of date.

索赔是有时间期限的，一般会在合同中明确规定，通常在货物到达后15~45天内。发现问题后要及时收集证据，在有效期内向对方提出索赔。不要因为过期而无法挽回损失。

(2) Pay Attention to Consultation Skills（注意磋商技巧）

In the negotiation of claims, you should both insist on principle and flexibility. Don't be unreasonable and embarrass the other party. Showing sufficient evidence prevents the other party from shirking its responsibility. Impress the other party to make full use of its value on reputation and yearning to long-term cooperation.

在索赔谈判中要软硬兼施，既要坚持原则，又要有一定的灵活性。切忌得理不饶人，让对方下不来台。出示充足的证据让对方无法推卸责任。充分利用对方对信誉的看重、对长期合作的向往打动对方。

Ⅵ Etiquette at the End of Negotiations（谈判结束阶段的礼仪）

1. Signing Ceremony（签约仪式）

In order to show the importance of cooperation and the importance of contracts, some large-scale cooperation projects will hold a signing ceremony. According to the needs of the simplification of the ceremony, decide whether to set up a signature table, arrange senior leaders to meet with members of the other delegation, and invite members of the press to attend. It is necessary for negotiators to learn the relevant etiquette rules and procedures.

为了显示对合作的重视和合同的重要性，一些大型的合作项目都会举办签约仪式。根据仪式繁简的需要，决定是否专设签字桌，安排高级领导会见对方代表团成员，请新闻界人士参加等。谈判者有必要学习相关礼仪规范及流程。

(1) Determination of Signatories and Participants（签字人与参加人员的确定）

Usually, the signing ceremony is attended by the members of the negotiating team, and the signatory is determined by the relevant parties through negotiation. However, the signatory is not necessarily a negotiator. It is usually a senior leader who can represent the company. It is also necessary to consider whether the identity of the signatory personnel is equal. In order to express the importance of signing the contract, some countries that value their identity will also invite some relevant persons to observe the ceremony. If you need to invite other people to participate in the signing ceremony, you need to obtain the consent of the other party, but also pay attention to the number of participants that should be equal.

通常情况下，由谈判小组成员出席签约仪式，由相关方协商确定签字人。但签字人不一定是谈判人员，通常是能代表公司的高层领导，同时也要考虑双方签字人的身份是否相当。为了表示对签约的重视，一些看重身份的国家还会邀请一些有地位的相关人士观礼。如果需要邀请其他人员参加签约仪式，需征得对方同意，同时也要注意各方参加人数应相当。

(2) Arrangement of the Signing Hall (签约厅的布置)

Signature tables and adequate seats should be provided in the signing hall. Print and bind the number of copies of the contract with the signatories and place them on the signing table with the pen. The flag of the respective country should also be placed in the middle of the table where the signatory is seated. Be careful not to misplace the flag, and the guest's flag should be placed on the right to show respect. Once there was an agreement between the two parties, at the time of the official signing, the flag of the other party was misplaced on the left side of the table. The head of the guest delegation therefore doubted the ability of the host party and refused to sign the contract, and the company lost a big business.

签约厅内应设置签字桌和足够的座椅。打印装订好与签字人数量相当份数的合同文本，与签字笔一起放置在签约桌上。签字人就座位置的桌子中间还应摆放各自国家的国旗。注意国旗位置不要放错了，客方的国旗应该放在右侧以示尊敬。曾经出现过双方达成协议后，在正式签约时，主方布置人员错将对方的国旗放在了桌子的左侧。客方代表团的团长因此怀疑主方的办事能力而拒绝签约，公司为此丢了一笔大生意。

In terms of seating arrangements, according to different needs, there are three common forms:

在座次安排方面，根据不同的需要，常见的有以下三种形式：

a. Side-by-side Arrangement (并列式)

This is the most common form of seat signing ceremony and is suitable for occasions where the media participates. The signing table is placed horizontally to the door, and the signing person is located in the middle of the table against the door. In accordance with the international etiquette of respect for the right, the guest's seat is arranged on the right side of the entrance, and the host's seat is on the left side of the entrance. If there is a signing assistant, whose location is outside the signatory. Other attendees are placed side by side behind their respective signatory personnel. See Figure 6. 1.

这是双边签约仪式最常见的座次形式，适用于有媒体参加的场合。签字桌面对门横放，签字人的位置居中设在签字桌后。按照国际上以右为尊的礼仪，把客方的座位安排在进门右方，主方座位安排在进门左方。如有助签人员，则其位置设在签字人外侧。其他出席人员的位置在各自签字人的后方并列安排。如图 6.1 所示。

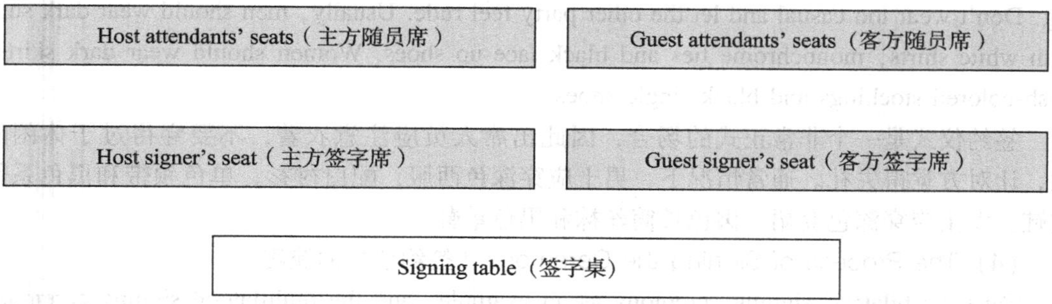

Figure 6.1　Side-by-side Arrangement

b. Face-to-face Arrangement（相对式）

The face-to-face signing table and signing staff seating arrangement is the same as the side-by-side arrangement, except that the attendant is not behind the signing staff, but opposite the signing person. See Figure 6.2.

相对式签字桌和签字人座次安排与并列式相同，区别在于其随员席不是在签字人的后面，而是设在签字人位置的对面。如图 6.2 所示。

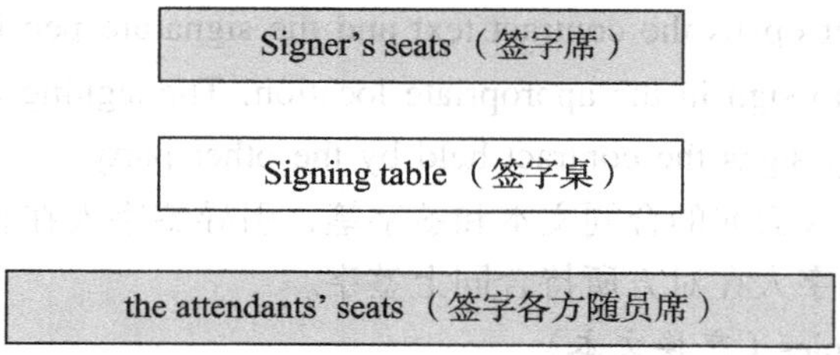

Figure 6.2　Face-to-face Arrangement

c. Chairman Arrangement（主席式）

The chairman arrangement is mainly applicable to the multilateral signing ceremony. The signing table is placed in the same way as the previous two forms. However, the signing table only has one free seat. All personnel attending the signing ceremony, including the signing staff, are sitting in the position facing the signing table. The signing personnel will then return to the original seat after signing the signature on the signing table. See Figure 6.3.

主席式的座次安排主要适用于多边签约仪式。其签字桌安置与前面两种形式一样。但签字席只设一个自由席位。所有出席签约仪式的人员，包括签字人员都坐在面朝签字席的位置。签字人员依次到签字席就座签字后，再返回原座位。如图 6.3 所示。

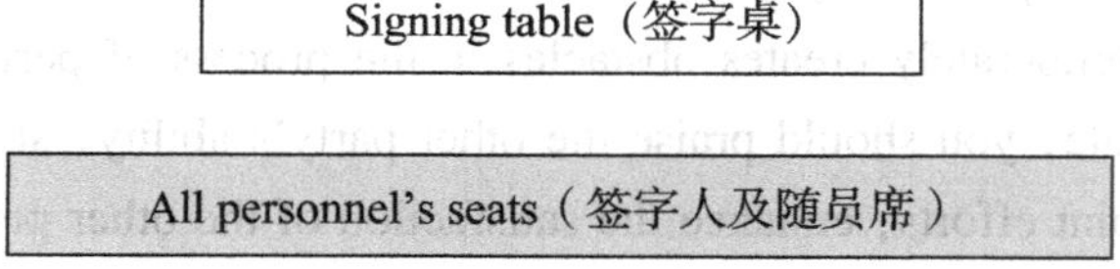

Figure 6.3　Chairman Arrangement

(3) Dress of Attendees（出席人员着装）

The signing ceremony is a very formal occasion, so attendees should pay attention to clothing. Don't wear too casual and let the other party feel rude. Usually, men should wear dark suits with white shirts, monochrome ties and black lace-up shoes. Women should wear dark skirts, flesh-colored stockings and black single shoes.

签约仪式是一个非常正式的场合，因此出席人员应注意衣着，不要穿得过于休闲随意，让对方觉得失礼。通常情况下，男士应穿深色西服，配白衬衫、单色领带和黑色系带皮鞋。女士应穿深色套裙、肉色长筒丝袜和黑色单鞋。

(4) The Process of Signing the Ceremony（签约仪式的流程）

Take the bilateral signing ceremony as an example, and the multilateral signing ceremony process is similar.

以双边签约仪式为例，多边签约仪式流程相似。

a. Starting Ceremony（仪式开始）

The parties who participate the signing ceremony enter the signing hall and take the seats in turn, and the signing personnel are seated at the same time.

各方参加签约仪式的人员步入签约厅依次就座，签字人同时入座。

b. Signing of the Contract（合同签署）

The signing assistant opens the contract text and the signature pen in front of the signatory and guide the signatory to sign in the appropriate location. The signing assistant then exchanges the text and the signatory signs the contract held by the other party.

助签人员打开签字人面前的合同文本和签字笔，引导签字人在合适的位置签字。再由助签人员交换文本，签字人在对方所持合同上签字。

c. Exchange the Copies（交换文本）

The signatories stand up to exchange the text of the contract with the other party, shaking hands and exchanging pen as a memento. The entourage applaud and celebrate.

签字人起立与对方换回己方合同文本，同时握手祝贺并交换签字笔以资纪念。随行人员鼓掌庆贺。

d. Drinking to Celebrate（饮酒庆祝）

When conditions permit, the ceremonial staff can bring champagne to the audience to meet each other. After the signing ceremony, the host party can also host a banquet to attend the event to celebrate the success of the cooperation. When you celebrate, be careful not to be too happy or just to congratulate yourself on your own success, and not to show off the means of forcing the other to give in. In order to prevent the other party from forming an understanding that your profit is more or it is manipulated by you so that it feels frustrated and even angry, and even fails to cooperate and deliberately creates obstacles in the process of performing the contract to counterattack and retaliate, you should praise the other party's ability, stress that the transaction is a win-win result of joint efforts, enhance the satisfaction of the other party, and actively fulfill the contract.

在有条件的情况下，礼宾人员可送上香槟酒，供在场人员互相碰杯道贺。签约仪式后，主方也可设宴款待出席人员，庆贺合作成功。庆贺时注意不要过于喜形于色，只顾祝贺己方成功，更不要炫耀迫使对方让步的手段，以免让对方形成我方获利更多或者被我方操纵的认识，从而感到挫败甚至愤怒，以致在履行合同的过程中不配合、故意制造障碍进行反击、报复。应该称赞对方的能力，强调成交是共同努力的双赢结果，提升对方的满足感，积极履行合同。

2. Banquet Etiquette（宴请礼仪）

Banqueting is a common way to express welcome, celebrate cooperation and promote mutual affection in international business negotiations. In the banquet activities, to follow the appropriate etiquette, especially the international general etiquette, can make the banquet activities achieve the desired results.

宴请是国际商务谈判过程中常见的一种表达欢迎、庆祝合作、联络双方感情的方式。在宴请活动中，应遵循恰当的礼仪，特别是国际通用礼仪，能使宴请活动取得预期的效果。

（1）Preparations for the Banquet（宴请的准备工作）

a. Determination of the invited guests. Before the banquet, the inviter should make clear the guests and the number to make sure of the number of tables and determine the level.

确定邀请的宾客。在宴请前，邀请方要明确请哪些人，请多少人，为订桌数、确定档次提供依据。

b. Determination of time and place. The choice of time should pay attention to the convenience of guests. Do not choose their holiday or family reunion day. The choice of location can consider the budget, the purpose of the banquet and the identity of the guests. Choose a restaurant with local characteristics, but do not choose the guests' hotel. The hotel where the guests are staying is like their makeshift home, and a banquet there likes a treat at the guests' house.

确定时间和地点。时间的选择注意主宾方便的时候，不要选在对方节假日、家人团聚的日子。地点的选择可以考虑己方的预算、宴请的目的及宾客的身份。选比较有地方特色的饭店，但不要在宾客下榻的酒店。客人下榻的酒店对他们来说就像其临时的住所，如果在那里设宴，会让人感觉是在客人家中款待他们。

c. Selection of dishes. When choosing dishes, we need to consider the main guests' taste, preference and taboo, and combine the local characteristics. If there are Muslims among the guests, do not order dishes with pork and alcoholic beverages. If there is European or American, don't order a dish with dog meat, game and guts.

菜品的选择。在选择菜品的时候，需要考虑主宾的口味偏好、禁忌，再结合当地特色。如果宾客中有穆斯林，则不要点配有猪肉的菜和酒精饮料。如果有欧美人，则不要点配有狗肉、野味、内脏的菜。

d. The sending of invitation card. The inviter shall prepare the invitation card and send it to the guests a few days before the banquet. The invitation card should include the inviter, the invitee, the subject matter, time, place, etc. If there is a request on the garment, it should also be noted on the invitation card. The guest who receives the invitation card should reply in time to facilitate the other party to determine the number of participants. The day before the banquet, the inviter should call the guests again to confirm the information.

发送请柬。邀请方应在宴请前几天准备好请柬并发送给宾客。请柬上应写上邀请人、被邀请人、事由、时间、地点等内容。如果服装上有要求，也应在请柬上注明。收到请柬的宾客应及时回复，方便对方确定参加人数。在宴请前一天，邀请方应再次致电宾客确认宴请信息。

e. Determination of seats. Formal banquets should be prepared with seating cards placed according to the identity of the guests. Usually, The closer you are to your host, the more honorable you are. The first seat on the right of the host should be reserved for the most distinguished guest. When the guests arrive, the receptionist should take them to the place where they are arranged.

座次的确定。正式的宴会应准备座位牌，根据宾客的身份确定座次。通常情况下，离主人越近的座位，身份越尊贵。主人右边第一个位子应留给最尊贵的客人。客人到达后，接待员应带其到安排好的地方就座。

(2) Dining Etiquette（赴宴礼仪）

a. Dress. Formal banquets usually need to be dressed, or you can refer to the dress code on the invitation card. Usually, women should wear dresses and men should wear suits. When seated, dress appropriately. Don't take off your coat or tie for comfort. If the indoor temperature is high, you can take off your coat and leave it when you enter the restaurant.

着装。正式的宴会通常需要穿正装，也可以参考请柬上的着装要求。在通常情况下，女士应穿礼服，男士应穿西服。入座后，也应保证着装得体。不要为了舒适脱掉外套或松开领带。如果室内温度较高，可在进入饭店的时候把大衣脱下寄存。

b. Time of arrival. Arrival time needs to refer to the invitation party's habit. Usually the guests should arrive on time or 5 to 10 minutes in advance. Guests should arrive half an hour later for a Latin American party.

到达时间。到达时间需要参考邀请方的习惯，通常情况下应准时到达或提前 5~10 分钟到。赴拉美人的宴会，客人则应晚半小时到。

c. Dining. When eating, be careful not to affect the person next to you. Keep a certain distance from the table and keep your elbows away from the table; don't make a sound when eating; don't talk with food; don't wave your cutlery; don't put your cutlery in random after eating, the knife and fork should be slanted on the plate, chopsticks should be placed beside the bowl, do not put them on the bowl to make it easy for the waiter to collect.

用餐。用餐时，注意不要影响到旁边的人。与餐桌要保持一定的距离，不要把手肘放在餐桌上；进食时不要发出声响；不要含着食物讲话；不要挥动你的餐具；不要在用餐后将你的餐具乱放，刀叉应斜放在盘中，筷子应放在碗旁边，不要放在碗上，以方便服务员收取。

When the host or main guest speaks, other personnel should stop eating, put down the cutlery and watch the speaker. When there are multiple tables of guests, people at other table should act on the main table, and do not toast before the toast at the main table.

在主人或主宾发言时，其他人员应暂停进食，放下餐具，注视讲话人。有多桌宾客时，其他桌的人应以主桌行事，不要在主桌祝酒前敬酒。

d. Departure. Other guests usually leave after the main guest has left. When leaving, greet the host, praise the party's careful arrangement, and thank the host for his hospitality. If you need to leave early, you should inform your host in private and leave without disturbing other guests.

离席。通常在主宾离开后其他客人才陆续离开。离开的时候，应向主人致意，称赞宴会的精心安排，并感谢主人的款待。如果需要提前离开，应私下告知主人，在不惊动其他客人的情况下离席。

3. Gift Giving（礼品赠送）

Gift giving is seen in many countries as an essential way to build and consolidate relationships. Gift giving is also an art. Different countries have different habits on the type of gifts, the giving occasion and opportunity. Only by knowing the etiquette, can we deepen the relationship.

送礼在许多国家被看作是建立和巩固关系必不可少的方式。送礼也是一门艺术。不同国家对礼物的种类、赠送的场合及时机有不同的习惯。只有深谙相关礼节，才能起到加深双方感情的作用。

（1）Selection of Gifts（礼物的选择）

Local specialty can usually be chosen as gifts, but they should be easy to carry without the company logo. When preparing gifts, consider the relevant policies of the country or enterprise where the recipient is located. If they think of gifts as bribes, don't pick ones that are too expensive to cause trouble. At the same time, we should pay attention to the cultural taboo of the recipient. For example, Latin Americans don't like to receive swords or handkerchiefs. The former means breaking off with the receiver, while the latter represents sorrow. And don't give anything too much private which will cause embarrassing.

通常可以选择当地特产作为礼物，但要注意方便携带，不要印有公司标志。准备礼物的时候，要考虑收礼人所在国家或企业的相关政策。如果他们把礼物看作贿赂，则不要选过于昂贵的礼物，以免带来麻烦。同时要注意收礼人所在国家文化上的禁忌。比如，拉美人不喜欢收到刀剑或手帕。前者代表要断绝关系，后者代表着悲伤。也不要送过于私密的东西，让人尴尬。

（2）Gifts Packaging（礼品包装）

Gifts usually require packing together with a card with a blessing and a signature. The color of the packaging should be noted for the preference and taboo of the receiver. Don't use black, brown and white wrapping paper for the Germans. Gifts for the Japanese should be packed in the proper color according to the occasion. Red, gold and white is for a happy occasion, and other things are in black, purple or black and white wrapping paper.

礼物通常需要包装起来，并附上带有祝福语和签名的卡片。包装的颜色应注意收礼人的偏好和禁忌。送给德国人的不要用黑色、棕色和白色包装纸。送给日本人的礼物要注意包装的颜色与场合相符，红色、金色和白色用于喜事，其他事用黑色、紫色或黑白相间色包装纸。

（3） Timing of the Gift Giving（赠送礼物的时机）

The timing of the gift giving is different in different countries, and the custom of the recipient should be taken into account to avoid misunderstanding and adverse effects. Gifts are usually given in Korea and Japan for the first meeting. Germany and Latin America usually don't exchange gifts until the negotiations are over, and if you give them in advance, they will think you have improper attention.

赠送礼物的时机在不同国家有所不同，应参照收礼人的习惯，以免产生误会，带来不良影响。韩国和日本通常初次见面就会赠送礼品。而德国、拉美国家通常在谈判结束后才交换礼物，如果提前送礼，对方会认为你有不当企图。

（4） The Way to Receive Gifts（接受礼物的方式）

The way in which gifts are received varies from country to country. In China and Korea, you can't open a gift in front of the giver. But in countries such as the United States and Brazil, it is appropriate to open a gift in front of the giver. We should also express our love of the gift and our gratitude to the giver, and write another thank-you letter when we receive gifts from the American.

接受礼物的方式在不同国家也不尽相同。在中国、韩国，不能当着送礼人的面打开礼物。但在美国、巴西等国家，当面打开礼物才是恰当的行为。还应该表达出对礼物的喜爱和对送礼人的感谢，收到美国人的礼物还应再写一封感谢信。

4. Farewell Etiquette（送别礼仪）

The host should figure out the departure time of the guests and go to the hotel in advance to accompany them to the airport. You can also arrive at the airport in advance to wait for the guests and say goodbye. The identity of the main farewell should be comparable to that of the guests. Pay attention to the guests leaving until you can't see the guests. Don't let the staff to leave or do other things right away once the guests turn around, making people feel not sincere. As a guest, before leaving the seeing-off staff's line of sight, you should turn back and wave goodbye again, and don't leave without heading back, so as not to lose your politeness.

送别来宾应该弄清楚对方离开的时间，提前到其下榻的宾馆，陪同前往机场。也可以提前到达机场等候客人并送别。主要送别人员的身份应该与来宾相当。注意目送客人离开，直到看不见客人身影。切忌客人一转身，送别人员就马上离开或做其他事情，让人感觉不够真诚。作为客人，在脱离送行人员视线之前，也应回身再次挥手道别，不要头也不回地离开，以免失仪。

Summary

The end of the negotiation can be judged from the conditions of transaction achieved, the time, the content of the consultation of the other party. There are three main ways to conclude negotiations: concluding a transaction, negotiation suspension or breakdown. Strategies to facilitate transactions include the concession method, compromise method, summarizing method, ultimatum method, deadline-setting method and package trading method. The drafting of the contract mainly includes the determination of the drafters and the determination of the drafting content; the review of the contract mainly includes the examination of the content and the audit of the signatory. Claim negotiation is a way to deal with contract disputes, which mainly includes the preparation before claim negotiation, the main contents of claim negotiation and notes for claim negotiation. Etiquettes at the end of negotiations include signing ceremony, banquet etiquette, gift giving and farewell etiquette.

谈判的结束可以从交易达成的条件、时间、对方协商的内容来判断。结束谈判有三种主要方式：成交、谈判中止和谈判破裂。促成交易的策略包括让步法、折中法、总结法、最后通牒法、设定期限法和一揽子交易法。合同的起草主要包括起草方的确定和起草内容的确定；合同的审核主要包括内容的审核和签字人的审核。索赔谈判是合同纠纷的一种处理方式，主要包括索赔谈判前的准备、索赔谈判的主要内容及索赔谈判的注意事项。结束时的礼仪包括签约仪式、宴请礼仪、礼品赠送和送别礼仪。

Module Ⅱ Terminology Practice

1. Clause: A separate section of a discourse or writing, specifically a distinct article in a formal document.

2. Quota: A fixed, limited amount or number that is officially allowed. Quotas are usually set by a government or by an organization of producers of a particular product. For trade quotas, governments set the quota to limit the import of a particular product, restrict the access to the domestic market by an offshore producer, and give the domestic producers the opportunity to improve their position in the market. Such protectionist policies in industries including steel, autos, and many consumer electronics products, have protected domestic industries from international competition.

3. Know-how License Contract: It refers to a license contract in the international technology trade that uses the right to transfer proprietary technology. Proprietary technology generally refers to secret technologies, knowledge and experience that are necessary for production activities and that are not open to the public and transferable, and that are expressed as engineering product design, process procedures, and operation methods that can be realized in economic life. It also often includes aspects of production management and business operations, especially the most critical part of the technology necessary to produce a patented product or to achieve a patented production method.

4. Compensation Trade Contract: The compensation trade contract is also called the "compensation trade agreement". It is an agreement signed by both parties of different nationalities on compensation trade methods, basic rights and obligations, etc. The main contents of the contract usually include: compensation trade items, equipment or technology specifications, compensation product specifications, quantity, pricing method, method of supply, time limit, credit in compensation trade and guarantee, transportation and insurance, the terms of liability of both parties and the resolution of disputes.

5. Investment Contract: An agreement or transaction in which a party invests money in a common enterprise, the profits from which are derived from the efforts of others.

6. Formal Contract: A contract made binding by the observance of required formalities regardless of the giving of consideration.

7. Forward Contract: A privately negotiated investment contract in which a buyer commits to purchase something (such as a quantity of commodity, security, or currency) at a predetermined price on a set future date.

8. Integrative Negotiation: A type of negotiation in which the parties cooperate to achieve maximum mutual benefit in an agreement. Long-term partnerships and collaborations between colleagues are often characterized by integrative negotiation. An integrative negotiation is more popularly known as a win-win negotiation.

9. Distributive Negotiation: A type of negotiation in which the parties compete over the distribution of a fixed pool of value. Here, any gain by one party represents a loss to the other. Popularly referred to as a zero-sum negotiation or a win-lose negotiation.

10. Exploding Offer: An offer with an expiration date.

11. Interests: The goals underlying a party's negotiating position.

12. BATNA: Acronym for "best alternative to a negotiated agreement". Knowing your BATNA means knowing the options of what you will do or what will happen if you do not reach agreement in the negotiation at hand.

13. Winner's Curse: After a deal has been reached, the nagging conviction that one could have negotiated a more favorable deal.

14. ZOPA: Acronym for "zone of possible agreement". This is the area in which a potential deal can take place. Each party's reservation price defines one of the boundaries of the ZOPA. The ZOPA itself exists, if at all, in the overlap between the parties, reservation prices.

15. Wiggle Room: The flexibility that may exist in a particular offer, whether it has to do with money or time frame. If you have no wiggle room, you should strongly convey the message that this is your best offer.

Module Ⅲ New Words

1. accomplishment *n.* 成就；完成；技能；履行
2. assume *v.* 假定，认为；承担；装出；呈现
3. authorization *n.* 授权，批准；批准（或授

权）证书

4. banquet *n.* 宴会，盛宴；筵席；宴请，款

待 *vt.* 宴请，设宴招待；宴饮，参加宴

会；*vi.* 参加宴会

5. breach *n.* 破坏；破裂；缺口；违背 *vt.* 攻破；破坏，违反
6. ceremony *n.* 典礼，仪式；礼仪，礼节；虚礼，客气
7. champagne *n.* 香槟酒；香槟酒色；平原；平野
8. concession *n.* 让步，迁就
9. confront *vt.* 面对；使面对面，使对质；碰到，遇到；比较
10. consistent *adj.* 一致的；连续的；不矛盾的；坚持的
11. contract *n.* 合同；契约；协议
12. dispute *vi.* 辩论，争论 *vt.* 就……进行争论，辩论；对……的真实性或有效性进行争论，怀疑；争夺，竞争；抵抗，抵制 *n.* 辩论；争端；（劳资）纠纷；罢工 *vi.* 激烈争辩；争执；争吵；吵架
13. distortion *n.* 扭曲，变形；失真，畸变；[心理学] 扭转
14. draft *n.* 汇票；草稿；选派；（尤指房间、烟囱、炉子等供暖系统中的）（小股）气流 *vt.* 起草；制定；征募 *vi.* 拟稿；绘样；作草图 *adj.* 初步画出或写出的；（设计、草图、提纲或版本）正在起草中的，草拟的；以草稿形式的；草图的
15. entourage *n.* 随行人员
16. execution *n.* 实行，履行，执行，贯彻；作成，完成，签名盖印使法律文件生效，执行法律；执行死刑，强制执行，执行命令；成功，奏效，效果
17. facilitate *vt.* 促进，助长；使容易；帮助
18. figure *n.* 数字；算术；人物；身材 *vi.* 计算；出现；扮演角色 *vt.* 计算在内；估计；推测；认为
19. identity *n.* 身份；[逻] 同一性；个性；[数] 恒等（式）
20. inconsistent *adj.* 不一致的，不调和的；前后矛盾的，不合逻辑的；反复无常的；歧出
21. indignant *adj.* 愤慨的；愤怒的；义愤的
22. liability *n.* 责任；倾向；债务；妨碍
23. litigation *n.* 打官司；诉讼
24. memorandum *n.* [外] 照会，备忘录；[商] 便笺，函；记录；[法]（契约等条文的）节略
25. memento *n.* 遗物，纪念品，用以回忆的东西
26. obligation *n.* 义务，责任；证券，契约；债务；恩惠
27. opponent *n.* 对手；反对者；敌手 *adj.* 对立的；敌对的
28. performance *n.* 表演；演技；表现；执行
29. personnel *n.* 全体员工；（与复数动词连用）人员，员工；人事部门
30. resent *vt.* 对……感到愤怒；怨恨；愤恨；厌恶
31. signatory *n.* 签字人，签约国 *adj.* 签署的，签约的
32. summarize *vt.* 总结，概述
33. terminology *n.* 专门名词；术语，术语学；用辞
34. transaction *n.* 交易，业务，事务；办理，处理；（一笔）交易，（一项）事务
35. unconfirmed *adj.* 未经证实的；未予确认的；未经认可的

Module Ⅳ Useful Expressions

1. cut the losses 减少损失
2. round off 圆满完成，结束

3. tie up 完成，解决
4. loose end 未了结的零星事务或问题
5. front runner（某阶段的）竞争领先者
6. up one's sleeve 藏有……锦囊妙计；留有一招
7. up to 取决于……的，须由……决定的
8. tighten up 使更严格，使更有效
9. total amount of concessions 让步的总和
10. close a deal 成交
11. confirm the agreement 确认协议
12. observe the contract 遵守合同
13. be entitled to do 有权做
14. speak highly of 高度赞扬
15. subject to sth. 以……为准
16. commercial integrity 商业诚信

Module Ⅴ Exercise

Ⅰ. Answer the following questions according to the text.

1. How to judge the end of the negotiation?
2. What are strategies to facilitate the transaction?
3. What are ways to conclude negotiations?
4. What are the main contents of a contract?
5. What shall we pay attention to when reviewing the contract?
6. What is the process of signing ceremony?
7. What are the common forms of seating arrangements in the signing hall?
8. How shall we prepare for the banquet?
9. What shall we pay attention to when sending a gift?
10. What shall we pay attention to when seeing guests off?

Ⅱ. Fill in the blanks with the expressions given below.

agenda　breakdown　close　extent　maximum　negotiation strategies　negotiation time　suspension　terms　time　trade　transaction

1. The difference between a successful negotiator and an unsuccessful negotiator is the ability to ________ a deal when it has reached its ________ level of distributing "enough" among all participants.

2. The deal is best closed when the ________ has been exhausted.

3. To obtain the final concession, we must grasp two problems: first, the ________ of the concession, and second, the ________ of the concession.

4. There are only three ways to conclude international business negotiations: ________, ________ and ________.

5. The end of international business negotiations can usually be judged by ________, ________ and ________.

Ⅲ. Please determine whether the following statements are True or False.

1. Setting deadlines could help briskness and the concentration of energy. (   )

2. It is not necessary that the parties be in agreement to the language and terms of the deal before its closure. (   )

3. The implications for the negotiation to have a deadline are negative. (   )

4. Declining the deal must be done with the greatest diplomacy because the potential for future dealings is very important. (   )

5. In the negotiations, as long as the main issues are settled, the writing agreement can be immediately acted upon to facilitate the signing of the agreement. (   )

6. Among the outcomes of the negotiations, only the signing of a contract has practical significance. (   )

7. A transaction price range is the best acceptable trading condition, and it is the lower limit of the price range that we have set in advance to conclude a transaction. (   )

8. If the majority of terms are agreed upon, the disagreement clauses are only a small part, it can be judged to be in the final stages. (   )

9. The compromise strategy is usually the intermediate condition of the sum of the differences between the two parties, as a strategy to continue negotiations or compromise. (   )

10. When the consultation is close to the prescribed time limit, the negotiation naturally enters the final stage and an agreement must be reached within the prescribed time limit. (   )

Ⅳ. Translate the following sentences into Chinese.

1. I think we have covered everything.

2. May I call your attention to Clause 4 of the Draft Agreement?

3. I hope you will understand that Subsection 8 will have to be amended.

4. I think we should include a Force Majeure Clause.

5. I think that Clause 1 does not reflect what we agreed last Friday.

6. I think Clause 5 is substantially the same as Clause 8. I think we could delete it.

7. It contains basically all we have agreed upon during our negotiation.

8. This copy is for you. Let's congratulate ourselves that this transaction has been brought to a successful conclusion.

9. I think we can call it a day.

10. We've made excellent/good/some progress.

11. Can I just run over the main points?

12. I'm sure we would all agree that we have had a successful meeting.

Ⅴ. Translate the following sentences into English.

1. 让我们仔细检查一下合同，看看是否一切都没问题。

2. 对于第二段，我持强烈保留态度。

3. 我认为第 9 条的措辞很容易让人误解，应该做一些改动。

4. 让我感到惊愕的是第 10 条居然一点儿也没提到货物滞留的事。

5. 就我看来，我们应该增加一个标准仲裁条款。

6. 如果一方未按本合同的条款执行，另一方有权终止合同。

7. 关于这一条你们还有什么意见？

8. 我们向前迈出了一大步。

9. 让我们再看一下主要观点。

10. 你方有需要补充的吗？

11. 你方能在下次会议之前起草这个吗？

Ⅵ. Separate the following sentences into three categories below.

ⅰ) summarizing ⅱ) follow-up action ⅲ) departing

a. So, we have agreed on an initial one-year contract on the basis of full support and minimal project work.

b. I'm sorry I have to leave abruptly.

c. Fax us a proposed schedule and we can talk it through in two weeks.

d. Now, can I just run over the main areas of agreement and those that are still left open?

e. So it only remains for me to thank you for coming over. It's been a very productive meeting.

f. Patrick, can you draft that and circulate it before the next meeting?

g. So, Anna has been keeping copious notes. She'll let you have a detailed summary.

h. Thank you very much for coming over today.

Ⅶ. Case Study

Case 1: The Import Policy Is Not Well Understood and Almost Suffered Loss

Time: 1998

Key Point: Import Policy

Background

Industry: Manufacturing

Subject: A Professional Foreign Trade Agency Company

Issue: On December 24, 1998, a professional foreign trade agency company in China was commissioned by domestic steel distributors to import hot-rolled coils.

On December 24, 1998, a professional foreign trade agency company in China was commissioned by domestic steel distributors to import hot-rolled coils. The import department manager asked the salesman to first implement the relevant national import policy to understand whether import was allowed and whether an import license was required and made inquiry to a certain international steel company. The salesperson informed the business manager that he could import but required an import license. On December 30, 1998, our foreign trade agency company signed import agency agreements and import contracts with domestic users and foreign companies, and then the letter of credit was issued by the foreign trade company. On January 13, 1999, the letter of credit was revised according to the requirements of the foreign party, and the shipment period was changed to March 15, 1999. On February 25, 1999, one steel distributor said that he heard that the specifications above 310mm were not allowed to be imported, and that the foreign trade company was required to assist in the implementation immediately. The company's business manager had consulted the relevant national management department to confirm that the state clearly stipulated that the hot-rolled coil import was not allowed for specifications from 310mm to 10,100mm including 310mm and 10,100mm. After consulting the salesman, the salesperson was consulting an import goods customs broker at the time and has not checked the relevant documents. The matter ended here, and the error was a foregone conclusion. On the same day, the business manager made a phone call with the foreign party and sent a fax to discuss the solution. He hoped to reach an understanding with the foreign party and said that our users were willing to pay $ 20 per ton of compensation and cancel the contract. However, the foreign party replied that the goods had been collected at port and would be shipped soon and asked us to pick up the goods on time and perform the contract conscientiously. The only thing they could cooperate with us is that they could postpone the delivery for one month so that we could go through the import approval procedures. In the face of the risk that goods couldn't be cleared, we had nothing to do. On March 9, 1999, the foreign party sent the navigation data of the cargo ship. It is expected to be shipped on March 1 and arrive on the port on April 21. According to the above schedule, we believe that the ship had the possibility of transshipment and pre-lending bills of lading. Immediately afterwards, our foreign trade company confirmed through the international shipping company that there was no cargo ship around March 1 of the Black Seaport. The earliest sailing schedule is May 20. On March 11, our foreign trade company sent a fax to the foreign party, telling the seller that if our company found that the bill of lading was pre-borrowed, it would refuse to pay the purchase price. On March 13, the foreign representative and employee of the foreign party in China came to the foreign trade company to negotiate the delivery, and asked our foreign trade company to cooperate with the pre-lending bill of lading, which was rejected by our foreign trade company. On March 23, the foreign party called: "We agree to cancel the contract because of the inability to load timely."

Questions

1. Why can't goods be cleared?

2. How did our company succeed in cancelling the contract?

Appendix

The state clearly stipulates that importing the hot-rolled coil for specifications from 310mm to 10,100mm is not allowed.

Case 2: The Signing Ceremony

Case Source: Ma Chunzi. *International Business Negotiation and Etiquette*. Beijing: Beijing Institute of Technology Press, 2017.

Preface

Time: In the 1990s

Key Point: The Country A's side was late for the signing ceremony.

Background

Industry: Industry

Subject: A Large State-owned Enterprise in Country A and a Large Japanese Company

Issue: A large state-owned enterprise with about 6,000 employees in Country A wanted to find a well-funded enterprise to be a partner in order to avoid the situation of bankruptcy.

A large state-owned enterprise with about 6,000 employees in Country A wanted to find a well-funded enterprise to be a partner in order to avoid the situation of bankruptcy. After many efforts, the company finally found a large Japanese company with international reputation. After a long and arduous bargaining between the two sides, the contract was finally drafted, and the employees of the whole enterprise were rejoicing. The Country A's personnel who thought that they were successful had a bureaucratic style in the signing ceremo-ny of the next day. The time of arrival at the signing place was 10 minutes later than the formal agreement between the two parties. When they entered the signing hall, the Japanese personnel had already lined up and waited for their arrival. The Country A's leader asked the Japanese personnel to sit on the signatory table. The Japanese staff all bowed to them neatly. Then they collectively withdrew from the signing hall. The Country A's leader was inexplicable because it was just 10 minutes late. Afterwards, the Japanese side submitted a formal letter to the enterprise in Country A, which wrote: "We will never look for a business partner who has no time concept. Those who do not comply with the agreement will never be trusted."

Undoubtedly, the cooperation between the two sides has stranded. The enterprise in Country A has paid a heavy price for its 10 minutes' delay—bankruptcy and nearly 6,000 people having been laid off.

Questions

1. Why did the Japanese staff withdraw from the signing hall?
2. What lesson can we get from this case?

Appendix

One of the signing etiquettes is to be on time.

Case 3: An Equipment Contract

Case Source: Ma Chunzi. *International Business Negotiation and Etiquette*. Beijing: Beijing Institute of Technology Press, 2017.

Preface

Time: In the 1990s

Key Point: Vague, Unquantifiable, Unfounded Clause

Background

Industry: Timber

Subject: A Timber Plant

Issue: A medium-sized timber plant in China is enjoying a booming business in recent years. However, the equipment of the plant is backward and the product technology is relatively old, which limits the development of the factory.

A timber plant in a forest area in Northeast China is a medium-sized wood ware factory with a booming business in recent years. In the past few years, relying on the guaranteed advantages of raw materials, traditional wood ware with relatively low manufacturing costs is popular in the market and has achieved considerable economic benefits. However, the equipment of the plant is backward and the product technology is relatively old, which limits the development of the factory. Therefore, the plant decided to invest heavily in the introduction of equipment technology to further improve production efficiency and open up a broader market. So it signed an equipment contract with a foreign woodworking machinery group through an agent of an international economic and technological cooperation company, with a total value of 1.1 million US dollars. In accordance with the contract, the foreign party would bring the equipment to the factory and the foreign person-nel would come to the factory for commissioning and installation. During the inspection, the Chinese side found that some parts of the machine had serious wear marks and the operating rate was less than 70%, which could not be put into production at all.

The Chinese side then pointed out to the foreign party that its product had serious quality problems and did not meet the contract mechanical performance guarantee targets, and asked the foreign party for a solution. The foreign party said that it would send strong technical personnel to the factory to solve the problem. Two months later, the working group sent by the foreign party went to the factory and replaced some parts that did not meet the standard. The machine was recommissioned, but the acceptance still did not meet the technical standards stipulated in the contract. After commissioning and studying, the foreign side agreed to go back to study, but there was no following for three months. Later, the factory was coordinated by the agency company, and the foreign personnel came to the factory for a commissioning. The acceptance still failed. Due to the installation and the commissioning equipment introduced, the Chinese side had almost stopped production, and there was no profit for half a year. In order to put into production as soon as possible, the Chinese side believed that it could no longer spin this round again, and was ready to make some concessions through negotiations, as long as the overall requirements were met. This was the case of the Chinese and foreign parties. After the Chinese made this proposal, they immediately agreed to sign the equipment acceptance memorandum.

The foreign company conducted three commissions. However, after commissioning, only one item met the standard, and the Chinese side believed that it could not pass the acceptance. However, the foreign company believed that the required standards had been met. Thus the two sides had initiated disputes.

Originally, there were serious problems with the quality of foreign products. The Chinese side had every reason to express a tough attitude and argued against it. However, after the disputes between the two sides occurred, the foreign side appeared to be justifiably strong, which made the Chinese side miserable. What is the crux of it?

Originally, in the memorandum signed by the two sides, with the consent of the Chinese side, some of the guarantee indicators were removed, and some of the original required indicators were loosely adjusted. In fact, China had made concessions. However, the concessions must be purposeful and valuable. The re-formed clauses needed to be clearly defined in favor of the Chinese. Otherwise, it may cause new passiveness. However, the memorandum had drawn up such clause standards: The degree of wear of the parts is "according to the smoothness of the hand"; certain parts "do not show obvious damage", etc. This vague, unquantifiable, unfounded clause had allowed the other side to take advantage of it. According to such vague regulations, other side insisted that it met the above criteria and that the two sides could not argue about this fact.

Questions

1. Why did the foreign side appear to be justifiably strong after the disputes?

2. Can you give some suggestions for the case?

Appendix

The details of the negotiation and the details of the contract should be clear.

Case 4: An Agent Import Contract

Case Source: Ma Chunzi. *International Business Negotiation and Etiquette*. Beijing: Beijing Institute of Technology Press, 2017.

Preface

Time: In 1999

Key Point: An Agency Import Agreement

Background

Industry: Chemistry

Subject: Company A, Company B and Company C

Issue: Company A had no import and export management rights at that time, so it entrusted Company C to import chemical raw materials.

In 1999, a private company in Zhejiang, China (referred to as Company A) and a chemical company in Singapore (referred to as Company B) reached a deal after consultation and imported a batch of chemical raw materials. Company A had no import and export management rights at that time, so it entrusted a domestic foreign trade company (referred to as Company C) to import them. Company A and Company C signed an agency import agreement, and Company C as the buyer of the import contract of this batch of chemical products, directly signed with Company B. The contract is signed, and the payment method is agreed to be effected by the buyer after receiving the goods by wire transfer (T/T). In fact, there was no direct negotiation and contract between Company C and Company A. After the shipment to Shanghai, Company A took the goods. However, after the legal representative of Company A died due to a traffic accident, the company's operations suddenly stopped, and soon the company went bankrupt, and the import payment was not paid out. In September 2003, Company B sued Company C in Shanghai and required Company C to pay the full payment according to the import contract signed by both parties. Because the agency import agreement submitted by Company C can't prove that Company A has directly reached a contract transaction with Company B, and Company A has been closed down, Company C can only negotiate the settlement of the payment dispute with Company B.

Questions

1. Why did Company B require Company C to pay the full payment?
2. Can you give some suggestions for the case?

Appendix

The foreign trade company accepts the agency agreement signed by the domestic customer, and then signs the import and export contract with the foreign company. It is an indirect agent. The name of the principal does not appear in the import and export contract, nor does it show that the foreign trade company is the agent acting.

This kind of indirect agent obscures the substantive achievement of the contract transaction. It is the fact that the principal directly negotiates and deals with the foreign merchant. The foreign trade company only acts as an agent to direct the import business, and has no decision on the main terms of the contract. In the case, there is no substantial participation of Company A in the trade between Company A and Company B.

Case 5: Failed Negotiations

Case Source: Jin Juan. *Intercultural Business Communication*. Beijing: Capital Economic and Trade University Press, 2010.

Preface

Time: In 1999

Key Point: Serious Arrangement Errors in Negotiation

Background

Industry: Trade

Subject: Company M and Arabs

Issue: Company M has no experience in dealing with Arabs.

Company M is a large company whose products are among the best of its kind in China. Its business has expanded to several foreign countries, but it is still blank in the Middle East because it has no experience in dealing with Arabs.

One day, a delegation visited Company M from Dubai, and Mr. Guo received it as the company's general representative. Since the delegation was very interested in the company's products, the two sides sat down to negotiate on the products.

During the negotiation, Mr. Guo was confused and bored because the Arabs asked for a pause every hour and then went to prey.

At lunchtime, the company arranged a sumptuous lunch for these Arabs. After the guests were all settled, the waitress began to introduce various dishes to these Arab guests in English. These Arabs were surprised and happy with the wide variety of dishes, but the good times didn't last long. When the waitress mentioned the specially cooked pork, the smile disappeared from the guests' faces. All of them were embarrassed, no one said a word, and quickly stood up and left the table without saying a word to anyone, even though there were some local dignitaries. Without notifying Company M, this Dubai delegation left the city where Company M was located that day.

A few days later, Mr. Guo heard the worst news: The Dubai delegation signed a contract with their competitor, Company C, and that contract was the one that Company M had failed to talk with the Dubai delegation at the time. Mr. Guo was also severely criticized by his boss for this serious mistake.

Questions

1. Why did the negotiation fail?
2. Can you give some suggestions to Mr. Guo?

Ⅷ. Role plays practice. Work in pair and converse according to the given information.

Task 1

Background

A and B were negotiating patent transfer rights. B asked for a technical license for products improvement and development. A guaranteed advanced machinery and technology but refused to grant B the right to sub-license. B argued the necessity to get the right to let other firms manufacture some items at a lower cost. A suggested to solve the problem on a sub-contract because he worried that the technology may be divulged.

Terms and Phrases

concrete	confidential	transfer the patent
technical secret	effective	constitute
accomplish	on-the-job training	technical target
adequate facility	scope	assimilate
duration	exceed	

Relative Expressions

1. Could you please provide us with…
2. Why are you opposed to granting…
3. I hope we can satisfy your requirement.

4. I can understand your thoughts.
5. We do not intend to grant you...
6. Let us work out something realistic.
7. We wish to stress that...

Task 2

Background

White: General Manager, California Global Development Co., Ltd.; Qian: General Manager, China's Shenzhen Music Kitchen Microwave Manufacturing Company. The two sides intend to establish a joint venture for the manufacture of household microwave ovens in Shenzhen. The joint venture is now entering into negotiations on the amount, proportion and mode of investment.

Terms and Phrases

authority	registered capital
time-consuming	account for
commit the money	play for kingdom
background	investment proportion
microwave stove	exclusively
construction funds	premises
circulating capital	allocate

Relative Expressions

1. I'm very happy to tell you that...
2. The joint venture is only entitled to use the land.
3. How much will the registered capital be?
4. How long does the venture run?
5. I suggest the total amount of the investment go...
6. What about the investment proportion of the two parties?
7. We will provide the factory with building, premises, some machinery and equipment.
8. We are prepared to contribute... percent, including the cash, machinery and equipment.

Chapter 7

Negotiation Styles in Different Countries

Work Objective

After studying this chapter, you will be able to:

- familiarize with the styles of negotiators from major trading countries;
- master the tactics to deal with foreign negotiators;
- know the social etiquette of major trading countries.

Case Guide-Reading

A Japanese company has a trade negotiation with an American company. At the beginning of the negotiation, the representatives of the United States introduced the situation to the Japanese side, while the representatives of the Japanese side kept silent and buried their heads in the record. After the U. S. representative finished speaking, he asked for the opinions of the Japanese representatives, who said, "We don't quite understand. Please allow us to go back and study." So the first round of talks ended. A few weeks later, the Japanese company changed a delegation and appeared at the negotiating table, declaring that it did not know the situation. The US side has no choice but to repeat it. However, after speaking, the Japanese representatives still said: "We can't reply immediately. Please allow us to go back to study." The second round of talks was suspended. A few weeks later, the Japanese side repeated the situation twice again. In the end, it only agreed to inform the US side of the result after going back. Half a year later, while the American company was in a state of anxiety, a delegation led by the chairman of the board of directors of the Japanese side flew to the United States suddenly. When the US side was unprepared, it asked for immediate negotiation and threw out the final plan. It forced the Americans to discuss the whole details in a hurry, so that the Americans were caught off guard and finally reached an agreement that was obviously beneficial to the Japanese.

Source：Dou Ran, *International Business Negotiation and Communication Skills*. Shanghai：Fudan University Press, 2009.

Module Ⅰ Text

Ⅰ Negotiation Styles in American Countries（美洲国家的谈判风格）

1. American Negotiation Style（美国人的谈判风格）

Most Americans are descendants of Europeans, and their style of action follows some of the characteristics of Europeans. But after hundreds of years of prosperity, they have also formed their own unique style. They opened up the border in the ridiculous New World and cultivated a strong spirit of enterprising. Without the imprisonment of the feudal system, they lacked a concept of hierarchy and emphasized equality for all.

美国人多数是欧洲人的后裔，他们的行事风格沿袭了欧洲人的一些特点。但在数百年的繁衍生息后，也形成了自己独有的风格。他们在荒芜的新大陆开疆拓境，培养了强烈的进取精神。没有封建制度的禁锢，使他们缺少等级观念，强调人人平等。

（1）Do Not Value Personal Relations with Partners（不看重与合作者的私人关系）

There is an American saying：“Business is business”. They don't like to confuse public affairs with private affairs, and they don't want to mix personal feelings into their business. Therefore, in business negotiations, they will not work hard to understand each other and establish personal relationships with partners. Transactions with new customers do not require intermediaries. If the other party tries too enthusiastically to communicate with them before the negotiation, they will feel that there may be problems with the negotiation target and the other party has bad intentions, hence they will become very vigilant. At the beginning of the negotiation, they will get to the point and not talk about business-independent topics.

美国有句俗语：“生意是生意”。他们不喜欢把公事和私事混淆起来，也不愿意在业务上掺杂私人感情。因此，在商务谈判中，他们不会在了解对方、与合作者建立私人关系上下功夫。与新客户交易也不需要通过中间人联系。如果对方在谈判前过分热情地试图与其联络感情，他们会觉得可能谈判标的有问题，对方居心不良，因而变得非常警惕。他们在谈判的开局阶段就会开门见山，进入正题，不会谈论与业务无关的话题。

（2）Strong Sense of Time（时间观念强）

Americans have a very strong sense of time. They look at time as wealth. They think that time will never come back. They must grasp it well and make full use of it. Therefore, the negotiations need to be well organized. They will set an accurate negotiation agenda and demand the other party to strictly follow the agenda arrangement. They want to be efficient and quick and do not tolerate repetitive delays. If things don't go well, they become very anxious and restless. To complete the negotiations on time, concessions may be made as the deadline approaches. For them, punctuality is a sign of respect for each other and attaching importance to cooperation. If a partner is late for the negotiation, they will be very angry and think that the other party is not sincere. Attention should be paid to participating in negotiations on time. If you can't make an appointment on time, you must inform the other party in advance and apologize.

美国人有非常强的时间观念，他们把时间看作财富，认为时间一去不复返，必须好好把握，充分利用。因此，谈判需要组织得很好。他们会设定准确的谈判议程，并要求对方严格按照议程安排进行。他们做事讲求效率，希望速战速决，不能容忍反复拖延。如果进展不顺利，他们会变得非常焦虑，坐立不安。为了按时完成谈判，可能在最后期限临近时做出让步。对他们来说，准时是尊重对方、重视合作的表现。如果合作方在谈判时迟到，他们会非常恼火，认为对方没有诚意。注意准时参加谈判，如果不能按时赴约，必须提前告知对方，并表达歉意。

(3) Direct Communication（直接的沟通方式）

Americans belong to a low-context culture. That is to say, they express their meaning mainly through oral language, and do not put their meaning in nonverbal expressions, moods and speaking environment. In negotiation, they like to express their views directly, and think that it is insincere to knock around and make vague remarks and frequently use the word "yes", "no", "surely", "certainly", "not at all", etc. When understanding opponents' opinions, they also focus on their language and ignore other nonverbal information. The other side can bargain bluntly and justifiably. Unless the strategy requires it, don't use silence to indicate rejection. Americans will find it difficult to adapt.

美国人属于低语境文化，就是说，他们主要通过口头语言表达自己的意思，不会把自己的意思放在非语言的表情、语气及说话时的环境中。在谈判中，他们喜欢直截了当地表达自己的看法，认为旁敲侧击、含糊其辞是不真诚的表现。经常使用"是""否""当然""一点也不"等词。在理解对方的意见的时候，也主要关注对方的语言而忽略其他非语言信息。对方可以直言不讳，有理有据地讨价还价。除非策略需要，不要用沉默来表示拒绝，美国人会难以适应。

(4) Negotiation Strategies（谈判策略）

Americans are more cautious about partner selection and will know about their ability to perform the contract in advance. During the negotiations, the Americans are enthusiastic, self-confident, eloquent, proactive, and accustomed to straightforwardly indicating their position. Before the negotiations, they will fully prepare scientific and accurate data to prove the feasibility of their own programs. They like to discuss the cooperation matters one by one, and they are good at making "package deals" and solving related problems that have not been agreed. They also focus on the overall consideration of trading conditions. Americans tend to believe that negotiation is a positive-sum strategic game benefiting both sides. Formality is not a deal affecting the negotiation for Americans, and they don't value rituals. Americans sometimes show emotion in negotiations, but these emotions will not affect their final decision.

对于合作伙伴的选择，美国人态度较谨慎，会事先了解对方的履约能力。在谈判中，美国人热情自信、口若悬河、积极主动，习惯直截了当地表明自己的立场。在谈判前，他们会充分准备科学准确的数据资料以证明自己方案的可行性。他们喜欢逐一讨论合作事项，擅长做“一揽子交易”，把没有达成一致的相关问题一并解决。他们注重从全局考虑交易条件；把谈判看作双方都会获利的正和策略博弈。他们不认为谈判会受程序正式与否的影响，不看重仪式。美国人有时在谈判中表现出情绪化，但这些情绪不会影响他们的最终决定。

Americans like detailed and specific contracts that guide everything about the negotiations. They tend to include everything they discuss in the contract. If there is any change in the transaction, there is also a need to revise and rewrite the contract to cover the new situation. They will also include in the contract what might have happened and how it might have been handled.

美国人喜欢详细而具体的合同，以用于指导有关谈判的一切。他们倾向于将讨论的所有内容写入合同。如果交易有任何变动，也需要修订并重新拟定合同以涵盖新情况。他们还会把可能发生的情况及处理办法写入合同。

(5) Ways of Personal Decision-making (个人决策的方式)

Americans emphasize individualism and everyone should be responsible for his actions. In the negotiation, the negotiating members have clear responsibilities. In their own jurisdiction, individuals have full decision-making power and do not need to consult other members but only need to agree on specific issues first with the boss. As a result, their negotiating team is relatively small and may even be single. They focus on their main goals and will not consider adapting their goals to the progress of other members.

美国人强调个人主义，每个人都应该为自己的行为负责。在谈判中，谈判成员职责明确，在自己的管辖范围内，个人有完全的决定权，不需要征求其他成员的意见，通常只需要先与上级就特定问题达成共识。因此，他们的谈判小组人数相对较少，甚至可能只有一人参加。他们专注于自己的主要目标，不会考虑调整自己的目标去配合其他成员的进展。

Because of the vast territory of the United States, Americans in different regions also have their own style characteristics. Americans in the east have a strong sense of competition and emphasize strict compliance with the law. Americans in the midwest are more concerned about friendship, and in cooperation with them, you can contact your relationship with each other in private. Americans in the western region value credibility. Americans in the southern region are more straightforward and emotional, but the pace of negotiations is slower, and we need to control our emotions and patience when negotiating with them.

由于美国地域广阔，不同地区的美国人也有自己的风格特点。东部的美国人有强烈的竞争意识，强调严格按照法律行事。中西部地区的美国人比较看重友情，和他们合作可以先私下交往联络感情。西部地区的美国人很看重信誉。南部地区的美国人更直爽、更加情绪化，但谈判节奏更慢，与他们谈判要控制情绪，保持耐心。

(6) Social Etiquette (社交礼仪)

- Americans generally don't exchange business cards unless they want to keep in touch. If they don't send back business cards, don't mind.

- To go to an American home, you can bring a bunch or a pot of flowers, or a bottle of wine.
- Don't rely too close when communicating with Americans. It is best to keep a distance of more than 1 meter, and don't touch their bodies casually to avoid being uncomfortable.
- Keep eye contact when communicating. They think this is a candid performance.
- Don't use laughter to express emotions other than happiness, the other party will not understand.
- 除非想保持联系，美国人一般不会交换名片。如果他们没有回送名片，不必介意。
- 去美国人家做客，可以带一束或一盆鲜花，或一瓶酒。
- 与美国人交流的时候不要靠得太近，最好保持1米以上的距离，也不要随便触碰他们的身体，以免对方不自在。
- 沟通的时候要保持目光接触，他们认为这是坦诚的表现。
- 不要用笑来表达高兴以外的情绪，对方会无法理解。

2. Brazilian Negotiation Style（巴西人的谈判风格）

Brazil is a multicultural country, mainly Indians, blacks and whites of European descent. People of different nationalities have their own characteristics of negotiation, but they also have the common characteristics of Brazilians, who are optimistic, good at negotiation and think that life is more important than work.

巴西是个多元文化的国家，主要有印第安人、黑人和以欧洲人后裔为主的白人。不同民族的人有本民族的谈判特点，但他们也有巴西人共同的开朗乐观、擅长谈判、认为生活重于工作的特性。

（1）Value Personal Relationships（重视私人关系）

Brazilians are collectivist-oriented and it is important for them to build a personal relationship of continuity and trust. They are willing to cooperate with people they know, love, and trust. Therefore, it is necessary to invest sufficient time and money to establish a strong relationship with them before the transaction. After getting acquainted with the other party, you may transfer to the business topic. You can express your desire for long-term cooperation. Let them feel that compared with business, you value themselves and their relationship which will help to gain their trust. Therefore, fixed personnel should be arranged to engage with them so as not to return to the stage of establishing relationships because of substitutions.

巴西人是集体主义导向的，对他们来说建立持续、信任的私人关系非常重要。他们愿意跟自己了解、喜欢、信任的人合作。因此，有必要在交易前投入充足的时间与金钱与他们建立牢固的关系。应该在与对方熟识后再转入业务方面的话题。可以向他们表达你方长期合作的愿望。让他们觉得比起生意来，你更看重他们本身及与他们的关系，这有助于获得其信任。因此，应安排固定的人员与他们接洽，以免因为换人而重新回到建立关系的阶段。

(2) Loose Time Concept(松散的时间观念)

Brazilians advocate a free lifestyle and have no strong time concept. Therefore, the negotiation process is usually slow and often delayed. They don't like to act in a hurry and don't like being urged. They see impatience as a shortcoming and feel rude. It usually takes a few negotiations to complete the decision. If you try to speed up the progress, they may feel invaded and bring bad results. Therefore, you must have sufficient patience and control your emotions during the negotiation process.

巴西人崇尚自由的生活方式,没有太强的时间观念。因此,谈判进程通常较缓慢,经常延误。他们不喜欢匆忙行事,也不喜欢被人催促,把没有耐心看作缺点,而且觉得很粗鲁。通常需要几次交涉才能完成决策。如果试图加快进度,可能会让他们感觉受到冒犯从而带来不好的结果。所以在谈判过程中要有充足的耐心并控制好情绪。

They are used to doing many things at the same time. When negotiating, they will jump between various topics, not in order. In this case, don't show upset. Always follow up on the negotiation process and often emphasize the conditions that have been agreed upon.

他们习惯同时做多件事情。在谈判时会在各种话题间跳来跳去,而不是按顺序进行。遇到这种情况,不要显露不快。要始终跟进谈判进程,经常强调已经达成一致的条件。

(3) Communication Style(沟通风格)

Brazilians are proud and sensitive, and it is important to maintain their face during negotiations and to respect what they are proud of and their self-esteem. Don't criticize them in public or confront them directly. If you want to win their favor, you should show your interest and enthusiasm. Do not show emotions that are out of control or impatient, which may harm their self-esteem.

巴西人骄傲而敏感,在谈判时维护他们的面子、尊重其引以为豪的东西和自尊非常重要。不要在公开场合批评他们或直接与他们正面对抗。要想赢得他们的好感,应真挚地表现出你的兴趣和热情。不要表现出情绪失控或不耐烦这种可能伤害他们自尊的行为。

(4) Negotiation Strategies(谈判策略)

Negotiating with Brazilians is not easy, but they will not be overly bargaining. They are tough and even aggressive negotiators who will conduct extensive bargaining and will not easily make concessions. They will expect the final price to be 40% lower than the original offer, so leave enough space for concessions and ask for the other party to make a return. To maintain calmness and courtesy, avoid conflicts, and often emphasize the relationship between the two sides. They like to force the other party to make concessions by increasing time pressure, so you need to have enough patience and perseverance. When bargaining, remember that they are more eager to enhance the intangible benefits of their power and status than economic gains.

与巴西人谈判并不轻松,但他们也不会过分讨价还价。他们是强硬甚至非常有侵略性的谈判者,他们会进行广泛的讨价还价,不会轻易让步。他们会期望最终价格比最初报价低40%以上,因此,要为让步留下足够的价格空间,在让步的同时应要求对方做出回报。要保持冷静和有礼,避免冲突,经常强调双方的关系。他们喜欢通过增加时间压力来迫使对方做出让步，需要有足够的耐心和毅力。在讨价还价时要记住，比起经济收益，他们更渴望提升其权力和地位这些无形的利益。

a. Deceptive Tactics（欺骗型战术）

Brazilians often use deceptive strategies. In order to be in a dominant position in bargaining, they will try to mislead each other, including passing false nonverbal information, pretending not to be interested in the entire transaction or a concession, distorting the price of a product or giving false demand and concessions. But even if you have seen the other party's lies, don't expose them or even imply them. They will feel that this is a personal injury. It is best to verify with information obtained from other local sources. But using excessive deception to intimidate them may be counterproductive and damage the relationship. They like to use the "good cop, bad cop" tactic. It is more effective to use this same tactic to deal with them, but if they are identified, it will bring catastrophic consequences. The "bad cop" member should no longer appear in the subsequent negotiations.

巴西人经常使用欺骗型策略。为了在讨价还价中处于优势地位，他们会想方设法误导对方，包括传递虚假的非语言信息、假装对整个交易或某次让步不感兴趣、歪曲某个产品的价格或给出虚假的需求和让步。但即便你识破了对方的谎言，也不要当众揭穿甚至暗示，他们会觉得这是对人身的伤害。最好用在当地其他渠道获取的信息进行核实。但是用过分使用欺骗的手法恐吓他们可能会适得其反，损害双方关系。他们喜欢用"红脸白脸"战术，用这种技巧应对他们也比较有效，但如果被识破，会带来灾难性的后果。唱白脸的人员不要再出现在后面的谈判中。

b. Stress Tactics（压力型战术）

They also often use stress tactics, including making final quotes, not giving in or nibbling policies. They may say that it's their final offer many times, but this is not the case. Therefore, be careful to show your own cards. They also use silence to express rejection or obtain concession to the offer. Don't use time pressure tactics or ultimatums, they will think that the other party is not willing to establish long-term relationships, or even end negotiations.

他们也经常使用压力型战术，包括做出最终报价、不让步或蚕食政策。他们可能会多次表示是最终报价，但并非如此。因此，要小心亮出自己的底牌。他们也会用沉默来表达对提议的拒绝或获得让步。不要使用时间压力型战术或最后通牒，他们会认为对方不愿建立长期的关系，甚至会终结谈判。

c. Confrontational Tactics（对抗型战术）

Brazilians sometimes appear aggressive in negotiations. They may threaten or warn, publicly express their anger, or even leave halfway to disrupt your position. But it is not recommended to fight them, because it is likely to hurt their self-esteem. It's best to express your determination and perseverance in a friendly and respectful manner.

巴西人有时在谈判中显得好斗。他们可能表达威胁或警告，公开表现他们的愤怒，甚至中途离场来打乱你的阵脚。但不建议与他们针锋相对，因为这样做很可能会伤害他们的自尊。最好友好而恭敬地表达你的坚定和坚持不懈。

Emotional tactics can be used frequently and effectively, such as making the other party feel guilty. When using these tactics, you should pay attention not to hurt their personal dignity. It's more effective to use the emotional appeal of personal relationships or emphasize how your proposal can increase personal satisfaction or glory.

可以经常有效地使用情绪战术，如让对方觉得内疚。对其使用这些战术时要注意不要伤害个人的尊严。以私人关系或强调你的提议能如何增加其个人满意度或荣耀这种情感诉求为借口比较有效。

d. Defensive Tactics（防御型战术）

They also often use defensive tactics such as hindering or changing topics, asking for inquiring or direct questions, making commitments, and maintaining firm positions.

他们也经常使用防御型战术，如阻碍或转换话题、提出探究性或直接的问题、做出承诺、保持坚定立场等。

（5）Ways of Decision-making（决策方式）

Most Brazilian companies are highly hierarchical and require people to act according to clear powers. The decision maker is usually the highest executive. Brazilian administrators rarely authorize others to exercise their powers. It is also difficult for outsiders to approach senior management. You can usually contact subordinates who have no decision-making power, but they may have a great impact on decision-making, so we should maintain good relations with them.

多数巴西公司等级森严，要求人们按明确的权力范围行事。决策者通常是最高执行官。巴西管理人员很少授权他人行使职权。外人也很难与高层管理人员接洽。通常接触的都是无决策权的下属，但他们可能对决策影响很大，因此要与他们保持良好的关系。

Their decision-making usually takes into account specific circumstances rather than general principles or laws. Before making a decision, they will consider the whole situation, but their personal feelings, experience and intuition are more convincing than experimental proof and other objective facts.

他们的决策通常考虑的是特定的情形，而不是普遍原则或法律。在决策前，他们虽然会通盘考虑，但个人感觉、经验和直觉比实验证明和其他客观事实更有说服力。

（6）Social Etiquette（社交礼仪）

- Don't make "OK" gestures to Brazilians which is an uncivilized action for them.
- Do not discuss political topics related to Argentina.
- Don't give a handkerchief for gifts as they think it will bring quarrels and unhappiness. Also don't wrap gifts in purple (for sadness) or brown (for death).
- Respect should be shown to people of high status.
- 不要对巴西人做"OK"的手势，对他们来说这是不文明的动作。
- 不要讨论与阿根廷相关的政治话题。
- 送礼不要送手帕，他们认为这会带来争吵和不快。也不要用紫色（代表悲伤）、棕黄色（代表死亡）包装。

• 对地位高的人应表现出尊敬。

Ⅱ Asian Negotiation Styles（亚洲人的谈判风格）

1. Korean Negotiation Style（韩国人的谈判风格）

The Koreans were deeply influenced by Confucianism before the founding of the country, and then influenced by western culture after the founding of the country. Therefore, the Koreans' negotiation style is a combination of the eastern and western characteristics. They don't like uncertain things, and emphasize status. In negotiations, they are not only face-loving and conflict-avoiding, but also independent, and speaking frankly in the negotiations.

韩国人建国前深受儒家思想影响，建国后又受到西方文化的熏陶，因此其谈判风格融合了东西方的特点。他们不喜欢不确定性强的事情，强调身份地位。在谈判中，既有爱面子、不坦诚、避免冲突的一面，也有独立性强，讲话直率的一面。

（1） Attitude Towards Personal Relationships with Partners（对与合作者私人关系的态度）

Koreans pay attention to personal relationships, and for the first time, it is best to find a prestigious middleman. Before starting to negotiate business, you should take the time to understand each other and establish a good relationship. They usually talk about some relaxed topics to create a harmonious atmosphere during the start of the negotiations. They have a strong hierarchy and status concept, and the negotiators sent should be equal to the members of the other party.

韩国人注重私人关系，初次接触，最好找一个有声望的中间人介绍。在开始洽谈业务前，应花时间相互了解，建立良好的关系。他们在谈判开局阶段通常会谈论一些轻松的话题来营造和谐的气氛。他们有较强的等级和地位观念，派出的谈判成员要与对方成员身份相当。

（2） Time Concept（时间观念）

If the Koreans are the host, they will arrive on time when negotiating. If they are guests, they will arrive later. The topics are generally not discussed in order. The decision-making process is slow.

如果韩国人是主方，他们谈判时会准时到达。如果是客方，则会迟一点到达。他们一般不会按顺序讨论话题。决策过程较缓慢。

（3） Communication Style（沟通风格）

Korea is a country of high-context cultures, and the Koreans tend to seek the true meaning of each other through informal contacts and nonverbal clues. Influenced by Confucian culture, they do not like too direct communication. Usually they will not directly reject the other party's request and will euphemistically express their opinions. Even if you know their lies, you should respond skillfully, not directly. Don't be too tough when you clarify your point of view. Show respect for them and maintain their face. Out of courtesy, they usually don't interrupt other people unless they are eager to engage in more indepth topics.

韩国属于高语境文化，韩国人倾向于通过非正式的接触和非语言线索寻求对方真实意思。受儒家文化影响，他们不喜欢太直接的沟通方式。通常不会直接拒绝对方的要求，会委婉表达自己的意见。即便你识破了他们的谎言，也要有技巧地回应，不要直接说破。阐明自己观点的时候不要过于强硬，应表现出对他们的尊重，维护他们的面子。出于礼貌，除非他们急于进行更深入的话题，他们一般不会打断别人的发言。

（4）Negotiation Strategies（谈判策略）

Koreans attach great importance to business negotiations, and will fully understand their opponents before the negotiations. They pay attention to the negotiating field and like to choose a classy place. At the beginning of the negotiations, they attached great importance to the construction of a good atmosphere. They also like the negotiation content to be structured. After the negotiation starts, they will usually discuss the main topic with the other party first.

韩国人非常重视商务谈判，在谈判前会充分了解对手。他们很注意谈判场地，喜欢选择有档次的地方。在谈判开始阶段，他们非常重视良好氛围的营造。他们也喜欢谈判内容条理化，在谈判开始后，一般会先与对方讨论谈判的主要议题。

Korean people are smart and strong, but they are polite and others are easy to overlook their shrewdness and perseverance. They like to deal with conflicts directly. Negotiators are aggressive and good at using emotional tactics such as anger or frustration. They will also make their opponents step back by winning pity or making them feel guilty, but not in return. They are impatient and can't stand long negotiations. But they themselves like to use up their opponents' energy by repeating and prolonging the "fatigue tactics" of negotiations. They are good at feinting in the East to assault the West and using time limit tactics. They also like to know other party's perseverance through private contact. They are good at finding contradictions among their opponents and using them to weaken their opponents. The quotation is generally reasonable.

韩国人聪明而强势，但他们很有礼貌，容易让人忽略其精明、坚持不懈的特点。他们喜欢直接处理冲突。谈判人员很有攻击性，很擅长运用愤怒或沮丧等情感战术。他们也会通过赢得对手的怜悯，或让对手觉得理亏，使其步步退让，却让对手没有回报。他们比较急躁，无法忍受长时间的谈判。但他们自己却喜欢通过不断地重复和延长谈判的“疲劳战术”来消耗对手的精力。他们还擅长用声东击西和期限战术。他们也喜欢通过私下接触了解对方的坚毅程度。他们擅长发现对手成员间的矛盾，利用其削弱对方势力。报价一般较合理。

（5）Ways of Decision-making（决策方式）

Koreans tend to make group decisions and are more conservative and unwilling to take risks.

韩国人倾向于群体决策，较为保守，不愿承担风险。

（6）Social Etiquette（社交礼仪）

- Do not invite female members to participate in amateur drinking.
- Pay tribute to those with higher status.
- Don't laugh or make exaggerated gestures in public.

- Do not directly reject members of the other party and damage their faces.
- Exchange of gifts is very common. Gifts must be returned when they are received.
- 不要邀请女性成员参加业余的饮酒作乐。
- 对地位更高的人表达敬意。
- 不要在公共场合大笑或做夸张的手势。
- 不要直接拒绝对方，使其颜面受损。
- 交换礼物很常见，收到礼物一定要回赠。

2. Japanese Negotiation Style（日本人的谈判风格）

(1) Relationship Takes Precedence over the Deal（关系优先于交易）

The Japanese believe that transactions are conducted more in the context of long-term relationships, in which relations take precedence over transactions. Serious business negotiations can only take place after being satisfied with the other party. Before actual negotiation, the Japanese will strive to get as much information as possible about the negotiators of the other party. When the two sides negotiated for the first time, they are used to being introduced by middlemen who had business dealings with both parties. In the opening stage, they may ask some more personal questions to understand each other to enhance trust. They hope to establish a strong relationship before the end of the transaction, so the negotiating opponents will be invited to the entertainment venue during the negotiation to enhance understanding. Their main way of negotiating is cooperation.

日本人认为交易更多是在长期关系的背景下进行的，其中关系优先于交易。只有在对对方感到满意之后，才能进行严肃的商务谈判。在实际进行谈判之前，日本人会争取获得关于对方谈判人员的尽可能多的信息。双方初次谈判的时候，他们习惯由与双方有业务往来的中间人进行介绍。在开局阶段，他们可能会问一些比较私人的问题来了解对方，以增进信任。他们希望在结束交易之前建立牢固的关系，所以谈判期间会邀请谈判对手去娱乐场所，以增进了解。他们的主要谈判方式是合作的。

It is recommended to repeatedly emphasize long-term interests and your commitment to them, as well as the business relationships you want to build. Keep in touch at all stages of business engagement, but be aware that in this country, the strength of the relationship depends not on whether someone likes you or not, but rather whether he thinks you are trustworthy and reliable. If the answer is yes, he may be willing to compromise. Trust can be built by entertaining together, giving gifts, and using influential intermediaries. In the event of disputes, it is better to invite the original introducer to mediate.

建议反复强调长期利益和你对他们的承诺，以及你想要建立的商业关系。在业务参与的所有阶段都要定期保持联系，但要意识到，在这个国家，关系的强度与其说取决于某人是否喜欢你，不如说取决于他是否认为你值得信赖和可靠。如果答案是肯定的，他可能会愿意妥协。可以通过一起娱乐、赠送礼物、利用有影响力的中间人等方式建立信任关系。出现争端时最好请最初的介绍人进行调解。

(2) Time Concept (时间观念)

Japanese do not value time, and working overtime is a common occurrence for them. Their negotiation is slow and protracted, and it is normal to continue until the evening. However, social and business occasions should be on time, and if you are late, you should inform and apologize in advance. It is best to contact them three weeks in advance.

日本人并不看重时间，加班对他们来说是常事。他们的谈判节奏缓慢、拖沓，持续到晚上也是正常的。但是社交和商务场合应准时，如果可能迟到应提前告知并深表歉意。最好提前三周与他们联系会面事宜。

(3) Communication Style (沟通方式)

The Japanese tend to avoid extremes and tend to adopt a moderate attitude to achieve harmony. The famous Japanese artisan Miyamoto Musashi taught his warrior class in his book *The Book of the Five Rings*: "A warrior of the late sixteenth and early seventeenth centuries should maintain the same way of doing things in any situation and keep the intermediate attitude." Although his proposal is aimed at warriors, it also affects the Japanese government and business people today, and thus moves to commercial negotiations. The main manifestations are that they generally do not want to say "no", respond ambiguously, and like long silence.

日本人倾向于避免极端，并倾向于采取中庸的态度，以达到保持和谐的目的。日本著名兵法家宫本武藏在其著作《五轮书》中教诲他那个时代的战士阶级："一个16世纪末和17世纪初的武士，在任何情况下都应保持同样的行事方式，并保持中间态度。"虽然他的建议是针对武士的，但也影响着当今的日本政府和商界人士，从而运用到商业谈判中。主要表现为极端情绪不外露，一般不愿说"不"，回应含混不清，喜欢长时间的沉默。

a. Do Not Want to Say "No" (不愿说"不")

Professor Chie Nakane, the Japanese cultural authority, pointed out that in addition to the completely reciprocal subordinate relationship, the Japanese almost never used the word "no". Even if he means no, he will use "yes" in a verbal form, while expressing the intention of rejection with nonverbal cues. The Japanese will say that certain things are "very difficult" to express rejection. If the Japanese say "I will consider it", his meaning is almost equal to "no". On the contrary, if the Japanese use the word "yes", it may not really be affirmative.

日本文化权威中根千枝教授指出：除了完全互惠的上下级关系，在其他情况下日本人几乎从未使用过"不"这个词。即使他的意思是不，他也会以口头的形式使用"是"，同时用非语言的暗示表达拒绝的意图。日本人会用某些事情是"非常困难的"来表达拒绝。如果日本人说"我会考虑它"，他的意思几乎就等于"不"。相反，如果日本人使用"是"这个词，可能不是真正表示肯定。

b. Respond Ambiguouly (回应含混不清)

In order to ensure consensus in decision-making, to preserve face, or to prevent possible changes in position in the future, the Japanese deliberately blur their final position in negotiations. If they feel that the objection may be embarrassing, they will suggest objections that are not relevant to the actual problem.

为了保证在决策中达成共识，保留颜面，或者预防以后可能改变立场，日本人在谈判时会故意模糊己方的最终立场。如果他们觉得提出的异议会让人尴尬，他们会提出与实际问题无关的异议进行暗示。

c. Like Long Silence（喜欢长时间的沉默）

In Japan, there is a saying that "silence is gold", which also reflects the concept of avoiding confrontation that they were instilled from an early age. The famous Japanese cultural authority Kanji Hatano has compared the quarrels between children in Europe and the quarrels of Japanese children. It has been found that children in Europe will quickly rebut, and Japanese children will remain silent even if they think they are correct. When there was a stalemate in the negotiations, the typical reaction of the Japanese was to keep silence, retreat or change the theme. For the Japanese, silence for a while can ease the conflict and give both sides the opportunity to rethink the issue.

在日本，有句格言叫"沉默是金"，这也体现了他们从小就被灌输的避免对抗的观念。著名的日本文化权威波多野完治曾对欧洲各国儿童的争吵与日本儿童的争吵进行了比较。他发现，一般欧洲儿童会迅速反驳，而日本儿童即使认为自己是正确的，也会保持沉默。在谈判出现僵局时，日本人的典型反应是沉默、退缩或改变主题。对于日本人来说，沉默一段时间可缓和冲突，让双方有机会重新思考这个问题。

It is recommended to stay calm and not to let the emotions get out of hand in the negotiations. Inflicting embarrassment on the Japanese may make their team feel embarrassed and may have disastrous consequences for business negotiations. If you have to talk to someone about an unpleasant personal topic, don't do it in public, and always convey your message in a way that keeps his self-esteem.

建议保持冷静，不要让情绪失控。给日本人造成尴尬可能会让其团队觉得丢脸，也可能对商业谈判造成灾难性后果。如果你必须与某人提起一个令人不快的个人话题，千万不要在公共场合这样做，并且总是以保持对方自尊的方式传达你的信息。

(4) Negotiation Strategies（谈判策略）

The Japanese negotiation style is very formal and there are few acceptable tactics. There is a Japanese saying: "The warrior is good at grilling fish, and the poor can only bake rice cakes." The former patiently waited until the right moment, and he turned the fish over with lightning-fast precision. On the other side, the poor man nervously licked his rice cake and flipped it over and over until it became crispy and fluffy. It can be seen that they are patiently waiting for the most suitable time. In the negotiations, they will not be affected by the negotiating agenda, will not rush to make a decision in the set negotiation deadline, but patiently wait for the best time. Don't make big concessions too early, they will think that you are not prepared or interested. Friendship, patience and persistence should be demonstrated during negotiations.

日本人的谈判风格非常正式，能接受的战术很少。日本有句谚语："武士擅长烤鱼，而穷人只能烘烤年糕。"一方面，前者耐心地等待，直到适当的时刻，他会以闪电般的精确度将鱼翻过来。另一方面，那个穷人紧张地拍打着他的年糕，一遍又一遍地翻转，直到它变得酥脆蓬松。由此可见他们对耐心等待最适合时间的看重。在谈判中，他们也不会受谈判议程的左右，不会在设定的谈判最后期限仓促做出决定，而是耐心地等待最佳时机。不要过早做出大幅度让步，他们会认为你没做好准备或没兴趣。谈判时应表现出友好、耐心和坚持。

a. Deceptive Tactics（欺骗型战术）

Japanese sometimes use and accept deceptive tactics, including pretending not to be interested in the entire transaction or a concession, distorting the price of a product or giving false demand and concessions. If there is an opportunity, the accuracy of the information can be confirmed through other channels. Or ask questions to find out the truth. It is best not to use the "good cop, bad cop" tactic, to give false needs and concessions should be cautious, any act aiming to fool the Japanese can ruin the established relationship.

日本人有时会使用并接受欺骗型战术，包括假装对整个交易或某次让步不感兴趣、歪曲某个产品的价格或给出虚假的需求和让步。如果有机会，可以通过其他渠道证实其信息的准确性。或通过提问来了解真实情况。最好不要用“红脸白脸”战术，给出虚假的需求和让步也要谨慎，任何愚弄日本人的做法都可能毁掉已经建立的关系。

b. Pressure Tactics（压力型战术）

The Japanese may use pressure tactics like starting with written quotations, keeping silent and time pressure. They may urge the other to give in by keeping silent for more than a minute. Time pressure tactics are also difficult to deal with. Once they know your deadline, they will be used to force you to give in. It may even be possible to start negotiations on the last day before you leave. But don't use time pressure tactics over them because they have enough patience and persistence to deal with it. Be careful with ultimatum tactics, which may make them feel humiliated. Don't use tactics such as frank start, uncompromising, and quotation with an expiration date.

日本人可能使用书面报价开局、保持沉默、时间压力等战术。他们可能会通过保持一分钟以上的沉默来促使对方做出让步。时间压力战术也很难应对。一旦他们知道你的最后期限，就会加以利用，迫使你做出让步。他们甚至可能在你离开前的最后一天才开始谈判。但不要对他们使用时间压力战术，因为他们有足够的耐心和毅力进行应对。要谨慎使用“最后通牒”战术，这可能让他们觉得没面子。也不要用坦诚式开局、不妥协、带有效期限的报价等战术。

c. Defensive Tactics（防御型战术）

Japanese may use defensive tactics such as changing topics, making inquiring or direct questions, making promises, and maintaining firm positions. They will ignore the tactics that hinder their access to certain information, and will repetitively repeat similar questions before they get a satisfactory answer. Sometimes it is possible to motivate the Japanese to reconsider their position by making a commitment.

日本人可能使用转换话题、提出探究性或直接的问题、做出承诺、保持坚定立场等防御型战术。他们会无视阻碍其获得确定信息的战术，在没有得到满意答案前，会不懈地重复相似的问题。有时候可以通过做出承诺来激励日本人重新考虑其立场。

(5) Decision-making Process Is Group Oriented (共识决策过程)

Although some decisions in Japanese companies are made by the decree of the top management, most of the decisions of the low-level or middle-level management are achieved through consensus. The same is true in the negotiations. The proposal must be approved by all relevant personnel and will not be decided on the spot until an internal agreement is reached. Once they agree to a proposal, they will be difficult to change because it requires the consent of all personnel.

虽然日本公司中一些决策是通过最高管理层的法令做出的，但低层或中层管理层的大多数决策都是通过共识达成的。在谈判中也一样，提议必须得到所有相关人员的认可，在内部达成一致前，不会当场做出决定。而一旦同意了一项提议，他们就很难改变，因为这需要所有人员的同意。

(6) Social Etiquette (社交礼仪)

• Unless there is a strong personal relationship, don't always make eye contact when talking. The Japanese think that low eyesight is a manifestation of respect.

• It is very important to exchange gifts. After the initial meeting and signing, you need to prepare gifts of different grades according to the status of the recipient. Don't open the gift in person. There are a lot of attention to the types and packaging of gifts, and it is best to consult locals when preparing for gifts.

• Exchanging business cards is a necessary meeting step. Ensure that everyone in the room receives your business card. The name card should be marked with title and position so that the other party can confirm your identity.

• Negotiations are conducted in formal and conservative clothes. Men had better wear a dark suit and tie.

• Don't refuse Japanese entertainment invitations. This is an important way for them to build strong relationships. If they are rejected, they will think that you are not interested in working with them.

• Do not discuss the topic of Japan's relations with Korea and China.

• 除非有牢固的私人关系，交谈时不要经常进行目光接触，日本人认为目光低垂是尊敬的表现。

• 交换礼物很重要，初次会面、签约后都需要，应根据受礼人的身份、地位准备不同档次的礼品，以示敬重。不要当面打开礼品。礼品种类和包装都有很多讲究，备礼时最好咨询当地人。

• 交换名片是必要的认识步骤。确保在场所有人都收到你的名片。名片上要注明头衔、职务，以便对方确认你的身份。

• 谈判时穿正式、保守的服装。男士最好穿黑色西服配领带。

• 不要拒绝日本人娱乐方面的邀请，这是他们建立牢固关系的重要方式。如果被拒，他们会认为你没有兴趣与其合作。

• 不要讨论日本与韩国、中国关系方面的话题。

3. Singapore's Negotiation Style（新加坡人的谈判风格）

Singapore is dominated by Chinese, accounting for more than 70% of the total, followed by Malays and Indians. This is a multicultural country. People of different nationalities have the same values, but they are also greatly influenced by their respective cultures. They advocate modesty, experience and teamwork.

新加坡以华人为主，占总人数的70%以上。其次是马来人和印度人。这是个多元文化的国家，不同民族的人拥有相同的价值观，但也受各自文化的很大影响。他们崇尚谦虚、经验和团队精神。

（1）Attitudes Towards Personal Relationships with Partners（对与合作者私人关系的态度）

Singaporeans are collectivist-oriented. It is very important to build an enduring, reliable private relationships. Most people want to build strong relationships before they reach a deal. The first meeting was to get to know and build relationships. The beginning of the negotiation will generally be familiar with each other through chatting. It's best to spend some time getting to know each other and get involved in serious business discussions after getting along well with each other. They want to build long-term business relationships with each other for many years. This kind of business relationship mainly exists in individuals or teams, so the stability of contacts should be guaranteed.

新加坡人是集体主义导向的，建立持久可靠的私人关系非常重要。多数人希望在达成交易前建立牢固的关系。初次会面以结识和建立关系为主。谈判开局阶段一般会通过寒暄相互熟悉。最好花些时间互相了解，相处融洽以后再转入严肃的业务讨论。他们希望与对方建立多年的长期商业关系。这种商业关系主要存在于个人或团队中，因此，应保证联系人的稳定性。

Singaporeans also attach great importance to face. Correcting the opinions of others, opposing the elders or superiors will make everyone feel embarrassed and humiliated, which is not conducive to the negotiation process. Don't talk to someone in public about unpleasant topics, but also pay attention to maintaining others' self-esteem when talking in private. Keep calm in negotiations and never show frustration in public.

新加坡人也很看重面子。纠正别人、反对长者或上级的意见都会使所有人觉得尴尬而丢脸，不利于谈判的进行。不要当众跟某人谈及不愉快的话题，私下谈论的时候也要注意维护别人的自尊。在谈判中要保持冷静，决不要当众表现出沮丧。

（2）Time Concept（时间观念）

It is best to contact the meeting two weeks in advance. Singaporeans are very punctual, and the Chinese are particularly concerned about not wasting others' time. Being late for no reasonable reason is a serious offense to them. If you are late, be sure to explain why and apologize. The pace of negotiations is slow and procrastinating. Be patient and control your emotions throughout the negotiations. They belong to a multi-time system. When they negotiate, they like to jump around in various topics, not one by one.

最好提前两周联系会面。新加坡人很看重准时，华人特别在意不去浪费别人的时间。没有合理原因的迟到对他们来说是很严重的冒犯。如果迟到了，一定要说明原因并深刻致歉。谈判的节奏较缓慢、拖沓。在整个谈判中要保持耐心并控制好情绪。他们属于多元时间制，谈判的时候喜欢在各个话题中跳来跳去，不会按顺序一个一个来。

(3) Communication Style (沟通方式)

Singaporeans speak low and gentle. They advocate ways of staying calm and controlling emotions. Silence has no negative meaning for them. In order to maintain their face, they like euphemistic communication. Objections and confrontations should be avoided publicly, so they seldom say "no", but use some vague wording to indicate negation. If they say "yes" in a hesitant or weak way, it also means rejection. Or they will deliberately ignore the question you asked. They only refuse when they are unwilling to do business with each other. Therefore, it is also necessary to communicate with them in a euphemistic way. Too directly will make them think that the other party is very rude.

新加坡人说话语调低沉、温和。推崇始终保持冷静、控制情绪的处事方式。沉默对他们来说没有负面意思。为了维护面子，他们喜欢委婉的沟通方式。应避免公开提出异议和对抗，所以他们很少说"不"，而是用一些模糊的措辞来表示否定。如果他们用犹豫或微弱的方式说"是"，也意味着拒绝。或者他们会故意忽略你的问题。他们只有在不愿意跟对方做生意时才会直接拒绝。因此，也要用委婉的方式与他们沟通，过于直接会使其认为对方很粗鲁。

Nonverbal communication is very important in Singapore, and we should pay close attention to their tiny hints, and they also pay attention to others' gestures. In addition to shaking hands, there is generally no physical contact. In addition to meeting for the first time, don't make frequent eye contact at other times otherwise, they will feel rude and invaded. Grimacing or shaking your head means different opinions. They may use laughter to cover up emotions such as jealousy, shyness, disapproval or grief.

非语言沟通在新加坡很重要，应密切关注他们的微小暗示，同时他们也很注意对方的手势。除了握手，一般不要有肢体接触。除了初次见面，其他时候不要频繁地目光接触，否则他们会觉得粗鲁、受侵犯。做鬼脸或摇头都意味着有不同意见。他们可能用笑来掩饰尴尬、害羞、不赞成或悲痛等情绪。

(4) Negotiation Strategies (谈判策略)

Singaporeans are shrewd negotiators, skilled in using various negotiation skills, good at patiently and firmly pursuing their goals, and good at utilizing differences among members of the other side for profit. Although the main negotiation style is competitive, they avoid confrontation and believe that negotiations should be conducted in a friendly atmosphere. Negotiators should be sufficient to demonstrate your importance to them and help build stronger relationships and speed up the negotiation process. Quotations should leave ample room for concessions.

新加坡人是精明的谈判者，能熟练运用各种谈判技巧，擅长耐心而坚定地追求其目标，善于利用对手成员间的分歧获利。虽然主要的谈判风格是竞争型的，他们却避免正面冲突，认为谈判应在友好的气氛中进行。参加谈判人员要充足，对他们来说这表现了你方的重视，有利于建立更牢固的关系并加速谈判进程。报价要为让步留下充足空间。

Singaporeans prefer a direct negotiation style, and deceptive tactics are not used much. Do not lie or mislead them and damage the business relationship between the two parties. They seldom use the "good cop, bad cop" tactic, which can be used to deal with them. To avoid losing face, be cautious in using strategies that give false demands or concessions.

新加坡人偏向于直接的谈判风格，欺骗型战术用得不多。不要撒谎或过分误导他们而损害双方的商业关系。他们很少用"红脸白脸"战术，可以用这种战术应对他们。为了避免丢脸，要谨慎使用给出错误需求或让步的战术。

(5) Ways of Decision-making (决策方式)

The decision-making of Singaporeans is usually a consensus-oriented group decision-making process. This process may involve many leaders reaching consensus after careful consideration. Therefore, the decision-making process is time-consuming and needs enough patience. Senior leaders have a great influence on the decision-making results, so we should try our best to win their support.

新加坡人的决策通常是共识导向的群体决策过程。这个过程可能涉及许多负责人在深思熟虑后达成共识。因此，其决策过程耗时较长，需要足够的耐心。高层领导对决策结果影响很大，应想方设法赢得他们的支持。

(6) Social Etiquette (社交礼仪)

- Special respect must be paid to the elders, who should be allowed to take the lead when they enter, and those present should stand up.
- Don't make loud noises in public. Talk in low voices during meals.
- You need to exchange business cards when you meet for the first time.
- Singaporeans care about their identity, so when referring to people with titles or doctoral degrees, you'd better add their titles.
- Business occasions should be conservatively dressed, and men should wear dark suits and ties.
- Don't touch someone else's head.
- Don't point at anything with one finger.
- 一定要特别尊重长者，长者或上级入场时应让其先行，在场人员应起立。
- 不要在公共场合大声吵闹，在用餐时应低声交谈。
- 初次见面时需要交换名片。
- 新加坡人在意身份，称呼有头衔或博士学位的人时，应加上他们的头衔。
- 商务场合应保守着装，男士最好穿深色西服配领带。
- 不要摸别人的头。
- 不要用一个手指头指东西。

Ⅲ European Negotiation Styles（欧洲人的谈判风格）

1. German Negotiation Style（德国人的谈判风格）

The Germans are characterized by calmness, diligence, self-confidence, rigor, and eagerness to do well in everything. They are cautious and planned. They have a strong professionalism, pursue efficiency and perfection, and have confidence in their own first-class product quality and precise technical standards. They value the reputation and credit of their collaborators. They like precise words and behavior, the style of negotiation is formal, and they don't like to make jokes.

德国人具有沉稳、勤奋、自信、严谨、好强的特点。他们行事谨慎，富有计划性；有很强的敬业精神，追求工作效率和尽善尽美，对自己的一流的产品质量和精确的技术标准充满信心。他们很看重合作者的声誉和信用。他们喜欢精确的话语和行为，谈判风格很正式，不喜欢开玩笑。

（1）Attitudes Towards Personal Relationships with Partners（对与合作者私人关系的态度）

Germans do not care about commercial cooperation with a party that has no personal relationship. It is believed that friendship and interpersonal relationships will complicate negotiations, so they will deliberately keep a distance from their partners. Don't give gifts before the initial contact or negotiation has made substantial progress, which will make them doubt your motives. They take business relationships seriously, and once you win their trust, two parties can work together for a long time.

德国人不在意与没有私人关系的一方进行商业合作。认为友谊和人际关系会使谈判变得复杂，所以会刻意与合作者保持距离。不要在初次接洽或谈判没有实质性进展前送礼，这会让他们怀疑你的动机。他们严肃对待商业关系，一旦赢得其信任，双方就可能长期合作。

（2）Time Concept（时间观念）

Germans have a strong sense of time and are very punctual. An advance appointment is required for the meeting. Don't be late for negotiations, so as not to arouse their distrust and disgust. When negotiating with Germans, you should pay attention to work efficiency, have strict plans for negotiation time, and have clear topics for each negotiation and don't delay it at will.

德国人有很强的时间观念，非常守时。会面需要提前预约。谈判时切忌迟到，以免引起他们的不信任和厌恶。在与德国人谈判时，要注重工作效率，谈判时间有严格计划，每场谈判都有明确的议题，不要随便拖延。

（3）Communication Style（沟通方式）

Germans pay attention to planning, efficiency, and do not like gossip unrelated to negotiations. Generally, after a brief introduction at the beginning, they cut into the main topic. They state their questions clearly and do not like ambiguous expressions. They see effective treatment as a sign of a person's capability. They think eye contact during conversation is a sincere expression.

德国人注重计划，讲求效率，不喜欢与谈判无关的闲聊，一般开局阶段简单介绍后就切入正题。他们陈述问题清楚明白，不喜欢模棱两可的表述方式。把有效处理问题看作衡量一个人能力的标志。认为交谈时的眼神交流是真诚的表现。

(4) Negotiation Strategies (谈判策略)

The Germans will be well prepared before the negotiations. At the beginning of the negotiations, it will take a long time to state their position, including the negotiating requirements and the issues that must be resolved. They are confident because of their developed industry and first-class product quality. This also makes them very convinced of the reliability of their quotations. They generally do not give in to the other party, even if there is, the magnitude is small. In order to achieve their overall goals, they can also show flexibility in some ways. They are very patient with bargaining and are good at using other competitive forces to force the other party to make concessions. The style of negotiation is tough, serious and direct. They pay attention to the details and you must be fully prepared before negotiating with them.

德国人在谈判前会做充足的准备。在谈判开局阶段，他们会花较长的时间陈述其立场，包括谈判要求以及必须解决的问题。他们因其发达的工业、一流的产品质量而信心满满。这也使得他们非常相信自己报价的可靠性，一般不会向对手做出让步，即使有，幅度也很小。为了达到他们的总体目标，他们也可能在某些方面表现出灵活性。他们关于讨价还价极有耐心，擅长利用其他竞争力量迫使对手做出让步。谈判风格强硬、严肃而直接。他们注重细节，与他们谈判前一定要做好充分的准备。

Be patient when negotiating with the Germans. They are very careful and, in order to ensure that their negotiating goals are met, they will not rush ahead with the negotiations until they are assured of their objectives. They do not use time as a tactical tool in negotiations to gain psychological advantage over their opponents through procrastination.

当与德国人进行谈判时，要有耐心。他们非常小心，在没有确保达到其谈判目标前，他们不会仓促推进谈判。他们不会在谈判中把时间作为战术工具，通过拖延获得对对手的心理优势。

Germans don't like to mix food, entertainment and work. As hosts, they are also good at creating a positive atmosphere through banquets at a certain stage of negotiation, or when the negotiations are over. But do not discuss business during meals until a strong relationship is established. After establishing a strong long-term relationship with the Germans, business can be discussed during meals and entertainment, but caution is recommended.

德国人不喜欢将饮食、娱乐和工作混在一起。作为东道主，在谈判进行到一定阶段或谈判结束的时候，他们也擅长通过宴请营造积极的氛围。但在建立牢固的关系之前，不要在用餐期间讨论业务。在和德国人建立了牢固的长期关系之后，可以在吃饭和娱乐期间讨论生意，但建议小心行事。

(5) Ways of Decision-making (决策方式)

The Germans emphasize personal responsibility, and decision-making is generally top-down and does not require collective discussion.

德国人强调个人负责，决策一般自上而下，不需要集体讨论。

(6) Social Etiquette（社交礼仪）

• Avoid using informal names, or address somebody by name, add their titles when you call them.

• The dress must be formally decent, preferably wearing a three-piece suit with a vest.

• Do not put your hands in your pocket. This is a very rude performance.

• Topics do not involve personal privacy, politics, and World War Ⅱ.

• Shake hands at the beginning and end of the talks.

• Don't give a gift for the first meeting.

• 避免用不正式的称呼，或直呼其名，有头衔的人要称呼头衔。

• 着装必须正式得体，最好穿带背心的三件套西服。

• 不要把手放在口袋里，这是十分无礼的表现。

• 话题不要涉及个人隐私、政治和二战。

• 会谈开始和结束的时候都要握手。

• 初次见面不要送礼。

2. Dutch Negotiation Style（荷兰人的谈判风格）

Dutch culture is diverse, and the Dutch are open-minded and will not impose their own cognition on others. This is a society that advocates equality and inclusiveness, and believes that anyone, regardless of their identity or influence, should be respected. Business is a very serious business for them, and business meetings should be very formal.

荷兰文化具有多元性，荷兰人思想开放，不会把自己的认知强加在别人身上。这是一个主张平等并有包容性的社会，认为任何人，不管其身份、影响力如何，都应该被尊重。对他们来说商务是很严肃的事情，商务会面应非常正式。

(1) Attitudes Towards Personal Relationships with Partners（对与合作者私人关系的态度）

The degree of commercial relations before cooperation is not too great in the Netherlands, and is not a necessary prerequisite for initial business cooperation. During the start of the negotiation, the time for chatting will not be very long. The discussion is mainly on business topics, and they are willing to understand each other in cooperation. Once trust is established, they will show loyalty to their partners and are willing to cooperate for the long term. Therefore, efforts should be made to leave them with a good impression of honesty and reliability.

合作前的商业关系程度在荷兰影响不是太大，不是初次商务合作的必要前提。在谈判开局阶段，闲聊的时间也不会很长，讨论主要集中在商务话题上，他们愿意在合作中了解对方。一旦建立起信任，他们会表现出对伙伴的忠诚并愿意长期合作。因此，应努力给他们留下诚实可靠的良好印象。

(2) Time Concept（时间观念）

Reservations should be scheduled one to two weeks in advance. The Dutch strictly follow the agenda and it is necessary to discuss the agenda in advance. They hate wasting time, and any meeting should be very punctual, and it should not be more than 5 minutes late. If it is possible to be late, you should inform in advance. It is very rude to notify the cancellation of a meeting in a short time in advance. Their negotiation process is faster, but the decision time is longer. It is recommended to be fully prepared for the negotiations.

应提前一至两周预约会面。荷兰人严格遵循议程安排，有必要提前讨论确认议程。他们讨厌浪费时间，任何会面都应该非常准时，迟到不宜超过 5 分钟。如果可能迟到，应提前告知。提前很短时间通知取消会面是非常失礼的行为。他们的谈判进程较快捷，但决策时间较长。建议为谈判做好充分准备。

They like to do things in an orderly manner, and don't like being bothered or multitasking. When negotiating, they usually discuss each item separately in the order listed, and are reluctant to revisit the conditions already discussed. Don't show annoyance or anger at this.

他们喜欢有条不紊地做事，不喜欢被打扰或一心二用。谈判时，他们通常会按列出的目标顺序分别讨论每一条，不愿意重新讨论已经谈好的条件。对此不要表现出懊恼或生气。

(3) Communication Style（沟通方式）

The Dutch speak at a moderate volume, not very lowly, nor particularly loudly. They rarely show their emotions in public and consider self-restraint a virtue. When talking, generally keep a distance of about 1 meter. They communicate more directly. Rather than speaking skillfully, they value going straight and being honest. They don't like ambiguous expressions, and they like to share their views, concerns, and feelings with others. They don't value face, they can openly accept others' pointing out mistakes directly. Therefore, it is better to be frank than to evade and deceive, and do not express rejection in a euphemistic manner. Being too polite makes them suspect that the other party is asking for something.

荷兰人说话音量适中，不会很小声，也不会特别大声。他们很少当众表露情绪，认为自我约束是一种美德。在交谈时，一般保持 1 米左右的距离。他们的沟通方式比较直接。比起说话有技巧来，他们更推崇直来直去和诚实。不喜欢模棱两可的表述，喜欢公开与人分享其观点、关注点及感觉。不看重面子，可以坦然接受别人直接指出错误。因此，直率比逃避和欺骗更好，也不要用委婉的方式表达拒绝。过于客气会让他们怀疑对方有求于人。

When communicating, they rarely use body language and have less physical contact. But eye contact should be frequent, let them feel your sincerity, and help to build trust.

在沟通的时候，他们很少用肢体语言，身体接触也较少。但目光接触应该频繁，让他们感觉到你的真诚，这样做有助于建立信任。

(4) Negotiation Strategies（谈判策略）

The Dutch see the negotiations as a process of joint problem-solving. The buyer and the seller are equal and are responsible for reaching an agreement. They focus on balancing short-term and long-term interests. The main style of negotiation is cooperative, but unless they have no choice, they are not willing to compromise. They believe in a win-win principle and hope that the other party will reward them with respect and trust. You should be outspoken while ensuring respect and cooperation. Logical reasoning and factual approach can be used to resolve disputes, and sometimes apologies can appease them. Although they are diligent, they are not as detail-oriented as the Germans, and they will strive to reach an agreement as soon as possible.

荷兰人把谈判看作共同解决问题的过程。买卖双方是平等的，都对达成协议负责。他们注重平衡短期利益和长期利益。主要的谈判风格是合作型的，但除非别无选择，他们不愿妥协。他们信奉双赢的原则，希望对方对其的尊重和信任予以回报。应该在保证尊重、合作的同时直言不讳。可用逻辑推理和摆实事的方式解决争议，有些时候，表示歉意也能安抚他们。虽然他们也很勤奋，但不像德国人那么注重细节，他们会争取尽快达成协议。

The Dutch's negotiation style is relatively straightforward and they rarely use deceptive tactics. Do not deceive or mislead them and damage the business relationship between the two parties. You can use the carefully planned "good cop, bad cop" tactic against them. Don't use the "limited power" tactic, because they will feel that they didn't find the right person.

荷兰人的谈判风格较直接，很少使用欺骗型战术。不要欺骗或过分误导他们而损坏双方的商业关系。可以对他们使用小心策划的"红脸白脸"战术。不要使用"权力有限"法，因为他们会觉得没有找对人。

They may use pressure tactics. When using similar tactics against them, you should clearly explain your offer and not be aggressive. Be careful with ultimatums. They don't think it's appropriate to accept them unless they are particularly interested in your offer and have a clear basis for it.

他们可能会使用压力型战术。对他们使用相似战术时，应清楚解释你的报价，不要咄咄逼人。要小心使用最后通牒。他们认为不妥当，除非对你的报价特别感兴趣并清楚其依据，才会接受。

Although the direct style of the Dutch sometimes appears aggressive and challenging, they will not be ashamed to deal with open confrontation. Excessive quotation is not appropriate for them and will dampen their enthusiasm for negotiation. The best initial offer should be in your trading range.

虽然荷兰人直接的风格有时显得有侵略性和挑战性，但他们不会羞于应对公开的对抗。过高的报价方式对他们来说是不妥的，会打击其谈判积极性。最好初次报价就进入你的成交范围。

They occasionally use emotional tactics, but it's best to stay calm. It is rare to talk about personal relationships in negotiations. They often use defensive tactics. Don't change it when you make a promise, or you will lose faith in them and cause the deal to be canceled.

他们偶尔会使用情绪型战术，但最好保持平静。在谈判中讲私人关系是很少见的。他们经常使用防御型战术。当做出承诺后就不要改变，否则会失信于他们而导致交易被取消。

(5) Ways of Decision-making (决策方式)

The decision of the Dutch company is a process of group discussion and all participants have the right to express their opinions. Usually the decision-making power is in the hands of low-level managers, without consulting senior managers. The main task of executives is to provide guidance and coordinate decision-making when needed. They have no final decision-making power. The Dutch take a long time to make decisions and need enough patience. It is more important to understand the company structure and win the support of all levels of people involved in the negotiations than to focus only on the top leadership. Once a decision is made, it is difficult to change.

荷兰企业的决策是群体讨论达成一致的过程，所有参与者都有权表达意见。最终决定权通常在低层经理手中，不用请示高管。高管的主要任务是提供指导及在需要的时候协调决策的达成，他们没有最终决定权。荷兰人做决策花的时间很长，需要有足够的耐心。了解其公司结构，赢得参与谈判的各层面人员的支持比只关注上层领导更重要。决策一旦达成是很难改变的。

The decision-making process of the Dutch negotiating at home and away from home are very different. They are well aware that the success of away negotiations requires quick decision-making. So the Dutchman who negotiates away from home usually has enough decision-making power to make a deal. If you want to speed up the negotiation process, you can invite the Dutchman to negotiate away from home.

荷兰人在主场和客场谈判的决策过程差异很大。他们很清楚在客场谈判要取得成功需要迅速地做出决定，因此，参与客场谈判的荷兰人通常都有足够的达成交易的决策权。如果想加快谈判进程，可请荷兰人到客场谈判。

They generally make decisions based on general principles without considering specific circumstances, and do not like exceptions. They believe that personal feelings and experience are not related to business negotiations, focusing on experimental proofs, logical parameters and objective facts.

他们做决定时一般根据普遍原则而不考虑特定情况，不喜欢例外。他们认为个人感觉和经验与商务谈判无关，关注实验证明、逻辑参数和客观实事。

(6) Social Etiquette（社交礼仪）

• In a restaurant, you should talk in a low voice. Excessive volume is a sign of impoliteness.

• It is impolite to interrupt others.

• In business occasions, don't call people by their first names. When addressing people with titles, you should add titles before their last names.

• Business cards should be exchanged for the first meeting.

• Don't give too expensive gifts. It's better not to give gifts when you first meet.

• For business occasions, people should dress formally and conservatively. In most cases, men should wear dark suits and ties.

• Business banquets are usually arranged at noon, during which it is not appropriate to discuss business.

- 在餐馆应小声交谈，音量过大是失礼的表现。
- 打断别人说话是不礼貌的。
- 在商务场合不要直呼其名。称呼有头衔的人，应在姓前加上头衔。
- 初次见面应交换名片。
- 不要送过于贵重的礼物，初次见面最好不送礼。
- 商务场合应穿着正式、保守，在多数情况下，男士应穿深色西服配领带。
- 商务宴请通常安排在中午，其间不宜谈业务。

3. Russian Negotiation Style（俄罗斯人的谈判风格）

（1）Emphasis on Personal Relationships with Partners（重视与合作者的私人关系）

Russians value personal relationships very much and are used to doing business with familiar people. Strangers need to get in touch with them through local people who are familiar with them, and then cultivate their feelings through private contacts. In the opening phase, you usually have to chat for a while. The main purpose of their first meeting is to evaluate the credibility of the other party, and will not make a cooperation decision at this time. Working with unfamiliar people, Russians will try their best to take advantage of it. And if you gain their trust, they will be more gentle and more cooperative when negotiating. Therefore, building a relationship of enduring and trust is critical to business success.

俄罗斯人非常看重私人关系，习惯与熟悉的人做生意。陌生人需要通过和其熟识的当地人和他们联系结识，再通过私下交往培养感情，才可能进行商业合作。在开局阶段通常要闲聊一阵。他们首次会面的主要目的是评估对方的可信度，不会在这个时候做出合作决定。跟不熟悉的人合作，俄罗斯人会想尽办法占便宜。而如果获得了他们的信任，谈判时他们会更有风度并更加合作。因此，建立持久和信任的关系对业务成功至关重要。

（2）Time Concept（时间观念）

Although the Russians need an appointment to do business, they are required to be on time during the negotiations. But they don't think of time as something very valuable, they need to be carefully calculated. Don't show signs of impatience even if the other person is late for the meeting one hour or longer time. They do not have a detailed agenda when negotiating, and the pace of negotiations is slow and loose. When negotiating, they may jump around in the topic, not in order. In order to achieve better results, they would rather delay the time and achieve their goals. You need to be prepared for long negotiations, and can also let them master the rhythm of negotiations.

虽然俄罗斯人办事需要预约，谈判时要求对方准时，但他们并不把时间看作非常宝贵的东西，需要精打细算。即使对方迟到一小时或更长时间，也不要表现出不耐烦的迹象。他们在谈判时不会制定详细的议程，谈判节奏缓慢、松散。在谈判的时候，他们可能在话题中跳来跳去，而不是按顺序处理。为了取得更好的结果，他们宁愿拖延时间，以达到目的。要有长时间谈判的准备，也可以让他们掌握谈判节奏。

（3）Communication Style（沟通方式）

Russians use gestures less when communicating, and they don't like to show their emotions.

But they are emotional, and the more familiar they are with you, the more generous they are. When you are in contact with them, you should use a firm, dignified and non-separate attitude to avoid being aggressive. Keep eye contact frequently when talking to them, which can convey your sincerity and help you gain their trust.

俄罗斯人在沟通的时候较少使用手势，也不喜欢让情绪外露。但他们重感情，对于越熟悉的人，越豪爽大方。跟他们接触的时候，要用坚定、有尊严又不疏离的态度，避免显得咄咄逼人。与其交谈的时候要保持目光频繁接触，这可以向他们传达你的诚意并有助于获得他们的信任。

(4) Negotiation Strategies（谈判策略）

Russians are good at negotiating, and in order to convince each other, they may exaggerate their abilities or make unreliable promises. Use tactics such as lying and sending false nonverbal information, pretending not to be interested in the whole transaction or a single concession, distorting the value of an item, or making false requests and concessions. They are also good at using "good cop, bad cop", limited power, time pressure and other tactics. They like to discuss many details, so prepare enough information.

俄罗斯人擅长谈判，为了说服对方，他们可能夸大自己的能力或做出不可靠的承诺。他们使用说谎、发送假非语言信息、假装对整笔交易或单一让步不感兴趣、歪曲物品的价值、做出虚假的要求和让步等战术。他们还擅长使用"红脸白脸"、权力有限、时间压力等战术。他们喜欢讨论许多细节，所以要准备足够的资料。

a. Use Competition（利用竞争）

Before identifying the final collaborators, the Russians will contact as many potential partners as possible to obtain different quotations and detailed information to facilitate their own evaluation of the transaction price. When competitors are under pressure to hold down their prices, they negotiate with the company they want with the lower terms.

俄罗斯人在确定最终合作者之前，会尽可能多地联系潜在伙伴，以获得不同报价和详细的资料，便于自己评估交易价格。并促使竞争者之间迫于压力互相压价，再用压低的条件与心仪的公司谈判。

b. Adhere to the Position（坚持立场）

The Russians looked at the compromise as a sign of weakness. They are very patient, persistent and stubborn negotiators. It is very difficult to get concessions from them unless the other party makes enough concessions or is particularly firm. They think that the negotiation is a zero-sum game, and one party's gain is equal to the other's loss. They may also make minor concessions while asking the other party to make major concessions. They always think that the other party's offer has a false component, and they try to bargain. Therefore, the price to the Russians should be increased by more than 40%, and sufficient information should be prepared to support your quotation in order to cope with the persistent price-cutting.

俄罗斯人把妥协让步看作懦弱的表现。他们是非常有耐心、执着和顽固的谈判者。要从他们那里获得让步是非常困难的，除非另一方做出足够的让步或表现得特别坚定。他们认为谈判是一场零和博弈，其中一方的收益等于对方的损失。他们也可能会做出轻微的让步，同时要求对方做出主要的让步。他们总是认为对方的报价有水分，想方设法讨价还价。所以，对俄罗斯人的报价要加上40%以上的溢价，要准备充足的资料支持你的报价，以应对其执着的压价。

c. Afterwards Conditionality（事后附加条件）

Russians like to come up with special service requirements that are not included in the quotation after reaching the final price with the other party. If you promise, you will increase your own costs. If you refuse, the conditions for negotiation may be completely abolished, the reinvention will be repeated, and the previous efforts will be lost. Therefore, when negotiating with them, it is best to discuss other conditions first, and then determine the price based on the services you need to provide.

俄罗斯人喜欢在与对方达成最终价格后又提出一些不包含在报价中的特殊服务要求。如果答应，会增加己方的成本。如果拒绝，则谈妥的条件可能全部作废，推倒重来，前面的努力付诸东流。因此，在与他们谈判的时候，最好先讨论其他条件，后面再根据需要提供的服务确定价格。

Be polite and firm throughout the negotiation process. Don't make big concessions too early, otherwise, it will arouse their expectations for further compromise.

在整个谈判过程中要礼貌而坚定。不要过早做出大的让步，否则会激起他们让你做出进一步妥协的期望。

(5) Ways of Decision-making（决策方式）

Russia is a country with a strong sense of hierarchy. Russians are accustomed to reporting to their leaders and making decisions from their superiors. Therefore, in the negotiations, they have limited power and it is difficult to make a decision immediately. If the other side's conditions are different from their own, they will not give in easily.

俄罗斯是个等级观念很强的国家，俄罗斯人习惯凡事向领导汇报，由上级做决策。因此在谈判中，他们权力有限，很难马上做出决定。如果对方的条件与己方有出入，他们不会轻易让步。

(6) Social Etiquette（社交礼仪）

• Don't make OK and "V" gestures to them. It is obscene in Russia.

• Do not put your hands in your pocket. They think it is a rude performance.

• When calling Russians, you can call their full names or "Mr." or "Ms." plus their surnames. Since they value their status, if they have titles or positions, it is best to use them instead of "Mr." or "Ms."

• Introduce with a firm handshake.

• Exchange of business cards is an essential step when you first meet someone. The title and doctoral degree (if any) should be clearly marked on the business card.

• 不要对他们做OK和"V"手势，在俄罗斯那是淫秽的意思。

• 不要把手放在口袋里，他们认为这是粗鲁的表现。

• 称呼俄罗斯人的时候可以叫他们的全名或者“先生”或“女士”加姓氏。由于他们很看重身份地位，如果对方有头衔或职务，则最好用其代替“先生”或“女士”。

• 介绍的时候要伴随坚定的握手。

• 交换名片是第一次见到某人时必不可少的一步。名片上要标注清楚头衔和博士学位（如有）。

Ⅳ African Negotiation Styles（非洲人的谈判风格）

Africa is a vast region. Most African countries have underdeveloped economies and strict grades. People engaged in business activities come from famous families and attach great importance to etiquette. The North African countries have different negotiation styles compared with South Africa whose economy is more developed.

非洲地域辽阔，多数国家经济不发达，等级森严。从事商务活动的人都出身名门，非常看重礼节。北非国家和经济较发达的南非相比谈判风格迥异。

1. Attitudes Towards Personal Relationships with Partners（对与合作者私人关系的态度）

Africans value their personal relationships with their partners and promote friendship through private contacts, which helps the negotiations to proceed smoothly. If they don't like you, you will have a hard time making progress in the negotiations. Socialization accounts for a large proportion of business activities in Africa. They learn about each other by watching events, travel, and hunting with business partners. In the beginning of the negotiations, you should take enough time to chat with them. Once they have a sense of trust in you, it is easy to solve the problems in the negotiations. Choosing a local agent to assist in the negotiation is very beneficial to the business.

非洲人很看重与合作者的私人关系，通过私下交往增进友谊，有助于谈判的顺利进行。如果他们不喜欢你，你将很难在谈判上取得进展。社交在非洲商务活动中占了很大比重。他们通过与商业伙伴一起观看赛事、旅游、打猎来了解对方。在谈判开局阶段，应花足够的时间与其寒暄。一旦他们对你有了信任感，就很容易解决谈判中的问题。选择一个当地代理商协助交涉非常有利于业务的开展。

2. Time Concept（时间观念）

North Africans are inefficient, procrastinate and have little sense of time, but they still need to make appointments in advance. At the beginning of the negotiation, they will talk for a long time about topics unrelated to their business. It may also be interrupted by phone calls or other visitors, but don't appear impatient or unhappy. In the middle of the negotiation, the host may also propose tea or talk about it next time, which should be approved. Negotiations with them should be patient enough to conform to their negotiation rhythm, and should not be too hasty to make them feel disrespected.

北非人工作效率低下，办事拖沓，没什么时间观念，但会面仍需提前预约。谈判时，开局时会长时间谈论与业务无关的话题。谈判也可能被电话或其他来访者打断，不要因此显得不耐烦或不高兴。谈判中途主人还可能提议喝茶或下次再谈，应该表示赞同。与他们谈判要有充足的耐心，顺应其谈判节奏，不要操之过急，使其觉得不受尊重。

South Africa has the strongest economic power in Africa, and most local businessmen are white. They work earnestly and have a strong sense of time and negotiation efficiency. An appointment is required before the visit. A little greeting at the beginning of the negotiation is enough.

南非属于非洲经济势力最强的地方，当地商人多数是白人。他们工作认真，有较强的时间观念、谈判效率较高。拜访前需进行预约。开局稍事寒暄即可。

3. Communication Style（沟通方式）

North Africans attach great importance to the ability of language expression. They like to interrupt others in conversation, but they have no malice. They like to exaggerate things, such as over-promises or terrible threats, and reiterate important things over and over again. They don't say "no" directly. They think it's impolite and tend to refuse it euphemistically. Their body language is also very rich, and they are close to each other when talking. Familiar people will have frequent physical contact with each other.

北非人很看重语言表达能力，交谈时喜欢打断别人，但并无恶意。他们喜欢夸大其词，如做过度的承诺或可怕的威胁，反复重申重要的事情。他们不会直接说“不”，认为这是不礼貌的，更倾向于委婉地拒绝。他们的肢体语言也非常丰富，交谈时挨得较近，熟人之间会有频繁的肢体接触。

South Africans, on the other hand, prefer direct speech, making it difficult to understand other people's euphemistic expressions.

而南非人则喜欢直白的说话方式，难以理解别人委婉的表达。

4. Negotiation Strategies（谈判策略）

The North Africans regard the negotiations as competitive, like bargaining, and take the extent of the other's concessions as a measure of the success of their negotiations. The initial offer should leave room for lengthy bargaining. They are reluctant to solve problems according to the law and do not like to discuss the details of cooperation too much. The content of the contract may be discussed and revised many times.

北非人把谈判看作竞争性的，喜欢讨价还价，把对手让步的幅度视为衡量其谈判成功的标准。初次报价应为冗长的讨价还价留有余地。他们不愿依据法律解决问题，不喜欢过多讨论合作细节。合同内容可能多次反复讨论、修改。

The South Africans are very familiar with the transaction project and are very serious about the terms of the contract, but do not like to bargain for a long time. They are generally more conceited. Don't apply the "ultimatum" method to them. They are very annoyed by being pressured, but will further delay the negotiation process. They also motivate others to make concessions by deliberately slowing down the pace of negotiations.

南非人则对交易项目了解得很仔细，对合同条款也很认真，但不喜欢长时间讨价还价。他们一般都较自负，不要对他们使用“最后通牒”法，他们对被施压会感到非常懊恼，反而会进一步拖延谈判进程。他们也会通过故意减缓谈判节奏来促使对方做出让步。

5. Ways of Decision-making（决策方式）

In Africa, it is usually negotiated by the responsible person, and they also hope that the other party is the one who can decide. Decision-making methods are centralized.

在非洲，一般由具有决策权的负责人出面谈判，他们也希望对方是能做主的人。决策方式属于权力集中型的。

6. Social Etiquette（社交礼仪）

- When calling them, add their titles.
- When shaking hands, eating and giving gifts, use the right hand. African Muslims believe that the left hand is used to deal with dirty things.
- Shake hands with every one present with enough strength for the first meeting.
- Don't talk about sex, religion, race and politics.
- Gifts can effectively promote the relationship between the two sides.
- Pork and alcohol should be avoided when Muslims are feasted and don't talk at meal time.
- In business occasions, people should wear conservative suits.
- In Arab countries, women should not participate in business activities or expose their limbs and hair.
- Don't cross your legs and point the sole to others.
- Don't spit in front of Africans who think spitting is a curse on their enemies.
- Don't talk business with Muslims during Ramadan.
- Don't yawn or sneeze in front of Egyptians. If you can't help it, turn your face and cover your mouth and apologize.
- 称呼对方时，加上其头衔。
- 与非洲穆斯林握手、进食、送礼时应用右手，他们认为左手是用于处理污秽事物的。
- 初次见面，应与在场所有人有力地握手。
- 不要谈论性、宗教、种族和政治话题。
- 赠送礼物能有效促进双方关系。
- 宴请穆斯林时忌猪肉、饮酒，不在用餐时交谈。
- 商务场合应穿保守的西服。
- 在阿拉伯国家，女性不宜参与商务活动，更不要裸露肢体和头发。
- 不要架二郎腿，不要把鞋底对着对方。
- 切忌当着非洲人的面吐唾沫，他们认为吐唾沫是对仇人的诅咒举动。

- 在斋月不与穆斯林谈生意。
- 在埃及人面前尽量不要打哈欠或打喷嚏，如果实在控制不住，应转脸捂嘴并致歉。

Ⅴ Australian Negotiation Style（澳大利亚人的谈判风格）

The main negotiation style of Australians is cooperative. They regard buyers and sellers as equal subjects and believe in a win-win result. They are willing to make compromises in order to advance the negotiations. The stage of collecting information and bargaining is usually smooth, but the decision is relatively slow.

澳大利亚人主要的谈判风格是合作型的，把买卖双方看作平等的主体，信奉双赢的结果。他们愿意为了推进谈判而做出妥协。收集信息和讨价还价阶段通常比较顺利，但决策相对缓慢。

1. Attitudes Towards Personal Relationships with Partners（对与合作者私人关系的态度）

While trust is important to Australians, they don't value business relationships. Existing business relationships are not a necessary prerequisite for initial cooperation. They tend to know each other in business cooperation. Both parties who do not have personal relationships can also conduct business. Because Australians don't trust people who only do business, letting them see your personal situation helps to gain their trust. Personal integrity and reliability can help you win their trust. They advocate equality, and their identity and status have little effect in the negotiations. It is beneficial to conduct business through local introduction, but it is not necessary. In the opening stage, they usually establish personal relationships through chat.

虽然信任对澳大利亚人来说很重要，但他们不太看重商务关系。已有的商务关系不是初次合作的必要前提条件。他们倾向于在商务合作中了解对方。没有私交的双方也可以开展业务。由于澳大利亚人不信任只做业务的人，让他们看到你个人方面的情况有助于获得其信任。个人诚信和可靠都能帮助你赢得他们的信任。他们崇尚平等，身份和地位在谈判中的作用不大。通过当地人介绍对开展业务有利，但不是必要的。在开局阶段，他们通常会通过闲聊建立私人关系。

2. Time Concept（时间观念）

When they meet, they want the other party to arrive on time. If there are no good reasons, it is impolite to be late for more than 10 minutes. If you are late for more than 5 minutes, you should call in advance to let them know.

在进行会晤时，他们希望对方能准时到达。如果没有充足的理由，迟到超过 10 分钟是不礼貌的。如果会迟到 5 分钟以上，应提前打电话告知。

3. Communication Style（沟通方式）

If Australians have a good relationship with you, they will tease you and you don't feel offended. They may sometimes be silent when they talk, but this doesn't make much sense. They like direct communication and don't feel that it is difficult to reject others. They rarely communicate in a concealed way, so you can understand their views from the literal meaning, and try to express your opinions in a literal way. When you are introducing a product or service, it is best to clearly indicate its strengths and weaknesses. Be careful not to express your opinion with an arrogant attitude. Although they are direct, they will express their meaning in a polite and friendly way. Therefore, they will express their clear expectations in a polite way.

澳大利亚人如果与你关系良好，会与你打趣，不要觉得被冒犯了。他们交谈的时候可能有时沉默，但这没有多少含义。他们喜欢直接的沟通方式，不会觉得拒绝别人很困难。他们很少用隐晦的方式进行沟通，因此从其字面意思理解其看法即可，也尽量用字面意思表达自己的观点。在介绍产品或服务的时候，最好明确指出其优缺点。注意不要用傲慢的态度表达你的观点。他们虽然直接，但会以礼貌友好的方式表达。因此，他们会用客气的要求表达其明确的期望。

Their gestures and body language are vivid. There may be physical contact, such as patting someone on the back to show friendliness. If you move your arms up with a thumb up, it is a rude gesture for them. Eye contact should not be too frequent, although watching others can be sincere, but staring at people will make them feel uncomfortable.

他们的手势和肢体语言生动。可能会有身体接触，如拍某人的背表示友好。如果竖大拇指的时候手臂向上动对他们来说是粗鲁的手势。眼神接触不要过于频繁，虽然注视别人可以显得真诚，但盯着人看会让他们感到不舒服。

4. Negotiation Strategies（谈判策略）

Australians like to negotiate directly and honestly, only occasionally using deceptive tactics. Don't lie to them or mislead them, which can affect or even undermine business relationships. It is also not recommended to use "good cop, bad cop" tactic, which will make them doubt your credibility. They don't like being pressured. Try not to use stress tactics. Do not give the final offer too early in the bargaining phase. They understand silence as cold, unfriendly, or uninteresting. Don't use time pressure tactics. It's not suitable for them.

澳大利亚人喜欢用直接坦诚的方式谈判，只偶尔会使用欺骗型战术。不要对他们撒谎或误导他们，这会影响甚至破坏商务关系。也不建议用红脸白脸战术，这会让他们怀疑你的信誉。他们不喜欢被施压，尽量不要用压力型战术。在讨价还价阶段不要过早给出最终报价。他们把沉默理解为冷淡、不友好或是不感兴趣。不要使用时间压力战术，这对他们不合适。

They also rarely use offensive tactics. Don't leave the game halfway or aggressively threaten, they will think it is offensive to the person, and may even end the negotiations. They often use defensive tactics such as blocking or switching topics, asking for inquiring or direct questions, making commitments, and so on.

他们也很少用进攻型战术。不要中途离场或咄咄逼人地威胁，他们会认为是对人身的冒犯，甚至可能终结谈判。他们经常使用防御型战术，如阻碍或转换话题、提出探究性或直接的问题、做出承诺等。

5. Ways of Decision-making（决策方式）

In Australia, decisions are often made by individuals, but they will consult others and seriously consider the opinions of others. Senior executives, if not involved in negotiations, are mostly involved in decision-making. Therefore, it is important to win support from top management and subordinates who may influence decision-making.

在澳大利亚，决策往往是由个人做出的，但他们会咨询别人，并认真考虑别人的意见。高层管理人员即便不参与谈判，也大多会参与决策。因此，赢得高层管理者和可能影响决策的下属的支持很重要。

When making decisions, they refer to a large number of general principles, not specific situations. Although they will be considered comprehensively, experimental evidence and objective facts are much more important than personal feelings and experience.

在做决策时，他们会参考大量的普遍原则，而不是特定的情况。虽然他们会通盘考虑，但实验证明和客观事实比个人感觉和经验重要得多。

6. Social Etiquette（社交礼仪）

- Don't praise someone in public, otherwise they will doubt your motives.
- Contact them one week in advance.
- When calling, the surname is usually preceded by "Mr. /Ms." instead of title.
- When you first meet, exchanging business cards is not a necessary procedure. Although you may not get a rebate, it is best to bring a business card and distribute it to everyone present.
- Don't discuss other people's private lives when you meet.
- There are few corruption and bribery in Australia. Don't give too expensive gifts.
- Australians distinguish their work from their life very clearly, and talk less about business issues during business banquets.
- Australians seldom give gifts in business occasions, especially when meeting for the first time, in order to avoid being questioned about motivation.
- 不要当众称赞某人，否则他们会怀疑你的动机。
- 提前一周联系与他们的会面。
- 称呼时，姓氏前一般加上“先生/女士”而不用头衔。
- 初次见面时，交换名片不是必要程序。虽然可能不会得到回赠，但最好带足名片，分发给在场的所有人。
- 不要在会面时讨论别人的私生活。
- 澳大利亚腐败、贿赂现象很少，不要赠送过于昂贵的礼物。
- 澳大利亚人把工作和生活分得很清楚，商务宴会期间尽量少谈业务方面的话题。
- 在商务场合澳大利亚人很少送礼，尤其不会在初次会面时送礼，以免被质疑动机。

Summary

This chapter introduces the American, Brazilian, Korean, Japanese, Singaporean, German, Dutch, Russian, African, Australian negotiation styles and coping suggestions from the attitude towards personal relationships with collaborators, time concept, communication style, negotiation strategies, decision-making way and different social etiquette in these countries.

本章从对与合作者私人关系的态度、时间观念、沟通方式、谈判策略、决策方式等方面介绍了美国人、巴西人、韩国人、日本人、新加坡人、德国人、荷兰人、俄罗斯人、非洲人、澳大利亚人的谈判风格、应对建议及各国不同的社交礼仪。

Module Ⅱ Terminology Practice

1. Agent: A person in charge with representing the interests of another in negotiations with a third party.

2. Die-hard Bargainers: People for whom every negotiation is a battle.

3. Multiphase Transactions: Negotiations that will be implemented in phases, or that have the prospect of subsequent involvement in the future. The context of the negotiations allows parties to negotiate based on follow-through and continuing communication.

4. Information Asymmetry: A situation in which one party has more information than another.

5. Positions: What the parties in a negotiation ask for, in other words, their demands.

6. Reservation Price: The least favorable point at which a party would accept a negotiated deal. The reservation price is derived from, but is not usually the same thing as, the BATNA. Also known as walk-away.

7. Strategy: A planned sequence of how one is going to approach a negotiation, including what the negotiator will offer and ask for (give and get).

8. Tactics: The specific methods for implementing a strategy.

9. Trade Off: To substitute or bargain one issue for another. This tactic is often used in sales negotiations.

10. Bluffing: A tactic in which one party in a negotiation indicates that it may be willing to do or accept something that it actually has no intention of following-through on.

11. Negotiator's Dilemma: The tension caused by the negotiator's attempt to balance competitive strategies—trying to discern when to compete where interests conflict, and when to create value by exchanging the information that leads to mutually advantageous options.

Module Ⅲ New Words

1. after-hours *adj*. 业余的

2. aggressive *adj*. 咄咄逼人的

3. compromising *adj*. 妥协的；让步的

4. conciliatory *adj*. 安抚的；说服的；调和的；调解的

5. deceptive *adj*. 欺骗性的

6. egalitarian *adj*. 主张平等的

7. evasive *adj*. 逃避的

8. integrity *n*. 正直，诚实

9. primary *adj*. 主要的

10. protocol *n*. 礼仪；协议

11. protracted *adj*. 拖延的；延长的

12. reciprocate *v*. 回报

13. taboo *n*. 禁忌

Module Ⅳ Useful Expressions

1. empirical evidence 实验证明
2. figure out 想出，弄清楚
3. final say 最终决定权
4. "good cop, bad cop" tactic "红脸白脸"战术
5. group oriented 团体取向
6. live up to 达到高标准；不辜负；实行；履行
7. logical arguments 逻辑参数
8. make headway 取得进展
9. quibble over 夸夸其谈
10. a short notice 提前很短时间通知
11. in line with 与……一致
12. shake someone up 使振作，激励
13. fight one's way 打开一条路前进，奋斗着前进
14. in depth 全面地，彻底地
15. have an eye for 能看出，具有识别……的能力

Module Ⅴ Exercise

Ⅰ. Answer the following questions according to the text.

1. What are the styles of US negotiators?
2. What are the styles of Brazilian negotiators?
3. What are the styles of Korean negotiators?
4. What are the styles of Japanese negotiators?
5. What are the styles of Singaporean negotiators?
6. What are the styles of German negotiators?
7. What are the styles of Dutch negotiators?
8. What are the styles of Russian negotiators?
9. What are the styles of African negotiators?
10. What are the styles of Australian negotiators?

Ⅱ. Multiple Choice. Please circle the letter corresponding to the correct response.

1. Relationship building is important in which of the following situations?

a. When the United States is involved in the negotiations.

b. When a Hispanic country is involved in the negotiations.

c. When Germany is involved in the negotiations.

d. When Great Britain is involved in the negotiations.

2. Which of the following statements regarding negotiation with Germans is incorrect?

a. Protocol is very important and formal.

b. Germans typically use a handshake at the beginning and end of meetings.

c. Germans tend to be detail-oriented and like technical people as part of negotiations.

d. In business, Germans are typically individualistic; however, as people they are very group-oriented.

3. Which of the following statements regarding negotiation with Japanese people is incorrect?

a. A business meeting should be arranged by an intermediary who has a relationship with both parties.

b. In Japan, social meetings are very important for building a relationship of trust and friendship.

c. Completing a deal quickly is important to the Japanese.

d. The Japanese use subtle and complex verbal and nonverbal cues.

4. U. S. negotiators tend to ________.

a. make fewer adjustments to their opponents' behavior and change their negotiation strategy less

b. change their negotiation strategy less and are less ethnocentric than their opponents

c. use a group-oriented negotiation style and make fewer adjustments to their opponents' behavior

d. use less ethnocentric behavior than their opponents and use a group-oriented negotiation style

5. Individuals who are not group-oriented may feel that group-oriented negotiators ______.

a. appear to stall, make individual decisions, and are not interested in the negotiations

b. appear to stall, are not interested in the negotiations, and give ambiguous statements

c. make individual decisions, are not interested in the negotiations, and give ambiguous statements

d. give ambiguous statements, are not interested in the negotiations, and are very rigid

6. Which of the following does not describe a Japanese negotiating team?

a. They allow insufficient time for the negotiations.

b. They come to the negotiation table with a large contingent of people.

c. They give concessions that are small.

d. They need to get to know their business partners.

7. U. S. negotiators tend to make ________ adjustments to their opponents' behavior, and

they change their negotiation strategy ________ than the negotiators from other cultures when dealing interculturally.

a. fewer; less b. fewer; more c. more; more d. no; less

8. In Western countries, the taboo number of gifts is ________.

a. 4 b. 9 c. 13 d. 14

9. ________ regard odd numbers as auspicious numbers and are not interested in even numbers.

a. Australian b. Chinese c. Korean d. Japanese

10. ________ avoid green and thinks it is an unlucky color.

a. American b. The Dutch c. Russian d. Japanese

Ⅲ. Please determine whether the following statements are True or False.

1. Don't send purple flowers to Brazilians, because the flowers of this color are mainly used in funerals in Brazil. ( )

2. In Japan, don't send lotus flowers, because it means memorial and is considered unlucky. ( )

3. Relationship building in the United States requires the use of an intermediary. ( )

4. Agendas are viewed positively around the world. ( )

5. Discussions can be both emotional and unemotional depending upon the cultures involved in the negotiation. ( )

6. A compromising negotiation style is a competitive approach to reaching an agreement. ( )

7. Overcoming cultural barriers is relatively unimportant when negotiating. ( )

8. Silence is an important part of Japanese nonverbal communication and should not be interrupted. ( )

9. When negotiating with Brazilians, remember that they are more individualistic than people from other Latin American countries. ( )

10. Negotiation protocol is different for different cultures. ( )

Ⅳ. Translate the following sentences into Chinese.

1. The quality of your shipment for our order is not in conformity with the agreed specifications. We must therefore lodge a claim against you.

2. Our investigation shows that damage was caused by improper packing. Therefore we have to refer this matter to you.

3. We shall lodge a claim for all the losses incurred as a consequence of your failure to ship our order in time.

4. We have substantial evidence for lodging a claim. Here's a report from a well-known public surveyor in London.

5. As requested, we will send you a replacement within a week and hope you will be pleased with the new lot.

6. Since I have seen rusty instruments with my own eyes, I agree to replace the defective ones as soon as I return home.

7. The wrong pieces may be returned by the next available steamer for our account. But it's preferable if you can dispose of them in your market because the woolen sweaters are of good quality and new design.

8. Since you bought the goods FOB Qingdao, we cannot entertain your claim for the losses occurred in transit. We propose you approach the shipping company or insurance company for compensation.

9. We regret to tell you that we can't entertain your claim as it is now far past the time stipulated in the contract.

10. Without the survey report issued by a reputable surveyor to support your claim, we cannot take your claim into consideration.

Ⅴ. Translate the following sentences into English.

1. 我们发现货物有某种严重缺陷。
2. 我们有足够的证据提出索赔。
3. 关于你方产品质量低劣的问题，我方要求你方赔偿2万美元。
4. 因这批货物褪色严重，严重浸雨，已经没法出售了。
5. 对此，我深表歉意。我公司指示我要尽快予以补救。
6. 我们对你方遭受的损失深表遗憾，同意赔偿你方2万美元。
7. 你方尽可放心，如果是我方的错，我方一定会改正。
8. 恐怕我方不能接受你方的索赔，因为你方无法提供足够的证据。
9. 恐怕我方不能赔偿你方损失，因为那是你方对产品使用不当造成的。
10. 货物损坏是在码头搬动装船时因操作野蛮造成的。

Ⅵ. Case Study

Case 1: The Importance of Understanding the Negotiation Style

Case Source: Liu Yuan. *International Business Negotiation* (3rd Edition). Beijing: University of International Business and Economics Press, 2008.

Preface

Key Point: American oil company manager almost ruined a major transaction because he did not understand the negotiation style of the Arab countries.

Background

Industry: Oil

Subject: American Oil Company Manager and Arab Company Representative

Issue: When the American oil company manager negotiated the details of the agreement with the representative of the Arab company, because he did not understand the negotiation style of the Arab countries, he repeatedly retreated when the other party approached, and almost missed an important transaction.

A US oil company manager almost ruined an important oil sale. He recalled the incident: "I met an Arab representative of the Organization of the Petroleum Exporting Countries and discussed with him some details on the agreement. He gradually came closer to me until he was only 15cm away from me. At that time, I didn't realize anything. I stepped back and saw that he was slightly hesitant, frowned, and then turned to me again. Close, I took another step back. Unexpectedly, I found out that my assistant was staring at me anxiously and shook his head to me. Thank God, I finally understood what he meant. I stood still and closed the deal in a position that I felt most uncomfortable."

Questions

1. In the United States, what business habits do you need to follow when meeting?

2. What inspired the case in this case?

Appendix

The Americans' legal concept is generally strong. On the streets, Americans cannot be seen crossing the road and spitting. As soon as they enter public places, smokers immediately extinguish the cigarettes. They believe that the law must be observed, so if their rights are violated, they will immediately use the law to recover what they have lost. Child abuse is going to be brought to court. When Americans find a fly in a restaurant, they will also be required to sue in accordance with the law.

Case 2: The Fashionable Dress Led to the Breakdown of Negotiations

Case Source: Lu Xiaohui. *Business Negotiation*. Zhengzhou: Zhongyuan Peasant Publishing House, 2007.

Preface

Key Point: The general manager of a large state-owned enterprise in China is self-righteous and fashionable, causing negotiations to fail.

Background

Subject: A Chinese Enterprise and a German Company

Issue: Zheng Wei, the general manager of a large enterprise in China, failed to understand the German business habits and negotiating style, and the negotiations failed.

Zheng Wei is the general manager of a large enterprise. On one occasion, he was informed that the chairman of a well-known German company was visiting the city and had the intention to seek a partner. So, he tried his best to ask the relevant departments to match the two sides. What makes Zheng Wei ecstatic was that the other party was also interested in cooperating with his company and hoped to meet him as soon as possible.

On the day when the two sides met, Zheng Wei deliberately made a modification to his image. According to his understanding of fashion, he wore a jacket, a jean, a baseball cap and a pair of ankle shoes. Undoubtedly, he hoped that he could leave the impression of being smart, strong and fashionable. However, contrary to his expectation, his self-perceived "fashion" is a bad thing, he has broken his big event.

Questions

1. What mistake does the general manager in this case make?
2. What is the German side's comment on this?

Appendix

The Germans have a strong sense of "seeking truth from facts", paying attention to reality and not advocating exaggeration. The Germans' living rooms are unpretentious and neat. All kinds of daily necessities, such as doors, locks, switches, etc., are solid and strong. They pay attention to practicality, and would rather be cumbersome and never have a watch. They also pay attention to the inner quality of a building, a piece of furniture, and a set of equipment. They pay attention to down-to-earth and never talk about it.

Case 3: Parisian Designer in Japan

Case Source: Li Xuemei, Zhang Wei. *International Business Negotiation*. Beijing: Tsinghua University Press, 2011.

Preface

Key Point: The female designer of the French company expressed surprise at the Japanese company's product-related issues.

Background

Industry: Clothes

Subject: French Company and Japanese Buyer

Issue: The female designer of the French company, Kristen, is very helpless with the many personal issues that have been asked by the boss of Japanese company.

A buyer of a Japanese women's chain store called a head office in a clothing factory in Paris and asked to send someone to Tokyo for an autumn show. In the past few years, the two companies have continued to do business. The Parisian company sent a female designer Kristen. On the third day in Tokyo, the company arranged the show. The female designer thought that since there was a long time to go, they could sit down and talk about business. So, after meeting the guest, she immediately put the slides, made the show, talked about the price, and then talked about how to promote. After half a day of tossing, she discovered that the Japanese side including the boss and the salesmen, all of whom were stunned and looked at her with no expression. After a moment of silence, the Japanese boss spoke and suddenly asked Kristen many questions. He asked her where she was studying fashion design, her past work experience, what her hobbies were, how long she had worked in the Parisian company, which were not related to business. Some topics turned too fast. At first, Kristen didn't want to talk about them. Later, she thought that if she wanted to continue this talk, she would have to answer them. The Japanese boss talked to her about how successful his relationship with the

French company was, how the two companies worked together, and how the French company sent senior executives to visit the Japanese countryside. Finally, the Japanese boss repeatedly told Kristen to remember everything he said that was useful when she returned to Paris to see her boss. Later, she called to tell her boss all the things, and said that she was not optimistic about the business of the negotiations.

Questions

1. Why are Japanese boss stunned? What do you think is wrong?

2. What are the negotiation style and characteristics of Japanese businessmen according to this case?

Appendix

Negotiation style involves different negotiation process, views on private relationship and topics for people from different countries.

Case 4: A Chinese Company and a Company in Africa Broke Down on Mineral Purchase Negotiations

Case Source: http://blog.sina.com.cn/s/blog_954e22a40102wfvg.html.

Preface

Key Point: A Chinese company has failed in the negotiations because it does not understand the negotiation style of Africans.

Background

Industry: Mineral

Subject: A Chinese Company and a Company in Africa

Issue: The style of negotiation and the knowledge of the local law department led to the failure of the negotiations.

A Chinese company wanted to buy minerals from Africa, a world-famous aristocratic family cooperative. After arriving in Africa, the African side arranged a series of activities. Only a few days later, formal negotiations began, but the time left for negotiations was very limited. The African side prepared seven contract editions during the negotiations, each with dozens of pages, and it was difficult to read them all in a limited time. After the intense bargaining negotiations between the two sides, at the moment when the two parties are about to sign the contract, the Chinese side has found a big problem in the contract. The original place of the lawsuit is Singapore, but as stated in the contract, a lawsuit should be lodged through a local court in Africa. Because of this problem, the two sides immediately turned their faces and the negotiations broke down completely.

Questions

1. What business habits and negotiation styles do African businessmen embody in this case?

2. Briefly state other business habits and negotiation styles of African businessmen.

Appendix

In order to succeed in conducting business negotiations with Africans, it is necessary to pay attention to the selection of high-quality negotiators, choose appropriate negotiation time and extensively collect information on the country's politics, economy, market, etc. The Chinese negotiators must have extroverted personality, behave in a civilized manner, be humorous, responsive, witty, and flexible.

Case 5: Ludwig's Trip to Asia

Case source: Jin Juan. *Cross-Cultural Business Communication*. Beijing: Capital Economic and Trade University Press, 2010.

Preface

Key Point: Different Negotiation Styles of Germans and Asians

Background

Industry: Trade

Subject: An Asian Company and a German Company

Issue: There's embarrassment and misunderstanding when the Asian representative negotiated with Ludwig.

Ludwig is the sales director of a medium-sized trading company in Munich, Germany. Recently, the company has a business in Asia to negotiate. Considering the importance of business, Ludwig decided to go in person. Before he left, he prepared well enough and carefully studied the products and the creditworthiness, capital status, management status and production capacity of the Asian company. He also asked the assistant to send his schedule to the other party, including the talks at each time and the specific content of the talks. However, at the talks on the first day, the Asian representative was three minutes late, which made him very unhappy. When the talks began, he clarified the intention directly and immediately entered the topic, while the Asian representative said too many polite words there: "Are you going well on the road?" "Are you used to living here?" "Can you adapt to the weather here?" And so on. Ludwig immediately reminded: "I think we should start the discussion immediately." After one day of negotiations, he felt that progress was not significant. That night, the Asian representative invited Ludwig to dine together, ordered many dishes, and said to him, "We have a very spectacular waterfall here, which is famous all over the world. Let's go together tomorrow!" Ludwig asked, "Did you receive my schedule? Is there a problem with the arrangement of my schedule?" "No, no." the Asian side showed an awkward expression. The next meeting was indeed in accordance with Ludwig's schedule, but the progress was slow. Ludwig had already revealed his whole cards completely, but the Asian side did not seem to follow his beat and was always supportive, or used procrastinating negotiating language such as "research" and "consider". Moreover, during the meeting, some private questions were asked: "Are you married? How old is your son? What does your wife do?" The questions of privatization which were raised during formal negotiations surprised Ludwig. It has been a week since Ludwig came to the negotiating site, but the contract has not been signed yet. He felt that the Asian representative had always been circling around the pond and even doubted the sincerity of the other party.

Questions

1. What negotiation styles does the German businessman embody in this case?

2. What negotiation styles does the Asian representative embody in this case?

Ⅶ. Role plays practice. Work in pair and converse according to the given information.

Task 1

Background

Our university intends to establish two computer rooms for students. Therefore, we need to purchase 100 desktop computers from HP Computer Company.

Our university and HP Computer Company has reached a consensus agreement in computer equipment and price. As the commencement date approaches, the preparatory work is requested to be completed before it. And all 100 desktop computers must be in place within one month in the new semester. However, HP Computer Company expresses it is tough to achieve this goal owing to the limited time.

Simulate negotiations so as to reach an agreement bogged down by this difficulty. You are divided into a few teams, representing two parties to carry favorable agreement as soon as possible.

Terms and Phrases

completion	unwilling	compromise
signature	observe the contract	honor
charge	unanimous	speak highly of
subject to		

Relative Expressions

1. What we hope to do today is to...
2. Perhaps you should...
3. We might be able to...
4. We've agreed on the following...
5. There's still the question of... to be solved.
6. Outstanding issues are...
7. As far as... is concerned, we agree...
8. It remains for me to thank you for coming and...

Task 2

Background

Suppose you are a businessman from the China National Medical Instruments Export Corporation. You've found your last consignment of medical instruments rusty. So you lodge a claim for the rust of the medical instruments. At the meeting,

(1) you show the on-the-spot records and photos to the seller;
(2) you present the view of the case;
(3) the seller acknowledges to compensate;
(4) the seller promises to ship the sound instruments to replace the defective ones;
(5) the seller agrees to pay the shipping expense.

Terms and Phrases

poor packing	faulty packing
encounter	put the blame on
sustain great loss	lodge a claim
remedy	crucial
appreciate	

Relative Expressions

1. I have to complain about...
2. You should be responsible for the loss.
3. We hope you will effect a full settlement of our claim.
4. We apologize for the inconvenience caused by...
5. We will arrange for the dispatch of the replacements.

教学支持说明

1. 教辅资源获取方式

为秉承中国人民大学出版社对教材类产品一贯的教学支持，我们将向采纳本书作为教材的教师免费提供丰富的教辅资源。您可直接到中国人民大学出版社官网的教师服务中心注册下载——http://www.crup.com.cn/Teacher。

如遇到注册、搜索等技术问题，可咨询网页右下角在线 QQ 客服，周一到周五工作时间有专人负责处理。

注册成为我社教师会员后，您可长期根据您所属的课程类别申请纸质样书、电子样书和教辅资源，自行完成免费下载。您也可登录我社官网的“教师服务中心”，我们经常举办赠送纸质样书、赠送电子样书、线上直播、资源下载、全国各专业培训及会议信息共享等网上教材进校园活动，期待您的积极参与！

2. 高校教师可加入下述学科教师 QQ 交流群，获取更多教学服务

经济类教师交流群：809471792
财政金融教师交流群：766895628
国际贸易教师交流群：162921240
税收教师交流群：119667851

3. 购书联系方式

网上书店咨询电话：010－82501766
邮购咨询电话：010－62515351
团购咨询电话：010－62513136

中国人民大学出版社经济分社
地址：北京市海淀区中关村大街甲 59 号文化大厦 1506 室　100872
电话：010－62513572　010－62515803
传真：010－62514775
E-mail：jjfs@crup.com.cn